PRAISE FOR
# *Outsiders*

"As the role of women undergoes yet another convulsion, it's good to read of five women who made a powerful contribution."
—Joan Bakewell, *The New Statesman*

"It was a relief, really exhilarating to read *Outsiders*. Gordon's composite biography brings to light the overlaps between the lives of five visionary women in their quest to give expression to truths that their original natures allowed them to perceive."
—Fenuala Dowling, *Aerodrome*

"Gordon succeeds in showing not only the pain but 'the possibilities of the outsider.' While distinctive in their voices, these writers converge 'in their hatred of our violent world,' exposing domestic and systemic violence. Their strength of spirit shines from the pages and through the ages."
—Anita Sethi, *Observer*

"Through sensitively recounted biographical details and literary readings, Gordon seeks to understand how these women became writers despite the obstacles in their way, and creates a web of connections, effected in part by their reading of each other's works, and the writings of Mary Wollstonecraft."
—Gail Marshall, *Times Higher Education*

"I love how Lyndall Gordon thinks and I love the clarity and reach of her writing, combining imaginative audacity with scholarly scruple. Her *Outsiders* builds into a lucid meditation on how certain writers become lighthouses for each other."
—Joseph O'Connor, *Irish Times*

"[A] stunning portrait of Woolf . . . one of the most sophisticated explorations of Woolf available and a perfect introduction for students and general readers alike."
—*The Virginia Woolf Bulletin*

"A lively and enterprising group biography"
—Catherine Taylor, *The Financial Times*

"A biographer of the imagination."
—Frances Wilson, *Mail on Sunday*

"The visionary, beautiful *Outsiders*."
—Karina Szczurek, *South African Sunday Times*

"Impeccably researched . . . an excellent read."
—*The Lady*

# Outsiders

# Outsiders

## FIVE WOMEN WRITERS
## WHO CHANGED THE WORLD

### LYNDALL GORDON

Johns Hopkins University Press

*Baltimore*

First published in Great Britain in 2017 by Virago Press
First published in the United States in 2019 by Johns Hopkins University Press

2 4 6 8 9 7 5 3 1

Printed in the United States of
America on acid-free paper.

Johns Hopkins University Press
2715 N. Charles Street
Baltimore, Maryland 21218-4363
www.press.jhu.edu

Library of Congress Control
Number: 2018955300

ISBN 978-1-4214-2944-1 (hardcover : alk. paper)
ISBN 978-1-4214-2945-8 (electronic)
ISBN 1-4214-2944-6 (hardcover : alk. paper)
ISBN 1-4214-2945-4 (electronic)

*Special discounts are available for bulk purchases of this book.
For more information, please contact Special Sales at 410-516-6936
or specialsales@press.jhu.edu.*

Johns Hopkins University Press uses environmentally friendly
book materials, including recycled text paper that is composed
of at least 30 percent post-consumer waste, whenever possible.

*For Paula Dietz*
*who upholds the civilisation the writers in this*
*book imagined for our future*

'Souls live on in perpetual echoes'

George Eliot, *Middlemarch*

# CONTENTS

# LIST OF ILLUSTRATIONS

# FOREWORD

Like many as a child, I made friends with characters in books. It's a strange tie between reader and writer. We come to know a lasting poet or novelist more intimately than we do people of our own place and time; closer in a way than love and friendship. Growing up in a provincial town, I was drawn to outsiders and especially to girls like Maggie Tulliver in *The Mill on the Floss*, a restless, intelligent girl who cannot find a home for her aspiring nature — much like her creator, George Eliot herself. Later, I loved Virginia Woolf's sightings of the night where she sees into hearts and minds of outsiders whose shadow-selves fade in the glare of day. I was a convert to Emily Brontë's full-throated contempt for 'the world without' in favour of 'the world within'. All were outsiders during their lifetimes, and painful though this was, their separations from society did release what they had to say.

As a child with an ill mother, I knew about pity for those set apart; but at the same time I was struck at an early age by the possibilities of the outsider who, like my mother, could use her apartness to see the world afresh. The outsiders who have meant most to me tell us not who we are, but who we might be.

I have chosen five extraordinary outsider voices rising in the course of the nineteenth century: a prodigy, a visionary, an outlaw, an orator and an explorer. To my mind, they came, they saw and left us changed. Each differs in her own place and situation, but what Mary Shelley, Emily Brontë, George Eliot, Olive Schreiner and Virginia Woolf also have in common is the way they inform one another, and us, across the generations. All five were readers before they became writers, which is to say each heard those who came before her in a chain of making. I want to look at the links in this chain as each successive woman brings to birth a new genus. On 2 January 1846, when Emily Brontë was writing *Wuthering Heights*, her unfettered voice powers its way past its time. She declares, 'No coward soul is mine.' The American poet Emily Dickinson, taking in that voice in 1881, and Virginia Woolf, hearing it in 1925, seize on the same word: this writer is 'gigantic'.

I'm curious how an outsize voice came to each of the five writers. How did they become writers despite the obstacles in a woman's way? Their lives appeared changeable to the point of metamorphosis. It was improbable that Mary Godwin at the age of sixteen should have found a great poet, Shelley, keen to encourage her wish to write. It was improbable that Emily Brontë should have had two sisters of congenial genius who contrived to publish her almost against her will. Doctors and nurses did not expect Virginia Woolf to recover from her mental illness in 1915, let alone emerge in the 1920s as a leading novelist. George Eliot could have been an evangelical teacher; Olive Schreiner could have remained a governess.

In each, I see at the outset of their lives a shadowy being, half-awake to untested potency, surfacing in a letter or murmuring to herself in her journal, but always improvising, indeterminate, as she veers from the path laid out by custom. Passion was part of their emergence, as was sexuality: George Eliot fell for a man who could not love her in the way she wished. Mary Godwin (later Mary Shelley) was headlong in her love for a poet to whom, she felt, she could 'unveil' all she was. Olive Schreiner was explicit about arousal, extraordinarily so for a single woman in the 1880s, to the future psychologist of sex, Havelock Ellis, who made notes as she spoke.

In the nineteenth century it was a truth universally acknowledged that nice women were quiet. They did not indulge in utterance in a public arena. To do so was immodest, unwomanly; assertion or egotistical display was thought unnatural. Remarkably then for three insubordinate spirits, their novels spoke instantly to their time: Mary Shelley's *Frankenstein*

(1818), George Eliot's *Adam Bede* (1859), and Olive Schreiner's *Story of an African Farm* (1883). The even bolder words of Emily Brontë and Virginia Woolf, however, did not reach a wide audience till well after their deaths.

These lives and books, as they commune with one another across time, converge in their hatred of our violent world. Emily Brontë brings home the horror of domestic violence together with the misogyny and hate-speech Heathcliff hurls at all comers. Both Mary Shelley and Olive Schreiner witnessed the barbarous impact of war on civilians. Virginia Woolf wakes from madness to the madness of war: the senseless slaughter going on in the trenches.

Four of these five writers began in unpromising situations. The exception is the first, Mary Shelley, who produced *Frankenstein* before she turned twenty. For though she became, like the others, an outsider – in her case, a social outcast – she started with an unprecedented advantage as the daughter of Mary Wollstonecraft, the pioneer of women's rights. Her father, William Godwin, was almost as famous as her mother, a political philosopher admired by the best writers of the day, Coleridge, Lamb, Byron and especially Shelley.

All five of my choices were motherless. With no female model at hand, they learnt from books; if lucky, from an enlightened man. Common to all five was the danger of staying at home, the risk of an unlived life. But if there was danger at home, there was often worse danger in leaving: the loss of protection; estrangement from family; exploitation; a wandering existence, shifting from place to place; and worst of all, exposure to the kind of predator who appeared to offer Olive Schreiner a life – marriage – when she went to work as a governess at the age of seventeen.

In a period when a woman's reputation was her treasured security, each of these five lost it. Each endured the darkness of social exclusion. How far was it willed – how far, for instance, did Emily Brontë will her unpopularity at a Brussels school, or was it involuntary? Were the acts of divergence necessary if each woman was to follow the bent of her nature? Mary Ann Evans fled a provincial home where a brainy girl was regarded as odd. In London, she called herself an 'outlaw' before she became one by living with a partner outside the legality of marriage. Yet it was during her years outside society in the late 1850s that George Eliot came into being.

Virginia Stephen (later Virginia Woolf) settled in Bloomsbury as part of a group. Her brothers, sister, and their mostly homosexual friends, E. M. Forster, Lytton Strachey and Maynard Keynes, provided a shield. In such stimulating company, Virginia and her sister turned themselves into unchaperoned young women, flaunting words like 'semen' and 'copulation' in mixed company until all hours of the night. It was scandalous, but not dangerous. Danger, for Woolf, was the threat of insanity, bound up with what Henry James called 'the madness of art'.

No one, of course, can explain genius. Women are especially hard to discern outside the performing spheres assigned to them in the past, the thin character of angels in the house. In contrast, Virginia Woolf explores the secret thing: women's enduring creativity as it takes its way in shadow; in her generation and before, it did not proclaim itself.

What we now know is that after these writers' lifetimes, families concocted myths, playing down the radical nature of these women. George Eliot's widower presented a flawless angel; at the opposite extreme, Schreiner's estranged widower branded her with his annoyance. The devoted son and daughter-in-law of Mary Shelley cast her in the Victorian mould of timid maiden and mourner. But voices sing out past the tombstones of reputation. The words of these five altered our world, seeding an evolved breed. We do more than read them; we listen and live with them.

To say I chose these writers was actually wrong; they chose themselves. For each had the compulsion Jane Eyre expressed when she said, '*Speak* I must'.

# 1

## PRODIGY

### Mary Shelley

'All being decided I ordered a chaise to be ready by 4 o clock,' the poet Shelley records. 'I watched until the lightning & the stars became pale. At length it was 4,' he goes on. 'I went. I saw her. She came to me.'

It was no common elopement when Mary Godwin, at sixteen going on seventeen, took off with Percy Bysshe Shelley. This milk-pale girl with her piercing, sidelong looks was a prodigy. She had published a narrative poem at the age of eight. Her father, William Godwin, spoke of her as 'somewhat imperious and active of mind'. When she stole from his London house on 28 July 1814, together with her stepsister Clara Mary Jane (called Jane at home, and best known now as Claire Clairmont), the two girls carried their writings. Mary had packed her papers in a box (together with her parents' love letters). She promised Shelley that he might read 'the productions of her mind'. And not just read: he was disposed to 'study' her writings. Two to three years later, buoyed by the poet as live-in mentor, she would produce *Frankenstein*, an extraordinary feat at the age of nineteen.

Mary, in a modest tartan dress, had met Shelley when he came to visit her father. He was tall, long-legged, with an open-neck in a time of cravats to the chin. His shoulders were a little hunched by the intensity of his stare. A protected innocent, Mary woke to an overwhelming passion for this stranger. Like the even younger Juliet, coming face to face with

Romeo in her father's house, Mary was at once absolute for love. 'I am thine, exclusively thine', she wrote secretly in her copy of his poem *Queen Mab*. 'I have pledged myself to thee and sacred is the gift.'

It felt as though her very being was defined by the completeness of her surrender, as she confided a few months later to Shelley's friend Thomas Jefferson Hogg: 'I who love him so tenderly & entirely, whose life hangs on the beam of his eye and whose whole soul is entirely wrapt up in him.'

Attentive and rather delicate, he had the appeal of a man unconcerned to prove his manliness. He was secure enough to admit the womanly elements in men's make-up. As Mary put it, he was 'soft as a woman; firm as the star of night'.*

It was not blind love; desire was folded in recognition. She felt 'interpenetrated' by his strangeness. Shelley struck her, as he struck everyone: he was like no other man. He had the visionary eyes of one who wants to reform the world. He wanted justice for those deprived of it, to do away with political and domestic tyranny, but to Mary, with her revolutionary parents, that was familiar. What was different about Shelley was a gentleness he felt and wished to spread towards all living things. A man should not retaliate for an injury; rather, his forgiveness should convert the injurer, so that it's not altogether a myth in the making when Mary spoke of 'my divine Shelley'.

A barrier to her passion only intensified it, like Juliet's ardour for the forbidden Romeo. Six years older than Mary, Shelley was married – contentedly, it appeared to Mary's father. It did not occur to William Godwin that this most precious of his five children, the one most like him in her rational self-command, could be so abandoned as to throw herself into adultery.

But common words – adultery, elopement, sex, even passion – are inadequate for what was under way. The single most important fact about Mary Godwin is that she was a prodigy whose intellect had flourished in

---

* She expresses in poetic terms what geneticists would later discover: the x element in the xy chromosome that determines the male (as distinct from the xx that determines a female). At the start of sexual differentiation – that is, from conception – the male is biologically a variation on the female, contrary to scripture transmitted by men.

a home with liberating ideas of child development – a home that was an innovative publishing house exclusively for children's books, with Mary herself the youngest by far of its authors. This promise drove all Mary did. When she and Jane galloped away into the dawn – the dawn of their new lives – they carried some books. Most were by Mary's mother, Mary Wollstonecraft, the author of *A Vindication of the Rights of Woman*, published in 1792, the year that Shelley was born. Shelley was her disciple, a man who looked on women as intelligent beings who would rise if freed from the constrictions of society, especially the marriage bond. The girls of Godwin's household were captivated by Shelley's attentiveness to their thoughts, while Shelley was drawn to possibilities furled in a daughter of Mary Wollstonecraft.

'What art thou?' he asks in his poem 'To Mary –'. 'I know but dare not speak.'

With Shelley alone Mary could 'unveil' what she felt herself to be. Playing into desire in the space between the two was a drama of knowing and mystery, speaking and the unspoken. Intending to revolutionise the world, Shelley meant to bring on women, and that was seductive to Mary. Outwardly, she appeared silent and serious, her thoughts 'a sealed treasure'. Shelley broke through that bar of privacy. His voice applauds her, opening new channels of thought. Where for her it had been 'exquisite pain' to check the flow of thoughts strange or changeful, now that flow moves and quickens as it should. With Shelley she lets loose a voice, as she puts it, that can assume a 'natural modulation' and 'communicate with unlimited freedom'.

Mary's 'sealed treasure' matched the 'secret store' Shelley as a youth had built up and armoured so as to walk about a public school where aggression mimicked a war-torn world. The inward power grew and with that a 'sense of loneliness'. As the son and heir of landed gentry, educated at Eton, Shelley was an insider who chose to be an outsider. He cherished his 'peculiarities' and allowed them to 'unfold in secret', aware he would be misunderstood 'like one in a distant and savage land'. His lone, tender being, alien to his conventional father, thirsted for the sympathy of one like himself, and this kindred being he found in Mary, young as she was.

Together, they stood by what Shelley called the 'inmost soul'. The nerves, Shelley found, are like chords struck to accompany 'one delightful voice' vibrating with his own.

Mary was at one with Shelley's dissemination of love; its energy empowered her all the more because it came not from on high but through sympathy. His manner was simple, so unstuffy that she could lie at ease on his breast or against his knees, as she did when the runaways reached the coast and put to sea.

Their immediate plan was to make their way on foot to Switzerland, starting in Paris. It was a stormy crossing of the Channel, with waves rushing onto the boat, but when they beached on the sands at Calais Shelley saw a broad, red swathe of light.

'Mary, look,' he said, 'the sun rises over France', as though he were proclaiming a new life.

She appeared to him 'insensible to all future evil'. How did it happen that two years later she'd conceive a novel about an evil that was monstrous in every sense?

*Frankenstein*, as all know, is about a scientist who puts together a larger-than-life man. What is his nature? What will he do? Unparented and shunned, he turns to violence and, empowered by his size, his havoc is appalling. 'Frankenstein' entered the language as a word for a dangerous experiment leading to loss of control. The novel has always had cult status, for its blend of horror with a universal issue. Is violence innate, or is it brought on by emotional deprivation: the impact of absent parenting and social prejudice? This is a question posed by a young woman whose situation made her enough an outsider to enter into the monster's frame of mind. For to take off with Shelley was to put herself outside society, and in the course of their travels she witnessed the barbarism of men.

At the book's core is the story of the monster from his estranged point of view. As with Macbeth, the author dares to grant a voice of human feeling to a killer, constructed in this case of human matter and yet visibly – terrifyingly – alien.

In the two centuries since its publication there have been innumerable variations in plays and films, but the myth of *Frankenstein*'s inception has held to this day. It is that Mary Godwin conceived *Frankenstein* suddenly, out of nowhere, in a dream induced by Shelley and Byron talking of Gothic fictions. This memory, offered by Shelley himself in the preface he wrote for the novel and expanded by Mary fifteen years later when both poets were dead, linked *Frankenstein* with those immortal names. In this way Mary was fixed in the shadow of the two men and the books they chose to read. But to open up the private story behind the frissons of far-off Gothic horror, we must go back to Mary's family: to the revered but somewhat blighted figure of her father; to what was pent up when her stepsister Jane succumbed to 'horrors'; and to Mary's own observations and emotions on the road to *Frankenstein* — all that led her to shape this great work.

Mary Wollstonecraft died ten days after giving birth on 30 August 1797. The motherless child became intensely attached to her father, who was no ordinary father or widower. At the time, William Godwin was a celebrity as a political philosopher. Two generations of thinkers read his revolutionary enquiry, *Political Justice*, and London men whose gifts would outlast the age — Coleridge and Charles Lamb — came to 41 Skinner Street in the City, where Godwin lived surrounded by books. Their talk was part of his daughter's education, and Mary was aware that a girl brought up by such a father to think for herself could outdo the limitations of female tuition.

Mary's father encouraged her first book, written when she was a child taken with a popular song. *Mounseer Nongtongpaw* is a comic-verse story about the blunders of an insular and absurdly thick John Bull when he travels to France during the brief peace of 1802–3.* Addressing the French in English, he takes their '*je n'entends pas*' to be information about a grandee called Nongtongpaw. Godwin published this in 1805, the year he opened his Juvenile Library on the rounded corner of Skinner Street.

---

* The Peace of Amiens between France, Britain, Spain and the Batavian Republic (the Netherlands) had brought a brief halt to the Napoleonic wars.

Godwin fancied that Mary looked like her mother, the love of his life, and a miniature does show a similar curl at the corner of her mouth and the same deeply dented upper lip. Yet Mary looked more like her father, with the high tablet of her forehead, pale complexion and long, elegant nose. She had her father's studiousness and taste for reading.

All the while Mary had to contend with a blow that had fallen late in 1801, when her beloved father remarried. From then on, Mary's closeness to her father was challenged by a stepmother whose temper the child could not trust. Her dislike was visceral: 'a woman I shudder to think of'.

Mary Jane Vial had passed herself off as a widow to account for her two fatherless children, Charles and Jane. (The name she'd assumed, Mrs Clairmont, possibly came from *Clermont*, a Gothic novel of 1798, one of a genre whose excesses thrilled Jane Austen's heroine in *Northanger Abbey*, completed in 1799.) The dubious name and murky past of Mrs Clairmont led Godwin to marry her twice on the same day in different London churches. Conceivably, being Catholic, she wished for a Catholic ceremony, but it's likely also that Godwin meant to secure legal cover for her varied identities. The second Mrs Godwin was already pregnant with Godwin's child, and he acted with a sense of responsibility (as he had done when he'd married Mary Wollstonecraft, then pregnant with Mary).

'Second Mamma', as Godwin introduced her, was an able woman wearing green glasses, who had worked as an editor and translator. Though her experience of the book trade made her a suitable helpmeet for Godwin, she turned out to be moody – 'the bad baby', Charles Lamb called her. She would alarm the family by walking out on them – and then would return.

When Godwin had been a bachelor who wrote for his living, he was poor – one reason not to marry until his forties. In Wollstonecraft's time, though troubled by money, they managed to scrape by and to be so happy together that though both had wedded reluctantly as a sop to public opinion, they were soon converted to marriage. It turned out differently with Second Mamma: all Godwin's friends thought her inferior to his first wife. His new wife's influence overwhelmed this highly intelligent and loyal man in that she changed his relations to people. He turned into an inveterate borrower.

Then Mary Jane's habit of twisting the truth vented itself on Godwin's daughters, especially the elder, Fanny, whom Godwin had adopted. Fanny was the child of Wollstonecraft's earlier partnership with an American, Gilbert Imlay, who came from a well-to-do shipping family in Philadelphia. They knew nothing of Fanny's existence, and Imlay's roaming life did not admit of childcare.

Her mother's death and replacement by Second Mamma, followed by the birth of a son, William Jr, left Fanny in a weak position, the only child amongst the five in the Godwin household with no blood tie to either parent. During the years when Godwin had been a single father, he had put into practice Wollstonecraft's belief that domestic affections should form the basis of education. One day, when he happened to be going away from home, he asked Second Mamma to kiss her stepdaughters, but only if she wished. The afterthought suggests that she was not naturally affectionate with the two little girls who came into her charge.

For her father's sake, Fanny tried to see Second Mamma's good points, but the girl's vulnerability as she grew older released a jab. Mrs Godwin took it upon herself to drive it home to Fanny that she was a burdensome extra. So it was that the frisking 'Fannikin', the child Wollstonecraft had adored, who had accompanied her mother on her journey to Scandinavia, who had been her mother's comfort and slept in her arms, grew up dispirited.

Beset by the cares of business, Godwin ceded control to his wife. While Fanny tried to placate her, Mary was less inclined to yield. Where Fanny seemed to will herself to become a never-to-be-rescued Cinderella at the mercy of Second Mamma, Mary opposed their stepmother.

There was growing friction as Mary grew up. What Godwin gave out doesn't ring true, that health was the reason to dispatch her at fourteen to Dundee, to the household of Godwin's friend Mr Baxter, who had two daughters. It's more likely that Mary had to get away. 'Health' could be a euphemism for mental health, a bent for depression both Wollstonecraft's daughters got from their mother.

It was while Mary was in Scotland that Shelley visited the Godwins at Skinner Street. As a rebel against all forms of authority he revered Godwin's politics. In 1810, at University College, Oxford, Shelley and his friend Hogg had published an essay on *The Necessity of Atheism*, and when pressed by the university authorities, they did not own up. The university had found itself compelled to expel them. Shelley's father, Sir Timothy Shelley, had cast him off – though unable (for legal reasons) to disinherit him.

The poet was determined on reform along Godwinian lines: to recover what eighteenth-century philosophers believed to be our natural benevolence. Godwin – and Shelley – believed people needed to liberate themselves from laws and social institutions designed to keep them down. Thus Shelley's pamphlet against religion.

Plaster bust by Marianne Hunt, who knew Shelley well

Shelley trusted that Godwin stood by his 1793 book *Political Justice* – only to find that Godwin himself had changed. The bloodshed of the French Revolution had convinced him not to confront power head on; rather to convert the next generation through writing and mentoring those who sought his counsel. When Shelley came to his door in 1812, Godwin took a cool view of his rashness. He rebuked Shelley for his anger at his father, and for rushing to publish further incendiary pamphlets – in favour of Irish rebellion – without considering the consequences. He was showing off, Godwin said with his usual candour.

Shelley was delighted. Far from put out, he wanted nothing more than to take in Godwin's moral stand. Where Shelley was heartened to find Godwin so bracing, Godwin was heartened to find in this follower a master of words who was also heir to two hundred thousand pounds, a fortune at the time.

Though Shelley came to Skinner Street as a follower of Godwin, he was just as keen to meet Fanny, the daughter whose early years had been shaped by Mary Wollstonecraft. Even before he and Fanny met, he invited her to stay for a summer with him and his young wife, Harriet, in Lynmouth on the north Devon shore. To Shelley's surprise, Godwin would not permit this – he said that he did not know a man until he had seen him face to face.

When Shelley came to dine, Fanny was eighteen, a young woman with long brown hair and a face marked by the smallpox she'd had as a baby. Neither of her sisters figured on that occasion. Jane, aged fourteen, was at boarding school and Mary, recently turned fifteen, was around at the time but uninvolved. For once Fanny was not overshadowed, even though Godwin put Mary forward. Mary was 'very much like her mother', he repeated to Shelley, whose wide-awake, rather prominent blue eyes were intent on Fanny. That evening she was not the subdued, anxious-to-please young woman she had become. Shelley's readiness to know her called out her mother's eager eloquence and honesty, an animation Mary Wollstonecraft used to praise in the blithe child Fanny had been.

Shelley was charmed by her humane sensibility, and by Fanny's idea – one he would make his own – that poets are the unacknowledged legislators of the world. The stoop to his shoulders was balanced by the upward surge of a long, rose neck, a fount for his words. He had the blatant eccentricity of a person unafraid of his opinions, offset by alert manners. Intense and thin, with a narrow chest and shoulders, he lived on a diet of bread and nuts plucked abstractedly and none too often from his pocket. He had curly hair, washed by dunking in a bucket of cold water and left dishevelled. The back of his head was rather oddly flat.

So partial to each other were Shelley and Fanny that when Shelley made another visit to Skinner Street, Mamma saw fit to send Fanny to stay with her less than affectionate aunts, Wollstonecraft's sisters. Had Fanny remained in place as a focus for his attention, Shelley might not have turned his susceptibilities to Wollstonecraft's second daughter.

After a second stay in Dundee, Mary came home in March 1814, and friction with Mamma resumed. Mary would escape to her mother's grave in St Pancras churchyard. It was her place to read and commune with the world's lost model of womanhood.

On 5 May, Shelley turned up at Skinner Street and there was Mary. He came seven times that month, took lodgings near by, in Hatton Garden, and then, on 8 June, brought his Oxford friend Hogg, now preparing for the Bar, to meet Godwin. While the two young men waited in Godwin's study, Shelley strode impatiently up and down, asking Hogg where Godwin could be, and then, softly, the door opened and a pale girl in tartan said in a 'thrilling' voice, 'Shelley', and Shelley exclaimed in a 'thrilling' voice: 'Mary'. At once he bounded out of the study to speak to her.

The spark between them was already live in looks and gestures when, as Shelley saw it, Mary took the initiative. On 26 June 1814, with Jane as none-too-vigilant chaperone, he came with Mary to her mother's grave, and there poured out his past.

Afterwards, Shelley told Hogg that no words could match that 'sublime' moment when Mary Godwin declared she was his. There was no mention of his marriage, if his report of this scene was accurate. But hints of marital unhappiness had come Mary's way: Harriet, he intimated, no longer loved him, and the child she was carrying might not be his. Even so, for Mary to declare her feelings was boldly unconventional.

Any hesitation Shelley had was dispelled by Mary's candour and readiness, as resolute as Juliet's – her conviction they belonged together. Her originality was apparent in her very motions and tones of voice, blending tenderness and, for all her conviction, a need to be convinced of an equal commitment. His response to this girl, whose fine, gauzy hair, loose on her shoulders, spun as she moved her head, caught fire. Afterwards he told her,

> *How beautiful and calm and free, thou wert*
> *In thy young wisdom, when the mortal chain*
> *Of Custom thou didst burst and rend in twain . . .*

Mary Wollstonecraft was part of this entrancement. 'I would unite / With thy beloved name', is how Shelley put it in a verse recalling the revolutionary daring of Mary's parents. This sixteen-year-old is the 'aspiring Child' of a mother whose fame

> *Shines on thee, through the tempests dark and wild*
> *Which shake these latter days; and thou canst claim*
> *The shelter, from thy Sire, of an immortal name.*

The day following Mary's declaration seemed to Shelley his real 'birthday' – probably the day they threw caution away, dispensed with Jane and made love for the first time.

Jane's presence had not been incidental. She was not only the chaperone convention required; Shelley had his eye on her too, had visited her at her boarding school and they had taken walks together. To think and act with an independent mind was central to Godwin's teaching, and in this Jane Clairmont was formed in much the same way as Mary. Jane, too, meant to write. In fact, she preceded Mary in conceiving a story of an outcast. She had in mind a young woman whom people call an idiot because she outraged convention.

Together, Mary and Jane were agog over Shelley's ideas. His appeal went far beyond infatuation, though that was part of it; these girls were prime disciples of Wollstonecraft, whose portrait in Godwin's study had gazed down on them as they grew up and whose tomb was to them a sacred spot. Shelley was at one with Wollstonecraft in his keenness that women should read and learn, and his willingness to share his advantages was rare in an age when advice books warned against higher education for the weaker vessel. The poet's eagerness and his enquiring mind burst on Mary and Jane as their chance to move beyond the domestic horizon.

Shelley at once revealed to Godwin his plan to be with Mary. His voice was high and slightly cracked. Since Godwin had rejected the institution of marriage in *Political Justice*, Shelley expected Mary's father to consent.

'He had the madness,' Godwin exploded to a friend.

Godwin found himself in a complicated position. His outrage was in conflict with his need for a loan of over a thousand pounds that Shelley was negotiating on his behalf. Later Godwin gave out that Shelley had not conveyed his intentions until after the negotiation was finished on 6 July, but his actual response was to temporise and then exercise his not inconsiderable powers of reason to quash what he took to be Shelley's initiative. Like many a parent of an ardent daughter, he recognised what we now call grooming. To him, it was nothing short of wicked.

Harriet Shelley, anxious about her husband's silence, then arrived from Bath where she, her sister and child had stayed on their own while relations between Shelley and Harriet were strained. Over the previous three months or so they had not lived together, although sexual intimacy was not entirely at an end, since Harriet had conceived their second child in late March. She announced her pregnancy in July, the very month that Shelley broke the news to her that his commitment was now as a friend, not a husband.

Since this interview was stressful, he made an appeal for 'consolation', even as he told Harriet, 'it is no reproach to me that you have never filled my heart with an all-sufficing passion'. His promise of continued affection and an assurance that she could find someone else urged his wife to accept the situation. Could she sympathise with Mary as one 'suffering' from 'tyranny'? And would she send over some handkerchiefs and their volume of Mary Wollstonecraft's posthumous works? It did occur to Harriet that Mary had been talking up her mother as a lure.

Pressed by two pleas, one from Harriet (by then five months pregnant), reinforced by Godwin's reasons, Mary appeared to back down. Mrs Shelley was given to understand that Mary would do what she could to stop Shelley's advances.

Shelley's response was to take an overdose of laudanum — not a lethal dose. At midnight the Godwin household was roused by Shelley's landlord; the Godwins rushed over to Hatton Garden and found Shelley already in the hands of a local doctor. Mrs Godwin nursed him all the following day.

Though physically separated, Mary and Shelley did exchange letters. At first these were smuggled out of the house by the helpful Jane, and then, when Godwin put a stop to this, further letters were delivered by the bookshop porter. There were secret meetings when Mary and Jane took their daily walk near the Charterhouse. On 25 July, Godwin wrote an appeal to Shelley. He judged the poet's feelings as 'caprice and momentary impulse over every impulse that is dear to the honest heart'. He thought Harriet 'an innocent and meritorious wife', and asked Shelley to spare 'the fair and spotless fame of my young child'.

It was unusual for Godwin to show his feelings, but as he made this plea for Mary, his emotional temperature rose. 'I could not believe that you wd. enter my house under the name of benefactor, to leave behind an endless poison to corrode my soul.'

Given the force of this letter and Shelley's respect for Godwin, nothing might have come of scenes from a summer dream had not morning sickness set in. Mary was pregnant. And so the pair — accompanied by an eager but unknowing Jane — took off for France.

To put herself under the protection of a married man was, on the face of it, a disastrous move. At this stage, Mary had no way of knowing how readily Shelley could be drawn to other women or be tugged by a lovely girl in an oppressive situation. Nor was Mary likely to have been aware that Shelley's grandfather, Sir Bysshe, had kept a separate establishment for a mistress and four children. The Shelley family retained their social position as the pink of propriety because they followed the code of the cover-up. Shelley's extra-marital union with Mary was not in fact unconventional in terms of his family's history; what was unconventional was his unconcern for discretion — at least at first.

Damage to the reputation of an inexperienced girl did not trouble him, as it hadn't troubled him when he'd eloped with Harriet Westbrook, a schoolgirl who had grown up in a protective family. On that occasion, he'd been free to marry. The second time, when he eloped with Mary

Godwin, he had a wife and children to consider, but the same impulsive-
ness was in play. He was leaving his one-year-old daughter Ianthe and
an unborn baby, and he can't have been unaware that a declared atheist
who was openly an adulterer would find it difficult, if not impossible, to
gain custody of his children unless he returned to his wife. Yet desertion
was not the way he saw it; he built up a fancy of having Harriet join his
party as an attached friend, like Jane. To ignore the issue of infidelity was
common for many in his upper-class milieu. But to take on middle-class
innocents like Harriet and Mary was bound to cause trouble.

As they left the house, Mary held up the chaise to do 'something'. At
the last was there some reluctance to leave home in this stealthy way, or
some compunction, which she kept from Shelley? She was no careless
feather-head like Lydia Bennet, skipping off with a knave to no one knew
where. In *Pride and Prejudice*, Lydia leaves a gleeful, uncommunicative note.
Mary went back to leave what we can be sure was an informative note for
her father, which he found on his dressing table an hour or so later.

Godwin's usual manner was calm, philosophic. Now a cheated father,
he raged with shame. Shelley was 'licentious', a 'seducer' as well as a 'trai-
tor' to his hospitality. Godwin had welcomed into his home this young
revolutionary, the unlikely son of a baronet, with sufficient expectations to
fund deserving projects like Godwin's under-funded publishing house. The
Juvenile Library had a superb list, including the Lambs' *Tales from Shakespeare*,
but was always in crisis over debt. Now it would look as though Godwin had
bartered his daughter to save his business. He could not forgive Mary.

Mary's note to her father must have told him where they were going
because, en route to Dover, she feared to be pursued. They had four horses
so as to move faster as the temperature rose – it was unusually hot. That
first day was a race to get away.

But Mary was mistaken. Her father did not come after her, and he cau-
tioned his wife, who did pursue Jane, not to approach Shelley, who might

be 'violent'. In fact, Shelley was gentle with women, and Godwin's idea suggests rather the unaccustomed violence of his own feelings.

Mrs Godwin caught up with the runaways at Calais. There it became plain that she was not acting for Godwin and his daughter. Her sole concern was to persuade her own daughter to come home. When Jane refused, Mrs Godwin said not another word. Shelley and Mary encountered her making her way back to the harbour; no one broke the gulf of silence. The message was clear: Mary Godwin must be shunned.

Why did Godwin not go after Mary? Why in effect did he cast her off, shutting the door on so young a girl? It was puzzling behaviour, and Mary herself found this inexplicable given the special bond between her and her father. The depth of their mutual feeling must be in some way behind Godwin's rejection of Mary, but his private thoughts are hard to fathom. The fact remains: he meant to erase her.

The lovers moved on to Paris. It didn't matter that they found the gardens of the Tuileries too formal and without grass. 'We returned & were too happy to sleep,' Shelley records on Tuesday, 2 August, in their joint *Journal*. The following day, when Mary read aloud from Byron's work, it was as though the intensity of their feelings made the poems their own. It was there in Paris that Mary opened her box of private treasures, her writings and her father's letters, for Shelley to see. 'She rested on my bosom,' he records, and the morning passed in 'delightful converse'.

Along with love and heady intimacy, books were central to their union. Mary and Jane were setting out on higher education, rather like high-flyers today going off to university. It was a travelling university low on immediate funds, but, for all that, ambitious in its intellectual reach. Generations ahead of aspiring young women with no access to higher education, here were two girls, still in their teens, crossing borders, carrying books, with stories in their heads yet to be told. Though their actions cost them dear, they had exceptional luck to have two great minds to guide their reading: first Godwin, now Shelley. Her father had urged Mary to be great and good; Shelley did the same. Along with their closeness as lovers, he was absolutely with her in all her studies.

Leaving Paris at the start of their walking tour, Mary and Jane wore black silk dresses. As they made their slow way towards Switzerland, Shelley read aloud from Wollstonecraft's autobiographical novel, *Mary: A Fiction*. Published in 1788, the novel coincides with the period when Mary's mother stopped being a governess and began as a writer in London. This is when she determined on being 'the first of a new genus'. The stated aim of the novel was to develop a character different from Richardson's Clarissa or Rousseau's Sophie, whose perfections 'wander from nature'. Wollstonecraft meant to demonstrate 'the mind of a woman who has thinking powers': such a creature 'may be allowed to exist as a *possibility*'.

As a governess who had already published her advanced ideas on girls' education, that shadow of possibility was feeling its way onto the platform of action through the character of Mary, a survivor of setbacks who means to 'dart into futurity'. The fictional model is consistent with Wollstonecraft's belief that a change in woman's character must precede her more public advance: 'still does my panting soul push forward, and live in futurity, in the deep shades o'er which darkness hangs.'

Women, this novel laments, live by a stock of worn-out narratives, unable to reshape their lives. Its hope is for a road to open 'by which they can pursue more extensive plans of . . . independence'.

At one run-down inn after another, Mary, Jane and Shelley formed a reading party. All were bent on absorbing *A Vindication of the Rights of Woman* and *The Wrongs of Woman* (Wollstonecraft's second novel, published posthumously in 1798), as well as *Mary* and Godwin's *Political Justice*. In putting their precepts into practice – including their rejection of marriage as a form of property – the three travellers were outdoing their elders in revolutionary purity.

They went fired with the words of Mary Wollstonecraft and her trust in reason: 'Those who are bold enough to advance before the age they live in, and to throw off, by the force of their own minds, the prejudices which the maturing reason of the world will in time disavow, must learn to brave censure.'

Their route took them through a landscape of famine and wretchedness in the wake of Napoleon's defeat in February of that year. Mary later remembered the heaps of white ruins that had been the town of Nogent-sur-Seine. A white dust lay over the gardens. The defeated were harsh and no longer washed, their inns so filthy that sometimes the travellers could not sleep. A bed might be no more than a sheet spread over straw. At Ossey-les-Trois-Maisons, when rats, she claimed, put cold paws on her face, Jane was driven to lie on Mary's and Shelley's bed.

In the once-beautiful village of Saint Aubin, the Cossacks had left not a cow – there was no milk to be had. Along the road they met a man whose children the Cossacks had murdered.

'Brutal force has hitherto governed the world,' Mary's mother had declared in the *Rights of Woman*. 'Man accustomed to bow down to power in his savage state, can seldom divest himself of this barbarous prejudice.' Her daughter echoes 'barbarous': 'Nothing could be more entire than the ruin which these barbarians had spread as they advanced,' Mary observes, 'perhaps they remembered Moscow and the destruction of Russian Villages [during Napoleon's attack on Russia in 1812]; but we were now in France, and the distress of the inhabitants, whose houses had been burnt ... has given a sting to my detestation of war, which none can feel who have not travelled through a country pillaged and wasted by this plague, which, in his pride, man inflicts upon his fellow.'

Though Mary had started out sure that love could conquer evil, she was forced to look upon this scene. She discerned how the crimes done to civilians are prompted by twisted self-pity, justifying the murder of innocents as revenge.

Water for washing was in short supply all along their way through France. There were no basins to be had and often they were able to wash only face and hands at a village pump. As they approached Pontarlier near the border, Shelley offered Mary a chance to bathe in the shallow water of a roadside stream. Mary's excuse was that she had no towel, so Shelley offered to bring some leaves to dry herself. The offer was quietly declined. It's the alert Jane who sets down this scene in her journal.

Mary says nothing of Godwin in the journal she kept with Shelley, but this need not mean that her father was not on her mind. Her dependence on Shelley would have made it impossible to jar him with regret for her father. Approaching her seventeenth birthday, 30 August, Mary was a pregnant runaway without support. Shelley did not intend to earn a living. For all his egalitarian ethos, he retained the mind-set of entitlement. His idea of an income was to wring an allowance from his father and to borrow (at a ruinous percentage) on the strength of his future inheritance.

One night at Pontarlier Mary remarked that men are always the source of a thousand difficulties, and tried to laugh with Shelley about their unreliable coachman.

Shelley asked her why she suddenly looked sad.

'I was thinking of my father, and wondering what he is now feeling.'

'Do you mean that as a reproach to me?'

'Oh! No!' she brushed this off. 'Don't let us think more about it.'

It occurred to Jane how much Mary loved her father. Again it's Jane who set down what Mary does not record. A carapace contained her rebellions, warmth, desire and loyalty (and in this she was similar to her father, keeping her in sympathy with him, even as he withdrew). Proud and sensitive, she was not one to put herself forward unless cherished and supported. This reticence was reinforced by deliberate discretion in view of the two indiscreet men in her life. Her father's memoir of her mother, including her attachment to Gilbert Imlay, had opened the way to vilification – Mary recoiled from 'the vulgar abuse of the inimical press'. But she was following her mother's example now, with this 'spirit of the elements taking earthy dress', a superhuman (as she saw him) selecting her as his mate, a fate that placed her as one apart from the laws that govern ordinary mortals in a way the ordinary must find questionable.

At Troyes, a medieval town about halfway along their route, Shelley had written to Harriet, inviting her to join his wandering party. To his disappointment, no reply awaited their arrival at Neuchâtel across the Swiss border.

Mary had need of a cool head in the face of all she had to undertake, not only to measure up to what was elevating in Shelley (his poetry and classical education), but also mundane things: morning sickness at the outset; bed bugs in filthy inns; their blunders in buying an ass, then a mule on its last legs; Shelley's disappointment when Harriet did not join his party; their mistake in committing themselves to rooms in an ugly, comfortless house in Brunnen; and, not least, their shortage of money, which forced them to turn back.

One more trial came on 27 August, after they departed from Brunnen for the town of Lucerne. Jane was shocked by reading *King Lear*, with its howling voice of an outcast betrayed by kin, and then, by way of diversion, she dipped into *Richard III*, the killer of kin. That night she had the first fit of what Mary called Jane's 'horrors'.

Jane's horrors were not helped by their mode of travel. The cheapest was to go north by water, so they made their way towards the Rhine. Their boat-mates at Mellingen, in northern Switzerland, filled Mary with disgust. These men were slimy, 'uncleansable animals', 'loathsome creepers'. It was like looking into a heart of darkness. On this riverboat moving up the Reuss to meet their main route along the Rhine, Mary was forced to counter Godwin's trust in man's gradual progress towards enlightenment. She could entertain no consoling hope. ''Twere easier,' she wrote, 'for god to make entirely new men than attempt to purify such monsters as these.'

Stage by stage, from Basel, along the widening Rhine, past craggy cliffs crowned by desolate towers, past Strasbourg and Mainz to Cologne, and from there by coach, they came at length to the Dutch coast. Their road now wound between canals full of enormous frogs. By the time they arrived at Marsluys (Maassluis), near Rotterdam, they were down to their last twenty *écus* of the ninety pounds they had. Waiting out a storm, they had to plead a passage across the Channel. The Dutch captains would not put to sea in so wild a wind; only an English captain called Ellis was willing to try. The cost was three pounds each. All they could offer were hopes that when they reached London they would pressure Shelley's put-upon financial manager Hookham or, as a last resort, the disaffected Harriet, to cough up.

It was during their two-day wait in Marsluys that Jane and Mary turned from writing journals to stories. Jane had long had her plot in mind, born of Wollstonecraft and Rousseau's *Emile* (his liberating book on education, an influence through Wollstonecraft and Godwin on Jane's own upbringing). She resisted, as Wollstonecraft had done, Rousseau's portrait of a woman as a coquette with no truth in her: 'It is indeed partial to judge the whole sex by the conduct of one whose very education tended to fit her more for a Seraglio than the friend & equal of Man.' Here is Jane's entry in her *Journal* for the following day, Saturday 10 September:

> Write a story – . . . Write all day – After tea write the fragment of my Ideot – This has been for years a favorite plan of mine – To develop the Workings & Improvements of a Mind which by Common People was deemed the mind of an Ideot because it conformed not to their vulgar & prejudiced views.

Mary's story was 'Hate'. The title is all we know, and that to read it filled Shelley with pleasure. If we want to speculate about the content, we might recall that 'hate' is what Mary felt for her stepmother. Did she have a sense of foreboding at the prospect before her: London, the home city she had meant to leave, the stepmother who made her shudder and the father who had turned his face away?

Back in London, Mary and Jane had to wait for two hours in a carriage while Shelley persuaded his wife (now living with her well-off parents in Chapel Street) to pay for their passage. It was a delicate negotiation because Harriet, seven months pregnant, hoped at first that her husband would come back to her. Somehow Shelley convinced her to trust him to arrange everything for the best. Shelley's group found lodgings at 56 Margaret Street, Cavendish Square, within reach of Mary's father who, not content with ignoring his daughter, forbade her sister Fanny to visit. In Godwin's view, Fanny's reputation might be tainted by contact.

All the same, Mary Godwin continued to inhabit her father's intellectual space. On 20 September she began to read *Political Justice* and then, seated at her mother's tomb, she read her father's 1809 essay on sepulchres. If she craved her father's care, she exercised a tight-lipped control. The irony with which she spoke of 'the good people of Skinner Street' is the only bitterness she permits herself.

She now had no friends apart from Shelley's circle; none of her own sex, apart from Jane. It's thought that in France she had written to Isabel Baxter, with whom she'd lived in Dundee, but Isabel now shunned her, perhaps unwillingly, on the say-so of her new husband, Mr Booth. Isabel and her sister Christy posted what Mary called a 'very impertinent' letter to Fanny. Christy, who had once lived in Skinner Street as Mary's friend, professed friendship, but Mary observed, 'we see how much worth it is'.

Mary's solution was to build a defensive bulwark made of books. The *Journal* turns at this stage into a record of reading. Mary had an urge for classical learning, which would reappear in Mary Ann Evans (before she became George Eliot) and Virginia Stephen (before she became Virginia Woolf), mopping up Greek in her back room in her father's Kensington house. For them, Greek epitomised the education closed to women. Though bullying at Eton had made the school a 'little hell', Shelley had emerged with a love of Homer and the Greek dramatists. With his help, Mary began to have Greek lessons soon after their return to London.

Later that September, Mary and Shelley stopped at a bookseller's in Holborn and bought a guinea's worth of books. That day her journal records reading her father's *Political Justice* as 'a letter' from him, a substitute for the letters he never sent. When she finished this, she turned to her father's first and best-known novel, *Caleb Williams*.

She read night and day. The worse her situation socially or emotionally, the more completely she aligned herself with the greatest minds. To turn to books was her way of restoring or renewing herself. Call it self-education, or call it the resource of women with no access to institutions of learning. Mary Godwin, the Brontës, George Eliot, Olive Schreiner, Virginia Woolf – all were on the margin or outside society in one way or another, and all were readers. Books were their companions across time, seeding a new kind of woman. And their freedom from contact made reading and writing more sustained than for other middle-class women caught up in social duties.

In her pursuit of reading as self-making, Mary Godwin followed what her mother had urged. In Wollstonecraft's *Thoughts on the Education of Daughters*, the daughter becomes a reader from her earliest years. She is destined to displace the old breed of obedience and passive dependence, 'designed to hunt every spark of nature out of [women's] composition'.

Shelley, meanwhile, was dashing about trying to raise loans. During October and November he had to dodge arrest for debt; it was safe to return to a settled address only on Sundays. Frenetic though these efforts were, Shelley knew that ample money would be his eventually. Nothing could deprive him of his position as heir to his father's wealth. It gave him the confidence to do as he liked.

One night – it was a Friday, 7 October – Mary went to bed early and their guest, the author Thomas Love Peacock, took himself off after dinner. When Jane and Shelley were alone, Jane broached her idea of a 'subterraneous community of women'. It can't be a coincidence that, the night before, Jane had read Wollstonecraft's letters.

Shelley switched the subject to Jane's weakness: her imaginary fears. 'Is it not horrible to feel the silence of the night tingling in one's ears?' he prodded. The way he sets down this scene in his and Mary's journal, he behaved like an enquiring scientist as he repeated his question to the increasingly uneasy Jane.

One o'clock struck. Shelley called it 'the witching time'. At two, as they finally said goodnight, Shelley bent towards Jane, his hand on the table. At that moment he could not repress a sense of his power.

'How horribly you look,' Jane cried, 'take your look off!'

Her room felt unsafe. A pillow left under her bed now sat on a chair and the conviction seized her that she'd lost control of her surroundings. Terrified, she rushed back to Shelley. In an intent, almost clinical way, as though this were an experiment, he inspected Jane's 'distorted' appearance, and next day he records his observations: the 'deadly hue' of her lips and cheeks; a face beaming 'with a whiteness almost like light'; her ears prominent and erect; her wide, staring eyeballs, with lids retracted to nothing, as though they'd been 'newly inserted into the sockets of a lifeless head'; and the skin of her face wrinkled all over.

Shelley chose this moment to break it to Jane that Mary was pregnant. At this, Jane shrieked and writhed on the floor. Shelley was forced to wake Mary and bring her to Jane. Only Mary's presence calmed her.

Shelley laid it on so thick that Jane protested it was not what she'd felt, and what she did feel we can't know beyond Shelley's willingness to exercise power over her mind.

Apart from this scene in Shelley's hand, the *Journal* looks away from Jane's 'horrors' — Mary's word is thrown off evenly. Next day, while he talked to Jane, Mary took up *The Wrongs of Woman*. It may mean nothing beyond the fact that Mary was always re-reading her mother, but it does bring back Mary's let-slip remark (when Shelley had invited Harriet to join them) on men as the source of trouble.

The set-up was volatile because Shelley meant to act out his dreams — often acts of rescue. He fantasised converting and liberating 'two heiresses' — his sisters Hellen and Elizabeth — to join his party on a prospective expedition to the West of Ireland to further his determination to change society. At the dangerous edge of this mission, he cultivated Godwin's theory that no man owned a woman, and encouraged Mary, now heavily pregnant, to sleep with Hogg. Once again Mary was tactful. She patted Hogg with civil excuses in the wings of flirtation. This hadn't occurred to her, she told him. She wasn't ready as yet.

As the virgin-companion in this group, Jane's alarms were valid. She had put herself under the protection of a man who believed in free love, who had attached her as necessary to him and who blocked her defection into her own radical dream for changing the world: a community of women as a political underground.

The Godwins took the view that Jane was tainted by her association with Shelley, but retrievable if she might be persuaded to leave him and put herself under parental protection. Her mother came, together with Fanny, to Margaret Street and stood outside her window. Since Godwin had forbidden contact, they could only stand there making a mute plea.

Jane was always proud of growing up in the philosopher's home. It did weigh with her that he judged her to be in the wrong. She wrote to Godwin, who promptly ordered her to return home. Jane hesitated. Her 'horrors' now came on more strongly. Was she waking up to her mother's words at Calais, the threat of becoming a lifelong outcast, as irretrievable as Mary? Having borne Jane out of wedlock, Mrs Godwin was well placed to warn against putting yourself in a man's power. Jane had chosen to follow Mary's lead, but was shaken by what the pair had kept from her: Mary's pregnancy, which made her more dependent than Jane had imagined.

In November, Fanny was dispatched to fetch Jane with a ruse that her mother was dying. 'Fanny will not see me,' Mary reports in the *Journal*. 'Hear everything she says however . . . Papa tells Fanny if she sees me he will never speak to her again — a blessed degree of liberty this.'

Jane went home to Skinner Street on 13 November. What happened there is not known, only that Mrs Godwin did not die, and on the third day Jane returned to Shelley. Mary describes herself as 'very ill' for the following three days, while Jane went 'hopping about the town' with Shelley. Hopping. The word registers the renewal of Jane's claim, animating Shelley's quicksilver moves. From November 1814, the month that decided her unconventional future, Jane began to try out variations on her first name, Clara: Clary, Clare — and finally settled on Claire Clairmont. The old Jane was all but finished.

That month, Mary's pregnancy would have begun to show. There was no plan to hide herself: she was visibly bearing an illegitimate child in her home city while her partner, still unable to pay his debts, was on the run, dodging prison. He slept in various hideouts, mainly at Peacock's house, which meant that Mary and her step-sister were left alone. Mary felt or allowed herself no regret for her situation. Her refuge from public opinion was the life she shared with Shelley. Separation heightened their passion during a brief meeting. Afterwards, on 2 November, when Shelley looked back on a few sweet moments together, he wrote to Mary: 'There is eternity in these moments — they contain the true elixir of immortal life.' He felt that each became wiser as letters flew between them declaring a surpassing love, with Shelley playing out the Romeo and Juliet drama of divided lovers: 'oh that I could "fright the steeds of lazy paced time"'.

From the end of October and into November it had, in truth, been a desperate time because Shelley could lay hands on no money, and was driven to beg from his increasingly estranged wife. As Harriet fearfully approached the birth of their child, recalling the pain of the first, Shelley reassured her that a second should be better, though he does not involve himself in any way as the father. There is no thought of the child to come. Harriet's father was angry enough to contemplate legal action. This called out a bitter reproach from Shelley. It was shameful of Harriet to permit such talk.

If Mary thought of Harriet, she was too cautious to comment on paper beyond one distant word: Harriet was 'odd'. Mary never misses a beat in her passionate staunchness and demonstrative love. She was enthralled to Shelley: 'Mary's many embraces and the brightness of her eyes give me a sweet thought as I reflect on them.' These private words in their *Journal* are set down in Greek, his way of combining love with their love of learning.

His genius, she said, 'far transcending mine, awakened & guided my thoughts'. She always deferred to his gift, and yet in his view she surpassed him in originality. Mary understood how rare it was to find this reciprocity – it spurred her ready mind. In the evenings, when their lives were settled, Shelley often read aloud: it might be 'The Ancient Mariner' or extracts from Godwin and Wollstonecraft. It's as though Shelley, Mary and Claire made a home in these works, and no contrary purpose in the runaway party, no amount of sexual passion, and no degree of cold-shouldering from Godwin could dislodge these mental returns to him.

Mary Godwin's attachment to her father suggests that *Frankenstein*'s emotional core – the Creature's anguish over his maker's rejection – preceded his forbidding appearance (as Mary would later recount it) in a waking dream.

In December 1814, when she was six months pregnant, Mary went to a lecture by André-Jacques Garnerin, a French physicist famous for daring jumps with the parachute he'd constructed. A fashionable London audience of gentry and nobility heard about experiments in electricity and gases. This too would be vital to *Frankenstein*: the arch-experimenter who will use the discovery of electricity to jolt his artificially constructed Creature to life.

Where, ironically, Mary's situation liberated her to move forward intellectually and in self-contained strength, Fanny was constricted, almost as though Mamma made her pay for her sisters' escape. One evening Mamma did not allow Fanny, aged twenty-one, to come down to dinner, as punishment for receiving a lock of Mary's hair. Mary records this on 17 December, adding 'Fanny of course behaves slavishly'. There was no escape for poor Fanny. Loving both Godwin and her sister, she was tugged between opposed camps. And she didn't have a lover to soften the pain.

Shelley's grandfather died in January 1815. Sir Bysshe had been an American, a kind of Gatsby.* In Newark, New Jersey where he was born, he had been nobody. Then he'd travelled to England, amassed a fortune (by marrying – successively – two heiresses), inherited Field Place and other Sussex lands, built a family seat, Castle Goring, and was made a baronet in 1806 while his grandson was at school. Shaking off a warning from the family lawyer to stay away, Shelley took himself to Field Place, where his father preferred to live. Sir Timothy Shelley, now come into his inheritance, forbade his son to enter the house, but Shelley did not leave. He sat outside, defiantly reading *Comus*,† whose main character is a profligate.

But sometimes his outcast condition did disturb him, and he fancied that his father and uncle were in pursuit, in league with creditors who meant to imprison him. Whether this was true or not, Shelley's debts were resolved when his father gave him an annual income of one thousand

---

* *The Great Gatsby* by F. Scott Fitzgerald. Bysshe Shelley, born in Newark, was the son of a miller's widow who had married an English immigrant, a poor and distant relation of an aristocratic family, who tried his hand at business without success and then posed as an 'apothecary' though he was nothing but a quack. Richard Holmes (*Shelley: The Pursuit*, p. 10) has called Bysshe a New World figure, tall, purposeful and filled with initiative. He eloped with the sixteen-year-old daughter of a wealthy clergyman and later acquired social cachet and land through a second elopement with the daughter of an aristocratic family.

† *Comus*, a verse drama by John Milton, was a masque performed at Ludlow Castle in 1634. Comus, associated with the Greek god of revelry, kidnaps a virtuous Lady and tries to persuade her to drink from his enchanting cup of sexual licence. The Lady presents the rationale for the chastity to which she holds.

pounds. He was then able to settle two hundred pounds a year on Harriet and give Godwin – who still refused contact – a further thousand pounds.

Mary had lived closely with Shelley's fear of pursuit, and this, together with paternal rejection, night horrors and experiments in electricity, was a crucial ingredient for *Frankenstein*. As early as the start of 1815, a year and a half before Mary conceived her tale, all were active in her imagination.

On 22 February 1815, Mary went into labour. She was attended by a Dr Clarke, very likely the eminent Dr Clarke who had been called in when her mother was dying of puerperal fever after Mary's birth.

Mary wanted her sister, and Fanny was sent for. She came and stayed all night – free to do so because the Godwins happened to be away.

The baby, a girl, was almost two months premature and not expected to live but she held on, nursing at the breast. Mary began to hope that the child would survive, and then one morning, seventeen days after the birth, Mary woke to find her baby dead. Again it was Fanny whom Mary wanted at this time of stress. Fanny came in the rain and the sisters took this chance to talk of 'many things'.

Mary said, 'I was a mother and now am not' and 'it is hard to lose a baby'. She could not stop thinking of 'the little thing', and one night dreamt the child was not dead, only frozen, and rubbed in front of a fire, it came to life.

Even now, Godwin did not relent. He did not come to his daughter. Nor did he write to her or recognise the existence of a grandchild.

Claire was no consolation. Her tie with Shelley quickened while Mary was laid low, and possibly took an erotic turn. (Godwin thought her in love with Shelley, along with Mary and Fanny – all three enthralled by the same man, inviting free love.) Claire's presence was increasingly trying for Mary, to the point of what looks like depression. Meanwhile, Godwin sent another message to Claire with suggestions for her future. If she wouldn't come home, she might take up a post as a governess or at least lie low with a respectable family with a view to rehabilitating her image. As it happened, a family whom the Godwins approached on Claire's behalf turned her down.

Claire sank the Godwins' plans by making two conditions: she must be permitted to proclaim her contempt for the laws of society, and to go on visiting Mary and Shelley.

In May 1815, to Mary's relief, Claire resolved to live by herself in Lynmouth, the distant, difficult to access harbour on the north Devon coast where Shelley and Harriet had once stayed. It was a lone spot for a girl of seventeen, and Miranda Seymour, in her biography of Mary Shelley, asks whether Claire had to go away because she was pregnant. Day after day she sat on the shore thinking life too much to bear. All the same, isolation was to shape a natural womanhood in the novel-in-progress she called 'The Ideot'.

By January 1816 Claire was back in London with about half her novel done, as well as an entirely different plan for her future from the efface-ment the Godwins had in mind. Her aim was to become, like Mary, the protégée of a poet. With a flurry of letters – using a pseudonym at first, then revealing her ties with Godwin and Shelley – Claire approached the most celebrated poet of the day.

Lord Byron had connections with Drury Lane theatre, and initially Claire asked to see him with a view to becoming an actress. Once he agreed, Claire admitted that what she really wanted was to be a writer. It would seem that during her exile in Lynmouth, she had used her dis-tance from London to enter more deeply into her story of a free-minded woman – one, she told Byron, formed outside society, whom the present counter-revolutionary world would revile, but whose true nature a dis-cerning reader would recognise. An early letter to Byron invites him to be this reader:

Will you judge candidly & impartially? Will you make allowance for my years? I do not expect you to approve – all I wish to know is whether I have talents which if aided by severe study may render me fit to become an author.

My intention was this – To draw a character committing every violence against received opinion – one, educated amidst mountains & deserts; who knew no other guide than herself or the impulses arising from herself. Who, notwithstanding the apparent enormity of her actions, should however appear highly amiable, full of noble affections & sympathies.

What Claire asked of Byron was not sex, not in the first instance, rather a writer's encouragement. Her ironically titled 'Ideot' blends her optimistic self with Rousseau's child of nature, Wollstonecraft's thinking woman and the unconventional actions of Mary Godwin. Her conception of a Crusoe sort of girl may have come also from *The [Swiss] Family Robinson*, published in the first English translation by Claire's mother for the Juvenile Library in 1816,* but given Claire's highly individual voice addressing Byron, we might take her unfinished novel to be a sort of precursor to the Brontës. The wild Catherine, the woman of the moor in *Wuthering Heights*, does not speak to the moody Byronic man, Heathcliff, through custom or conventionalities; her voice comes from one bared soul to another.

To Byron, Claire confided a plan to embed her young woman's story in the narrative of an old clergyman. He's charitable enough to believe her to be at heart a Christian. To the pious reader, the tale would appear a warning against radical opinion, but Claire expects free thinkers to see the reverse – to endorse her revelation of woman's nature.

Claire spoke with pride of an indirect narrative. She told Byron that she'd adopted this method from the ambiguity of different points of view in Gibbon's *Decline and Fall of the Roman Empire*. Gibbon's tome was not designed for female readers; it was for men with a classical education, so that when Claire lets this drop she's making an intellectual claim, unaware that intellect in a female would hardly appeal to Byron. At best, it could be but a freak of nature, a joke. The mathematical brain of Byron's

---

* This translation from the German is still considered the best, and is the one used by Penguin Classics.

wife, Annabella Milbanke ('the Princess of Parallelograms'), had been incidental to her appeal as an heiress.

Byron had more than enough approaches from women, but it caught
his attention when Claire mentioned her stepfather. He had admired
Godwin's novel *St Leon* and was struck too by Claire's tie with Shelley,
whom as yet he had not met. Since Claire declared her belief in free love,
Byron assumed that she was Shelley's mistress along with Mary. Many
years later, when she looked back on her youth, she said that all she had
from Byron was ten minutes of happy passion.

'I shall ever remember the gentleness of your manners & the wild originality of your countenance', she told him.

Byron chose to believe that only a bad girl from an atheist home would
have offered herself in this way. He did not value Claire enough to waste
his supply of 'cundums' (only aristocrats could afford them) on a girl who
came 'prancing' to his rooms. It's Byron who smeared her as an oversexed
lightweight. He resented Claire for the wrong he did her by taking advantage of an underage hopeful. After all, 'a man is a man', was his excuse.
To be fair, he had no idea that she was following Mary's scenario: the girl
prodigy who gives herself to a poet; he then falls in love with her and
becomes her mentor.

The scandal of incest with his half-sister Augusta Leigh forced Byron
to leave England on 25 April 1816. There was some understanding, at least
on Claire's part, that they would meet again in Switzerland, where he
was bound. It was both a similar and an entirely different situation from
that of Mary when Shelley took her abroad. Byron did *not* invite Claire's
company. She continued to hope that she might be more to him, and
persuaded Shelley and Mary, who were thinking of Italy, to travel instead
to Switzerland.

The Shelley party left early in May. It now included a four-month-
old baby, Mary Godwin's second child, born in January 1816, whom
she'd called William after her father in an attempt to touch him, or at
least affirm their bond. Byron came to meet them at Sécheron on Lake
Geneva. They settled across the lake at Montalègre: Mary, Shelley and
Claire rented the Maison Chappuis, looking towards the dark Jura peak.

There, they turned from reading Latin and Italian to Byron's poems. Shelley read aloud their favourite canto of *Childe Harold*. They were only a few hundred yards from the Villa Diodati where Byron, together with his doctor-companion, John William Polidori, set up for the summer. Byron would come down to their villa or welcome them at the Diodati with a good-humoured smile.

When tourists trained telescopes on the Shelley–Byron set-up across Lake Geneva, rumour reported a harem. Back in London people were told how Byron was living with 'two wicked women'. Tablecloths drying on the line outside the Diodati were said to be their petticoats. The writer Mrs Inchbald, who in 1797 had snubbed Mary Wollstonecraft, newly married and visibly pregnant, now wrote one of her cutting letters to Godwin to say that she was curious to know whether it was his daughter or his *adopted* daughter – or might it be both – who was presently in Switzerland. Her tones of icy civility drove home the shame. This would appear to be confirmed by Claire's renewed intimacies with Byron and by the presence of baby William ('Will-Mouse', as they called him), but sexual ties co-existed with what was rarer: the closeness of these two young women to the rock-face of writing. They heard the elemental sound of the two poets' voices together like thunder and rain.

The sisters set to work to make fair copies of Byron's newest poems, the fourth canto of *Childe Harold* and 'The Prisoner of Chillon'. Though copying was a traditional role for women, it was heady for Claire and Mary to participate in a writing party with two of the greatest Romantic poets.

For Claire, sleeping with Byron meant a relationship; for him, it meant less than his previous flings with titled ladies of his own class. One was Lady Caroline Lamb, who was boyishly thin. Byron, who was bisexual, is said to have felt more for young men at Harrow and Cambridge. A woman should not be seen to eat, Byron considered; she might nibble at a chicken wing and sip a glass of champagne. Claire was not like this: her sole portrait (said to be a good likeness) shows a vivid physicality, with warm cheeks and black curls.

In Geneva that June, Claire discovered she was pregnant. Shelley supported Claire both in promising to see her through the pregnancy and with a new will, which was to give her the massive bequest of, in all, twelve thousand pounds.

It was at this point that the Shelley party made a concession to social opinion with a plan for a cover-up. They would stay at a distance from London, and Claire would assume a married name until the child was born. After weaning, the child would go to Byron and Claire would return to her maiden identity. What they failed to grasp is the bond of mother and child. And though Byron agreed to the plan, he had no idea how to be a father. His own had been a drunken gambler, who had deserted him – a boy with a club foot – together with his mother.

Paternal irresponsibility is central to the tale that Mary Godwin began in Geneva that June. It was a wet summer, and when it rained the party would linger late at the Diodati, and sometimes, if the rain persisted, sleep there.

Fifteen years later Mary would look back on conversations between Shelley and Byron as the prompt for her fiction about a scientist who ventures to put himself on a par with the Creator. This version of what happened plays up the two famous poets and casts herself as silent listener. True, no doubt, but it plays down what she had taken in over the preceding years.

One rainy night, 16 June 1816, she, Shelley, Byron, Polidori, and probably Claire too, sat late around a fire, reading German ghost tales. Byron suggested they each write a ghost tale. Mary couldn't think of anything suitable; then a night or two later she had a waking dream and on the instant realised this would do.

'When I placed my head on my pillow, I did not sleep', Mary recalled. 'I saw – with shut eyes, but acute mental vision – I saw . . .' What she saw was a man detached from social ties and bent on a dangerous experiment. At this point he was nameless; later she would call him Frankenstein. As he comes into view he's kneeling beside 'the thing he had put together' from the body parts of corpses.

'I saw the hideous phantasm of a man stretched out', she remembered. He stirred 'with an uneasy, half-vital motion'. Frankenstein, horrified, rushes away. He obliterates this with sleep, but when he opens his eyes the

Creature 'stands at his bedside . . . looking on him with yellow, watery, but speculative eyes'.

The Creature has approached him for recognition and nurture, but Frankenstein feels only horror and disgust. Where Frankenstein's parents had felt 'the deep consciousness of what they owed towards the being to which they had given life', he can see no connection with his own creation. He cannot see how his own unnatural aspect mirrors the unnaturalness of his experiment: a man bent on 'the creation of a human being'. As he does this work — for the benefit of mankind, he tells himself — his cheeks grow pale and his body emaciated, with 'eyeballs starting from their sockets' as he digs up graves for body parts and tortures living animals in order to unlock the secrets of physiology. And as he makes himself monstrous in this manner, he shuns others. He forgets friends and cuts off 'feelings of affection until the great object, which swallowed up every habit of my nature . . . should be completed'. He ignores the woman he expects to marry because he is bent on procreation without a woman. One of Mary Godwin's most brilliant strokes was this parallel of a monster of sorts creating a monster, bound together as unnatural kin.

When Frankenstein is devastated by the Creature's turn to violence — his murder of Frankenstein's five-year-old brother — he calls him a 'daemon' or 'devil'. These labels imply the otherness of evil. But the Creature will challenge this.

Frankenstein encounters his monster on the glacier at Chamonix, a solitary, untameable setting which Mary, Shelley and Claire visited in July 1816, soon after Mary's waking dream. Here we hear the monster's voice, his full-throated and, it must be conceded, justified outrage at his maker: 'you, my creator, detest and spurn me, thy creature, to whom thou art bound by ties only dissoluble by the annihilation of one of us . . . I entreat you to hear me before you give vent to your hatred on my devoted head.'

Hatred, he says. The word 'hate' resonates like a gong in the utterance of the Creature, reminiscent of Mary Godwin's story 'Hate', which she wrote on the Dutch coast in September 1814, when she was returning to her hometown as an outcast. *Frankenstein* treats hate as an emotion that yearns to be dissolved. In the heat of rage, her Creature offers a startling counter to hate. He's 'devoted' — a word pulsing, well below the surface, with the author's own attachment to her father in the face of rejection.

'I am thy creature', the Creature repeats. He lays it out to Frankenstein that he is alone, 'miserably alone'.

Frankenstein is compelled to grant the justice of this protest. 'For the first time . . . I felt what the duties of a creator towards his creature were, and that I ought to render him happy before I complained of his wickedness.' He consents to listen to him.

The Creature's testimony is similar to that of the criminal, Jemima, in *The Wrongs of Woman*: deprived of nurture, Jemima perceives herself 'an outcast from society'. It's as though Mary's novel speaks to her mother's, assenting to the necessity for domestic affections. At the climax of his story, the Creature hides in a hovel next door to a family and spies on their harmony. He would befriend them — would join the family of man — and yet he hesitates to show himself. This is the formative test: should he fail to disarm this loving family, he tells himself, 'I am an outcast in the world forever'.

Before the Creature tells his story he's called 'a fiend'; afterwards, he's a 'being'. 'The being finished speaking', Frankenstein informs us. He is touched against his will.

Though unwilling to defy Godwin, whom she adored as much as Mary did, Fanny wrote to her sisters in Geneva, declaring that she loved them more 'because I found the world deserted you . . . I love you for yourselves alone.' A letter from Mary had been 'very precious to me'.

Recently, Fanny had met her mother's Irish friend George Blood, who spoke of Wollstonecraft as 'a superior being'. His praise had roused Fanny from her melancholy: 'I am determined never to live to be a disgrace to such a mother.'

Sadly it was at this moment that Mamma saw fit to wound Fanny by telling her, as Fanny reports to Mary, 'I am your laughing stock – and the constant beacon of your satire.' Her melancholy deepened, and for this she blamed herself. If she could overcome her 'faults', she told Mary, she might find 'beings to love and esteem me'.

Fanny was unable to bring Mary and her father together. Nor was she able to help Godwin when, obedient to his wish, she pleaded with Shelley and her sister to rescue him from financial ruin. Compassion for both sides led her to take these responsibilities upon herself. Her failure to effect a solution, as well as her exclusion from the Shelley party – they took no notice of hints that she might like to join them –deepened her distress.

A family story lies behind *Frankenstein*, one of unresolved estrangement. It was Mary's feat to voice something of this via the resonant voice of a monster reproaching Frankenstein for his rejection. Through fiction she could express the emotion her reserve suppressed in her letters and journal. Unlike her fictional monster, she preserved a decent pride in her refusal to complain. Her entries in the *Journal* do not reveal her feelings about her father, and she could not risk confiding in Claire. Her self-control was highly developed in a girl of eighteen, especially one overcome by love and vulnerable too in her pregnant state, without care or advice. So it was that Mary breathed real emotion into the routine terrors of the Gothic novel. Her other feat was to use a popular genre to dramatise a philosophical debate.

On one side is the biblical view of our depravity after the Fall, which means that a new-made creature cannot be acceptable to society until he has been chastised and corrected. Frankenstein's new-made Creature takes the contrary view: he claims innate benevolence, which experience then corrupts. This is the radical position of Godwin and Wollstonecraft, originating in Rousseau and finding its perfect expression in Wordsworth's 'Ode on Intimations of Immortality in Early Childhood', where the child comes to life 'trailing clouds of glory' from the perfection of pre-life.

This is the Creature's challenge to his uncaring maker: he's saying, in effect, neglect me at your peril, for then you are guilty of making a criminal. Frankenstein's neglect of nurture co-exists with another human flaw: the selfishness of single-minded ambition. The novel's subtitle is *The Modern Prometheus*. Frankenstein demonstrates a Promethean reach for godlike powers in a way that can divorce a man from pity and tenderness, qualities Wollstonecraft had proposed as a corrective to the wrongs of power.

In the test her daughter sets up, the women in her story – Frankenstein's mother and his sisterly wife-to-be – are figures of selfless attention. Can these women, fortified by benevolent men like Frankenstein's father, hold off the horrors welling up from things ill done and done to public harm, which those in power tend to perpetrate? Sadly, no. *Frankenstein* takes a darker view of human fallibility than that of Wollstonecraft, who shared the hopes of revolutionaries. Hope was harder to sustain for her daughter in a counter-revolutionary period, and all the more so in the presence of her Creature's brutal acts.

The Creature moves against a target perceived as 'enemy'. His evil is less an aberration (as reassuring spin-offs would have it) than a fable about violence. Mary Godwin's experience crossing France in 1814 undercut her trust that love could conquer the forces against it. Her awakening included the devastation of civilian life inflicted by war; her Creature comes to kill innocents, like Cossack thugs in killer mode. Weird though the Creature looks, in actuality there is not much difference between his physical cruelty and the common cruelties of armed men, and the unarmed everywhere who perpetrate acts of domestic violence.

But that's not all. What's even more ominous is his speech that upholds aggression: the actor spouting words – the familiar ritual of terrorists and tyrants as they puff themselves. More evil than instinctive aggression is the calculated kind, a 'being' we recognise as human repeating the self-justifying words that block humanity, and in doing so transform man into monster.

———

Mary's life changed as she wrote and revised the novel during the second half of 1816 and spring of 1817. On returning to England, the party settled in Bath to begin the cover-up of Claire's pregnancy. There, Claire called herself 'Mrs Clairmont'. The Godwins were not to know, nor Fanny, nor anyone but themselves and of course Byron. Claire, attached still to Byron, wrote warmly, determined to encourage good relations for the sake of their unborn child. Byron preferred to have no more to do with her, and his derision of 'The Ideot' led Claire to kill 'that hateful novel thing I wrote'.

Meanwhile, back in Skinner Street, Fanny foresaw, as she put it to Mary, 'my unhappy life' as drudge to her Wollstonecraft aunts, who ran schools in Dublin. At this time Shelley's withdrawal of financial help for Godwin moved Fanny to defend Godwin's philosophy that those with means should support those who are in want.

'My heart is warm in your cause', Fanny wrote to her sister, 'and I am anxious, most anxious that Papa should feel for you as I do both for your own, and his sake'. The following day Mary received this 'stupid letter from F'.

Four days later, on 8 October 1816, Fanny passed through Bath on a westward journey. She had dressed carefully in a blue striped skirt and white bodice, with a brown pelisse and brown hat. She had a meagre eight shillings – not enough for a passage to Dublin – in her reticule. Next to her skin she wore her mother's stays.

It's not known what happened during the hour or two when Fanny arrived by the morning mail in Bath. Fanny did want to see Mary, since she sent word ahead. Mary, of course, was the only one in the family with whom she had a blood tie. But, for whatever reason, Mary did not meet her sister. Nor did she ask Fanny to stay, because of her commitment to keep Claire's pregnancy a secret. It's possible that Shelley came to see Fanny at the coaching inn, but there was still no invitation to join his party.

From her next stop, in Bristol, she sent warning notes to Shelley (to come and see her buried) and to Godwin ('I depart immediately to the spot from which I hope never to remove'), but she did not say where she was. Both, alarmed, set out to trace her. Fanny, meanwhile, took a coach to Swansea. There, at the Mackworth Arms, she sipped some tea. By now it was night, and she asked for a candle. By its dim light she wrote:

I have long determined that the best thing I could do was put an end to the existence of a being whose birth was unfortunate, and whose life has only been a series of pain to those persons who have hurt their health in endeavouring to promote her welfare. Perhaps to hear of my death will give you pain but you will soon have the blessing of forgetting that such a creature ever existed as

Before she swallowed the overdose of laudanum or before oblivion overtook her, she thought of those she loved, and to save further trouble, she tore off her name and let the candle consume it.

Next morning, Fanny's body was discovered. It was not identified, not from the stockings marked 'G', nor the stays marked 'MW'. Godwin gave out that Fanny had gone to join her aunts in Dublin. Privately, he told a family friend, Mrs Gisborne (who had looked after Fanny and baby Mary after their mother's death), 'that the three girls were all equally in love with [Shelley] and that the eldest put an end to her existence owing to the preference given to her younger sister'. It has to be a simplification, distancing the Godwins from responsibility for Fanny's suicide.

She was not the only casualty of Shelley's and Mary's union. A month later, on 9 November, Harriet Shelley, who thought her husband a 'monster', drowned herself in the Serpentine in Hyde Park. Pregnant, she had left her parents' house and taken lodgings under an assumed name. The news of Harriet's end did not come until December when her body was discovered. Shelley was ready to brand Harriet a prostitute; it helped to brush off guilt. He took to having an evening glass of ale to ease thoughts of her.

Two weeks after Shelley heard of his wife's death, he married Mary

Godwin at St Mildred's Church, Bread Street, on 30 December 1816. Neither of them wanted to marry, but Godwin sent his daughter a message that if she didn't do this, he too would commit suicide.

Shelley married, he explained to Byron, to assuage Mary's feelings about her father. Reconciliation with Godwin was instantaneous. He was relieved to the point of elation – so elated that, uncharacteristically, Godwin boasted of the improbable marriage of his penniless daughter to the son of a baronet and heir to an estate. Godwin must have known that money had nothing to do with the union, but in his relief from shame he took the view that this marriage meant a place for Mary in society after all. He actually used the word 'respectable' in the positive sense – bizarre for so radical a philosopher and even more bizarre had Godwin known that the bride, aged eighteen, was pregnant for the third time. After the wedding the bridal pair dined at Skinner Street, signalling Mary's return to her paternal home for the first time since 28 July 1814. She spent the whole of the following day with her father.

Such a change of heart is what Mary's outcast Creature most wants of existence: to be reunited with his maker and to be recognised as a 'being' with the human need for affection. And so it was that while the cast-off monster took shape in the shadow of thwarted need, the once cast-off Mary Godwin found it possible to disarm her father. She could do so only in her public identity as Mrs Shelley.

The transition from Mary Godwin to Mary Shelley went on unseen within a chrysalis, a creature who held on through the suicides of Fanny and Harriet – all that damage in her vicinity. Present too was a bent for fantasy in Shelley, a tendency to excess verging on madness – 'mad Shelley', he was called at school. When Charles Clairmont, Mary's stepbrother, accompanied the couple to view Shelley's rooms at University College, Oxford, he'd thought ironically of Shelley's expulsion as seen by the university authorities: a student who 'pored with the incessant & unwearied application of an Alchemist over the artificial & natural boundaries of human knowledge' and brooded over perceptions that came from the 'impudent penetration' of a 'monster'. It's an almost uncanny prefiguring of the intent of Frankenstein in his workshop.

Yet Mary's love for Shelley, her books and writing was indestructible, an alternative existence that she could enter and shut the door. Shelley's world-changing ideas and poetic greatness filled her sails with the wild wind of his words, his intimacy with the prodigy she knew herself to be, his love for her as 'mine own heart's home' and his enthusiasm for what she had to say. He read *Paradise Lost* aloud to Mary, a poem that Frankenstein's Creature read in his settled period of self-education: the Fall from innocence as the sequel to Creation. Three challenging lines from Milton's poem were included as an epigraph:

> *Did I request thee, Maker, from my clay*
> *To mould me man? Did I solicit thee*
> *From darkness to promote me? —*

Mary Shelley completed *Frankenstein* in April 1817, and the following month her husband made a fair copy of a few pages. The manuscript shows how Shelley made felicitous touches to her wording, but only a few. There's restraint in his marginalia. He read and re-read attentively, sensitive to Mary's imagination.

Addressing an unnatural father, pleas for sympathy fountain in great arcs from the black lips of the Creature. It's part of the monster's ambiguity that he can be human in this way, assertively civilised.

Mary Shelley's greatest feat is this solemn, high-toned language, at once imposing and a little absurd. For the Creature's language is decked out in magniloquence, imitating the refinements of formal education. Our ears pick up the artifice, in keeping with the artifice of his body. Mary Shelley conveys language as a self-conscious construct in the mouth of some who feel deprived of a privileged education; such self-consciousness is common also to the language of the colonial or foreigner who feels a need to validate his identity. Mary Shelley's modulation of this voice is nothing short of genius: it could easily fall into the respectable voice of narrators in Gothic fiction, a voice designed to authenticate the far and strange. On the other hand, the voice could easily become absurd, a caricature of itself, debasing the monster's claims. Instead Mary Shelley, at her most inventive, grants a genuine profundity to the Creature by drawing on the biblical language spoken by Godwin's devout family – a language Godwin himself would have exercised in his youth as a Dissenting clergyman – while the force of the Creature's outbursts came from the unspoken emotion of a daughter cast off by her father for more than two years.

Shelley is an ambiguous figure in Mary's story. To the fore there is a 'superior being'. For a man of that time he was wonderfully generous to a woman writer, urging her on, discussing, and encouraging her to turn what was originally to be a short tale into a novel.

As an imaginative mentor, he was Mary's perfect mate, yet she had to cope with his susceptibility to other women (elevated as a credo of love). In addition, there was a vein of high-handedness or self-absorption, evident in his treatment of Harriet – what she had called his lack of tenderness when he'd visited after their son Charles was born. He showed no interest in the child – the future heir – except as a means to extract more money from the Shelley estate.

One of Shelley's motives for marriage to Mary Godwin had been to gain custody of the children he had with Harriet. Her family fought him off in court with a case stressing his negligence as a father: the fact that he had failed to visit his children for more than two years. After the hearing went against him early in 1817, Ianthe, aged four, and Charles, aged two, were sent to a foster home which, for the children themselves, was the worst outcome. The further questionable fact is this: Shelley did not exercise his legal right to monthly access, though he had a settled life at Albion House in West Street, Marlow. He did not see these children again.* We can't know what Mary thought of Shelley's

---

* Later, in 1821, when Shelley had to write to his children's guardian, Dr Hume, on a money matter, he showed no care for them beyond a formal query as to their health and intellectual development. Typically self-absorbed, he is more concerned with 'the unexampled oppression' he himself suffered in 'being forbidden the exercise of . . . parental duties'.

dismissiveness, but this was the situation when she entered into the final stage of *Frankenstein*.

Now it was that she turned up the volume of utterance, as the Creature and Frankenstein enter the last rounds of their clash. In the closing scenes, Frankenstein must die of regret for the destruction his irresponsibility has unleashed, and his Creature must stare stricken at the lifeless father figure – or doppelgänger – he has pursued. Their fates are locked together and in a sense reflect each other. Many would come to think of Frankenstein as the name of the monster, who in fact remains nameless, alarmingly unplaced, with no face of his own.

One definite marker: the monster is gendered. Frankenstein constructs him as a male. What is a male? What is a female? The monster asks Frankenstein to make a female to assuage his loneliness, a dark variation on the biblical fable of Eden. The female proves more complex than Frankenstein expects. He discovers that he can't simply produce a female on the basis of his expertise in making the male, and as well as hunting up other organs – presumably the different reproductive organs – this challenge requires study and research. It takes a long time.

Frankenstein aborts the female at the last moment because her offspring could endanger the future of our species. In the end her nature remains unknown. The possibility that she might take on the violence of the male fills Frankenstein with fear.

The scene of this abortion speaks to our present debates on the right to life versus the law in certain countries, which condones what is called termination. The word itself dodges the reality of killing as experienced by a live creature, in the same way as soldiers' lingo of 'taking out' an enemy's life distances a killer from responsibility. A verbal denial of empathy may be at the core of what causes post-traumatic stress when fighters return to domestic existence. Frankenstein comes into his full character as monster when he tears apart the female-in-the-making. Mary, who had a baby gestating inside her as she completed the novel, compels her reader to look at an unfinished being as its life is taken from it. 'The remains of the half-finished creature, whom I had destroyed, lay scattered on the floor, and I almost felt as if I had mangled the living flesh of a human being.'

In turning a light on this dark scene, Mary Shelley writes as the daughter of Mary Wollstonecraft, who as a child had feared her father's domestic violence, not for her own sake but for his prime victim, her helpless mother. As a governess, Wollstonecraft spent a few weeks at Eton in the 1780s. There she witnessed the brutalisation of boys through the public school system that removed them from home and mother in order to shape them for rule and conquest.

The source of the monster's heartless aggression lies in something that happens before he's alive: Frankenstein's removal of himself from domestic ties, relying on ingenuity alone. In dramatising this, Mary Shelley confirms her mother's case for domestic nurture, together with Wollstonecraft's condemnation of 'the cold workings of the brain'. To cultivate brain at the expense of fellow-feeling is a travesty of our nature. It was Shelley's gentleness and his imaginative awareness of others that made him, in Mary's view, above lesser men.

Shelley touched up the last speech of the monster and the last sight of him on an ice-raft. In Mary's draft the Creature wants the flame of a funeral pyre to consume his body, which 'will give rest & blessings to my mind'. Shelley's fair copy gives the mood of despairing suicide an almost defiant resonance when he has the Creature declare that he will 'exult in the agony of the torturing flames' and adds a note of elegiac grandeur: 'The light of that conflagration will fade away. My ashes will be swept into the sea by the winds. My spirit will sleep in peace; or if it thinks will surely not think thus. Adieu.'

His ice raft lies close to the vessel. In Mary's draft he pushes himself off and the narrator reports, 'I soon lost sight of him'. Shelley's fair copy cuts these more mundane details but retains Mary's sombre final words so that, working collaboratively, they fix the last scene in the reader's mind: 'He was soon borne away by the waves, and lost in darkness and distance.'

The Creature, embodying uncontrolled violence, lives on in regions beyond our sight in the uninhabitable ice fields towards the North Pole. There's no knowing when he will reappear. He's both invisible and embedded in us in so far as Mary Shelley has granted a voice to hate alternating with longing for impossible love. For this Creature is not lovable; he's too wrapped in his self-regarding rage to stir love. Frankenstein doubts if a mate would respond as the monster expects. More likely, she'd hate him.

Shelley praised the recessed stories and framing plot of a navigator on a voyage of exploration that will risk peoples' lives. The navigator comes upon Frankenstein pursuing the monster across the arctic wastes. Dying, Frankenstein tells him his horrific story. Hearing this story as it evolved, Shelley looked into Mary's eyes 'deep and intricate from the workings of the mind' and heard an unspoken 'prophecy' in the sound of her gentle voice. His assent to her distinction, one that burns 'internally', made Shelley indispensable to Mary. While she submitted *Frankenstein* for publication in the late summer of 1817, Shelley completed the long poem that became *The Revolt of Islam*. His exquisite dedication of the poem to Mary pictures them as two lasting stars above the destructive fury of men: 'thou and I', he tells her

> *. . . can look from our tranquillity*
> *Like lamps into the world's tempestuous night, —*
> *Two tranquil stars . . .*
> *That burn from year to year with unextinguished light.*

The image of lasting stars looks back to an erotic scene in the poem. As the revolutionary lovers, Laon and Cythna, come together physically, his neck near hers, he's intent on her marble brow and 'dark and deepening eyes', which appear to him phantoms of one star, reflected as in a well. Joined as that star, they swam, he says, 'in our mute and liquid ecstasies'.

Love-making shields them from their own cold looks. Twined limbs and wild oblivion lift the lovers momentarily beyond fear and time, followed by the 'quick dying gasps' and the 'sweet peace' that did 'almost fill / The depth of her unfathomable look'. Almost, he says. How candidly he conveys what he can't compass in the orgasmic moment: 'I know not.' His sensitive assent to a part of a woman she withholds as her own, even as he responds to the 'blood that / Burned within her frame', explains why

Mary continued to be enthralled by Shelley. More than love-making, more than mentoring, he imagined 'the life meeting'.

*Frankenstein* was offered to John Murray, the well-known publisher of Byron, Scott and Jane Austen. Murray turned it down, as did Shelley's publisher, Charles Ollier. In August 1817 the novel was accepted by John Lackington, a friend of Godwin, whose list included the supernatural. The author's identity was kept secret and Shelley handled all negotiations with the publisher.

On 2 September, two days after her twentieth birthday, Mary gave birth to her third child, Clara Everina. Clara was the name, hardly mentioned, that she'd given to her baby who died, and the second name was that of Everina Wollstonecraft, her mother's favourite sister. Mary was breast-feeding as her book went through the press. Her mother had practised and promoted breast-feeding, an unfashionable practice in her time; her daughter's combination of nursing and writing was yet another way that her mother lived on in her.

That September in Marlow, Shelley wrote a preface to *Frankenstein*, as from the author, declaring that though the monster is physically impossible, the situation is true to human nature in the same way as *The Iliad*, *The Tempest*, *A Midsummer Night's Dream* and especially *Paradise Lost* are true. One aim is to extend this kind of poetic licence to the newer and as yet humbler genre of prose fiction. It's likely that Mary needed a poet as confident as Shelley to make this claim, but the other aim he states is within a woman's traditional compass: to demonstrate the necessity for the 'domestic affections'. When the proofs appeared in October, Mary gave Shelley, then in London, the freedom to correct them as he saw fit. While in London, Shelley also offered Claire's novel — almost certainly 'The Ideot' — to two publishers, one of them Lackington, who both turned it down. Sadly, with Wollstonecraft in eclipse, the marketplace was bound to reject a work that put forward her ideal of female self-sufficiency.

Meanwhile, Mary's father read *Frankenstein* in proof. 'An astonishing production from a girl of twenty', was Godwin's verdict.

*Frankenstein* was published anonymously on 1 January 1818. 'The author' dedicated it 'respectfully' to 'William Godwin, author of *Political Justice*, *Caleb Williams*, etc'. Certain reviewers picked this up to dismiss the novel as Godwinian. It was savaged by John Wilson Croker (now remembered only for crushing Keats with an ill-judged slam).

Godwin thought *Frankenstein* too good to have mass appeal. He was wrong. There was a discerning review from Sir Walter Scott in *Blackwood's Magazine*, who thought Shelley had written it. Shelley put Scott right, revealing the author's identity. The permanent impact of this work, conceived by the silent young woman in the shadow of Shelley and Byron, was to outdo them in lasting popularity.

Mary Shelley's fame as the author of *Frankenstein* never outweighed her reputation as an unacceptable woman – not in England; not during her lifetime. Claire's parallel but different fate turned on cover-up. The plan of shielding her from Mary's disgrace led to a series of disasters, as Shelley, Mary and their 'blue-eyed darlings' (or 'the chicks') moved with Claire from place to place in the course of 1818–19.

Initially, the Shelley party passed off Claire's baby, Allegra,* as the daughter of a friend, who was staying with them in the country – at Albion House -- for her health. But there was further talk of a Shelley harem. Allegra was a merry, strong-willed child with a cleft chin like Byron's. Claire and her child adored each other, but the time was coming to hand Allegra to Byron. This was the initial reason for going to Italy. Allegra was fifteen months old when, on 28 April 1818, her Swiss nurse, Elise Duvillard, carried her away from Claire in Milan and delivered her to Byron in Venice.

---

* At first Claire called her Alba, the dawn. Allegra was the name Byron chose.

The Shelley party then crossed Italy to the coastal region of Leghorn and then the hills around Bagni di Lucca. What happened behind the scenes of the next ten months is too sealed for any certainty – there was none at the time and none since. What can be verified is that on 27 December 1818 a baby, registered as Elena Adelaide Shelley, was born in Naples and left there in foster care. That Mary Shelley was officially the child's mother was part of the concealment. This was certainly not Mary's child, but was it Shelley's? Or had he adopted a local child on impulse? That would not be out of character, but why then hide the fact? The nursemaid, Elise Duvillard, gave out that this was Claire's child with Shelley. He denied it as blackmail and refused to pay hush money. Elise, retaliating, divulged her story to Mrs Hoppner, the wife of the British consul in Venice, which meant that it came to Byron's ears. When Mary denied the allegation in a seething letter to Mrs Hoppner, she said, 'my marriage was ever undisturbed'.

This was untrue, at least so far as Mary privately blamed Shelley for the tragic fate of her one-year-old daughter. In August 1818, Shelley and Claire had travelled back across Italy to see Allegra. Byron was permitting Claire and the child to spend a month together from mid-August at his rented villa at Este, near Padua. To deflect Byron's and others' suspicions about the tie between Shelley and Claire, Shelley had told Byron a lie. He had said that Mary was with them. To make good his lie, Shelley had required Mary to join them immediately. She'd complied on 5 September, bringing the two children, though baby Clara had been unwell. Shelley then persuaded Mary to travel on to Venice to see Byron. These journeys in the heat of the Italian summer had been too much for the ailing baby and Clara had died on her mother's lap as they waited for a doctor. She was buried on the Lido.

After parting again from Allegra, the Shelley party had moved to Naples, and then when they came to depart Mary records 'a most tremendous fuss'. Had that fuss to do with leaving Elena behind? The day before they left, 27 February 1819, Shelley registered a daughter's birth – supposedly two months earlier, on 27 December 1818 – and baptism. He kept correspondence relating to Elena secret from Mary, using false names. Their party never saw the child again, and her death was registered in

June 1820.* At this time Shelley felt as though a consuming destruction were 'as an atmosphere which wrapt & infected everything connected with me'.

Byron chose to believe that Claire was Elena Shelley's mother. This was damaging for Allegra, as Byron was inclined to treat her as an offshoot of a wanton mother, a child in need of correction – while Byron himself cavorted with Venetian women. In Venice the once-merry Allegra grew pale and began to wet her bed. To what extent Byron believed Elise's report of Elena no one knows, but it did occur to him that Allegra might not be his after all – in which case, he'd make her his mistress when she grew up.

The Shelley party moved on to Rome, where on 7 June 1819 Will-Mouse, aged two and a half, died of fever. 'My happiness ended here', Mary inserted later in the *Journal* she stopped writing. Wordless, bereft of all three children to whom she had given birth and feeling unfit to live, she sank into depression. The world now felt like quicksand, sinking under her, yet beside her was Shelley, 'this bark of refuge'.

If he did not sink with her, he explained, it was as much for her sake as his own. His poetry can penetrate her desolation and call her towards life. One extraordinary poem, 'Misery: A Fragment' pictures the love-making of a couple too close to the dead to release themselves from mourning. The woman is an 'unwilling, silent bride', whose 'imperial brow | Is endiademed with woe'. When her lover leads her to a bridal bed spread beneath the grave, he senses her latent desire: 'Ha! thy frozen pulses flutter'. In this dark place, ice and sensual fire come together:

---

* It was only after Elena's death that the blackmail began. Richard Holmes deduced (in *Shelley: The Pursuit*, p. 465ff) that the support that Shelley would have paid for Elena would then have stopped. He suggests, p. 471, that Elise could have been the mother, that she gave birth in January 1819, and that her rogue husband (to whom Elise was married in Naples, where both left the Shelleys), put out to lose the money, instigated the blackmail. Seymour poses the question why Elise should have concocted her story for the Hoppners, and suggests that she could have been upset by the death of the child and wished to blame Shelley. But then, after throwing her net widely and sifting the evidence with scrupulous care, Seymour (p. 227) regards the least complicated explanation as the most convincing. It is that Shelley chose to adopt what he termed a 'Neapolitan charge' and that the 'fuss' was because Mary did not wish to take this child on.

*Kiss me; — oh! thy lips are cold:*
*Round my neck thine arms enfold —*
*They are soft, but chill and dead;*
*And thy tears upon my head*
*Burn like points of frozen lead.*

They move together 'like spectres wrapped in shrouds'.

Shelley composed his lyric drama *Prometheus Unbound* between the deaths of Clara in September 1818 and that of Will-Mouse in June 1819. Extraordinary that during this harrowing time Shelley should offer a counter to Mary's dark version of Prometheus. In place of the annihilation of Frankenstein (the *Modern Prometheus* of her subtitle), the soaring language of Shelley's *Prometheus Unbound* offers healing love.

*Love, from its awful throne of patient power*
*In the wise heart, from the last giddy hour*
*Of dead endurance, from the slippery, steep,*
*And narrow verge of crag-like agony, springs*
*And folds over the world its healing wings.*

To read Shelley's finale is to understand why Mary afterwards held by her image of him as above the dross of ordinary existence. Without denying the validity of her destructively self-absorbed Prometheus, she upheld his answer — for all its universality, also a personal answer to her grief and anger. It would be a victory of the spirit, he argues,

*To forgive wrongs darker than death or night;*
*To defy Power, which seems omnipotent;*
*To love, and bear; to hope till Hope creates*
*From its own wreck the thing it contemplates . . .*

While Mary took in this creed, grief still held her in its grip. Shelley's poetic drama *The Cenci* centres on a tragic woman called Beatrice. His portrait of her in his preface, written in August 1819, is rather like Mary with her high forehead, arched brows and pale, composed face that is an 'impersonation' of who she is, veiling her private torment. For Beatrice, a pure soul, had been forced into incest as the victim of her father. To escape his clutches, she murders him.

At this time, Godwin reproached his daughter for lack of fortitude. 'Alas!' Mary Shelley wrote in a new novel about a daughter's yearning for her father, 'he, my beloved father, shunned me, and either treated me with harshness or a more heart-breaking coldness.' Something 'malignant' seemed to have blinded him to her – in real life this would have been her stepmother. *Matilda*, welling out of a dark pit during the second half of 1819, is a deathbed confession by the daughter of a disconsolate man who had lost his wife, the love of his life, in childbirth, shortly after their marriage – the very situation of Godwin in relation to Mary Wollstonecraft. 'Oh, my beloved father! Indeed you made me miserable beyond all words, but how truly did I even then forgive you, and how entirely did you possess my whole heart while I endeavoured ... to soften thy tremendous sorrows.' This is Mary Shelley's message to her father, who thought the incestuous love at the centre of the story too scandalous for publication.

Incest is not enacted. It's a form of heartfelt attachment born of loss and grief: a passion, yes; sexual jealousy, certainly; but the father's possessiveness is not erotic. It seems closer to desperate romantic longing – an extension of the father's craving to find his lost love in her daughter. Matilda and her father consider themselves outcasts, alien to humanity, and doomed to die. Their speeches are too prolonged not to become tedious, and yet resonating through the cries of these fictional beings, there are gleams of confessional truth. Equally revealing is Mary Shelley's candour about the state of extreme depression, which she suffered at the time she wrote this novella.

While Matilda withers at her father's bitter words, a poet called Woodville tries to console her with gentle benevolence. 'You must not shut me out from all communion with you', he pleads. To some extent she can respond: 'The poetry of his language and ideas ... held me enchained ... It was a melancholy pleasure to me to listen to his inspired words; to catch for a moment the light of his eyes; to feel a transient sympathy'. But in the end it's unreal beside her father's desertion. Locked in depression, she has become unreachable, and she suspects Woodville of prompting her expressiveness for some drama he will create in a poem.

Mary would not blame her own father: 'often did quiescence of manner & tardiness in understanding & entering into the feelings of others cause him to chill & stifle those overflowings of mind from those he loved which he would have received with ardour had he been previously prepared'.

When Frankenstein's Creature demands a mate, he expects the 'sympathies necessary for my being'. Mary had this, and could reasonably expect it to be life-long. But all happiness came to an end when Shelley drowned while sailing in the Bay of Spezia in July 1822. His death, when Mary was only twenty-five, left her 'alone! Oh, how alone!' for the rest of her life – another twenty-six years.

During the second half of her life, her *Journal* changed because it became her sole companion – apart from her last child, Percy Florence, who had been born in Florence towards the end of 1819, the sole child who remained to link her to what the Creature had called 'the chain of existence'. For a woman with her history, whose husband was no longer there as protector, her status as a married woman could not gain her acceptance. Her first move was to Genoa, where the English shunned her – 'bitterly', Shelley's friend Edward Trelawny observed.

Her father-in-law required her to bring her son home to England if he was to benefit from hand-outs. Though Mary complied in 1823, Sir Timothy Shelley refused ever to meet her.

Mary knew in advance that 'humiliation' awaited in England, a country she expected to 'hate more & more (if that be possible)'. She lay low and buried her resentment for the sake of Percy Florence. The only outlet was the *Journal* she kept in her desk, together with Shelley's poem 'Adonais: An Elegy on the Death of John Keats', his poetic affirmation of the risks genius takes on course to immortality:

> *. . . my spirit's bark is driven,*
> *Far from the shore, far from the trembling throng*
> *Whose sails were never to the tempest given;*
> *The massy earth and sphered skies are riven!*
> *I am borne darkly, fearfully, afar*
> *Whilst burning through the inmost veil of Heaven,*
> *The soul of Adonais, like a star,*
> *Beacons from the abode where the Eternal are.*

Where Shelley had marked out public opinion as an unspecified 'throng', Mary blamed 'masculine insensibility'. She believed herself 'disdained' as 'a woman – poor & unprotected'. She brought up the issue with a woman artist, Amelia Curran, who had painted portraits of Shelley, Claire, Allegra and Will-Mouse in Rome. Did she deserve to be shunned because of defects in her character? At other times, she veered towards misanthropy.

She said, were it not for the 'matchless lost ones who redeem their race I should learn to hate a sex who are strong only to oppress – moral only to insult –'. How she longed to be assured that she was 'not utterly disjoined from my species'.

Could England be her country, she asked herself. In Paris, a writer like herself would be fêted. She was young, lovely in her person, her manners quiet and civil, and she had written a novel that would outlast the ages. Yet here, in London, her achievement did not alleviate her isolation.

'Why is the companion of Shelley companionless,' she asked herself. 'I am young still . . . but I may not love – any but the dead.' Finally, on 30 January 1825, two and a half years after Shelley died, she accepted public shame as a position nothing could budge.

'I am an outcast,' she concludes. Shakespeare's Sonnet XXIX supplied the words for her despair: in disgrace 'with fortune & men's eyes / I all alone beweep my outcast state –'. In 1826 she published a novel called *The Last Man*. This tale of the last man to survive a plague is infused with the author's solitude.

And yet, always, she was able to call back her mother's resilience. She would stiffen her resolve with Cicero: '*nihil timens, nemini credens — semper invictum*'. Fearing nothing, trusting no one — ever unsubdued. To help her to bear up publicly she had to fudge her unmarried years with Shelley. In her 1831 preface to her revised edition of *Frankenstein*, a deft reference to 'my husband' implied that her marriage had taken place before the journey to Switzerland in 1816.

Ahead of other women writers through the nineteenth century and well into the twentieth, her inner and outward life had to be separate. This is a breed forced to reside in shadow, finding relief in obscurity. Despite Mary's professionalism in publishing a novel or biography every few years, and despite her need for the income this brought, she was familiar with 'the desire to wrap night and the obscurity of insignificance around me' rather than appear in print '— the subject of *men's* observations'.

Sealed thus in darkness, she was sustained by the memory of her eight years with Shelley, who had seen *Frankenstein* as one of the most original works of the day. Nothing could dent that assurance. She turned down two approaches of marriage — from the American actor John Howard Payne in 1825 and from the French writer Prosper Mérimée in 1830 — and held to continued communication with like women: Claire Clairmont and Margaret Mount Cashell, an Irish pupil and disciple of Mary Wollstonecraft. Their unmasked selves, like hers, walked invisible.

The road to *Frankenstein* had been an experiment in female self-making. Mary Shelley had shaped a writing self by drawing on strands of her own experience for a work of outsider art. At the same time her daughterly respect for Godwin, together with maternal responsibility, took her on a different course from that of a Creature who succumbs to anger. His change to the bad, arguably, is not caused by neglect so much as by the resentful story he tells himself, requiring acts of revenge. This mentality expounds the brutish history of mankind.

If Mary Shelley's youth was an experiment, Claire Clairmont tried out a parallel experiment as the more outspoken disciple of Mary Wollstonecraft. It's easy to read her letters to Byron as a common story of infatuation, but a lot there has to do with ambition. It did not occur to her to be other than open, in the Wollstonecraft–Godwin manner, about what she wished to do. Byron's withering response to her novel was a gust of personal spite conjoined with the traditional brush-off of women who presumed to write. Mary Shelley was silent in Byron's presence; she admired his poems and made fair copies without expecting him to recognise her own gift.

Though Claire envied Mary Shelley's achievement, she had the sturdiness to take a proto-feminist pride. Envy, she said, 'yields when I consider that [Mary] is a woman and will prove in time … an argument in our favour. How I delight in a lovely woman of strong & cultivated intellect.'

Claire seems not to have attempted fiction again for a long time. She did write a satire on Byron called 'Hints for Don Juan' (conceived in February 1820) and 'Letters from Italy' (between April and August 1820). Neither has survived. Many years later, in 1836, she published a story called 'The Pole'. But her public achievement lay in music. When their party had settled in Pisa early in 1820, Shelley engaged a music master, Zannetti, who trained Claire to performance standard. In Pisa, she tried out the overture to Rossini's new opera, *La Cenerentola* (1817); she sang arias from Mozart; and her voice, Shelley said, was 'like the breath of summer's night' on starry waters. At the end of the aria, her lingering note suspended a poet's soul 'in its voluptuous flight'.

Here Shelley celebrates Claire Clairmont, calling her by her nickname, Constantia,* in one of his greatest poems, 'To Constantia, Singing'. More than any verifiable fact, more than what Claire concealed to the end of her life, when she said how she longed not to depart without telling 'what my tongue has never yet ventured to tell', this poem reveals the 'blood and life' in Claire that inspired Shelley. It was not the cerebral excitement of revolutionary ideas but a response to a woman's voice, felt on the pulse:

> *Thy voice slow rising like a Spirit lingers*
> *O'ershadowing it with soft and lulling wings,*
> *The blood and life within thy snowy fingers*

---

* Constantia was from *Ormond* by the American novelist Charles Brockden Brown.

*Teach witchcraft to the instrumental strings*
*— My brain is wild — my breath comes quick —*
*The blood is listening in my frame,*
*And thronging shadows, fast and thick,*
*Fall on my overflowing eyes;*
*My heart is quickening like a flame;*
*As morning dew, that in a sunbeam dies,*
*I am dissolved in these consuming extasies.*

Where Byron had jeered at 'the odd-headed girl' with her black crop, Shelley perceives a young woman who carries him beyond the moons 'Upon the verge of Nature's utmost sphere'.

'Constantia turn!' he commands. 'Yes! In thine eyes a power like light doth lie.' Even as her voice is laid to sleep between her lips, that power lingers in her breath and springing hair.

'Constantia' was not shown to Mary. Shelley published it under the pseudonym 'Pleyel' in the *Oxford Herald*. Claire was too close to Shelley for Mary's comfort. It can't be known if he and Claire were lovers, but undoubtedly there was some quickening between them. When Mary's grief for her children displaced Shelley from the centre of her attention, he thought of jaunting off with Claire to the Middle East. Later, Claire claimed that she knew Shelley in some ways better than his wife did.

Claire's other perfect tie was with Allegra. 'My life,' she said of this fair-haired little girl. Claire's tragedy was not Byron, but parting from Allegra, who was to belong to her father and have the advantages of a peer's daughter. Claire pined for her and worried about leaving a child with so irresponsible a man.

Nothing could convince Byron of Claire's maternal fitness. He placed Allegra, aged four, in a convent at Bagnacavallo, twelve miles from Ravenna, with a view to correcting the child's faults 'so far as nature allows'. She was 'vain' and 'stubborn', the nuns were told. It was the convent's rule to immure a girl till she was sixteen. So Byron placed Allegra permanently beyond her mother's reach; ignored Claire's reminder of an agreement that their child would never be left without a parent until she was seven; turned away from Claire's repeated pleas to be permitted to visit; and then turned his face from the child's own plea to see her father when she was ill. There, unvisited, Allegra died of typhus in the spring of 1822.

Byron dispatched her body to England and had her buried at his school, Harrow. The body was left in an unmarked spot outside the chapel door, separated from those who lie in consecrated ground. No swaggering bully or sexual abuser would have been excluded as Allegra was.

Claire received the news with the calm of one to whom nothing worse could happen. She would hate Byron for the rest of her life – beyond life, she said. Her loss, followed two months later by that of Shelley, stripped Claire of all that mattered. Illness was added to grief. Her glands were tubercular, she was told, but she had to find work.

On 20 September 1822 she boarded a coach for Vienna, expecting to teach English alongside her brother. Charles Clairmont found her employment, yet no sooner did she start than she was tracked by spies of the Austrian Chancellor, Klemens von Metternich. They declared her a dangerous radical for her past with Shelley, denied her a teaching licence and gave her notice to leave Austria. Over the winter of 1822–3, Claire grew 'skeleton thin'. Mary Shelley, who had no source of income beyond the minute amount she earned from writing, sent her twelve pounds when Byron refused to help.

She travelled on to Russia to be a governess in a remote place where no one knew her dark history. Claire is now remembered for her unconventional relations with Shelley and Byron. More significant, though, for women of the future is the independent course she took at this point, propped by her bonds with other independent women. 'The party of free women is augmenting considerably,' she put it to Mary. 'Why do not they form a club and make a society of their own. The women who go astray have generally so much talent and sensibility, so much genuine goodness of heart, collected into a club their society might become famous ... for its art and refinement'. Though Margaret Mount Cashell in Pisa, Mary in London and Claire in Russia were physically apart, their tie, maintained through letters, did realise what Claire had dreamt up in her night-time confab with Shelley: 'a subterraneous community of women'.

———

Mary's muteness, like Claire's, did not mean submission to the blows of fate. 'I beleive [sic] that we are sent here to educate ourselves,' she said. After Shelley died, she supported herself and her son by her pen, encouraged by Margaret Mount Cashell, who told her, 'Composing is certainly the best antidote to melancholy.'

Her next novel was called *Valperga*, a feminist variation on the genre of historical fiction popularised by Walter Scott. Her father edited her work and when it was published in 1823, she gave him the profits. Godwin was there of course on her return to London that year; she stayed a little while with the Godwins in their new premises on the cobbled east end of the Strand, and during the first week, her father accompanied her to a staging of *Frankenstein* — but she could not speak to him of depression after he'd silenced the depression she had suffered following the death of Will-Mouse. She was considerate enough not to trouble Godwin, and took it upon herself to help in times of crisis, for his Juvenile Library was never free of debt.

The pressure of muteness opened the floodgate of an extraordinary interior utterance. The 'Silent' voice of Mary Shelley's 'Journal of Sorrows' vents the emotions of transformation and loss. She sees herself as a human embraced by a superhuman who then departs, leaving her ill at ease in the old dispensation. She is marked as other. As such she can address the shade of Shelley, who understood her. But for the most part she does not believe in converse with the dead, so that she speaks as a solitary. It's a voice that takes over from the full-throated lamentations of the Creature, or a voice his aborted mate might have had, unleashing its aria of thwarted existence.

Mary Shelley's journals and Claire Clairmont's letters are where their powers as writers came to reside. After Shelley's death, these private letters and journals are the vessels that carry what had to be unspoken if these women were to survive. It is as though the sheer pressure of silence brought out, in each, the heightened utterance of literature in the private genres open to women for whom public speech was denied.

Mary Shelley conceived of a women's history and proposed the idea to John Murray in 1830. It could have been a realisation of Claire's idea of the subterranean links of women throughout the past. As a learned woman and as her mother's daughter, no one could have been more suited to bring this topic to the surface of history, but Murray turned it down. Women's history would remain buried until Olive Schreiner conceived it afresh in the late 1880s and then finally Virginia Woolf brought it to light in 1929 — a whole century after Mary Shelley — through the agency of her own press.

Next to *Frankenstein* and her *Journals*, Mary Shelley's third great achievement was her edition of Shelley's poems in 1839. Forbidden by Shelley's father to append a memoir of the poet, she slid a trove of biographical detail into her annotations. She notes how Shelley's 'passion for the reformation of mankind' co-existed with his penetration of character so that he was 'never a dupe'. He could read character in a look, a gesture, a phrase, and was not disappointed by ingratitude or betrayal because he expected it.

When Godwin eventually died he was buried, as he'd wished, with Mary Wollstonecraft in the churchyard of Old St Pancras, where they had married. Too young — in her early fifties — Mary died of a brain tumour in 1851. By that time the railway had broken through the churchyard and her son, Percy Florence, had had the bodies of Mary Wollstonecraft and Godwin moved to the vault of St Peter's church in Bournemouth, where he lived. Mary Shelley was buried between her parents.

The devoted Percy, now come into his inheritance as Sir Percy, together with his equally devoted wife, Lady Shelley (née Jane St John), took up the cause of publicising the poet. Over the following decades they changed the image of Shelley from dangerous revolutionary to that of Ariel, a doomed, ethereal spirit, while their image of Mary Shelley was suffused with Victorian sentiment. A painting pictures her in 1814, on that fateful June day when she met Shelley at her mother's tomb. It was what the Victorian public wished to see: a modest maiden holding back from the overtures of the poet as he leans towards her. So it happens that the full volume of her inward voice fades for a century or more. But it's there. Open her *Journals* to encounter it.

The Lover's Seat: Shelley and Mary Godwin in
Old St Pancras graveyard by William Frith (1877)

To her, 'the most contemptible of all lives is where you live in the world
& none of your passions or affections is called into action'. Fearlessly, she
resolved to 'descend into the remotest caverns of my own mind – carry
the torch of self knowledge into its deepest recesses'. Yet this venture was
not self-absorbed, not like that of the doomed, unnatural Frankenstein.
For she reached out with 'a kind of tenderness' to like minds, who could
share her need to 'tear the veil of this strange world & pierce with eagle
eyes beyond the sun'.

# 2

# VISIONARY

## Emily Brontë

Violence in *Frankenstein* seems far away: a one-off Gothic monster. More threatening is violence at home. In her great novel, *Wuthering Heights*, Emily Brontë imagined a house of men with a code of aggression. Two women live there: a cowed cook and a captive young widow stripped of her property. Kicks and blows have left her listless. This is observed by a visiting servant, Nelly Dean. Her position as a subordinate does not allow her to make any change, but her voice as witness carries a resistant narrative. Bared to her steady eyes is a world gone wrong.

Nelly has once been nurse to Hareton Earnshaw, the rightful heir to Wuthering Heights. He has been ousted and raised as an illiterate lout, grunting a few foul words. The hate and the bruised dependants, breaking the façade of family ties, repelled public opinion when the book came out in 1847 – and all the more once it was known to have come from a woman.

The author kept to herself. Emily Brontë was determinedly private, even at home in the Parsonage. Facts about her life are scant, prompting biographical fancies to do with wafting over heathery moors or vague forms of mysticism or literary dependence on a man: her brother Branwell was thought at one time to have written *Wuthering Heights*. Some have fancied a romance to account for the deathless love of Heathcliff and Catherine.

On the face of it, here was a woman to whom little appears to have happened, living out her short life (she died aged thirty) in a provincial hill village. Contemporaries saw her as silent, antisocial and overbearing towards her sister Charlotte when they travelled abroad. It continues to be something of a mystery as to how her greatness emerged. How did she come to the violence of her novel and conceive a mother and daughter whom Virginia Woolf thought 'the most lovable women in English fiction'? And how did she open out from graveyard lament to become one of the greatest visionary poets of all time?

In April 1820 she was nearly two years old when seven carts laden with the Brontës' goods bumped up the steep cobbled street of Haworth in the West Riding of Yorkshire. They came to rest at a small Georgian parsonage, built in 1779 at the top end of the village, with moorland stretching above. The parents and their six children felt, in the words of the Revd Patrick Brontë, like 'strangers in a strange land', implying a change as momentous as Exodus. Patrick Brontë came from County Down in Ireland; Maria, his wife, from Penzance in Cornwall. Their families were distant, and in moving here they had left behind the more sociable parish of Thornton, near Bradford.

From the start, the Brontë family seems to have been on its own, perhaps because Mrs Brontë, ailing since the birth of her last child, was too weak to be active in the parish, but more likely because the old families, the Greenwoods, the Taylors and the Heatons (ranked as gentlemen since the eighteenth century), did not take up Mr Brontë with anything like the hospitality he'd enjoyed in Thornton. Michael Heaton of Royd House, Oxenhope (who'd inherited his property through his mother) and his older brother Robert Heaton of Ponden House, two miles across the moor on the far side of Stanbury, were hereditary trustees of church lands, the main source of the stipend for the incumbent of Haworth. For the rest of their lives the Brontës would retain a sense of themselves as strangers, even though their parsonage was part of the village. It did not escape them that in Haworth there was 'not a single educated family'.

The strangeness was not, at origin, romantic, for it had to do with their father's swift change of class. A generation earlier, a family by the name of Brunty or Prunty, including a Catholic grandmother, Eílis [Alice] McClory, had migrated from the south to the north of Ireland. Patrick, tall, red-haired with pale blue eyes, was the eldest of ten children. In a two-room bothy with a mud floor, he read by the light of a flickering rush, and his love of books changed his life. It moved him from a lowly position, apprenticed to a blacksmith at the age of twelve, to village schoolmaster at sixteen. Five years later his religious intelligence caught the attention of Thomas Tighe, vicar of Drumballyroney, and so Patrick's vicar. Tighe was a graduate of St John's College, Cambridge, and in 1802 he sent Patrick Brunty there to read classics and theology. He went as a sizar, a servant to more affluent students, aided by a ten-pound annuity with the backing of the Evangelical reformer William Wilberforce. So there in the enormous grandeur of St John's was young Mr Brunty, learning to handle firearms alongside a peer of Ireland, the young Lord Palmerston. Gun-practice at the time was carried out with a view to defence against the threat of invasion by Napoleon.

While a student, Brunty changed his name to Brontë, possibly because in Greek it was the voice of thunder but more likely because he identified with fighters. In 1799, Admiral Nelson had been made Duke of Bronti (in Sicily). Patrick Brontë was studious, eloquent and a supporter of the Evangelicals, dedicated to renewing the church. His decision to be a minister led to a gentleman's position in the Church of England.

He married Maria Branwell, from a merchant family, in 1812. She was then twenty-nine and visiting a cousin in Yorkshire, where Mr Brontë held successive posts. Maria, whose parents had died, contributed an annuity of fifty pounds. Though the Branwells' middle-class status was superior to that of the Brunty family, it may not have been superior enough for a man whose peasant roots were disguised by his assumed name and hints of ancient ancestry. Mr Brontë never mentions the Branwells. He was friends with Tory gentlemen who distrusted the uneducated worker and who opposed Luddite revolutionaries in the Yorkshire mills in 1812, when they broke the new machinery that took away their jobs.

Maria's portrait in profile shows a slight woman with a strong nose and under-lip, in a dainty white dress with the high waist of the time. Emily

Jane, born on 30 July 1818, was their fifth child, after three daughters and a son, Branwell; a last daughter, Anne, was born in January 1820.

This was when Mr Brontë was offered a perpetual curacy in Haworth at two hundred pounds a year. There was a drawback to Haworth, which the church trustees may not have mentioned: the village was excessively unhealthy, even by the unsanitary standards of the day, with no sewers and polluted water running over the graveyard in front of the Parsonage. The average life expectancy was twenty-five.

At the Parsonage, all the children, except for baby Anne, were packed into a narrow room, no bigger than a passage, above the front door. On the other side of the wall Mrs Brontë died slowly from stomach cancer between January and September 1821. Her husband had never witnessed anyone in such pain – so agonising it tried her faith. Her death was expected almost daily. Sometimes she cried out, 'Oh God, my poor children – Oh God my poor children!'

Emily was the youngest in what was called 'the children's study', cut off from her mother and with a father worried and withdrawn. The sound of children's 'prattle' distressed him, so the five kept unnaturally quiet.

The moors offered an extreme contrast between the children's constraint in a tiny room and exposure to unlimited space when they emerged. This alternation between restriction and freedom, laid down in their earliest years, would shape the sisters' writings.

As the children wandered farther, each ridge rose against the sky, with its invitation to discovery. They found the 'fairy-cave' under the great boulders of Penistone Crags, what would become a heaven for the young Heathcliff and Catherine Earnshaw in *Wuthering Heights*.

As the children roamed, reports reached them of more challenging spaces. The Arctic explorations of Ross and Parry in the 1820s caught the fancy of Emily and Anne, and led eventually to a private world they would invent when they were ten and eleven. Fixed in Emily's earliest consciousness was this act of forging a path through uncharted territory.

Emily was three when her mother died. Her father's attempts to remarry failed. His appeals to an old flame, Miss Burder, are self-justifying and elaborately courteous. Mr Brontë was not one to draw out a woman, and it is not surprising that Miss Burder preferred to remain single. So there was to be no mother at the Parsonage, and when men visited they rarely brought their wives. Aunt Branwell, their mother's single, elder sister, was there to run the household, a small figure in large, old-fashioned caps who was displeased with her move from Cornwall to Yorkshire and dreaded the cold of the uncarpeted passages. She was not maternal, rather someone to respect and obey. Her nieces had to sit for hours in her over-heated room, sewing their samplers.

Was it in any way an advantage for the sisters to have no endearing model of femininity when they were girls? Later, when Charlotte's schoolfriend Ellen Nussey visited the Parsonage she found the sisters 'unpretending' and Emily 'lovable'. Her beautiful eyes, sometimes dark grey, sometimes dark blue, had an intent gaze which Ellen found keen and intimate. She remembered Emily at a 'Meeting of the Waters' on the moor, her fingers stirring the tadpoles, and making up dramas of leaders and cowards – no coward soul hers. If, as a girl, Emily was not withdrawn, we might wonder when she became so and why.

For three years following their mother's death the children looked to the eldest, Maria. Hers was a mind of rare grace, given to reading and thinking. From the age of seven to ten, Maria became her father's companion. She read *Blackwood's Magazine*, discussed its political essays and shared her father's thoughts on earthly existence as preparation for eternal life. She brought to this a conviction that humans might be higher beings than they are.

At ten, Maria and the next sister, Elizabeth, aged nine, were sent to a school for the daughters of poor clergymen. Even though it was a charity school Mr Brontë still had to pay fourteen pounds per child. Once they were joined by Charlotte and Emily, the cost amounted to a quarter of his annual income. It was more than he could afford, and his daughters knew that it was the best he could do to provide for their future. They had no money, which meant that they would be unlikely to marry, and so must prepare themselves for the lot of the governess – the position open to more or less educated middle-class women who had to earn their livings.

The newly established Clergy Daughters' School at Cowan Bridge was in Lancashire, fifty miles from Leeds along the road to the Lake District. It was a low-lying spot, chill and damp. Charlotte Brontë later told Mrs Gaskell that the scenes of Lowood institution in *Jane Eyre* were an accurate record of the torments that took place there. She added that she didn't include the worst because it would not be believed.

The school's founder, William Carus Wilson, fancying himself a benefactor, devised a regime of punishment, semi-starvation and hardiness. He was a clergyman who saw girls as weak and sinful, and his school would attempt to stamp out their nature by birching them into submission. In doing so he was hand in glove with the sadistic God of his books for children, a God who took care to destroy children's bodies for the good of their souls. The Brontë girls either fell prey to tuberculosis or the latent disease took hold under such conditions.

On 10 August 1824, when Mr Brontë took Charlotte, aged eight, to join her sisters, he noticed nothing wrong; nor did he notice the decline of his two eldest daughters when six-year-old Emily joined the school in November. Mr Brontë's oblivion seems so peculiar that it suggested a misleading idea that he did not take Emily himself. But it's conceivable that he would have seen three brave faces while he performed the orotund courtesies that had marked his rise. It's worth noting that Mr Brontë's Thornton friend and Charlotte's godmother, Mrs Franks, also visited the starved little girls on her wedding tour in September 1824 and picked up no effect of the hunger Charlotte would never forget.

Her sisters had to witness Maria's repeated humiliation by a teacher called Miss Andrews. Though Maria excelled in lessons, she was got at for untidiness. Miss Andrews would pounce on dirty nails even though frozen water had made washing impossible. The cowed girls had to watch Maria fetch a bunch of twigs, loosen her pinafore and receive several strokes on the neck. The beatings of Heathcliff in *Wuthering Heights* could have a source in the beatings Emily witnessed at Cowan Bridge, and the shock of seeing this done to the responsible sister who had replaced their mother.

In February 1825, after eight months at the school, Mr Brontë fetched a wasted Maria and brought her home. Unlike her mother, she looked forward to death. She had been steady in her endurance of cruelty and this character stamped itself on her sisters' memory. Reporting her death on 6 May to the school, her father wrote, 'She exhibited during her illness many symptoms of a heart under divine influence.' This is in the margin of the school's admissions register, next to Maria's name as the seventeenth pupil. News of her death may have prompted the school to dispatch Elizabeth with an escort. She too arrived home in a state of terminal illness. Only then, on 1 June 1825, did Mr Brontë remove Emily and Charlotte. They were at home when Elizabeth died twelve days later.

Nothing is recorded of Elizabeth's funeral but Emily, aged almost seven, would have been old enough to take it in. It can't be proved, but I think that she was marked ever after, as Charlotte was, by what happened at Cowan Bridge. 'The heart is dead since infancy', Emily wrote years later.

Grief and insistent memory, intense enough to induce apparitions of the dead, inhabit Emily's poetry and fiction. A poem dated 14 June 1839 (when Emily was nearly twenty-one) is in the present tense, signalling how tenaciously that past lives on: 'hearts greet kindred hearts once more', and then a sudden silence chills the room. All eyes turn to the door, while words die into whispers, as the kindred hearts listen for the voices of the dead: 'a sound / We know shall ne'er be heard again', but 'in vain — in vain!'

Repeatedly, longing calls up the beloved dead,

> *And think we feel their presence near,*
> *And start to find they are not here . . .*

Hovering at the interface of life and death, haunted minds intensify their sense of severance from those 'who have been our life — our soul —' by binding them together.

This poem, surely a result of the death of two sisters, anticipates the tantalising visitations of the dead Catherine at the beginning and end of *Wuthering Heights*. Catherine's ghost will eventually take possession of

Heathcliff and draw him closer to her hovering spirit as he vacates his body. To be with the dead is to recover his soul.

It is reasonable to wonder if the Cowan Bridge disaster and retentive bonds with her dead oldest sisters helped to shape the polarities of Emily's later fiction and poetry: 'so hopeless is the world without; / The world within I doubly prize'. In time, she found a way to translate the conflict of the visionary inner world and the distorting 'world without' into a family story.

The characters and events in *Wuthering Heights* are told largely by the downright servant on the scene. Nelly's voice is so homey that she serves to domesticate what in the story is strange and eerie. To some extent Nelly was based on the Parsonage servant, fifty-three-year-old Tabby – Tabitha Aykroyd – telling tales of local characters, which gripped the four Brontë children around the fire. She dealt out candid views on whom she liked or not, and fed the children well. Emily was attached to the kitchen, with its fire and Yorkshire accents, and would make the kitchen a dramatic centre in her novel. During the unbroken years at the Parsonage, from the summer of 1825 to the start of 1831, the children moved between the physical hearth of the kitchen and the upstairs life of the children's study where, in 1826, their imaginative union began.

That summer Mr Brontë gave Branwell a box of twelve soldiers. They provoked 'plays' of exploration, collaborative tales, some of which the children wrote down in tiny booklets that mimicked publications. The soldiers established themselves in a number of lands, one belonging to each of the children: Parry's land belonged to Emily, and Ross's land to Anne. Branwell drew exquisitely detailed maps with coloured outlines, as in Goldsmith's *Geography*. In one play, 'Tales of the Islanders' (1829) the children chose famous men to live there: Emily's choices were Walter Scott and his biographer Lockhart.

Emily and Charlotte began a different sort of 'bed-play' at the end of 1827, continuing into 1829. These 'very nice' night plays were too secret to be written down. Then, when Charlotte's godmother sent her to Roe Head School in 1831, Emily began further plays with Anne. This was the start of their Gondal saga. Emily and Anne had been dissatisfied with the minor roles assigned to their heroes by the dominant pair, Charlotte and Branwell, and they were bored by Branwell's battles and Charlotte's languishing heroines. Gondal's chief actors were headstrong women; it was ruled by the ruthless Augusta Geraldine Almeda, who ruins men. War in Gondal, unlike Branwell's pomp and parade, was stark. Gondal was an island in the North Pacific, with a setting and climate rather like Yorkshire: moors, mists and frozen gloom. Its people were hardy. Freedom was their blessing; prison their hell. Emily's Gondal poems of freedom and prison developed directly into the great poetry and fiction of her maturity.

Scott, Byron, Shakespeare, Milton, Bunyan, Dr Johnson and Wordsworth were amongst the writers on their father's hanging shelves between his study windows. These shelves contained no women writers: no Fanny Burney, no Mary Wollstonecraft, no Mary Shelley, no Jane Austen. Mr Brontë's time for his daughters' education was secondary to what he saw as his prime task: to teach his son Greek and Latin. His daughters sometimes participated in these lessons. (There survive translations from the Latin in Emily's hand and later Anne, as a governess, could offer Latin to the children she taught.) But Mr Brontë's chief contribution to his daughters' education was the encouragement he gave to reading, and the freedom he allowed them in their choice of books. Now and then they probably tramped four miles each way to the nearest circulating library, at Keighley, and the Brontë biographer Winifred Gérin suggests that Emily in particular borrowed books from the fine library belonging to the Heaton family at Ponden House. Gérin's idea is echoed by many who would like to link Emily's skill at the piano with the five musical sons at Ponden, as well as a rumour that the eldest, Robert, pined after Emily, but there is no evidence whatsoever. What we do know is that Emily read the heroic works of Scott, the nature poetry of the English Romantics and the revolutionary radicalism of Shelley, and that she, like Branwell and Charlotte, was immersed in Byron, with his melancholy loners.

In a sketch of 1834 Charlotte pictures Branwell, in the role of boastful Benjamin Wiggins,* scorning his sixteen-year-old sister Emily as 'lean

---

* Branwell made Charlotte furious in the end, and early on she's satiric in the face of his Byronic posturing.

and scant, with a face about the size of a penny'. Charlotte wrote this at
the time Branwell painted his portrait of his three sisters, and it may be a
satiric comment on his version of their appearance – her own as 'dumpy'
and Anne, to one side, as 'nothing'. Emily is the prettiest, with her deli-
cately pointed nose and small, pointed lips. She is taller than her sisters.
Branwell was to be the dominant figure in the family group and then, for
reasons unknown, he painted himself out. At that stage the whole family
looked to Branwell to be the achiever.

By shutting himself in his study and absenting himself from meals,
Mr Brontë managed to know little of his daughters' potentialities, and
he knew nothing of their writings until, eventually, Charlotte brought
him a published copy of *Jane Eyre*. He was astonished. His ambitions had
been fixed on his son, and Charlotte perhaps spoke for her sisters as
well as herself when she contrasted her father's attachment to Branwell
with blindness to his daughters' promise. Of course he was not unlike
most other fathers through the ages; it was the son who mattered. If his
daughters were jealous or resentful, they did not show it, and their sense
of duty was bolstered by genuine affection. They shared their father's grim
sense of humour, respected him and protected the privacy of his study.
There he sat, undisturbed, with his two pipes and his spittoon, making
copious notes on purgatives which 'give tone to the bowels' in the margins
of *Domestic Medicine*, writing unremarkable didactic verse (laced with hellfire
and endless woe) and preserving his domestic oblivion with solemn appeals
to God in the strong Scotch accent of the north of Ireland.

At nine o'clock, when Aunt Branwell went to bed, the sisters put away their
sewing, blew out the candles, and began to pace the shadowed dining room.
Their walk was free and rapid, keeping time with their thoughts and feelings. Ellen Nussey participated in this scene and reported it vividly. Emily
and Anne marched with their arms around each other's waists. To Ellen,
they seemed like twins interlaced in their affinities. She and Charlotte made

another pair. For those whose days were constrained by household tasks, night offered an untrammelled time to voice, touch and join with like minds. For the sisters (as later for Emily Dickinson in her Amherst room – starting at three in the morning with 'My wheel is in the dark', and still later for the mathematical heroine in Virginia Woolf's *Night and Day*), night was for thinking. Ellen assumed the sisters blew out the candles for economy. But darkness was a liberating cover; invisibility a form of freedom.

For three happy years, from the summer of 1832, when Charlotte left Roe Head, Charlotte taught Emily and Anne at home. She had particular success with her favourite subject, French, for later Emily's French was good enough to benefit from advanced study abroad. Mr Brontë bought a piano for his daughters and Emily took the lead with arias by Bellini scored for piano, Meyerbeer, Weber and Handel's oratorios. Most of these were arranged as duets, inscribed with the names of Emily and Anne. Then, in July 1835, with the expense of Branwell's training to be an artist ahead, Charlotte resolved to do what she could for Emily. She would return to her school as a teacher, and her post would pay for Emily's education; Emily, prised from Anne, would join her at Roe Head.

Incipient patterns took shape as Emily turned seventeen. Charlotte was about to lose her brother as a regular imaginative partner in their Angrian saga, and from this time she would invent schemes to co-opt Emily. More serious from Emily's point of view was the pressure to leave home.

One test of emergence as a writer is when the force of custom – the wrong narrative – takes over a person of promise. Emily's wellbeing depended on the security of home, with walks on the moor, sometimes with Anne, in order to get into the right 'humor' for writing. To leave home was an ordeal. Was it her experience at Cowan Bridge that made Emily unfit to take on 'the world without'? Or the sense of being out of step with the village? Yet she, like the others, knew that their father could not afford to keep them; they must prepare, once again, to garner the education that would enable them to earn their livings outside in the world.

So, on 29 July 1835, two sisters emerged again from the Parsonage into what Mr Brontë called 'this delusive and ensnaring world'. No one in 'this land of probation', he said, 'could lie beyond the reach of temptation'.

These were rather odd fears for two young women going to the safety of Miss Wooler's school, where Charlotte taught grammar to 'dolts' and Emily forced herself to face each day. Mr Brontë's pious warning showed no awareness of the real danger: homesickness.

Emily lasted three months. Silent, tall, at seventeen one of the oldest pupils in the school, she had little or nothing of Charlotte's hunger for knowledge, nor her gift for friendship. When she woke in the morning thoughts of home rushed upon her. Here, at Roe Head, she was the recipient of Charlotte's largesse, but Emily was not made to be a submissive dependant. To be in that situation sapped her strength. She could hardly bring herself to eat, and Charlotte feared her sister would die. By mid-October, a pale, wasted Emily was back at Haworth.

A poem speaks of 'those first feelings that were born with me', which obliterate all derivative schemes of existence:

> *I'll walk where my own nature would be leading:*
> *It vexes me to choose another guide.*

When the rules of schooling and adulthood forced her to relinquish her childhood nature, she shrivelled, unlike Anne. Of the four surviving children, Anne was the only one who could, without complaint, bear long periods in uncongenial society. Her judgements, severe and caustic though they were, did not shake her mind. She shared Emily's detachment but was able to disguise it, and even make use of it in her novels.

It's worth recalling that Anne did not experience the helplessness of a child of six or seven trapped with other girls, shivering and hungry, within school walls. Emily's collapse had its dark side laid down in memory: to leave home meant more than homesickness and loss of liberty; to be once more at school must have brought back fears. This has to be a guess, but it would explain Emily's failures to adapt despite her will to endure. It's as though to leave home was to be exiled from herself.

The pattern repeats. As with Maria and Elizabeth, Emily would deteriorate physically until she was like to die. Then the powers that be sent her home. In 1838–9 Emily began wasting once more in her only teaching post, in a large school at Law Hill near Halifax. She told Charlotte that her hours were six in the morning until eleven at night.

'This is slavery', Charlotte declared to Ellen. 'I fear she will never stand it.'

As predicted, Emily declined further and left the school in March 1839, after about six months. At Cowan Bridge, at Roe Head and then during her few months as a teacher, Emily had to cultivate privacy with an invisible wall to protect it. Behind that wall a voice issued in mournful poems. It's not gone unnoticed that she wrote many poems at Law Hill, but these are repetitious – a drear voice reiterating gloomy scenes. Law Hill was not a place where a latent voice could soar. How, after that, did her mournful voice become a resistant one?

Once home again her assured blast sounds decisively in her first great poem, written early in 1841 when she was twenty-two:

> Riches I hold in light esteem
> > And Love I laugh to scorn
> And lust of fame was but a dream
> > That vanished with the morn –
>
> And if I pray, the only prayer
> > That moves my lips for me
> Is – 'Leave the heart that now I bear
> > And give me liberty.'
>
> Yes, as my swift days near their goal,
> > 'Tis all that I implore –
> Through life and death, a chainless soul,
> > With courage to endure!

The breath of liberty in her nostrils, she could climb above Haworth and cross and re-cross a landscape too rough for cultivation. It was not a romantic scene. The land was soggy and bleak. Yet to be there was to be close to creation as yet untouched.

The sequel took place by night, when nature came to her with elemental drama. In a poem of July 1841, the tempest roaring at her window brings a 'voice divine'. Poured into her, that voice sweeps all else aside.

This is a story of a writer without a mask. So little does society impinge that she presents the purest instance of rising genius. An imaginative fount is abundantly in play; but apart from this, she walks invisible. It is difficult or impossible to reach her except through her writings. She will not say some of the things you and I would most like to know. What was her life like? How did it feel to be in a social position that was as new as the Brontës' assumed name? In the dreamlands of the children they were Genii or, in Emily's poems, Royals; to emerge from dreamland was to find a social hierarchy where she was no one. The Heatons, for instance, like other old families in the vicinity of Haworth, had been embedded in their milieu for centuries; they intermarried and socialised within that milieu, and when there was a significant funeral, that of the elder Robert Heaton in 1846, the substantial guest list did not include members of the Brontë family. After twenty-six years they still were not, in this insider sense, accepted.

Better than tacking together a few torn bits of biographical record may be to ask questions, even if we can't expect to answer them, and try to match Emily Brontë with other elusive writers with a view to learning more about that crucial 'world within'.

So again, the question: how did Emily Brontë take her leap to her visionary elevation? It can't be explained by books that talked to her – that approach puts her under the sway of men with a decided public face like Scott and Byron.

A more fruitful approach, I feel, is what Virginia Woolf can tell us of an extreme outsider whom she calls Rhoda in her novel *The Waves*. Like Emily, Rhoda is withdrawn and speaks but rarely. This is not of course Emily specifically, rather an insight into a supremely imaginative woman. Like Emily, Rhoda will not and cannot surrender the purity of early childhood. School tugs Rhoda to mimic the ways of other girls but here she's hopeless. At no stage of her life can Rhoda construct a convincing public face. Instead she lives in shadow as a creative phenomenon, 'the nymph of the fountain, always wet'. Her shadow-life is a condition of a full-on imaginative life. Rhoda's habitat, like Emily's, is amongst the permanent forms of nature. That inward voice she hears does not sound aloud and it has no face.

Another matching enigma, a more obvious one, is the visionary Emily Dickinson. Twelve years younger, Dickinson acquired a rare and treasured copy of the Brontës' *Poems*. She felt kin in particular to Emily Brontë in the authority both gave to 'the world within', and in the welcome Brontë grants to a 'Spirit' from a timeless existence beyond the world we know. Like her sister Maria, Emily Brontë saw life as preparation for eternity, but for the younger sister this feeling was more elemental than religious in the traditional sense. She calls the Spirit her 'slave' and 'comrade' as well as her 'King'. Having shunned 'the common paths that others run towards the worldly divinities of Wealth, Power, Glory and Pleasure', she recounts how she gave her spirit

> ... *to adore*
> *Thee, ever present phantom thing —*
> *My slave, my comrade, and my King!*

How surely, how daringly she speaks to a 'thing'. As comrade, this thing gives her 'intimate delight'; as slave it bends to her 'changeful will'. The poem opens in doubt whether there are words for a thing so ineffable, but by the end she exults in her eloquence, since her 'own soul' can do it. So the last couplet is a tease — her repeated plea is by now superfluous:

> *Speak, God of Visions, plead for me*
> *And tell why I have chosen thee!*

She's made it plain that visions come to a rebellious loner bold enough for the encounter.

Dickinson takes this further, in a poem in which a dreamer wrestles all night (like Jacob in the Bible) with a divine stranger, and finds, come morning, that he has 'worsted God'.

In strict terms, both poets are heretical, defying the dictum that the meek shall inherit the earth. Claiming to lack words for this divine encounter, Emily Brontë asks an angel to confer language: to 'plead for me' – to 'speak and say / Why I did cast the world away'. But it's only a show of humility, for she proceeds to speak for herself, and speak she must those startling words, 'slave' and 'comrade' (as well as the traditional king), to explain the ways of God to man. It's a changing relation, like that of Dickinson's 'Spirit', who was 'never twice alike, but every time another — the other more divine'.

Words fail but meanings still exist, as in Dickinson's dashes, pushing words apart to inject a resonant silence: 'And yet — Existence — some way back — / Stopped — struck — my ticking — through —'. Here are visionaries crossing the frontier of language.

But how did poetry and visions sit with their lives? Since they had daily lives as nineteenth-century women, we might ask what concessions each made to conformity. When the Parsonage servant, Tabby, lamed her leg and had to take a rest in the winter of 1839–40, Emily, together with her sisters, took up housekeeping with alacrity – it was preferable to guarding their manners in schools and others' houses. Emily was in charge of the kitchen and baking, while Charlotte chose to sweep the floors and do the ironing, impervious to Aunt's wrath when she burnt the clothes in her first effort.

Emily Dickinson too took to domesticity with her prize-winning Indian bread, her father's favourite pudding and the gifts she sent to neighbours in Amherst, often flowers from the conservatory her father built for her. She was more fortunate than Emily Brontë in a father who excused her from household tasks so that she could devote morning hours to poetry. She played spoofing games with images of femininity, particularly in her largely fictional 'Master' letters to a bearded man. Sentimental hearts are taken in by her 'Belle of Amherst' image or the pathetic poet who writes a letter to the world which does not write to her. No. Her eruptions belie these caricatures of femininity.

Emily Brontë did not go in for spoofs. She despised the world so entirely that she made no concessions, not even to amuse herself or tease future readers. A memory of what it feels like to follow the wrong course – for me, a narrative of expatriation that led to collapse – lends itself to what Emily could not bring off however hard she tried. The masks required by schools took her to the limits of endurance.

Charlotte had a solution. She conceived a plan for Emily and her sisters to earn their livings together: why not open a school near by – possibly at Dewsbury, with Miss Wooler's support, or at the Parsonage? Charlotte, who in truth longed for further education, proposed that she and Emily go abroad for six months to study French, German and, in Emily's case, music, with a view to their prospectus. This scheme was in the air from July 1841, when Emily turned twenty-three. Not having earned her living for over two years, she was bound to agree to Charlotte's venture. Charlotte secured a loan of fifty pounds from Aunt Branwell, and after much debate the sisters settled on the Pensionnat Heger in Brussels. So it was that on 8 February 1842 Emily and Charlotte set out via London and Ostend, escorted by their father.

The school was in a narrow, cobbled street below the fashionable rue Royale and park. Steep steps, narrower and steeper than the Belliard steps today, led down to the rue d'Isabelle. There, Mr Brontë left his daughters in the care of Monsieur and Madame Heger. Where Charlotte had come to stretch her wings in a 'promised land' of 'exquisite pictures' and 'venerable cathedrals', Emily had to brace herself for another ordeal.

At twenty-three and twenty-five they were ten years older than the ninety schoolgirls with whom they studied. They sat together in the quietest corner at the back of the second of three classes, the sole foreigners (with one exception) amongst the sixty girls in that room. In the refectory, with its two long tables and suspended oil lamps, they were served French food including pears cooked in wine, fresh from the grove of pear trees in the school's garden – unlike food at the Parsonage, where Tabby boiled the potatoes to a sort of sticky glue. At 8 p.m. there were *pistolets* (delicious small rolls) before bed. Upstairs in the dormitory, where the sixteen or so boarders slept in narrow, curtained beds, Emily and Charlotte were granted more privacy at the far end of the long room.

Each Sunday they attended the Protestant Chapelle Royale in the place du Musée. The Revd Jenkins, who officiated as the British Chaplain in Brussels (and as Chaplain to the Protestant King Leopold) invited the sisters for Sunday lunch, where Emily did not utter a word. In her home character at the Parsonage, Charlotte was tart and laughing, but with the Revd Jenkins and his family she too was ill at ease, turning her head away in accord with Emily. The Jenkinses' son, sent to escort the sisters, was put out by their forbidding silence.

They did not attend Catholic prayers at the school nor the nightly *lecture pieuse* about saints and martyrs. Charlotte later described how Emily's 'upright, heretic and English spirit' recoiled from Catholicism. I've wondered if it was Emily's hostility to Catholicism, shared by Charlotte, that infected their relationships with fellow pupils. I've wondered too if their religious antagonism had an Irish vehemence via their father. They told themselves the Belgians hated the English. They returned the hate and made few friends, apart from the English Wheelwright sisters, who were at the school, and even they did not take to Emily. She was universally unpopular, though one pupil, Louise de Bassompierre, gave her a drawing of a tree and said years later, '*Miss Emily était beaucoup moins brilliante que sa soeur mais bien plus sympathique.*'

For these reasons, they kept to themselves and during the recreation hour from five till six they walked apart, often in an alley at the back of the school's garden, which bordered on a boys' school, the Athenée Royale. This walk was out of bounds to others. Pupils noticed — one of the few, oft-repeated observations that has come down to us — how Emily, though much taller than Charlotte, leant on her as they walked, and seemed to exercise a power over her. 'Unconscious tyranny' was the strongly-worded impression of Constantin Heger, and he was not alone.

Pupils at the school, most of them from the fashionable classes, remarked the absurdity of Emily's big shoulder-enhancing sleeves and straight skirt. The look of the late 1820s and 1830s suited her height, but fashion in the 1840s had replaced it with sloping shoulders and narrow sleeves, with skirts springing out from a low tucked waist like a rounded bell. Emily had a grave beauty, but to these contemporaries she appeared 'lank'. That word, lank, tells us more about fashion than about Emily. Opinion was hardly mollified by her much-quoted retort to teasing girls, 'I wish to be as God made me.'

Her refusal to conform suggests that when she undertook the Brussels venture, by which time she knew her limits, she resolved to bare what she was. It would help to avoid the collapses of the past, brought on by forced obedience. Not to contort herself to fit the artifice of femininity may have been the only way she could take on 'the world without' a fourth time. This was to be her last attempt at being away. Where going abroad had proved an impetus for Mary Shelley's prodigious development, Emily Brontë's originality depended on staying at home.

All that's certain is that Charlotte, alert to Emily's deviance and history of decline, wished to protect her. But Emily did not want to be managed by her sister and there was another issue: Charlotte's attempts to detach her from Anne.

Anne was never included in Charlotte's plan. She was put aside with a vague promise that her turn would come. At this time she was holding up in her second post, teaching the daughters of the Robinson family at Thorp Green Hall near York. She remained there during 1842 while her older sisters were in Brussels, and took advantage of this life in the shade by visiting her store of observations with a view to a realistic novel about the wrongs of a governess. A boy she called Tom finds a nest of chicks and boasts how ready he is to 'wallop 'em! See if I don't!' Tom's uncle crows at this promise of manliness beyond 'petticoat government'.

Mary Wollstonecraft, as a governess, writing her first novel, *Mary*, testifying to a woman of vastly superior intelligence in the 1780s; Anne Brontë in a Yorkshire country house, raising a vehemently adversarial inner voice soon after the Woman Question took off in 1840;[*] and then Olive Schreiner, as a governess on a remote African farm in the later 1870s,

[*] See Chapter 5.

pressing on with a feminist novel – here and there, in unlooked for places, the new breed sprouts.

Emily's musicianship was such that Mme Heger was moved to offer her a music post in the school, and at the same time, in July 1842, she offered Charlotte a place as English teacher. The offer was an exchange, not a salary: in return for teaching in the school, the sisters would have board and lodging and free tuition in French for a further six months.

M. Heger, called 'Monsieur', tutored them privately. He was thirty-two when they arrived, only nine years older than Emily. He had black hair and always dressed in black. There was a tigerish tension in his blue eyes, a confrontational readiness in a way that suggested a challenge at once dramatic and severe. He proved a crucial mentor for Charlotte, and had an even higher estimate of Emily. As Shelley had insight into what burnt internally in Mary Shelley, here – unexpectedly – is another rare man. For Monsieur perceived in this awkward young woman an intrepid navigator with the will to go on. What he saw was the daring. It's like the navigator-narrator in *Frankenstein*. Because such a venture was closed to women, Heger thought Emily should have been a man.

In the summer of 1842, by which time he had grasped the extraordinary potential of the Brontës, Heger devised a new method of instruction. He would read aloud from the classics of French literature so that his English pupils might discern the author's motive and 'principle' and, at the same time, catch the feeling and rhythm of French. He asked them to write '*Imitations*' in the same style, with the same subtlety of 'nuance'. The masterstroke was to demand that they apply this feeling, rhythm and nuance to subjects of their own choosing.

He told them: 'It is necessary, before sitting down to write on a subject, to have thoughts and feelings about it. I cannot tell on what subject your heart and mind have been excited. I must leave that to you.'

Emily objected. She did not wish to imitate anyone.

Monsieur overrode the objection, whereupon Emily showed her native fist by choosing the Anglo-Saxon leader Harold, at his most diehard before the battle of Hastings, when he feels it in him to resist the Norman invasion.

In turn, M. Heger showed his mettle as a teacher unthreatened by manifestations of Emily's will. He was the first outside the Parsonage and for decades to come to recognise her genius.

Alien and resistant though Emily was, her *devoirs* suggest there were gains to be had from the control and terseness Monsieur demanded: observation or fact as a basis for emotion, drama, ideas. Her portrait of Harold required some factual basis. Her essays 'Le Papillon' ('The Butterfly') and 'Le Chat' ('The Cat') required attention to an actual creature. Emily argues in a playfully unyielding voice that the Cat, self-interested, cruel, hypocritical, is the animal most like humans, not dogs, who are too good. We may consider whether the essay, a genre with its feet on the ground, was for her a mere exercise, or whether the essays of 1842 offered a bracing alternative to 'divinest anguish'. Did work for an exacting teacher wake her from what one of her Gondal characters calls the wish to 'indulge in Memory's rapturous pain'?

Only one Gondal poem was completed in Brussels, with two others completed on her return to Haworth. There's the usual replay of grave-yard scenes and grief for loved ones under the sod – grief which 'never heals with years'. Though Gondal figures change from poem to poem, character is thin and it's the anguish of loss that drives the poems. And then suddenly, in the midst of what reads like routine woe, lines jump out, dated 17 May 1842, as Gondal drama mutates towards the central drama of *Wuthering Heights*: the Fall from innocence. There's the regret of an adult who has betrayed a childhood integrity:

> *Dear childhood's Innocence, forgive,*
> *For I have done thee wrong!*

She worked hard to attain passable French (including letters of invitation and refusal, so stiffly formal as to walk a tightrope of politeness above offence), the rudiments of German and proficiency in drawing, but above all she benefited from her music master, M. Chapelle, brother-in-law to M. Heger and a teacher at the Royal Conservatory in Brussels. In return for this privilege, Emily may have felt obliged to offer those music lessons at the pensionnat. It's consistent with her ungraciousness – call it determination – that she insisted on teaching during the recreation hour so that she did not have to give up her own time for study. She was impervious to her pupils' annoyance. Charlotte was relieved that the Hegers, at least, perceived Emily's quality despite what she calls her sister's 'singularities'.

They returned to the Parsonage in November, after Aunt Branwell died. The Hegers wrote to Papa, a warmly appreciative letter urging the sisters' return, but Emily resolved to take Aunt's place as housekeeper and to manage the investment of what the sisters had inherited, while Charlotte returned to Brussels. What had been 'the children's study' was now Emily's room, where she pursued her imaginings.

All through 1843 she was once again the only sister living at home. After her music training in Brussels, she played a lot of Beethoven: his sonatas and three of the symphonies, transcribed for piano. One of the symphonies was No. 7, and how fitting for her the charged second move-ment with its tension between mounting passion and order: the contraries of two houses, one given to abandon, the other to decorum, in her novel.

All the while her one-time imaginative partner Anne was still at Thorp Green, where she pressed on with her novel about a governess who lives for a 'world within'. Anne's phrase may anticipate Emily's 'world within' in her 1844 poem 'To Imagination'. Their unheard voices echo in the space between their works.

Certainly, Anne's lone, 'plain' governess anticipates Charlotte's Jane Eyre, and it seems that Anne, drawing on her more sustained experience of 'the world without', took the lead as novelist. Her 'passages in the life of an Individual' became *Agnes Grey* (1847), published in a volume together with *Wuthering Heights*. We can't know when Emily first conceived the latter, but it would not be surprising if the latter were in mind well before the earliest evidence that she was writing it in the spring of 1846.

Its story turns on the wrongs that result from a calculated mar-riage, and it so happened that while Emily had been away in Brussels an instance of such a marriage had taken place in the vicinity of Haworth. The Heaton papers reveal that a son of Michael Heaton, called Robert,[*] married Mary Ann Bailey, who gave birth rather soon afterwards, on 13 September 1842.[†] Unusually in the Heaton papers, there is no record of the precise date of the marriage, only the year. Whether or not Emily Brontë took note of this Heaton marriage we can't know, only that it offered material for the flagrance with which *Wuthering Heights* questions the base reasons behind the binding marriage contract. Certain names in *Wuthering Heights* — Heathcliff and Hareton — are close to Heaton. Incidentally, a Mary Earnshaw was part of the Heatons' extensive circle.

In April 1843, Emily takes on the voice of a betrayed woman to declare a repeated resolve: 'thy love I will not, will not share'. Her voice sees through falsehood: 'But, oh, thy lies shall ne'er beguile!' This empowers the speaker to detach from 'wrongs' that do, she admits, tear her. Instead the speaker will turn her face to 'the heaven of glorious spheres' rolling 'on its course of light / In endless bliss through endless years'. Endless bliss. Endless years. We are close enough to hear her vehement breath.

In a poem dated 10 February 1844, the 'spirit', alert to heaven, can calm a 'resentful mood' venting a 'demon's moan'. A 'savage heart' must be concealed: 'What my soul bore my soul alone / Within its self may tell.'

All this while, Charlotte had to bear a forbidden passion for her married 'master', M. Heger. A month before Emily's resentful moan, Charlotte had returned, tight-lipped, from Brussels, and now began her long, secret agony over her severance from Monsieur and his curtailed response to her pleas for continued communication. At times she managed to mask her insistence as need for advice in setting up a school. The sisters put out a leaflet in the summer of 1844, announcing a school at the Parsonage, with Latin, French and music on offer and Emily Brontë in charge of

---

[*] This Robert, born in January 1818, was a nephew of Robert Heaton of Ponden. His birth date is sometimes cited as earlier, but I follow the date listed by his mother, Ellen Heaton of Royd House.

[†] I have not managed to trace her background. In the Heaton papers the Baileys do not appear amongst the old, established families with whom the Heatons were accustomed to associate, and (like the Brontës) they were not amongst those invited to the elder Robert Heaton's funeral in 1846.

housekeeping. No pupils came. By mid-1845, with Anne back from Thorp Green, all three had given up on teaching.

One day in the autumn of 1845, when Emily was not about, Charlotte looked at her poems copied into two notebooks. She was astounded by a voice unlike any other woman Charlotte had ever read: no feminine diffuseness; no tremulous warbling. This voice was terse and with a strange music of its own. It came to her with the force of a trumpet.

As Charlotte feared, her sister was outraged by an invasion of her privacy. She saw Emily's character as 'not one, on the recesses of whose mind and feelings, even those nearest and dearest to her could . . . intrude unlicensed'.

It was Anne who broke the tension. Watching the standoff between her sisters, she brought out her poems for her sisters to read. Her voice of endurance touched Charlotte with its pathos – here was another accomplished poet – and it flashed on Charlotte that though her own poems fell short of Emily's genius, the three of them could put together a volume of verse.

Emily continued for some days to protest that her 'rhymes' were not for publication.

Charlotte spoke up for 'honourable ambition'. A mind like Emily's, she argued, must have some residue of their childhood hope to be authors. Anne was a support. She and Emily concurred in omitting Gondal. Many of their poems had been voicings by the characters of that land, but the poems for the volume were to stand without Gondal contexts.

The sisters were aware that women writers were unlikely to have a fair hearing. To protect their work, they resolved on pseudonyms. And so the Brontës' first book, *Poems by Currer, Ellis and Acton Bell*, came out in May 1846.

The book was privately printed for the sum of thirty-one pounds and ten shillings, money available from their aunt's bequest. Though only two copies were sold by June, nearly forty were sold over the next two years and the authors posted copies to Wordsworth, De Quincey, Hartley Coleridge, J. G. Lockhart and Alfred Tennyson. Unknown to the sisters, they were read by Charles Dodgson (later known to the public as Lewis Carroll, author of *Alice in Wonderland*) and by Florence Nightingale, who transcribed some of the poems into a notebook of favourites and recalled later how struck she was by Emily's experience of wind, stars and visions that kill her with desire.

From then on the sisters were united in their secret purpose. Branwell was also writing poems and was in fact already in print (in the *Bradford Herald* and the *Halifax Guardian*), but there was a deliberate decision on the part of the sisters not to include their brother in their plan. Often expansively drunk, Branwell could not be relied on to keep their secret, but there was more to the problem.

After losing a number of jobs, he'd joined Anne as tutor at Thorp Green. There Anne had witnessed Mrs Robinson glad-eyeing her brother, exciting his susceptibility. Dismissed in July 1845 by an ailing Revd Edmund Robinson, who died soon after, Branwell deluded himself that all Lydia Robinson wanted was to give herself (and her property) to him. At length, she dispatched her coachman to warn Branwell away. The well-connected widow remarried and swanned about high society as Lady Scott. The Brontës saw her as a wicked woman who had injured their brother, while he went on drinking at the Black Bull, taking drugs and disrupting the Parsonage. Emily witnessed a Fall at close hand, which she could draw on for her portrait of drink-sodden Hindley Earnshaw, the owner of Wuthering Heights, as he loses his grip.

Once, when Branwell set fire to his bed and lay there stupefied, Emily was tough enough to pick him up and carry him downstairs. This was the family situation as his sisters sealed off, so far as they could, and launched into publication. On 6 April 1846 they informed Aylott and Jones, the London publishers of the forthcoming *Poems*, that each was writing a novel.

In *Wuthering Heights* scenes of home cruelty disrupt the Earnshaw and Linton families through two generations: the humiliation and whipping of a dark street boy, Heathcliff, taken into the Earnshaw family; and the violence that Heathcliff, in turn, inflicts on his wife, who finds him a 'monster'. After she runs away and dies in hiding, he terrorises his sickly son and then the very young Cathy Linton, whom Heathcliff traps and forces to be his daughter-in-law. At first she tries to find an ally in her boy-husband, who is also her cousin, but he's too beaten down, too feeble in spirit as well as body to be other than self-protective; he treats her with unkind petulance. Another cousin is the degraded Hareton, Hindley Earnshaw's son, whom Heathcliff has ousted from his birthright and brought up to follow his lead as foul-mouthed brute.

The violence, we know, is far from all. Heathcliff is more famous for his passionate bond with Cathy's mother, Catherine Earnshaw. When Catherine said, 'I *am* Heathcliff', she stressed that their love offered no visible delight. Their sameness is not romantic nor is it erotic; it's strange — and yet there's a familiar element.

As Mary Shelley's monster is human enough to fix on a father figure, so Heathcliff fixes on a sister figure, who bonds with him in child-hood. The pair's affinity endures after each makes a worldly marriage prompted by class and, in Heathcliff's case, greed. Catherine marries the gentlemanly but lifeless Edgar Linton, while Heathcliff elopes with Edgar's sister, Isabella. Heathcliff, who has an eye to Isabella's future property as her brother's heir, despises her, and from the start wants to bash her 'curd' face black and blue. Isabella, meanwhile, is romancing this brute in her fancy. She ignores Catherine's warning. Nor is she deterred when Heathcliff hangs her dog before they gallop away. But marriage to Heathcliff brings this home. Within twenty-four hours Isabella finds her husband scarcely human, a 'goblin' or 'fiend'.

Heathcliff's havoc has, of course, a history. Blending with horror is pity for his outcast youth. As with Mary Shelley's Creature, the more we know of his past, the more ambiguous he appears. Heathcliff manifests human nerves and grief when he finds Catherine damaged by her marital cage. What humanity he has resides in their love. Catherine says of Heathcliff: 'If all else perished and *he* remained, I should still continue to be; and, if all else remained, and he were annihilated, the Universe would turn into a mighty stranger. I should not seem part of it.' To her, Heathcliff is not a monster; he's her very self, interfused with their moorland setting. Catherine's words are close to Emily Brontë's sublime allegiance:

*Though Earth and moon were gone*
*And suns and universes ceased to be*
*And thou wert left alone*
*Every Existence would exist in thee*

This is from her best-known poem, 'No coward soul is mine',* dated 2 January 1846 — at the time she was writing *Wuthering Heights*. When Catherine dies after giving birth, Heathcliff does feel a stranger in the universe, as he beats his head all night against a tree. But then this moving grief turns to violence: he shakes his wife until her teeth rattle; he throws a knife at her. It lands in her neck and Isabella herself has to pull it out.

Insistently, the story leads us back to aggression empowered by physical force. We are braced and exhilarated by the effrontery with which Emily Brontë sees through power and lets it declare its baseness. Heathcliff admits that the more his victim writhes, the more he wants to squash its entrails. He 'experiments' with the limits of his wife's fear to the point where she wishes to die. Are we to blame Heathcliff's aggression on lack of nurture, the plausibly simple (or simplistic) excuse of Frankenstein's monster? Or do we understand Heathcliff to be Nature itself, red in tooth and claw?[†] Is violence then innate?

For two fertile years, from late 1845 to late 1847, Emily's voice came from behind the shield of Ellis Bell. Sadly, this protection was smashed in the course of 1848. It was not only disheartening that *Poems* sold so few copies and that her crooked publisher failed to return the fifty pounds that she and Anne had to advance against sales of their novels, and further that

---

* Virginia Woolf quotes stanzas from this poem to top the case she makes for professionally disempowered women in *Three Guineas*. See below, pp. 280–1.
† If so, Emily Brontë anticipates Tennyson's 'red in tooth and claw' of *In Memoriam* (1850), nine years before Darwin spells out this aspect of evolution in *The Origin of Species* (1859).

reviews condemned *Wuthering Heights*, but then in July 1848 Charlotte and Anne chose to reveal their true identities. They went in person to present themselves to Charlotte's astonished publisher, George Smith, at 65 Cornhill in London. Their purpose was to scotch rumours that the Bells were one man, publishing his supposedly inferior works, *Wuthering Heights* and *Agnes Grey* (December 1847) and *The Tenant of Wildfell Hall* (June 1848), on the strength of *Jane Eyre*'s huge success the previous October.

Emily refused to accompany her sisters. She was furious. Her privacy was gone.

Once the Bells were outed as female, they came into question as 'coarse'. The foremost literary reviewer, George Henry Lewes, summed up the adverse reaction in an unsigned review in the *Leader*: 'Books, coarse even for men, coarse in language and coarse in conception, the coarseness apparently of violent and uncultivated men – '. Even Charlotte's defender, Mrs Gaskell, when it came to writing her friend's life, put forward the notion that Charlotte had touched 'pitch' but had been purified by suffering. Angelically pure is the way Victorians wished ladies to be, and Mrs Gaskell was determined to redeem Charlotte's reputation for unladylike passion and vehemence.

Lewes, impressed with *Jane Eyre*, had corresponded privately with Charlotte, and Emily wrote to him too (though it's not known what she said). Lewes then attacked Charlotte's feminist novel *Shirley* (1849), on gender grounds. She protested to him about this public betrayal of her gender. Thackeray also got at her, while pretending it was a joke. When she visited London, he called her 'Currer Bell' in company. Next day, when he called, she had it out with him. Then he deprecated the unladylike rage. Much as he admired her writing, Thackeray thought it driven by a spinster's 'hunger' for a man. If she had a husband, he said, she'd have no need to write.

Emily's unsociable habits and unwillingness to please must be seen in this gendered context, which makes her no freak: rather a woman courageous enough to resist absurd norms.

In *Wuthering Heights* Catherine first appears as a ghost calling in vain at the window of Wuthering Heights. While alive, she had shifted between the abodes of men: the violent Heights and the lifeless decorum of the Grange. Her buried self, disembodied, demonstrates the impossible choice that faced women, denying them full-bodied existence. An element of Emily entered into Catherine's outsider self enduring beyond her lifetime.

Nelly Dean has an intimation of such endurance as she looks at the faces of the dead: 'I feel an assurance of the endless and shadowless hereafter – the Eternity they have entered – where life is boundless in its duration, and love in its sympathy, and joy in its fullness.'

The novel's fame is for a love that can cross the barrier of death. The union that haunts and torments the lovers of the first generation is recovered in their afterlife. Domestic affection is the alternative, and this wins out in the second generation. The novel opens and closes with the second generation, and the meaning of the book lies not only in the rage that destroys the earthly existence of first generation; it is in an end to Heathcliff's rule. His death in 1802, a year after the novel's opening, brings reconciliation and release to Cathy and to her kinsman Hareton, whom Cathy woos from the emotional prison of his loutishness. We watch the brute world at the Heights become kinder.

One night in my twenties I set the alarm to wake me for 'the late, late movie' on TV at 4 a.m.: William Wyler's 1939 *Wuthering Heights* with Laurence Olivier as Heathcliff. I have not forgotten the disappointment of that long-ago night in New York. The movie conventionalised the strangeness into a cliché of romantic love between an ill-cast actor and a Hollywood star, Merle Oberon, with her pouting, kissy mouth. Worse, domestic violence is played down in so far as Isabella does not run away and die – Hollywood would have her remain at Heathcliff's side, the troubled but loyal little wife. Worst of all, they cut the second generation.

After that, I used to ask my students why the second generation is vital to the novel. Most did see that though Hareton and Cathy are not as extreme as the lovers of the first generation, they aren't tame; their domesticity is a condition of restored order. Cathy teaches Hareton his letters and they bend together over a book, and literacy transforms him. Nor have the graces of Cathy's upbringing been wiped out by Heathcliff's attempt to make her a 'slut'. Her awakened sympathy for Hareton is consistent with the care of Nelly Dean, whose even voice has carried us through the hate that nearly wrecked their world.

The strangest scene in *Wuthering Heights* is Heathcliff digging up Catherine's coffin to look on her face once more. Afterwards, he arranges for his body to be buried beside hers with the sides of their coffins opened so that their dust can merge. The graveyard scene has some resonance for an unexplained incident a while after the novel came out.

There was tension mounting to a rift between the Heaton brothers and the Revd Patrick Brontë, whose letters to the Heatons are coldly formal. When Michael Heaton, chairman of the church trustees, died at the age of seventy on 5 March 1860, Mr Brontë refused to inter him in the Haworth churchyard, where all the Heatons and five out of six of Mr Brontë's children had been buried. The immediate reason was that the ground was full, but two days later an order was obtained from Whitehall to bury Michael Heaton with his wife and ancestors, and here is the puzzling fact: Mr Brontë still refused. What's more, he exerted his authority over his curate and son-in-law (Charlotte's widower) Arthur Bell Nichols, who also refused.

It's worth recalling how precarious the Brontës had always been. For forty years Mr Brontë's position had been merely that of a perpetual curate, and his home belonged to the trustees, the Heatons amongst them. Was there some slight that hurt the Brontës' thin skin when it came to their rise in the class system? Or had the rift come about through Emily's use of sorry episodes in the Heatons' past?

The Heatons are linked with *Wuthering Heights* in a more immediate way than the dubious notion that Ponden House was the model for the elegant Thrushcross Grange. The long, stone building is more like a farmhouse, more like Wuthering Heights, particularly the separate 'Old House' where there was a tree with a branch that beat against a window, as in the novel. The main house, originating in the Tudor period (older, in fact, than the

'Old House')* was renovated in 1801, the year that opens *Wuthering Heights*. The novel's plot suggests that it was not only the house that attracted Emily's attention but also the disruption of an interloper. Initially Henry Casson was there in a serving capacity, like the young Heathcliff. It's thought he was higher than a servant, more probably a manager of the estate. He worked for a young Heaton widow, and by inducing her to marry him gained control of the property for nearly twenty years in the mid-seventeenth century. The rightful heir, his stepson, then a child, was sidelined in the same way as Hareton Earnshaw, who for the space of his youth loses control to the usurper.†

Heathcliff's abusive union with his social superior, Isabella Linton, may have a source in a more recent drama: the marriage in August 1813 of Elizabeth Heaton to a Bradford delivery boy called John Bakes. The

---

* In 1513 Wilfred Heton was granted two acres by Henry VIII and the original house was built in 1541. The 'Old House' was built in 1634 by Robert Heaton (1587–1641) for his son and heir, Michael Heaton (1609 –43). The 'Old House' was demolished in 1956.

† How much or how little Emily Brontë knew of hearsay is a matter for speculation. There is the oft-repeated story about Jack Sharp who had built Law Hill. He had been adopted by John Walker of nearby Waterclough Hall and then ousted by the rightful heir. He went in for revenge against Waterclough. Emily could have heard this when she was at Law Hill in 1838–9 and the suggestion is that she used him as a model for Heathcliff. But Sharp was a distant stranger; the Heatons she knew.

The facts of the Heaton episode are these: Michael Heaton died unexpectedly in his early forties in 1643 (perhaps in the Civil War), only two years after the death of his father. He left no will though there was an inventory of his possessions. Not long before, in December 1640, he had married a co-heiress, Ann Scarborough, the descendant of medieval Lords of the Manor at Glusbury Hall in North Yorkshire. At twenty-six, Ann Heaton was left with a two-year-old girl and a one-year-old boy and, according to her elaborate marriage settlement, a right to half the estate. So here was what in law was called a femme sole, an independent woman of property under neither husband nor father. In about 1650 she consented to marry a man who was far beneath her socially: his son by a former marriage was apprenticed to a blacksmith. Nothing was done by Casson to put his stepson's rights on a legal footing, and it was not until 1663, when the heir came of age, that his rights had to be recognised. All the time this child was growing up, his stepfather acted as though he were master of the estate and appropriated the furniture and goods as if they belonged to his wife and were by matrimonial right his. As an adult his stepson, Robert Heaton (1642–1714), was compelled to buy back his father's goods. There was a half-brother, John Casson, who lived at Ponden – he remained a bachelor – and only resigned his claim on the property on his deathbed in 1710. He must have been too weak to sign since he left only the shaky squiggle of 'his mark' on the quitclaim. So it was that the Heatons were not free of the Casson entanglement for two generations.

marriage was a disaster, and Elizabeth (like Isabella) died young, in March 1816.*

The third Heaton story is post-*Wuthering Heights*. It involves Michael Heaton's eldest son, Robert, who was Emily's exact contemporary. When Mr Brontë refused to bury Robert's father, this was the member of the family whom he would have opposed most directly. Was there some special animus, possibly to do with the hushed-up wedding date in 1842? Or was there resentment against the Heatons as a family? Or had it to do in some way with Emily's dark re-enactment of Heaton mismatches in *Wuthering Heights*? This remains a mystery, and my guess — it can be no more — is that the mystery involves the Brontës' sense of themselves as strangers who, for all their gifts of mind and imagination, were never admitted to the Heatons' circle.

Catherine Earnshaw in her ghostly aspect is literally outside, calling at the window of Wuthering Heights, thrusting her child's hand through the broken pane and unable to enter. The novel is filled with calling, speaking, witnessing and listening: we hear the tale from Mr Lockwood, the tenant of Thrushcross Grange, who hears it from Nelly Dean. As in *Frankenstein*, horror is brought home, domesticated, by narrators who are all the more reliable for their ordinariness. In this way Emily Brontë both draws us in as listeners and keeps her distance.

Catherine's is a posthumous voice, recessed behind the voices of others who report her words. Nelly wonders at beings whose gusts of life extend what's familiar. Catherine speaks subliminally to our submerged selves. In time that posthumous voice, at once far off and intensely close, woke the public's ear.

---

* Again, it's impossible to know how familiar Emily Brontë was with the detail of this story. As with Ann Heaton and Henry Casson, Elizabeth's attraction to a social inferior may have sufficed to provide material for the novelist's imagination. There's no suggestion in the Heaton papers of physical abuse, rather callous arrogance. Scorning 'trade' for himself, Bakes put his frail young wife to work in the shop his father had provided in Gomersal, and then when she was emaciated, coughing — dying, as it proved, at the age of twenty — Bakes dumped her and their child at Ponden and left at once. He was carousing from one pub to another, and had a habit of arriving in the middle of the night, waking the family so as to cadge funds for drink. Elizabeth's mother died a few months after her daughter, and her father the following year.

During her lifetime Emily had resisted Charlotte's management – an elder-sister protectiveness, as Charlotte felt. It was agonising for her to stand by helpless as Emily wasted away with tuberculosis during the last months of 1848.

Emily went to bed at the usual time of ten each night and came downstairs punctually at seven each morning, to the day of her death; despite paroxysms of coughing and pain in her side, a hastening pulse and panting after the least exertion, she would not concede illness. If Charlotte asked how she was, she did not reply. She refused to see any 'poisoning doctor'. Charlotte had to witness 'the conflict of the strangely strong spirit and the fragile frame before us – relentless conflict – once seen, never to be forgotten'.

After Emily died on 19 December 1848, Charlotte controlled her sister's reputation. She selected and revised Emily's poems for an edition by her own publisher, Smith Elder, in 1850, and at that time wrote a preface for a new edition of *Wuthering Heights*. Charlotte felt called upon to apologise for the novel as flawed; she deprecated the creation of Heathcliff: a writer should not lend her imagination to a 'demon'. At a stroke her authority as the more famous sister cuts down the familiarity of domestic violence – she's siding with public opinion that prefers to look away. Neither the public nor Charlotte were prepared to condone a voice that spoke out against the Victorians' idealisation of marriage.

In the same way but even more firmly, Charlotte deplored Anne's telling portrait of domestic violence in *The Tenant of Wildfell Hall*. If anything, the secret violence of Arthur Huntingdon, behind the closed door of his affluent home, is worse than Heathcliff's. Like Frankenstein's monster, Heathcliff has been warped by rejection, but Arthur's malice is without motive. He twists his wife's resistance so as to shift the blame for his downhill course onto her, as she records: 'he says I drive him to it by my unnatural, unwomanly conduct'. He hates innocence, and takes pleasure in hurting his wife and flaunting his freedom to corrupt their child. He does this because he can; the law empowers him, and Arthur is literally drunk on power — he's drinking all the time. Helen writes in her diary about false manliness:

> My greatest source of uneasiness, at this time of trial, was my son, whom his father and his father's friends delighted to encourage in all the embryo vices a little child can show . . . – in a word, to 'make a man of him'.

In running away from her husband, and taking their child with her, Helen is acting against the law. She and her son are her husband's possessions and he has the right to reclaim them. Helen must take refuge under a pseudonym, and in a place where she's unknown. When *Wildfell Hall* came out, its defiance of the law was considered scandalous. In the introduction to the second edition, Acton Bell made a plea for people to abandon the 'delicate concealment of fact – this whispering, "Peace, peace" when there is no peace'. But then, in 1850, by which time Anne too had died of TB, Charlotte brushed off the subject as an error of judgement. She meant the effects of dissipation and alcoholism on the family, as Anne had experienced in Branwell. So it was that, two years after her sisters died, Charlotte devised an image of them as ladies not that different from those whose supposed refinement kept them from seeing brutal scenes.

Heathcliff calls his bookish daughter-in-law a 'slut'. He hates Cathy as the daughter Catherine had with Edgar Linton, and his smear denies her respect as a member of family with a right to protection. Our century is at last waking up to physical abuse on a measureless scale, but to readers in the mid-nineteenth century, Heathcliff's mind-set was too outré and brutish for readers.

After Emily died, Charlotte tried to placate opinion with an image of reclusiveness and the untaught simplicity of a country girl. Her wish to protect encouraged, as Lucasta Miller shows in *The Brontë Myth*, an unintended eclipse of her sister for the next thirty or so years until, at the end of the century, New Women took to a more forceful model.

Emily, Charlotte had declared, was too removed from life to know what she was doing. This was untrue. For one thing, Emily had a sure grasp of the law as she relays how Heathcliff acquired all the property of two families. Remarkably, she brings into play historical laws of property and wills operating during the period in which the novel is set, 1771 to 1803 – laws that changed during the 1830s.

A legal man, Charles Percy Sanger, brought this to light in his 1926 essay 'The Structure of "Wuthering Heights"', which also shows the symmetry of the two interconnected family trees. Sanger worked out the intricate network of dates underpinning events; his listing reveals how accurately the novelist deployed unmentioned dates as she wrote: there was a careful, chronological schema holding together a headlong drama of violence and passion, moving backwards and forwards over thirty years.

Sanger had been a Cambridge contemporary of Leonard Woolf, who heard this as a paper read to the Heretics, a society at the University. He and Virginia Woolf, already a huge admirer of Emily Brontë, published the essay at their Hogarth Press and it gave readers an unexpected angle on a growing recognition of her greatness in the twentieth century.

For all Charlotte's determination to play down her sister's 'singularities', there had been contradictory truths. Before Emily died, Charlotte had spoken of 'a certain harshness in her powerful and peculiar character' as what drew her to this sister. And immediately after she died, Charlotte had defended Emily hotly in private.

'Because Ellis's poems are short and abstract, the critics think them comparatively insignificant and dull,' she said to an editor at Smith Elder. 'They are mistaken.' Emily's sublimity and her harsh strength had been a law unto itself. 'Stronger than a man, simpler than a child, her nature stood alone.'

Then, under the cover of fiction, Charlotte offers a striking insight. It comes in her characterisation of the bold, free-spoken Shirley (in her feminist novel of 1849), modelled, she said, on Emily. Shirley had her manner of sitting on the rug reading, with her arm round her rough dog's neck. This was Emily's fierce dog Keeper with his 'strangled whistle', called Tartar in the book.

Shirley portends a far future. Her rhetoric is less polite than the speech of feminists like Harriet Martineau in the 1840s and 1850s, who hoped to disarm men with their rationality and virtue. Shirley's voice is openly confrontational, more like the voices of women's liberation in the 1970s. It's not the way women spoke in 1811–12, the time *Shirley* is set. In *Sense and Sensibility*, which Jane Austen published in 1811, Marianne is brought to a point where she can no longer contain herself in public. She must speak out to the caddish Willoughby, who has abandoned her to marry for money. It's clear in these early years of the nineteenth century that confrontation is more injurious to a girl's peace of mind than the custom of self-silencing. Marianne's near-scream at the heart of her drama and her collapse into illness shows it to be potentially fatal for a woman to question women's weak position. What Charlotte dares to do in 1849 – only nine years after the public rise of the Woman Question – is to empower Shirley, conferring on Emily's private boldness a fictional agency.

Inscribed in Shirley is a hidden nature graven in secret script: this is where a bereaved Charlotte speaks through her book to the woman Emily had the spirit to be. She's speaking, in a sense, to Emily's still-living ghost and to that element of Emily that went to make Catherine Earnshaw.

Here is Shirley's answer to questions about her exceptional freedom: 'In showing my treasure, I may withhold a gem or two – a curious unbought, graven stone.' Unbought. The script is innate, not acquired. In Emily's terms, what's unbought is the God within her breast who grants the power of 'undying life'.

This voice of the poems remakes faith, discarding the codes of religion with her assault on dogmatism, heaven and false humility. Organised religion has held the monopoly on souls; Emily reclaimed them. When Heathcliff cries 'I *cannot* live without my soul!' he means the undying love he had shared in youth with Catherine Earnshaw. *Wuthering Heights* explores a strange passion warped by social plots: Catherine's Fall into a tepid marriage with Edgar Linton; Heathcliff's Fall into plots of power, especially the revenge plot, which brutalise his nature. In betraying each other, the lovers lose themselves and wander in the wilderness – Heathcliff as scheming monster, Catherine as ghost.

In the end, Catherine and Heathcliff recover their heaven, which is not a resting place for the obedient; it is union in spirit. For Emily Brontë, this union can be sustained only through death. She took an extreme position: she saw the impossibility of spiritual wholeness in a violent world, which she utterly shunned. Like Maria Brontë, Emily longed for the release death could bring. For her, wholeness had an absolute existence beyond life; within this world, it remained a possibility immanent in the rocks of the immutable moor, the landscape closest to her heaven.

'Gigantic' is the word that came to two brilliant readers, Emily Dickinson and Virginia Woolf. 'Gigantic Emily Brontë', Dickinson said in 1881. A generation later, Virginia Woolf's voice soars — like an answering aria face to face with Emily Brontë:

> She looked out upon a world cleft into gigantic disorder and felt within her the power to unite it in a book. The gigantic ambition is to be felt throughout the novel — a struggle, half thwarted but of superb conviction, to say something through the mouths of her characters which is not merely 'I love' or 'I hate', but 'we, the whole human race' and 'you, the eternal powers . . .' The sentence remains unfinished.

Emily Brontë's last poem, in May 1848, written in the wake of the revolts in Europe, deplored bloodshed on the part of brutes who destroy civilian lives and homes with the ruthlessness only possible to those who become inured to the horrors they perpetrate. The opening line, 'Why ask to know what date, what clime?', is a rhetorical question. It declares violence, 'Power-worshippers from earliest time / Foot-kissers of triumphant crime', to emanate from the trained hardness of militarisation throughout the world and through all the ages.

Twenty-five years ago a biographer tried to nail Emily Brontë as anorexic; now it's Asperger's syndrome. It was ever thus. The personal will remain largely unknown. What we can know is her understanding of a woman's life, and it's this: there is no institutional habitation for a woman so bared as Catherine Earnshaw, as bared as nature itself in its bedrock stretch; neither the Heights, under the defective authority of her boorish brother, nor Thrushcross Grange, under her weak husband, can be her home. She is an orphan of the moors, a ghost shut out by Lockwood, who finds her fierceness terrifying.

Lockwood can be, if not unlocked, at least informed by Nelly Dean. Through her matter-of-fact voice, Catherine fills out as an ambiguous character shaped by what Virginia Woolf would come to call poetry of situation. It's a form of poetry peculiar to the novel because it depends on character,[*] nowhere more telling than where Catherine, deadened by her marriage, tears her pillow with her teeth and pulls out its feathers, then leans from the window of her marital bedroom at Thrushcross Grange, longing to fly away to her child-self. What's at issue is the artifice of female adulthood, imposed, imitative, impure. She looks towards her childhood home, Wuthering Heights, where she had been hardy and free.

Heathcliff speaks to that bedrock nature. He calls her out, not as a mate of the body, nor to take a place in a defective marital construct, but a brother-man to walk the moors with her in perpetuity, in somewhat the way that Frankenstein's Creature will always roam the ice beyond human habitation. Their untrammelled wildness is not part of our daily existence, but they lurk at the periphery, waiting to make their incursions into our domestic enclosures: thwarted desires and rage and bared utterance, now and then knocking at the windows of our souls.

---

[*] Virginia Woolf sees poetry of situation when character conveys to us a 'vision of presence outside the human beings', as does Captain Ahab in *Moby-Dick*.

# 3

## 'OUTLAW'

### George Eliot

The 'one marvel' that struck Henry James on arriving in England was George Eliot.

Once a self-proclaimed 'outlaw', by 1869 she reigned as pre-eminent novelist. Taking his turn at her side amongst a throng of visitors, James heard the voice of a 'counselling angel'. Her low-toned confidence and the tender expression on her long, pale face was superior, he observed, to the run of women, too many of whom took on a fashion for female helplessness 'like a species of feverish, highly-developed invalids'.

At her house, The Priory, opposite Lord's cricket ground in the solid northern suburb of St John's Wood, George Eliot was at home each Sunday to the leading lights of London, who came to pay homage. These included the evolutionist Thomas Huxley; the pioneering social psychologist Herbert Spencer; Gladstone, the Liberal leader; and the man of letters Leslie Stephen, who later would tell his daughter Virginia (eventually Virginia Woolf) how, when it came to his turn with George Eliot, this one-time Cambridge don had found himself on his intellectual toes.

Virginia Woolf heard tell of the novelist from her father, from Aunt Anny (Lady Ritchie, the daughter of Thackeray), and from other Victorians like Edmund Gosse who were part of the capital's intellectual elite. All pictured a grave celebrity, now in her fifties, dressed in black

satin, with a green-shaded lamp on the table beside her, along with
German books and ivory paper-cutters. These elders had seen a woman
'who has been through her struggle and issued from it with a profound
desire to be of use to others, but with no wish for intimacy'. At that pin-
nacle, her struggle dropped away.

How did it come about, this veneration of a woman once shunned for
ignoring the legality of marriage? Wives had shunned her the more, in the
way Mary Shelley had suffered nearly all her life. How then had George
Eliot made her way back into society?

Her glory as wise angel would be sealed in a monumental biography
published by George Eliot's financial adviser and, briefly, spouse, John
Cross, in 1885, four years after her death. Gladstone called it 'a Reticence in
three volumes', while William Hale White[*] protested that the angel of the
biography was unrecognisable, fading out the 'insurgent' journalist he'd
known as Marian Evans. Just as the wild reputation of Mary Shelley was
tamed after her death by her son and daughter-in-law, and Emily Brontë's
by her sister Charlotte, so was that of George Eliot – but, like those earlier
writers, that tamed story did not last.

Back in the early 1850s, as a fellow lodger in the Strand, she had told
William Hale White that it was worth learning French in order to read one
book, Rousseau's *Confessions*.[†] This, to White, fitted her 'entire' unconven-
tionality in her thirties. In a back room, with hair loose over her shoulders
and proofs in one hand, she had sat with legs over the arm of her chair.
To swing up her legs in that way, she could hardly have worn the stiffened
petticoat of the crinoline – a dress that required toes-together decorum.

Among her circle at that time was a new breed of emancipated young
women intent on the vote, learning and an end to laws blocking the full
development of human nature. The word 'feminist' now entered the
language. Bessie Parkes, aged twenty-two, was to become a prominent
feminist and to found an 'outsiders' school' for both sexes and for the

---

[*] Later known as the novelist writing under the name Mark Rutherford.
[†] She said the same to Emerson when they met in 1848 and he asked what book had made
the deepest impression.

children of Jews, Catholics and free-thinkers. At one soirée in the Strand, Bessie eyed Marian Evans. She detected a woman with the brain to overtake others of their sex.

'I think she will alter', Bessie remarked to Barbara Leigh Smith, aged twenty-four (who would publish a book on *The Laws in England concerning Women*, propose votes for women and co-found Girton College, Cambridge). It was 1852; evolution was in the air. As Bessie saw it, Miss Evans, in her early thirties, was on the cusp of a development that might reveal a creature of a higher order.

'Large angels take a long time unfolding their wings; but when they do, soar out of sight. Miss Evans either has no wings or, which I think is the case, they are coming, budding.'

This is a story of change. For Marian Evans to turn into George Eliot, she had to overcome obstacles of birth, setting and education. She did not find her novelist's voice until her late thirties; she was thirty-seven when she wrote her first tale. Unlike Mary Shelley and the Brontës, she did not have the advantage of a bookish home. Her language was distorted by the rhetoric of her evangelical schooling, and for many years this blocked her voice. Her early letters are deadly.

Apart though George Eliot was, her transformation happened within a wider development of womanhood at a particular time. Though a backlash against woman's rights had seemed to blot out Mary Wollstonecraft, Mary Shelley regenerated her mother's 'new genus' through her own self-supporting independence. Mary Ann Evans[*] was born in November 1819, the month Mary Shelley gave birth to the son who survived. Where Mary Shelley had the fame of her mother to fill her sails, as well as a radical, thinking father, nothing out of the ordinary

---

[*] 'Mary Anne' on her birth certificate, but she signed her name Mary Ann. Later she called herself Marian.

was expected of an 'unpromising woman-child' born in rural obscurity. Nothing, that is, but to do a woman's duty, to marry and reproduce – if some man could be induced to take on a girl who was plain and disturbingly learned. To change, she had to detach herself from her girlhood prospect as 'a failure of Nature'.

Often thought an oddity amongst her sex, she mulled over what new thing a woman might be. This self-shaping was taking place fifteen years before John Stuart Mill challenged norms of gender with his declaration in 1869: 'What is now called the nature of women is an eminently artificial thing – the result of forced repression in some directions, unnatural stimulation in others.'

Mary Ann was a second daughter of a second marriage. Her Evans grandfather in Staffordshire was a carpenter, and so at first was her father's brother Samuel. Before she was born, her father Robert Evans had moved to Warwickshire, as agent to Francis Paget Newdigate, the owner of Arbury Hall. The Evans family lived at South Farm on the Arbury estate and then, when Mary Ann was four months old, moved to the substantial Griff House, near Nuneaton. There was an older sister Christiana (Chrissey) and a brother, Isaac. Robert Evans was able in his practical way and proud of his forward 'little wench'.

But from the age of five or six Mary Ann was at boarding schools that narrowed what a girl could utter. One was at Nuneaton, two miles from her home. Two miles only. Not too far to travel each day. Did her mother not want to have this girl at home? Mary Ann says little of her mother, who had been Christiana Pearson, the daughter of a mill owner, and whose Pearson sister was to be the source for narrow-minded Aunt Glegg in *The Mill on the Floss*. Mary Ann's sense of herself as 'unpromising' reflects the conventional view of a brainy girl.

In the absence of a mother, she had a strong attachment – it would outlast her schooldays – to the chief teacher at Nuneaton, an evangelical called Maria Lewis, who spouted pious platitudes. Mary Ann gave herself to cant with all the fervour of her nature. The child's ear was not yet tuned to language that dies on utterance; it came to her as education, and her eagerness to learn was great. And so it happened that a verbal prison closed around this girl for years to come – a far cry from the dash of the Brontës or the polish of Mary Godwin, educated in a home that was a publishing house.

Mary Ann learnt to utter high-toned sentiments enunciated with elaborate correctness. As the years passed she cultivated this manner with an ever-grander vocabulary. Such an education would have warped a lesser girl, as George Eliot would demonstrate in *Middlemarch*, in the figure of Rosamond Vincy, a mannered showpiece of a girls' school. Doctrines dinning in her ears throughout her schooldays urged girls to subdue ambition as egotism, to cultivate proper modesty and to channel other gifts into obedience to God's voice. But none of this could blunt the girl's thirst for knowledge with a scope few women besides Mary Shelley had achieved.

When Virginia Woolf looked back at gifted women, she placed them as 'the daughters of educated men'; Jane Austen, the Brontës and Virginia Woolf herself had that advantage, and Mary Shelley too of course, and across the Atlantic, Margaret Fuller and Emily Dickinson. From earliest childhood their ears were tuned to the language of books with its ease and verve. Jane Austen was always on course to write that crisp sentence: 'Mr Collins was not a sensible man.'

Mary Ann Evans lacked this ease throughout her schooling. And it was not only lack; there was damage. Although her doctrinal schooling might appear harmless, the unformed mind is shut down. It's the reverse of the educational innovations of Wollstonecraft and Claire Clairmont. Mary Ann did not feel what she mouthed, and the poor girl blamed herself for not measuring up to the pious emotion that Miss Lewis expressed so readily.

Schools trained her further to clog a self-consciously stilted language with irreproachable quotations, mostly from the Bible. Ambition does lurk behind this display but it's awry. She could have become a female Casaubon, the pedant wound in laborious sentences, whom the mature George Eliot will find pitiful. Once, when she was asked who was her model for Casaubon, she pointed to herself.

During adolescence and after she went in for an austere Calvinism, exercising its dramas of giving up – in one instance, she rationalised giving up domestic novels. Unconvincing as this is – the saintly performance of a young girl trying out a role – she did have a point about some of these shallow books, which she would shove away later in her essay 'Silly Novels by Lady Novelists'.

Mary Ann was called home from school in 1835 when her mother fell ill. In February 1836 her mother died. Soon after, when Mary Ann was about seventeen, she went with her father on a visit to his brother Samuel in Derbyshire. In those days of poor rural roads, there were few unnecessary journeys for country folk, as in *Adam Bede* (where the fictional Loamshire and Stonyshire adjoin one another but feel far apart to their inhabitants). Mary Ann had not met these members of her family before, and there, in a humble cottage, she encountered an aunt in whom she glimpsed the possibility of being a different sort of woman.

Her uncle's wife Elizabeth Evans was said to be strange. She had been a Methodist preacher, vehement and, according to Mary Ann's father, failing in discretion. A woman should have yielded, he believed, to the Wesleyan Association, who had barred women from preaching in 1814. Elizabeth Evans had refused to stop. She had a calling. In a mirror she had seen a face with a crown of thorns.

Born in 1776, she'd started out a lace-mender in Nottingham. At the turn of the nineteenth century she had converted to Methodism, a movement for spiritual renewal that was not all that different from the Evangelical movement within the Established Church. Samuel Evans, himself a convert, first saw her as a pretty, black-haired young woman in a Quakerish dress, standing up to preach. The two married when Elizabeth was twenty-eight, and moved to Derby. When women were forbidden to preach, and Elizabeth was outlawed by her Derby congregation, she and Samuel moved to Wirksworth, also in Derbyshire, where they joined the Arminian Methodists, who gave Elizabeth 'full liberty of prophesying'. While Samuel ran a silk mill, Elizabeth continued preaching until 1835, when she and her husband were in their sixties. This was the year before her niece came to visit.

Mary Ann met a small woman with bright, dark eyes and grey hair, 'very gentle and quiet in her manners – very loving'. It was her aunt's 'spirit of love' that struck her; she saw her as 'a truly religious soul, in whom the love of God and love of man were fused together'. No cant there.

Elizabeth had been ill and Robert Evans invited her to recuperate at their home, to his daughter's keen delight. One sunny afternoon in the course of their 'sittings' and walks, Elizabeth related how, when she had been twenty-six, she'd visited an unhappy girl in prison. In 1802 this girl, Mary Voce, had been convicted of murdering her baby. Elizabeth Evans stayed with the girl all night in Nottingham Gaol and rode with her to execution. Many years later, her niece recalled 'the deep feeling I had under this recital'. The story was to be the germ of her first novel.

Elizabeth Evans did provoke one immediate change. Mary Ann felt 'corrupted' by an obligatory religious drama. She burst out to her aunt, 'I make the most humiliating and appalling confessions with little or no corresponding feeling.'

It was like trying to cleanse herself of false emotion by speaking with a directness to match her aunt's. 'I do not attach much value to the disclosure of religious feelings', she said. The forced gush, pumped out for so long, had left her inert.

'My soul seems for weeks together completely benumbed and when I am aroused from this torpid state, the intervals of activity are comparatively short. I am ever finding excuses for this in the deprivation of outward excitement and the small scope I have . . . '

She confessed further to an 'insatiable desire' for praise, and 'ambition' behind it – frustrated ambition.

'"Unstable as water, thou shalt not excel" seems to be my character instead of that progress from strength to strength'.

Yet even as she castigates herself her voice breaks free – casting off the tedious performance for the benefit of Miss Lewis. Vital to her development was her aunt's candour and the slow-growing seed of sympathy.

———

That year, her sister Chrissey married and Mary Ann, at seventeen, became her father's housekeeper. While she made butter and fed the hens, she taught herself Latin and persuaded her father to allow twice-weekly lessons in Italian and German.

At that date there was nowhere for an English girl to continue her education. In America, the first women's college, Mount Holyoke,[*] had just then come into existence. But in England the first Oxbridge college for women would not be founded until 1869, by which time George Eliot was fifty and well along her starry path as a novelist. Back in the 1830s, she'd had to devise a course of study for herself. All the while Mary Ann had the intelligence to see that learning is not an acquisition for show but a means to 'truth', and truth for her had to be tested by observation – an acumen she would introduce into the novel as 'realism'.

The other catalyst for change was a decision to move in 1841. Mary Ann told her aunt how restless she felt at Griff House. To Maria Lewis she had to present her restlessness as a failure of character: an inability to pray when her intelligence rebels against housekeeping. To stir currant jelly was enough to set this off.

Mr Evans saw her problem as a need to marry. He resolved to do something for his daughter, now going on twenty-two, with no one eligible in the vicinity. His plan was to pass on his home and post to his son, Isaac, and move to Coventry. There was a family consensus that it would be well to put this discontented young woman in the way of a wider society, where she might find a husband.

She was not pretty in the ordinary way. Later, in *The Mill on the Floss*,

[*] Founded in 1836, the college was at first called South Hadley Female Seminary.

her most autobiographical novel, she would follow the effect of perceived plainness and freakishness on a girl, Maggie Tulliver, who is
gifted with intelligence in an era before higher education was open to
women. Mary Ann caricatures her own looks: witch, hag, a failure of
femininity. Yet her portraits are not plain. They show a long sensitive
face with abundant brown locks folded inwards towards her cheeks.
Her lips are full, and unthreatening eyes look steadily at you. There's
no assertive charm, no performance, no attempt at an image: only the
charm of discernment.

Her father went to some expense to rent a house at Foleshill on the
edge of Coventry. They moved in March and for more than six months
Mary Ann felt the 'indifference' of the town. How lonely it was when
her father went away for a week. But then, by a stroke of fortune, their
neighbour, Mrs Pears, turned out to be another thinking woman, and
put Mary Ann in touch with a group of Coventry intellectuals. Mrs
Pears's brother, Charles Bray, was a ribbon manufacturer with a fine
house, Rosehill, overlooking Coventry, and his wife, Cara, was the
sister of Charles Christian Hennell, author of *An Inquiry Concerning the
Origins of Christianity*. This book took a historical view of the scriptures
and came to the conclusion that the Bible mingled a good deal of
myth with what was valid. By the time the Brays invited Mary Ann
to dine, in November, she already had a copy of the second edition
of Hennell's *Inquiry*. The effect was nothing short of conversion – a
counter-conversion against doctrine, and not Christian doctrine alone
but against the closed mind. Her counter-conversion was encouraged
by friendship with the Brays, who as Unitarians were less concerned
with the divine nature of Jesus as with his humanity. They worked for
progressive causes: humane treatment for the insane, wider suffrage
and education.

Mary Ann embraced the Brays as well as Mrs Bray's sister, Sara Hennell,
with all her ardour. They became her adoptive family and more: her
'guardian angels'. With them she felt free to express her nature – an open-
ness similar to what Elizabeth Evans invited. In both relationships there's
a release from the rhetoric and a shift towards honest directness, which

with the Brays and Sara Hennell is lightened by rueful humour. Her ease with them is a measure of the security she came to feel in the fond way they took her in as one of their own.

So Mary Ann was embedded in a new set of friends. A letter to Maria Lewis carries a warning amidst the shared sentimental language of flowers, Mary Ann as twining 'Clematis' and Maria as 'Veronica': her unsuspecting teacher-friend may be 'startled' by a soul-change that could cause a difference of 'opinion'. This warning takes the moral high ground: if the friendship should end it will be the teacher's fault for 'ex-communicating' her. The positioning is so deft, the moral ground so assured, that Maria Lewis is left no room for protest.

Mary Ann still invited this friend to stay during her Christmas holidays. But while she's there, on Sunday 2 January 1842, Mary Ann refused to go to church. This is a famous confrontation of daughter and father, but the presence of her old friend intensifies the drama. The tie with Maria unravelled. Mary Ann shed her, as a creature undergoing metamorphosis discards its former shape and habitat.

Robert Evans was shocked. After all, he'd moved to Coventry for her sake, and instead of entering into society in the way he'd hoped, she was shaming him. For there was talk; eyes followed Mary Ann; and advice about conceit was not wanting.

An explanatory letter to her father in February again takes the moral high ground: she would obey him in everything, she says, except in this matter of conscience; she would 'cheerfully' accept it if he cast her out, and would find lodgings in Leamington, where she would support herself as a teacher; and she was grateful for his love and would continue to love him as ever. Since his expense for her sake had proved unjustified, he was welcome to cut her from his will and to give her portion to her brother and sister.

Her tone of a patiently righteous victim did not heal the breach. Early in March the next year, her father spoke to their house agent about putting their Coventry home on the market; he intended to live on his own property in the country.

At this moment Isaac came to Mary Ann's rescue. He considered their father was treating her harshly, and invited his sister to return to their childhood home. She stayed at Griff for a month as an unhappy append-age to the household, and then in May returned to her father. Isaac's wife brought about a compromise: Mary Ann would accompany her father to church, silencing her resistance, while he, for his part, went to the agents to countermand his plan to give up on her. Elizabeth Evans paid a visit, but this time Mary Ann was not receptive. In retrospect, she regretted it: she had been in 'a crude state of free-thinking'.

Mary Ann expected to do something useful with her brains. Teaching held no appeal: she had considered it only during the clash with her father. The 'ambition' she'd owned in a shamefaced manner to her aunt is not explicit. If she thought of writing novels when she was young, she never mentions it. Her first efforts show an inclination for research and scholarship, feeling her way into a woman's anteroom to a life of the mind. It was like the space that gentlemen's clubs used to set aside for visiting ladies. Ladies were expected to be self-effacing; their voices should not obtrude. Only two years earlier, in 1840, when a contin-gent of American women delegates crossed the Atlantic to attend the World's Anti-Slavery Convention in London their credentials were refused. The first day of the convention was taken up with what came to be known as the Woman Question, with this day marking the start of a renewed woman's movement, forty years after the branding of its founder, Mary Wollstonecraft, as wild and wanton. But women appeared defeated that day in 1840. The delegates, including Lucretia Mott (now in the National Women's Hall of Fame in Washington DC) and Sarah Pugh, were permitted to attend only in women's traditional role as listeners.

So it was that a gifted young woman coming to adulthood in the early 1840s had to ask herself not only what can I do, but also what will a woman be allowed to do? While Mary Ann had been her father's housekeeper at

Griff, she had undertaken a chart of ecclesiastical history. A religious task was an acceptable occupation, and the dowager of the Newdigate estate gave this her blessing with a view to a publication that would contribute funds to the local church.

Another venture, starting in 1843, takes up what had been an unpublished venture of the Shelleys: to translate the Latin text of Spinoza, the Dutch precursor of the Enlightenment. An outsider of independent mind, Spinoza was congenial to Mary Ann. He had found himself cast out of his own close-knit Sephardi community in Holland for questioning the nature of divinity and the provenance of the five books of Moses (the opening books of the Hebrew Bible). He was excommunicated with formal curses for his unorthodox opinions: Jews were forbidden to speak to him or to read his writings.

Mary Ann's intellect was quickening through books that broke the paradigms of their day, Spinoza in the seventeenth century and Rousseau in the run-up to the French Revolution. These outsider-insurgents, along with her outspoken aunt, were her models. She was determined to defy her Christian community, her father, her one-time teacher and her own constructed voice.

Mary Ann had the security of an alternative family in the Brays. Through them she met an educated young feminist, Rufa Brabant, a translator and the daughter of a biblical scholar. When Rufa married Charles Hennell, Mary Ann was her bridesmaid, and there at the church in London Mary Ann met Rufa's father, Dr Robert Brabant.

He was embarked on a massive study of scriptural myths. Mary Ann felt honoured when he took to her at once and invited her to take Rufa's place. No more than a few days later, she was on her way south to his home in the Wiltshire town of Devizes. There she found herself in 'a little heaven', with 'Dr Brabant being its archangel', as she put it to the Brays. The great doctor, as she saw him, asked her to make herself at home in his library, and compliments lapped about her all day long.

Each day they read Greek and German together, and there were daily walks and talks. He decided to call her 'Deutera', which means 'second', she said, but sounded to her like 'daughter'. She was never tired of his company, and she asked her father for permission to extend her stay. In her enthusiasm, reinforced by a clear conscience as to the purity of her motives, she overlooked her effect on Dr Brabant's wife.

Mrs Brabant, who was blind, had received their guest kindly and laid on all manner of comfort, but she was not deaf to her sister Miss Hughes' suspicions of Miss Evans. Even though there was no affair, a husband's admiration for this younger woman and his liking for her company were hurtful. Mrs Brabant became jealous. So it was that Mary Ann found herself hustled out of heaven a fortnight early. Mrs Brabant let it be known that if Miss Evans ever came to their house again, she would go.

Dr Brabant, wanting a quiet life, let his guest take the blame – the Brays and Sara Hennell thought he behaved badly. Mary Ann had nothing good to say of him from then on; when their paths crossed, her voice was ironic. And he never completed that great book, a failure George Eliot would explore with scrupulous justice in *Middlemarch*. The ardently willing Dorothea, who longs to learn Latin, Hebrew and Greek, looks past the scholar's unappealing exterior to the intellectual treasures her imagination conjures up. It turns out that what the scholar, Mr Casaubon, wants from marriage is no more than an able but uncritical woman to prop his self-esteem and make herself useful as an unpaid secretary. The reader learns not to reject Mr Casaubon for the white moles on his face and the noise he makes drinking his soup, but for his blinkered egotism.

For Mary Ann, the Shelley idyll of learning was not to be. If she was shaken by expulsion from the Brabant household, she resolved not to show it. Her silence was rewarded when Rufa passed on to her the task of translating *The Life of Jesus* by the German Higher Critic (as questioners of the Bible were known) David Friedrich Strauss.

'I am sure,' Mary Ann remarked to Cara Bray, 'he must have some twinges of alarm to think he was dependent on the most contemptible specimen of the human being for his English reputation.'

A year later she had ceased to sit down to Strauss with any relish. Six pages a day, inching sentence by sentence across fifteen hundred pages, with a statue of the risen Jesus in front of her. Her face was pale and sickly as she pressed on, despite dreadful headaches. It took two and a half years of 'soul-stupefying' toil, blocking any other initiative. The frustration remained in her memory for the next twenty-five years, until she channelled it into fiction: Dorothea Casaubon's tormented obligation to subject her intelligence to working on her husband's 'Key to All Mythologies'.

During the years that Mary Ann toiled over Strauss, nothing fertile was possible. But she had the grit to keep going. She longed to cross the gender barrier and join with thinking men. A traditional route was translating — women were permitted an entrée to intellectual life in their handmaid capacity. Mary Wollstonecraft, for one, did masses of translating before she crossed into the male territory of political writing, and even then she brought out her *Vindication of the Rights of Man* and the more famous *Vindication of the Rights of Woman* anonymously. She had exceptional support from her publisher, Joseph Johnson, 'the father of the book trade' in the later eighteenth century. Even the boldest of women did need the help of a well-placed man, whether it be a publisher or, in Jane Austen's case, an enlightened father.

For the time being, Mary Ann Evans had the help of Sara Hennell, whose German was good enough to check the translation as it went along. Sara praised its accurate delicacy. The book was published (without the translator's name) in June 1846 and became one of the influential books on religious thinking in England. Chief backer and chair of the committee to raise funds for the translation was Joseph Parkes MP, father of Bessie.

The book's publisher was the entrepreneurial John Chapman, operating at the heart of literary London. He was sufficiently impressed with Mary Ann Evans to welcome her for a stay in his London house.

After her father died in 1849, Mary Ann was ready to make a move. There was a stint in Geneva, birthplace of her hero Rousseau; then, on her return to England in 1850, a disconcerting visit to her brother. This visit confirmed for her that she no longer belonged with her family — she doesn't specify her brother, but that's whom she means when she says that Griff was disappointing, the country 'dismal' and the people 'dismal'. Feeling unwanted, she came to a decision to leave the Midlands for good.

She told Sara, 'I am determined to sell everything I possess except a portmanteau and a carpet bag and the necessary contents and be a stranger and a foreigner on the earth for ever more.'

The plan was to try her hand as a reviewer in London, encouraged in this venture by the success of her immensely learned review of *The Progress of the Intellect* by R. W. Mackay and published by Chapman. The review is really an essay soaring and diving around the book's philosophic reach.

Lodgings in Chapman's house at 142 The Strand, in a prime position ten doors from Somerset House, with back rooms overlooking the Thames, cost two pounds and ten shillings a week for one of the better bedrooms with an additional three-and-six for fires and the same for boot cleaning and 'attendance'. Mary Ann had now the means with a modest income from the two thousand pounds she inherited from her father (a good deal less, even taking inflation into account, than the five hundred pounds a year that in 1929 Virginia Woolf considered a minimum for a woman writer already equipped with a room of her own).

The room was comfortable and Chapman made her more than welcome. He was a good-looking man (actually called 'Byron' in his youth) with an air of intellectual refinement. At twenty-two he'd married a stout, well-off woman called Susanna, who was fourteen years older, against the wishes of her family. Chapman was a charmer. He liked women's company – along with his eye to their attractions. After a trial stay of two weeks, Mary Ann resolved to return to London for an indefinite time.

She set out from Coventry in high spirits on 8 January 1851, this independent woman just turned thirty-one, who meant to enter the intellectual life of the capital. The journey by rail went smoothly until the train reached Weedon, when 'a coated animal' climbed into her compartment. As Mary Ann described it, 'I thought of all horrible stories of madmen in railways, but his white neck-cloth and thin, mincing voice soon convinced me that he was one of those exceedingly tame brutes, the clergy.'

Chapman met her at Euston, and at once took her to hear Michael Faraday lecture on the magnetism of oxygen at the Royal Society. It made her long to attend a course of lectures on geometry given by Professor Francis William Newman* at the Ladies' College in Bedford Square. When she mentioned this to Chapman, he promptly bought her a ticket. She would not allow him to pay, and though the cost was beyond her budget she didn't regret it. It was worth stinting on white gloves and even clean collars for the sake of up-to-the-moment scientific knowledge. As with Mary Shelley, science was part of an appetite for knowledge beyond the scope of their sex.

Mary Ann was drawn to the alert Chapman in somewhat the way that Charlotte Brontë had been drawn to Constantin Heger when she'd lived in the Pensionnat Heger in Brussels. As Charlotte Brontë puts this in one of her Brussels poems, unvoiced ambition – the laurel descending on a favourite's head – prompts an emotional attraction. It's heady for such a woman to be seen for what she feels herself to be.

Mary Ann's attention, fixed on Chapman, had little left for Susanna Chapman, her two children and their nominal governess, pretty, temperamental Elisabeth Tilley, who was Chapman's mistress. Too little, it turned out. Once more, as with Mrs Brabant, jealousy reared its head and there were ructions in the household. Chapman was often in Mary Ann's room, taking lessons in German and Latin, and they were spied holding hands. Their physical attraction made itself felt. Mrs Chapman and Miss Tilley, who together ran the lodging house, joined forces to turn Miss Evans out.

So, a second humiliating eviction: on 24 March 1851 Mr Chapman escorted a tearful Mary Ann to Euston to catch her train back to Coventry.

What did he feel for her? She ventured to air this before the train left.

He was not put out by the question. He held her in affection, he said, but his emotional commitments were to his wife and Miss Tilley, whom he loved in different ways. His diary suggests how taken he was with

---

* Brother of the famous convert to Roman Catholicism John Henry Newman, and one of the founders of the Ladies' College (later Bedford College).

deploying his considerable charm in the presence of a heaving breast. He was in his element in emotional scenes.

Did a *ménage-à-trois* disturb Mary Ann? We don't know, but my guess is that it did not — or no more than it took to adjust her tie to Chapman. George Eliot's later embrace of marital fidelity should not obliterate two facts that tell us how, in earlier days, she'd tolerated infringements of fidelity on the part of both sexes. Nowhere in her correspondence with the Brays does she mention the unmentionable: that Mr Bray fathered two illegitimate children during his marriage to Cara. There was 'Baby', who had stayed with the Brays for a few weeks in 1845 before being returned to her mother. Baby had granted Mary Ann 'a most gracious reception'. She had carried Baby about, inviting Baby's smiles and took her 'to pay our respects to the Cow'. And then there was Nelly (Elinor), born in about 1846 to Bray's mistress ('Mrs Charles Gray') and adopted by the Brays. They had no child of their own.

Mary Ann was again unconventional in 1848 when she took a dim view of Jane Eyre's refusal to live with Mr Rochester, tied to a mad wife.

'All sacrifice is good', Mary Ann said, but the law was absurd to tie a man to 'a putrefying carcass'.

Where Jane finds it in her to pity Mrs Rochester, Mary Ann's 'putrefying carcass' is over-the-top, a deliberate expression of defiance. This voice tells us how strong she could be in person, how sharp and adamant at times.

Soon after her retreat to Rosehill and the consolation of staying there, Chapman sent her a packet of letters from his wife, berating him for his intimacy with Miss Evans. Mrs Chapman was now suspicious of a continued correspondence with her husband about a catalogue of Chapman's publications, with summaries of each book, which he'd asked Mary Ann to put together. She instructed Chapman to tell — or, she hoped, *re*-tell — his wife that she was doing an unwanted task solely because Mr Chapman had requested it. Her point is that, this time, the husband should take his share of responsibility. She would have Mrs Chapman know that Miss Evans would go on doing what Mr Chapman asked of her, but 'with the utmost repugnance' and from the moral high ground of refusing payment. Though men found her low voice appealing, she could be adamant, as here in a lofty letter intended really for Mrs Chapman (interspersed with confidential notes to Chapman), and we can see why the womenfolk of men she favoured found her threatening. The letter is signed Marian Evans, her new version of her name.

It's typical that she then regretted taking an injured tone. 'Pray be candid,' she wrote to Chapman, 'that is the first, second and third thing I require, though I am a woman and seem pettish.' Such unprofessional behaviour would not do if she was to find a place in a man's world.

The challenge was to use her emotional energy in a controlled way, neither damping it down nor allowing it to consume the mind. It's similar to the challenge – how far can a respected female go – teased out by the young Emily Dickinson in her playful, highly gendered 'Master letters' to a bearded man, whom she casts as something of a Brontë 'master', combining the erotic tug of Rochester with the sadistic edge of Heathcliff. One model for 'Master' was the editor Sam Bowles, to whom Dickinson dared to say, 'You have the most triumphant face out of paradise.' With intent eyes and black beard, Bowles was immensely attractive to women, and all the more because he was well disposed to those with intelligence. An additional attraction for a writer was his work as publisher. In the early 1860s, Bowles published a few of Dickinson's best poems in his newspaper. A decade earlier, Chapman was proud to have published Marian's influential translation. All the same, she knew when to pull back from emotional licence, as Dickinson was to do, detaching herself and reading Bowles correctly, for in private he disliked the touchiness of a solitary woman writing in her bedroom.

Marian was sensitive enough to be touchy to a painful level; she had to cope with feelings close to the surface. That struggle pants through her letters, as swells of outrage or frustration or self-despair divert her into gloom. This internal struggle may be one reason why she delayed writing fiction for so long – with veiled glances at 'work' unattempted. What is work? She conveys to Bray without saying it that editing, for her, was a distraction. The delay was associated with recurring despair over her long, expressive, undoll-ish face. (Her host in Geneva had tried to heal her depression there by painting a prettified portrait, with criss-cross lacing over the bodice.) Inevitably, given her gifts, there was contempt for women's exaggerated passivity; their helplessness cultivated as an appeal to male protection.

Portrait of Mary Ann Evans (1849) by her host in Geneva, François Durade

In the face of all this, Marian's reason always held the reins. Thanks to her command of reason, the potential break between her and Chapman in the spring of 1851 was no more than a blip.

Mr Chapman kept her in mind for a new venture. In May 1851 he bought the *Westminster Review* and persuaded Marian to write a prospectus: the *Review* was to question religious dogma and promote national education, universal suffrage and judicial reform.

This was the period when revolts swept through Europe. Marian's response had put her heart and mind behind this. She admired the animation of the French who, she believed, really did want social reform. The English, by contrast, were 'slow crawlers' and their military would never sympathise with workers. Monarchs, including Victoria, were museum pieces. Yet, thankfully, the British Constitution would not obstruct liberty.

Chapman's renewed sense of Marian's distinction and his accord with her ideas led him to a step no man had ever taken: he offered her, a woman, the editorship of what was to be a leading London quarterly. Up front, Chapman was to be the editor, but he didn't have the intellectual edge needed to restore the *Westminster Review* to the prestige it had enjoyed under John Stuart Mill in the late 1830s. Marian Evans was to take this on anonymously, her gender unmentioned, in the official role of assistant editor.

Chapman's next move, in August, was to talk his womenfolk into taking Miss Evans back in a professional capacity. For her part, she accepted a relationship as helpmeet and never wavered in the support she gave to Chapman in good times and bad. His finances were shaky, and sometimes there would be nothing left to pay the top contributors of the day whom Marian commissioned: Harriet Martineau (who corresponded with Charlotte Brontë), John Forster (friend and eventually biographer of Dickens) and James Anthony Froude (friend and eventually biographer of Carlyle). Passionate though she was, Marian had her capacity for calm. Returning to the Strand on 29 September 1851, she told Sara: 'I am training myself up to say adieu to all delights. I care for nothing but doing my work and doing it well.'

Soon her table was 'groaning with books'. The first issue was due in January and she would edit nine more over the next two and a half years. By the third, the summer issue of 1852, which was to be the best yet, she was gratified to hear it said that the *Westminster Review* was now truly preeminent, outdoing even the prestigious *Edinburgh Review*.

In lieu of payment, Chapman offered her a life. His weekly Monday nights gathered together the progressive intellectuals of the capital, including John Stuart Mill, Karl Marx, the Italian liberator Giuseppe Mazzini, George Henry Lewes, who was co-editor of a weekly newspaper called *The Leader*, and Harriet Martineau. While Marian was at work, Carlyle dropped by to suggest Robert Browning as a contributor.

Within a month of her arrival, she met the philosopher Herbert Spencer, her contemporary, whose first book, *Social Statistics*, Chapman had just published. It predicted that humans would become so adapted to living in society that the state would fade away. Spencer's office was across the Strand. As subeditor of *The Economist*, he reviewed music, theatre and opera. This meant free tickets to performances, and one of the first of many invitations to Miss Evans was to see *The Merry Wives of Windsor*. George Henry Lewes, who was reviewing that night for *The Leader*, joined them in the box and his withering comments jollied them through a tedious performance. He made bold to say the play should be compressed into one act, and better still not produced at all.

George Henry Lewes: feminist friends would be astonished
to hear that he proved a 'considerate' lover

When Marian turned to hear him she saw 'a miniature Mirabeau'.[*] He was short, with untidy chin-length hair, light brown in colour, and a jet of sarcastic words spurted from his lips. His wide nostrils and red, full lips, half-covered by a straggling moustache, led Jane Carlyle to dub him 'Ape', and the image stuck. He was scarred by smallpox. His contemporaries call him ugly, yet his verve made this attractive. Marian later said that a *laideur divinée* [divine ugliness] appealed to her. Photographs show a rather worn face with no trace of hardness, though the stiffness of early photography did not allow for the mobility of his facial expressiveness – more French perhaps than English (for he'd lived in France in his youth). His unrelenting vivacity made him seem to Marian rather skimmingly light.

She was more impressed by the distinguished appearance and serious-ness of Mr Spencer, his brain heaving with enormous thoughts. A residue of her Brabantian leanings fixed her attention on the grand scheme, a thinker opening up the physiological basis of psychology in his second book, *Principles of Psychology* – this is what he talked about when Marian met him. He saw development not in terms of the individual but of the species. Specific strands of brain tissue, an association of ideas, he argued, could be passed from one generation to the next. Spencer applied a pre-Darwinian idea of evolution to psychology and sociology.

Soon after, Marian accompanied him to Kew Gardens on what she called a '*proof*-hunting' expedition. She comments humorously on his insistent theories. 'Of course, if the flowers didn't correspond to the theo-ries, we said, too bad, "*tant pis pour les fleurs*".'

The company of men seemed preferable at first. Soon, however, Marian began to meet women who were to make transforming contributions to society. There was the young Florence Nightingale, just returned from her study of nursing at Kaiserwerth (near Dusseldorf), who came to call. Marian liked her loftiness of mind, reflected in her form and manners. She had with her a staunch aunt, Juliet Smith (known affectionately as

---

[*] Honoré Gabriel Riqueti, comte de Mirabeau, an intellectual who had been a moderate leader in the French Revolution. As a thinker, he was a hero of Mary Wollstonecraft. After he died he was denounced for aristocratic connections.

Aunt Ju), who backed her nursing intentions and was to visit her at Scutari during the Crimean war. And Marian was 'agreeably impressed' with Florence Nightingale's first cousin, the Barbara Leigh Smith whom Marian had met already at Chapman's salon.

Yet despite these promising contacts, and despite achieving what she'd hoped to do, Marian was often low. These moods were linked with headaches and bursts of weeping she calls 'hysterics' – the sexist medical term reserved for women's mental sufferings. Parted now from the Brays, she feared loneliness as a single woman in her thirties. Her new friends, though also single, were for the most part younger, blither, more self-confident as the daughters of educated and wealthy men, securely placed in the upper middle class.

Marian distrusted her ability to make friends. In March 1852, she burst out in gratitude to a women's rights activist, Clementia Taylor, who'd suggested a visit and appeared to Marian one of those 'life-preservers – which relenting destiny sends me now and then to buoy me up'. 'For you must know', she went on confidingly, 'that I am not a little desponding now and then, and think that old friends will die off, while I shall be left without the power to make new ones. You know how sad one feels when a great procession has swept by one, and the last notes of the music have died away, leaving one alone with the fields and sky. I feel so about life sometimes. It is a help to read such a life as Margaret Fuller's.'

Margaret Fuller, an American, had been the first woman ever to enter public life as a literary journalist. She had been encouraged by Emerson, whom Marian had in fact met. They had breakfasted together at the Brays in 1848. Emerson had seen Marian as 'a young woman with a calm, serious soul' and Marian had looked up to him as 'the first *man* I have ever met'.

Margaret Fuller had worked for the *Dial*, the journal of the New England Transcendentalists, led by Emerson. After the *Dial* folded she had earned her living as a journalist in New York, then moved to Italy. There she'd lived with an Italian, Giovanni Ossoli, and borne a son. Tragically, in 1850 she, together with her child and Ossoli, were shipwrecked en route back to America – all were drowned off Long Island.

Reading Fuller's memoirs, Marian recognised herself in a woman who

in youth had lived for work alone, too brainy to be more than a friend
to men. One entry in Fuller's journal touched her to the quick: 'I shall
always reign through the intellect, but the life! the life! O my God! Shall
that never be sweet?'

A sweet prospect of her own was continuing to emerge in the figure of
Herbert Spencer. Like Marian, Spencer was a self-taught intellectual from
a Midland town. He favoured votes for women and deplored militarism
and imperialism – he would oppose the Anglo-Boer War at the end of the
century. He's barely remembered today, but in the 1850s he was on his way
to becoming an eminent Victorian whose weighty philosophical-science
sold a million copies.

This well-looking bachelor enjoyed Marian's gifts of mind combined
with womanly gentleness. She proved a discerning companion for a
reviewer's evenings at concert halls and theatres. He had only to step
across the Strand with tickets in hand – it might be Donizetti's opera
*I Martiri* at Covent Garden – and she was ready to go, two unattached
people free of domestic obligations.

But by April 1852 they were meeting so often that Spencer began
to worry. It occurred to him to clarify the situation in case of
misunderstanding.

Marian apparently reassured him that it had never been her habit to
imagine that a man was in love with her.

Had he insulted her by suggesting that she might be in love when he
was not?

To his relief, Marian took this 'smilingly'. The more truthful he was,
she said, the more she liked him – rather more than she was allowing.

With nothing now to deter them, they began to be together every day.
Marian reported to the Brays that he was 'a good, delightful creature' and
she always felt better for seeing him. As family might, the Brays invited
Spencer for a stay in Coventry; he and Marian agreed that he should
come when she was already there. They could not travel together, Marian
explained to the Brays, because of gossip circulating in London that she
and Spencer were engaged.

The hospitable Brays also invited George Henry Lewes to visit, but

Marian did not want him. She asked the Brays to find a time when she would *not* be there because, she said, much as she liked Lewes, he was too 'Londonish'. His fizzing *mots* would disrupt their conversation.

Marian didn't especially take to London society. She had always ridiculed herself as ugly, a freak creature who shrank from exposure in a ballroom where other women waltzed round and round in swaying crinolines. She could not afford to freshen her wardrobe, and refused Bessie Parkes's invitations to balls, saying she might look like 'a wilted cabbage'. It was all right to be a 'dowdy' at dinners where the focus was on conversation — there, she was in her element. In fact, she was striking rather than dowdy. Her dinner dress was black velvet and she was the sole woman guest amongst politicians and authors in the Savile Row house of Mr Parkes. 'She would talk and laugh softly, and look up into my father's face respectfully, while the light of the great hall-lamp shone on the waving masses of her hair and the black velvet fell in folds about her feet.'

Yet the more Spencer sought her out, and the more she liked him, the deeper she plunged into wells of self-despair. She felt she looked 'haggard as an old witch' or like one of those hags by the wayside in Italy; only worse, she said, for want of dark eyes and black hair to offset skin like parchment.

At some point between May and July 1852 it came to her that if Spencer took up with someone else she must die. It was a joke, yet not quite a joke when she told Sara that she might have to commit suicide once the revises for the summer issue were safely delivered. Continuous companionship now made the prospect of loneliness all the more acute, and two past evictions by wives had made her painfully aware that if Spencer married she would again be frozen out, bereft of that intimacy even if sadly it were innocent.

Attentive as Spencer was, he volunteered no sign of attraction. Did the problem lie with her looks or did the problem lie in Spencer? Maybe she was going about with a man whose temperament was cool verging on chill. During a heatwave early in July she teased him with gratitude for 'that tremendous glacier of yours' providing her with 'lumps of ice'.

Since they were so well suited as companions, she wondered if it might be possible to devise a permanent tie based on rational companionship. She mulled over this while on holiday at Broadstairs, on the Kent coast. And so it happened when Spencer came to visit her (twice) at Chandos Cottage that she ventured to put her hope on paper. She knew how startling a proposal from a woman would be. Unusually, there's no date, no signature. Shedding formalities and hot with purpose, she plunges into the cold without her customary address to 'Dear Friend'.

I know this letter will make you very angry with me, but wait a little, and don't say anything to me while you are angry. I promise not to sin any more in the same way.

My ill health is caused by the hopeless wretchedness which weighs upon me. I do not say this to pain you, but because it is the simple truth which you must know in order to understand why I am obliged to seek relief.

I want to know if you can assure me that you will not forsake me, that you will always be with me as much as you can and share your thoughts and feelings with me. If you become attached to someone else, then I must die, but until then I could gather courage to work and make life valuable, if only I had you near me. I do not ask you to sacrifice anything – I would be very good and cheerful and never annoy you. But I find it impossible to contemplate life under any other conditions. If I had your assurance I could trust that and live upon it. I have struggled – indeed I have – to renounce everything and be entirely unselfish, but find myself utterly unequal to it. Those who have known me best have always said that if I loved any one thoroughly my whole life must turn upon that feeling, and I find they said truly. You curse the destiny which has made the feeling concentrate itself upon you – but if you will only have patience with me you shall not curse it long. You will find that I can be satisfied with very little, if I am delivered from the dread of losing it.

I suppose no woman ever before wrote such a letter as this –
but I am not ashamed of it, for I am conscious that in the light
of reason and true refinement I am worthy of your respect and
tenderness, whatever gross men or vulgar-minded women might
think of me.

This is curiously like Jane Eyre's defiant proposal to Rochester, with
an eloquence that breaks through the self-silencing expected of a lady.
Both Jane and the real-life Marian are unlike other women in their
candour, unable to go on waiting for a man to speak. Refusing to falsify
their nature, both rebel against submissiveness to a gender code based on
female passivity.

Spencer thought of their tie as 'intimate', but he did not mean
physical intimacy. Marian did not fail to understand this in so cool a
character with a mind to his health, and she found a way around it.
It's often assumed that she asked Spencer to marry her, but she doesn't
mention marriage; instead she lays out a partnership of comfort and
continuity.

Spencer did respect this overture. He said nothing, not even in his
*Autobiography* published when George Eliot was famous; nothing until after
her death, when he confided to a friend what he'd felt: 'Just what I had
feared might take place, did take place. Her feelings became involved and
mine did not. The lack of physical attraction was fatal. Strongly as my
judgment prompted, my instincts would not respond.'

He gave her a similar response at the time. She was devastated but her
next letter to Spencer is even more extraordinary. She had the maturity
to turn humiliation into sympathy for the man who hurt her. She's
astonishingly calm and resolute. Her formality in addressing Spencer by
his surname is not detached; it's designed to retrieve the relationship on
a different footing.

Broadstairs Thursday Evening [29? July].
    Dear Mr Spencer
    It would be ungenerous in me to allow you to suffer even a

slight uneasiness on my account which I am able to remove. I ought at once to tell you, since I can do so with truth, that I am not unhappy. The fact is, all sorrows sink into insignificance before the one great sorrow – my own miserable imperfections, and any outward hap is welcome if it will only serve to rouse my energies and make me less unworthy of my better self. I have good hope that it will be so now, and I wish you to share this hope if it will give you any satisfaction.

If, as you intimated in your last letter, you feel that my friendship is of value to you for its own sake – mind on no other ground – it is yours. Let us, if you will, forget the past, except in so far as it may have brought us to trust in and feel for each other, and let us help to make life beautiful to each other as far as fate and the world will permit us. Whenever you like to come to me again, to see the golden corn before it is reaped, I can promise you such companionship as there is in me, untroubled by painful emotions . . .

Ever yours faithfully

Marian Evans.

Only five months after Bessie Parkes discerned Marian's potential 'wings', we glimpse, for the first time, the quality of feeling that was to make her novels fly: no longer that 'crude state of free thinking', instead a renewal of empathy, an ideal for human conduct, yet beyond the reach of most.

It's tempting to pity Marian's attachments – Dr Brabant, Chapman and now Spencer – and to put them down to feminine clinginess. Certainly, she owned to a need for someone to lean on, but that in itself is not peculiar. I think her need had to do with her originality, rather than weakness. Like other original women, Mary Shelley, Claire Clairmont and Charlotte Brontë, she sought an established mentor (equivalent to patrons of old) who would affirm the possibilities surging in her. Was she naïve to the effect of her sexuality? Was she naïve to her own needs, even? Maybe not. But Spencer was not for her.

Work once more brought calm, as she conferred – colleague to colleague – with Chapman about missed opportunities for the *Review*: rival quarterlies had got in first with the Pre-Raphaelite movement in art and with a subject that continued to attract Marian: the plucky life of Margaret Fuller.

This was how she saw she too had to be, 'plucky' as a substitute for happiness. No one, she resolved, was to know what she suffered. That she did suffer is plain from stray remarks: an apology to Cara Bray for being 'irritable and out of sorts' when Cara came to stay in August, and a confession to Sara that she was 'in a croaking mood' early in September – she had to 'wait and wait' for it to pass.

It occurred to her how cut off she was from her family, and she ventured to write to her much older half-sister, Mrs Henry Houghton, with an appeal to be in touch. 'I live in a world ... so remote from the one in which we used to sympathise with each other, that I find positive communication with you difficult. But I am not unfaithful to old loves – they were sincere, and they are lasting.'

Throughout the late summer and into the autumn of 1852, she was making deliberate efforts to restore her 'better self'. One of her first efforts was to defend George Henry Lewes against an attack by Harriet Martineau (as rival commentator on the sociologist Auguste Comte). Lewes pops up no less than four times in a letter Marian wrote on her return to London at the start of September.

She had been repeatedly dismissive of Lewes. In 1852 she'd accompanied Spencer to a set of tableaux devised by Lewes, which she found far too long. She had taken the first two volumes of Lewes's new novel *Rose, Blanche and Violet* to Broadstairs but left the third volume behind: 'I don't care to have it', she'd remarked to Spencer. Though Lewes contributed to every number she edited, starting with a piece she commissioned on lady novelists, she considered his articles 'defective'. The lightness of his manner made him appear superficial.

Spencer's articles, on the other hand, were rather too heavy. His subject was evolution, and he promised to lighten his next, for the October issue, by introducing more quotes to break up his page. Marian awaited it with the resignation of a child opening her mouth for a 'stone' sweet. That's all that crosses her lips in the aftermath of Spencer's rejection. No one was to know. All she reveals to Sara is that, back in her Strand room, she feels like a mad person with four walls closing in on her; her hands are wet with perspiration. But she doesn't die; she takes herself away, to Edinburgh and then to Ambleside in the Lake District, to stay with Harriet Martineau at her home, The Knoll, where Charlotte Brontë had stayed two years before. Martineau gives Marian a smiling welcome – a model of a contented single woman. And then Marian moves on to Rosehill. There, with the Brays, she is sure to be loved, and this restores her: she feels 'brave' and ready again for work.

On her return to London, in October, Lewes handed her a critic's bouquet. In his own journal, *The Leader*, he included two and a half columns in praise of the *Westminster Review* under new hands. It was once again what it had been under John Stuart Mill, he said. 'It is now a Review that people talk about, ask for at the clubs and read with respect. The variety and general excellence of its articles are not surpassed by any Review.'

Lewes had founded *The Leader* in 1850, together with his best friend Thornton Hunt, the son of Shelley's friend Leigh Hunt. As a child Thornton had stayed with the Shelleys at Albion House, and remembered Mary as untidy, distracted and cross, as well she may have been while trying to complete and sell *Frankenstein* and having, at the same time, to contend with a houseful of guests, including the Hunts' numerous unruly offspring.

Lewes was married to the beautiful and well-born Agnes Jervis. In 1850 the youngest of their four sons died in infancy, and a month later Mrs Lewes bore a boy, Edmund, by Thornton Hunt. Lewes gave the new-born his name. The decision upheld a code of sexual freedom, which Lewes shared with Agnes.

When, two years later, Agnes gave birth to another child by Hunt, Lewes came to accept that his was a marriage in name only. All the same he was a father, and still the supporter of his wife and her mixed brood, for the law did not permit divorce once a husband condoned adultery. Lewes did not talk about his situation – it was not generally known.

He had advantages neither Marian nor Spencer had enjoyed: a classical education at Dr Burney's school in Greenwich; a period at medical school, which woke his taste for science; and a polymath alacrity that led him into a variety of literary fields: playwriting, fiction, criticism. In a keen review of *Jane Eyre*, he'd recognised elements of autobiography fuelling the novel from well below the surface, and Charlotte Brontë had been glad to correspond with him – until they fell out over his preference for Jane Austen, and his criticism of her next and more overtly feminist novel *Shirley* as the flawed work of a woman. Later, when Mrs Gaskell documented this clash in her *Life of Charlotte Brontë*, Lewes was tactless enough to tell Mrs Gaskell that, when it came to the highest achievements, women could not match men. It was part of the armoury against women who encroached on male territory, and such a man will make exceptions for a few individuals. In an unsigned review of *Villette* in the *Leader*, he did continue to recognise the power of Charlotte's writing.

In March 1853, after Lewes had published his admiring review, they met at a gathering. Charlotte asked Mrs Gaskell *not* to point him out; she wished to identify him herself, and did so as soon as he came into the room. On seeing his face, her anger dissolved almost in tears because he looked 'wonderfully' like her dead sister Emily, 'her eyes, her very nose, the somewhat prominent mouth, the forehead, even at moments, the expression'. He sat with her most of the evening, taking in her conversation, but then put her down to Marian as 'a little, plain, provincial, sickly-looking old maid', which is to say he did not elicit, as others did, the glow of her eyes and the full charm of her tartness.

Marian waved 'plain' and 'provincial' away, for she was overcome by *Villette*, 'a still more wonderful book than *Jane Eyre*. There is something almost preternatural in its power.' Here was Lucy Snowe, who goes beyond what a plain, provincial woman is deemed to be. When she's asked, 'Who are you?' she answers truly, 'I am a rising character.'

Here is an alternative model to the feminist imitation of the dominant order. Charlotte Brontë imagines a rare woman who can rise on her own terms, developing slowly from within so as to release a different kind of agency and passion, and a moral being distinct from convention. What are women to be? Even the novelist is not prepared to say. 'Pause. Pause', the novel ends, leaving the question open for a time to come. It's a question George Eliot would take up.

Marian approached Lewes to review *Villette*, and was disappointed by his 'unsatisfactory' bias towards Mrs Gaskell's *Ruth*. In Marian's view, Mrs Gaskell could not do 'the half tints' of real life.

Marian was herself a creature of half tints. That astute observer Bessie Parkes was touched by the way Marian would sit close, look straight into her eyes and detect a hint of arrogance. At the same time love for a friend, Marian said, blinded her to any fault.

She had indeed been selfless in her unpaid support for Chapman and in the consideration she'd offered Spencer when she'd forced herself to back away. 'Egotism' – understandable if we call it ambition – had been the inward enemy she had tried to subdue all through her youth, and then it happened that ambition won out during a family crisis. In December 1852 her sister Chrissey's husband, Charles Clark, a doctor in his early forties, had suddenly died, leaving her with six children. Marian went back to the Midlands to help, and there she decided that Chrissey wasn't so badly off with the rent-free use of a house their brother owned. Marian's quick return to London upset Isaac. This is how she presents their quarrel:

> I had agreed with Chrissey that, all things considered, it was wiser for me to return to town – that I could do her no substantial good by staying another week, while I should be losing time as to other matters. Isaac, however, was very indignant to find that I had arranged to leave without consulting him and thereupon flew into a violent passion with me, winding up by saying that he desired I would 'never apply to him for anything whatever' – which, seeing that I have never done so, was almost as superfluous as if I had said that I would never receive a kindness from him.

Marian turns her brother into a Victorian caricature of paternalistic authority, an image that has stuck ever since (reinforced by their later differences), but the fact remains that he was left with the day-to-day impact of Chrissey's blow.

One other fact left Marian guilty. It was the age-old custom that an unmarried sister — having no life of her own — would lend a hand. This obligation was in the air in April 1853, when Chrissey told Marian she was 'rent' by a suggestion that her children be removed from her to an infant orphan asylum. Marian toyed with an idea that 'we' should send Chrissey's eldest son, who couldn't have been more than fourteen, to Australia. Obviously, Marian meant to fund this, or to help do so. Or should she go with Chrissey and all her family, to settle them, and then come back?

The facts were these: Chrissey had about a hundred pounds a year (from the sale of her husband's medical practice) and six dependants; Marian had two hundred pounds a year and no dependants. Should Marian join Chrissey and pool resources, in which case there would be enough for everyone? But this would mean an end to all that Marian had achieved so far. The impossibility of this hit her, releasing an outburst directed against the provincial life she'd managed to leave. This outburst, in confidence to Cara, uttered words she normally silenced: 'hideous' provincials, 'ignorant bigots'. Later, George Eliot was to dramatise this through the slowly accumulating scenes of Middlemarch, a fictional town in the Midlands with its small-minded stagnation, its obstruction of Dorothea, the idealistic wife of a landowner, and its resistance to Dr Lydgate, the idealistic medical man, who both try, in their different ways, to bring in reform.

> ... To live with her [Chrissey] in that hideous neighbourhood amongst ignorant bigots is impossible to me. It would be moral asphyxia ... Then I dare not incur the material responsibility of taking her away from Isaac's house and its attendant pecuniary advantages.

And then, characteristically, she calms down and sees that her brother is better than he appears when angry. She can tick herself off:

Yet how odious it seems that I, who preach self-devotion, should make myself comfortable here while there is a whole family to whom, by renunciation of my egotism, I could give almost every-thing they want. And the work I can do in other directions is so trivial!

Having examined this contradiction, there comes, swift on its heels, a confidence to Cara about what in particular is drawing her back to London. It's that she's taking 'doses of agreeable follies', mainly with Mr Lewes. The word 'unsatisfactory' about his review of *Villette*, on 18 March 1853, was the last adverse comment she would ever make about him. From 28 March her tone changes markedly. There was a pleasant evening, with 'Lewes, as always, genial and amusing. He has quite won my liking, in spite of myself.'

At a time when Spencer had withdrawn into mildly steady friendship and when she could not please her family without destroying herself, here was an enthusiast who favoured her — and not the superior, learned sort she usually admired. After falling successively for men who could not love her, here was someone ready to do so. These days, when Spencer came to call he sometimes brought his 'excellent friend' Mr Lewes along, and then, once, when Spencer got up to go, Lewes said he'd stay.

'Mr Lewes is especially kind and attentive and has quite won my regard after having a good deal of my vituperation', she comments to Sara. He was 'much better than he seems — a man of heart and conscience wearing a mask of flippancy.'

Heart and conscience. Clearly, by now she knew. My guess is that this was the time — between the French theatre that April and a performance of Rossini's *William Tell* — that Lewes revealed his situation: locked by law to Agnes and the children born to her and her lover. There was now a third child by Hunt on the way, and Hunt's wife was also giving birth almost simultaneously. Marian was singled out for this confidence. From now on her 'vituperations' against Lewes melted into gratitude for the kindness of this scarred man.

As a playwright and reviewer Lewes could take her behind the scenes at the theatre, and he took her behind the scenes in his personal life too. In a sense, behind the scenes is exactly where George Eliot would take the novel, away from the grotesque melodrama of Dickens and into the drama of interior life that in many ways was opened up by *Villette*. There, amidst the mundane doings of an English schoolmistress in a foreign city, is a woman's passion, acute but concealed. Passion of this sort was on her mind when Marian went with Lewes to see the French actress Rachel* in *Adrienne Lecouvreur*. Rachel is called Vashti† in *Villette*, and Lucy Snowe is both gripped and appalled to see desire as she understands it exposed on the stage. It opens up that question of a woman's desire: how far can a modest woman express the quality of her feeling?

It's not desire itself that's in question, for *Villette* makes it plain that desire exists in a woman's nature; it's a question of what a partner will encourage. In the novel the princely gentleman, seated beside Lucy Snowe at the theatre, would be put off by any sign of unladylike alacrity.

All that's certain is that Lewes sat beside Marian on a Saturday night in June 1853 when she expected to see – and disappointingly did *not* – the torrential feeling that Charlotte Brontë had witnessed in Rachel. Was un-acted desire in the air?

From the start of 1853, Marian wanted to leave the setup at the Strand. When she declared her work to be 'trivial', what did she mean? She was acting both as commissioning editor and copy-editor. She also wanted more privacy and less dependency on Chapman. He begged Marian to stay until the April issue of the *Review* came out. Her commitment to Chapman was hard to break; the *Review* would suffer if she left.

Until then, a busy editor had to protect her time, and in the course

---

* Rachel Félix, known as Mademoiselle Rachel.
† The king's defiant wife in the Bible's book of Esther.

of 1853 she was too busy for social duties. Marian could joke about social calls. 'I sometimes wonder if you expect me to return calls and repay civilities like a Christian', she teased Bessie, 'or whether it is sufficiently understood between us that I am a heathen and an outlaw.'

In the end it took until November 1853 for Marian to move from the Strand to independent lodgings at 21 Cambridge Street, Hyde Park. There, at last, she was free of Chapman's financial and domestic tensions and free too of unpaid toil, though it's conceivable that Chapman had let her stay rent-free in return for her work. She now had to pay nine pounds a month for her room. Chapman paid her fifty pounds for a translation of Ludwig Feuerbach's *The Essence of Christianity*: two shillings a page – which she thought pathetic, but she needed the income. She toiled over this, complaining of headaches, for the next eight months. All the while, though, she found herself 'exceedingly comfortable' in a room of her own and glad to discover that she no longer had to find a social life through Chapman. She had frequent guests, including Chapman himself, the steady Herbert Spencer, Harriet Martineau and of course Lewes.

Her regard for Lewes rose that November when he visited Cambridge and found that students had taken up his book *A Biographical History of Philosophy* (newly issued in a second edition). Over the next few months he was overworking to pay Agnes's bills – Hunt made no financial contribution to the care of his three children – and was prey to headaches and ringing in the ears. Carlyle spotted the difference between the two groups of offspring, and he didn't keep this to himself: Hunt's children were dark; the Lewes boys fair. There appears to have been no chance that Agnes's father, Swynfen Jervis (a high-society MP with an estate on the border of Wales), would help. The burden fell entirely on Lewes, who had no money apart from his earnings as a writer. Conceivably, the pressure – with no end in sight – intensified his symptoms to the point of collapse. This would explain his doctor's order to take two months off, starting in mid-April 1854. While he was away, staying with a friend in the country, Marian wrote his columns and reviews for the *Leader*.

Idleness didn't suit Lewes – he was no better for it. What did appeal to him was the prospect of writing a biography of Goethe (going back to an essay he'd produced on Goethe and science for the *Review*). The biography required research in Weimar, and Marian thought to travel with him and to translate the German passages he wished to quote. In July 1854, at the time her translation of Feuerbach came out (the only one of her books to carry her given name, Marian Evans, on the title page), she and Lewes made a decision that was to shape the rest of their lives: they would take off for Weimar together.

'I am preparing to go to "Labassecour"'* was all she told Sara. As she prepares for departure she slips into the guise of solitary Lucy Snowe sailing abroad. Only Bray, who lent her a hundred pounds, and Chapman are aware that she will not travel on her own.

As the late summer darkness fell on 20 July 1854 she closed the door for good on her lodging at 21 Cambridge Street. She carried a travelling bag and with her other hand she signalled to a hansom cab. The coachman set her down at St Katherine's Wharf, and she climbed aboard the *Ravensbourne*, a new fast steamer bound for Antwerp. By then it was after eleven o'clock. She stood alone – no other passenger in sight.

Twenty minutes passed. Fear mounted. Could something have prevented Lewes from joining her?

Then she saw his face looming through the dark, as she put it in her journal, 'looking for me over the porter's shoulder'. Soon they were gliding down the Thames. They spent all night on deck, pacing arm in arm until they saw dawn break between two and three in the morning as the steamer passed up the Scheldt. She marked the 'first faint blush of the dawn reflected in the glassy river' and then the sun rose 'and lighted up the sleepy shores of Belgium'.

As with Mary Godwin landing at Calais that July morning forty years before, this was the dawn of a new existence. To have crossed the Channel was a crossing from a single to a paired life.

* Charlotte Bronte's Brussels in *Villette*.

———

Each day of their slow movement towards Weimar was like a wedding tour with a companion to share the sights and pleasure in returning 'home'. Home from their first day in Antwerp was to be together in their room, to open a window and gaze out on the 'evening red melting away over the Scheldt and its shipping', and in Brussels on the fifth and sixth day, Tuesday and Wednesday, 'melting' again in the noon heat: 'lying melting in our beds through the middle of the day'. On the seventh day Marian gazed at the amphitheatre of wooded hills around the river valley at Liège 'in a state of rapture'.

Chapman did not expect Lewes to be faithful. With his 'Londonish' air of cynical vivacity, Lewes was not regarded as a safe prospect for a woman. Marian's feminist friends thought him a 'sensual' man — not a compliment. To them it meant careless roving. Without the legal protection of marriage, a woman was more liable to be abandoned, and then too there was the danger of unwanted pregnancy — most wives had a baby every year or two. All this is in the air when Jane Eyre refuses to live with married Mr Rochester.

You're an orphan, he reminds Jane. 'Who cares what you do?'

'I care for myself', is Jane's retort. Mr Rochester's history of French mistresses is hardly reassuring.

Marian rejected Jane's view from the start. She was prepared to trust Lewes, and she wrote from the Continent to assure Chapman she was not mistaken. It was a mature, considered reading of a man's character; different from Mary Godwin's departure with Shelley, with the unhesitating abandonment of the young. Two years later Marian confided to Barbara Leigh Smith — a young woman played on by Chapman's seductive repertoire — how happy Lewes made her. Barbara, reporting to Bessie Parkes, said they would have to revise their opinion of Lewes.

'Marian tells me that in their marital relationship he is unsensual, extremely considerate.' Barbara adds that they practised birth control and intended to have no children.

When it came to contraception, this couple was half a century in advance of common practice. We recall that back in 1815 Byron owned 'cundums' and that only aristocrats could afford them, mainly to shield a man from venereal disease. There was no notion of offering reciprocal protection, and not the remotest idea of birth control, in contrast to the responsible forethought of Lewes and Marian as they began to live together.

Books sealed their bond. Each day it was their habit to read aloud to each other, sometimes for hours. Like Mary Godwin and Shelley setting out for France in 1814, they carried a load of books.

Trains took them to Brussels, Namur and Liège. En route to Cologne, Dr Brabant joined them in their railway carriage and arranged for David Strauss to come to their hotel at breakfast next day. With these encounters, all charm of rapport vanished. Cologne was the only place Marian found 'dismal'.

'Strauss looks so strange and cast-down,' she reports to Bray, 'and my deficient German prevented us from learning more of each other than our exterior which in the case of both would have been better left to the imagination.'

Her German was not deficient. It did not occur to her that the strange manner of Strauss could have been a foretaste of what a single woman living with a married man must expect.

It didn't take long for gossip to circulate. When Marian and Lewes had strolled on deck as they crossed the Channel, they had chanced on Edward Noel, related to Byron's wife and an intimate of the Brays, especially Cara. The news soon reached Thomas Woolner, a sculptor who was part of the Pre-Raphaelite Brotherhood. He was scathing to the Scottish poet William Bell Scott, one of Lewes's oldest friends: '. . . blackguard Lewes has bolted with a—'. 'Slut' is it, or worse? He calls the couple 'stink pots of humanity'. George Combe, a phrenologist, regretted introducing Marian to friends. For her to have acted as she did led Combe to enquire if there might be insanity in her family. Carlyle spoke reprovingly of a 'strong-minded woman' who lures a husband away from his wife and children.

Stung by degrading reports of their 'running away', Marian took the high ground. For herself, she was 'entirely indifferent', she declared to Chapman, but since this did not apply to Lewes, she was hot in his defence.

> 62a Kaufgasse, Weimar
> [15 October 1854]

... This [running away from his wife and family] is so far from being true that he is in constant correspondence with his wife and is providing for her to the best of his power, while no man can be more nervously anxious than he about the future welfare of his children ...

The phrase 'run away' as applied to me is simply amusing – I wonder what I had to run away from. But as applied to Mr. Lewes it is more serious ... He has written to Carlyle and to Robert Chambers, stating as much of the truth as he can without too severely inculpating others ...

I have nothing to deny or to conceal. I have done nothing with which any person has a right to interfere. I have surely full liberty to travel in Germany, and to travel with Mr. Lewes. No one here seems to find it at all scandalous that we should be together ... But I do not wish to take the ground of ignoring what is unconventional in my position. I have counted the cost of the step that I have taken and am prepared to bear, without irritation or bitterness, renunciation of all my friends ...

Your obliged friend
Marian Evans

Lewes considered returning to London to refute the 'run-away' report, but feared the worry might undermine his precarious health. Instead he made two decisions in Weimar. When he learnt that Agnes was soon to give birth to a fourth child by Hunt, he resolved on a separation. It means that Marian gave herself to Lewes before he planned to separate from his wife, and this suggests how entire her trust in him had been – or the risk she'd dared to take.

Lewes's other decision was to give up the *Leader* as soon as he could. In the future he would rely on writing books for his main income. Marian was at hand to encourage this. In effect he had a first-class editor at his side. And further, she pledged her independent earning power to share Lewes's burden of responsibility.

A new family crisis touched her more than scandal did. Chrissey's second son, aged about fourteen, had been removed from school and put to work. He was 'naughty' and lost his job; then was sent to sea and within a few months he drowned. Marian was troubled not only for Chrissey's sake but because she could not afford – in every sense – to involve herself. She had chosen to support Lewes and his dependants. Perhaps she reasoned that Chrissey had Isaac.

Tucked away in the bag she'd packed to leave on 20 July was a chapter of a novel. It was like the box that Mary Godwin had packed when she left with Shelley, intending to show him the 'productions' of her mind. Marian's novel opened in a rural village in Staffordshire, the setting of her Evans family a generation or two back. She had yet to bring out the dramatic possibilities of obscure lives and unheard voices. This manuscript lay silent amongst her things during their three months in Weimar.

They expected the precinct of a court and were surprised to find themselves in a 'dull, lifeless village' with 'rough, straggling' houses, skinny sheep and only one small bookshop. But to their joy they discovered the composer and virtuoso pianist Franz Liszt in residence as Director of the Court Theatre and Kapellmeister (a position once held by Bach). When they went to see him, they met his mistress, a Polish princess, Carolyne zu Sayn-Wittgenstein, who had persuaded Liszt to give up performing to delirious audiences and concentrate on composing. She was plump, with blackish teeth, and arrayed for breakfast in a white gown lined with orange and a violet-trimmed cap.

Marian sat where she could see Liszt's hands on the piano as he entranced his guests with one of his religious *fantaisies*. 'For the first time in my life I beheld real inspiration', Marian wrote in her journal, 'for the first time I heard the true tones of the piano.' As he played he looked as grand as a Michelangelo prophet, she thought, but in repose his face had a tenderness that might serve as a model for a St John. She described his looks to Bessie as the divine ugliness when 'the soul gleams through it, which is my favourite kind of physique'. Twenty years later Liszt would be a source for the musician Klesmer in *Daniel Deronda*. After Marian's initial awe, she found herself able to tell Liszt her ideas and feelings.

Lewes's chief purpose in Weimar was to interview everyone he could find who had seen Goethe. There was Gustav Schöll, Director of the Art Institute, who had edited the letters and essays of Goethe, and was full of accurate information, and Kräuter, Goethe's last secretary. Goethe's daughter-in-law Ottilie gave Lewes entrée to the poet's study and bed-room, which were not open to the public.

Meanwhile, they had to support Agnes Lewes and her six children. Lewes sent them the twenty pounds he still earned each month for his columns in the *Leader*, and Marian was grateful to Chapman for his offer of paid work. For his October issue of the *Westminster Review*, she prepared the first of an extraordinary run of essays between 1854 and 1856. The best response to slander is to be happy, and for her to be happy was to fill the mind.

What's going on in her mental cocoon is not visible in her *Journal*. It records mainly her daily doings: the sights she sees and the people she meets. Nor is it visible in the *Letters*, where she's absorbing and defying her outcast position. The transformation lies in the shadow of certain essays not only her adaptation to realism, picking up on advances in art, but also in the way she's stretching herself against the model of advanced women in the past and shedding what's silly in her sex.

It can't be entirely irrelevant that before Marian left her post at the *Westminster Review* Thomas Huxley, the evolutionist who was shoulder to shoulder with Darwin, appeared at Chapman's Monday gatherings on his return from his own exploratory voyaging. As editor, Marian Evans sent Huxley biological publications for review. It was a historic moment when these intellectuals stood on the cusp of the world-changing idea that humans had not been placed on earth by a divine being but had developed from lower species across aeons of geological time. Here was scientific underpinning for Marian Evans to develop further the possibilities she sensed inside her.

It struck her that French women in the seventeenth and eighteenth centuries had advanced beyond women anywhere else. The essay 'Woman in France: Mme de Sablé' looks at the way men from all walks of life came to women's salons for the quality of understanding they offered. Mme de Sablé was 'a woman whom men could more than love – whom they could make their friend, confidante, and counsellor, the sharer not of their joys and sorrows only, but of their ideas and aims'.

Through such a woman Marian Evans can explore what she herself had been for Spencer and was now all the more for Lewes. She has in mind a marriage of true minds, and in Weimar, in August 1854, writing from the test ground of her own experience, she conjures up an image of female empowerment. She singles out French women for their confident centrality in their culture, their influence on a language that can unite an extreme of sensibility with an extreme of conciseness; and as she admires above all their rapid vivacity of mind, we glimpse a variant creature moving below the surface whose habitat will not be the shallows: a solid, deep-sea creature, slower, more patient in her judgement and with an encompassing breadth of mind.

For such a creature to surface she must swim away from the shoals. Most women's books are fit to be discarded, Marian Evans makes bold to declare in 'Mme de Sablé'. She's even more dismissive in her 1856 essay 'Silly Novels by Lady Novelists'. Their pious, high-society nonsense comes about because 'ladies' don't express their own nature and desires. In literature, where 'every fibre of nature' is involved, a woman has something specific to contribute. A developed woman will distil her subtlest essence: 'sympathy'. Here she finds her watchword. The rising author haunts this essay.

Chapman was not encouraging about the far-reaching feminism of 'Mme de Sablé'. He did publish it in his October issue, but he said nothing, and for a while did not offer Marian more work. To earn a much-needed income, she turned once more to translating. When they moved to Berlin in November she began to translate Spinoza's *Ethics*, taking over this formidable task from Lewes, who had accepted a commission to do it.

Was a buried wish to write fiction part of her attraction to Lewes as an established critic of the genre? In her bag there still lurked that scene for a novel, and one night she let drop to Lewes that she just so happened to have it with her. She read it aloud to him, and from then on he urged her to try her hand at fiction. Here was the vital response, not blocking or withering. It was what Shelley had done for Mary Godwin, and Charlotte for Emily Brontë.

When the time came to return to England, Marian had no illusions about what to expect. So long as the pair remained on the Continent they felt welcome in society. Lewes had numerous contacts and no one cut them for openly living together. But back home, women with reputations to consider would not be free to call.

As they crossed the Channel on 14 March 1855, Marian joked that a friendly bout of seasickness made her glad to see the cliffs of Dover. She found lodgings at 1 Sydney Place in Dover, intending to stay there as 'Miss Evans' while Lewes went on ahead to London. Marian's condition for joining him was that he obtain from Agnes a promise that she would never again wish to live with him as his wife.

'No, never', Agnes agreed. She added that she 'would be happy if her husband could marry Miss Evans'.

In fact a marriage, though barred by law, is exactly what Marian had to pretend to have. To present herself as another 'Mrs Lewes' meant that she didn't see herself as a mistress; it had to be a permanent tie. All the same, we have only to picture the constantly pregnant Agnes going about London as the legitimate Mrs Lewes. Ostensibly, she was pregnant by her husband. Her own liaison with Hunt was kept under wraps, and she remained outwardly respectable. Not so Miss Evans living with Mr Lewes.

Marian was aware that women who'd been her friends could not write to her, and arranged for her correspondence to go via Chapman or Lewes. All the while, she made statements about accepting her outcast status, affirming her resolve not to blame former friends for shunning her. 'I wish it to be understood', she wrote in 1857, 'that I should never invite anyone to come and see me who did not ask for the invitation.' She was steeling herself against the loss of friends, but in this very act she provoked those closest to her, Cara Bray and Sara Hennell.

Cara accused her of taking the marriage laws lightly. Marian denied it. Her commitment was so grave that she refused the social code of cover-up. Had she continued to live as 'Miss Evans' and conducted a discreet liaison, she would not have been ostracised. The paired life she was bent on took immense courage. In Victorian stories a 'fallen woman' could regain sympathy only if she died and did so repenting. Marian Evans, though, meant to thrive as 'Mrs Lewes'. That's what she felt herself to be and what she insisted others call her.

On their return to London, the new 'Mrs Lewes' and her husband took lodgings on the periphery of the city near Kew, and there she lived unvisited. Lewes came up to town once a week, but over the next few years Marian went but twice: once for work, to see Chapman, and the other time to the Zoological Gardens with a view to Lewes's explorations of marine biology. She said, 'I have no calls to make', and joked about resorting to a call on the molluscs. She was now, as she'd put it later, 'cut off from what is called the world'.

Where Marian could brush off George Combe as absurd and ignore Chapman's fears for the fidelity she expected from Lewes, she was upset by the shock to Cara and Sara. Her very fear of this had led her to ward off a rebuff by writing defensively via Charles Bray: she was braced to lose her friends.

Cara and Sara, who had loved her like a sister, accused her of not confiding in them, only in Mr Bray. Marian was unable to explain this to their satisfaction. What she offered made things worse because she said that what she'd told Mr Bray (about the extramarital children born to Agnes Lewes) was not for women's ears. She tried to put it over that she'd intended to protect them. Naturally, Cara (bringing up her husband's own extramarital child) and Sara (an active feminist) were astonished and offended. They thought, mistakenly, that Marian cared more for Bray than for them, and that she was 'boasting' of her control over bitterness and too willing to give up her oldest and closest friends. Marian adopted the same patiently forbearing voice as when her father had been about to cast her out. The more she went on in this voice, the more at odds both sides became. It didn't help for Marian to declare her love and gratitude. After one letter of protest Cara did not write again for a year. Sara did write, and they struggled to put their correspondence back on its confidential track, but Sara felt that she was writing to 'someone in a book, and not the Marian we have known and loved so many years'.

The new Mrs Lewes saw little of these old friends and never saw Rosehill again. It was a place to revisit only in memory. At Christmas 1855, when she went to Nuneaton to stay with her sister, Bray asked her to come by. She replied with the stiffness of hurt that she could not come when the invitation was issued only by the master of the house.

At first she kept her position from her siblings. It was not until 1857, three years after she went away with Lewes, that she wrote to inform her brother. The immediate need was for Isaac, who handled her inheritance, to deposit the income in Lewes's account (reinforcing her identity as his wife). Despite her plea that she had done Isaac no harm, he cast her off without a word. Sadly, he also exercised his authority over Chrissey, as a widow dependent on him, to forbid further contact with their wicked sister.

Three women stood by her. Rufa Hennell was quick to call at 8 Victoria Grove Terrace, Bayswater, when Marian joined Lewes in May 1855 for a brief transit in London. Bessie Parkes was next. She came all the way to their new lodgings in Clarence Row, East Sheen, a suburb of Richmond, and left Marian in 'a glow of joy', so glad was she to see this friend. Unfortunately, Bessie had enquired for 'Miss Evans', and Marian wrote afterwards to remind her that she was not known in their lodgings by her real name, for to use it would risk eviction. In fact, at the end of that same month she and Lewes did leave. It's probable that the landlady had caught a whiff of irregularity. In October they moved to 8 Park Shot, Richmond. Marian was anxious not to jar their friendly landlady. She warned any potential caller never to ask for 'Miss Evans'.

Later, Barbara Leigh Smith came to stay for a week when Lewes and Marian were at Tenby in Wales during the summer of 1856. The intimacy of the way Marian spoke to Barbara about 'considerate' sex took place after she had been cut off from almost all contact with women.

Feminists alone stood by Marian during the years she lived outside society. George Eliot has not been regarded as a feminist, largely because she was honest enough to criticise women. Yet in 1856 she supported the English feminists who put together a petition to Parliament for the Married Women's Property Act, permitting wives to retain their earnings instead of handing the money over to husbands. Marian remarked to Sara that it would raise the position and character of women. 'It is one round [rung] of a long ladder stretching far beyond our lives.'

Marian had intended to write on Margaret Fuller ever since reading her memoirs in 1852. She admired a 'loving woman's heart' that does not undervalue small acts of domestic care. In this period as an outcast, she picked up an earlier book by Fuller, her *Woman in the Nineteenth Century*, which had made its first appearance in 1843.

She saw in Fuller a 'strong and truthful nature, refusing to exaggerate women's moral and intellectual qualities as she makes calm pleas for removing artificial restrictions so that the possibilities of woman's nature may have room for full development'.

At the same time she read Mary Wollstonecraft's *Vindication of the Rights of Woman*. Copies were scarce in Victorian England, she observed. She read it with surprise to find Wollstonecraft 'eminently serious, severely moral' in her impatience with silly women.

Where Mary Shelley had looked back to Wollstonecraft as a daughter-disciple, Marian Evans looks back to the Wollstonecraft who was critical of female frivolity and cunning intrigues dictated by vanity. As Marian sums it up, Wollstonecraft wished women to assimilate knowledge thoroughly so as to bring about the growth of character. She held to this tough line in her discussions with Mrs Taylor: '"Enfranchisement of women" only makes creeping progress and that is best, for woman does not yet deserve a much better lot than man gives her.'

It's harsh, but both Wollstonecraft and Fuller had observed men in subjection to unreasoning wives. Marian too regrets this kind of ignorant narrowness, as she puts it in her essay 'Margaret Fuller and Mary Wollstonecraft': 'so far as obstinacy is concerned, your unreasoning animal is the most unmanageable of creatures'. George Eliot was to flesh this out in *Middlemarch* in her portrait of Rosamond Vincy, the blinkered wife who undermines her husband and helps to make it impossible for him to exercise his medical far-sightedness. As the essay puts it, where her weakness is not controlled by a woman herself it will *govern*. The precious meridian years of many a gifted man are wasted in routine toil so as to keep up an 'establishment' for a wife 'who is fit for nothing but to sit in her drawing-room like a doll-Madonna in her shrine'.

Unlike Marian, many Victorian feminists distanced their politics from Wollstonecraft because they wished to dissociate the Woman Question from slurs on her private life designed to discredit her revolutionary ideas. In fact she had been a woman of natural dignity who impressed men like Dr Johnson and William Godwin, but Pitt's propaganda machine branded her a slut. Women, including writers, backed away. Respectability was crucial to the political agendas of nineteenth-century feminism, with its focus on legal obstacles to gender equality.

Hardly conducive to an image of respectability was the matter of passion. It was off the map for first-wave feminists, and many remained single. Harriet Martineau broke with Charlotte Brontë over Lucy Snowe's fiery nature. But Marian Evans did not forget her own sense that she must 'die' if Spencer were not loyal to her. George Eliot was to recall this level of despair in *Deronda*, when the singer Mirah dips her cloak in the river. In this scene she looks back to Mary Wollstonecraft one rainy night in October 1795, soaking her clothes on the brink of the Thames, hoping to sink quicker, after Gilbert Imlay left her. Mirah, like Mary, is restored to life; each lives to know a good man and to unfold what she has to offer.

———

Marian's isolation from October 1855 until February 1859 proved fertile for work. There was a daily pattern: breakfast at 8.30; reading alone till 10; writing till 1.30; walking till 4; dining at 5, and then reading aloud for three hours each evening. As with Mary Shelley, this expansion of the mind through reading fuelled the writer.

All the while she continued to help Lewes. His writing career took a lift from the time they joined forces. *Goethe* was well received, and at the time that Marian finally completed her translation of Spinoza (on his behalf) in February 1856, Lewes moved on to marine biology. He went in for hands-on research in response to a stinging comment from Huxley that Lewes was merely a 'book scientist'. There, curious to behold, is Marian dangling her feet in the rock pools of Ilfracombe in the spring of 1856. Holding her dress out of the water, she collects specimens with Lewes, molluscs, annelids and zoophytes, which they place in glass jars and phials in every corner of their room. These Lewes examines under the microscope they'd acquired, and each morning they jump up to check for overnight develop-ments (or deaths). In this way, she said, 'we seem to have gained a large influx of new ideas'.

On an inland walk in the Devon woods, her eyes fix on a caterpillar who is 'spending its transitional life, happily knowing nothing of transi-tions', on a bush.

This absorption in zoology interrupted her work, Marian told Barbara Leigh Smith. But wasn't zoology part of it – an evolutionary narrative co-existing with her own transitional life? Later that summer, at Tenby, Lewes urged her again to write fiction, and then, on 22 September, she tried her wings. Swiftly and with extraordinary command of a new medium, she took flight and soared into her first story, 'The Sad Fortunes of the Revd Amos Barton'.

This story stakes out a territory she would make her own: she would look at country clergymen not from a theological point of view but in their everyday lives, as Jane Austen had done. She would apply the

domestic subjects of Flemish art to a series of *Scenes of Clerical Life*. She
defies the expectations of 'madam', the reader of silly lady novelists: no
high-society romance, no melodrama, no false piety, no extreme poverty.
Instead her focus is on family life: the well-intentioned but mediocre
clergyman (closely based on the fortunes of John Gwyther in her native
Chilvers Coton*), the caring mother whose health is failing in the course
of a seventh pregnancy, and the realistic portraits of children, from the
anxious eldest daughter Patty to Dickey and Chubby, the youngest boys
who respond to the soft touch of Milly's hand but can't take in their
mother's ordeal, and the red, seven-month baby who breathes for a few
hours. Its death is followed by Milly's death and burial. The reader is
brought to feel in Milly a natural kindness beyond the docile angel in the
house.

This may be what Marian had kept in mind since her time in Berlin,
early in 1855, when she'd proposed an essay for the *Westminster Review*, 'Ideals
of Womankind', a topic, she told Chapman, she wished to treat. The portrait of Milly Barton offers a domestic parallel with active feminists and is
in line with Wollstonecraft's insistence on domestic affections. The reader
is left haunted by the pain of the dull man who has lost Milly.

Lewes, as well as Marian, was unsure whether she could manage the
emotional demands of a deathbed. When she reached this point in the
story, he took himself off to London, leaving her alone to see what she
could do. On his return, late that night, she read the scene aloud. They
both cried; then he came across and kissed her, saying, 'Your pathos is
even better than your fun.'

Their relationship was more than a marriage. To her, Lewes was a
mentor: his scientific acumen was a stimulus to the realism she wished to
achieve. Even more so was his enthusiastic reciprocity: his embrace of her
emotional attunement that opened her ear as a writer to 'the roar from
the other side of silence'.

---

* The Revd John Gwyther, who recognised himself in Amos Barton, had been the local
minister in Mary Ann's childhood. Like Amos, he was not popular, both for his insistent
Evangelicalism and for his crush on a newcomer to the parish, a 'Countess'.

Lewes offered the story to the distinguished Edinburgh publisher John Blackwood, whose father had founded *Blackwood's Magazine* (the periodical Maria Brontë had read avidly). Lewes was already a contributor to 'Maga', which had recently brought out the first part of his *Seaside Studies*. Lewes did not divulge Marian's name, nor the fact that she was a woman. He made out that he was representing a diffident friend and spoke of the friend as 'he'.

Blackwood was a cautious Scot. It was his way to say a manuscript 'will do' and that he would read it a second time so as not to be carried away by a first reading. Rather stiffly he congratulated the author 'on being worthy of the honours of print and pay'; at the same time he thought it a 'defect' to end with the fates of the children in the story. A 'lame' finale, he called it, not perceiving how each child's loss and on-going life carries the heartbeat of a mother's unregarded work into futurity.

The author's confidence was shaken. Lewes advised Blackwood that his friend was 'unusually sensitive, and unlike most writers is more anxious about *excellence* than about appearing in print – as his waiting so long before taking the venture proves. He is consequently afraid of failure though not afraid of obscurity.' Blackwood's coolness had not encouraged the author enough to press on. Lewes found it necessary to explain 'the sort of shy, shrinking, ambitious nature you have to deal with'.

Blackwood was big enough to take the hint. His tone warmed. His wife, he conceded, had endorsed the roles of the children. Others were critical. One of Blackwood's trusted advisers thought the author might be a scientific man, 'not a practised writer', and that there was too much sniffing and dirty noses.

Though stung, Marian defended her realism. Her knowledge of science was as superficial as that of most 'practised writers', she said, yet she could not agree that scientific exactness should be incompatible with art. People who disliked the homely truthfulness of Dutch painting would not like any particular work of that school.

The first part of 'Amos' appeared in *Blackwood's Magazine* in January 1857. Lewes crowed over his 'hatched chick'. She was published anonymously (as were all writers for 'Maga'), and readers assumed the author was a man, almost certainly a clergyman. Signing a letter to Blackwood as 'the Author of Amos Barton', she promised the second of the *Scenes* shortly. In the meantime, on 4 February 1857, she chose a pseudonym and George Eliot came into being. 'George' was the twin hatched with George Henry Lewes, while 'Eliot' was a random choice. This masculine cover freed her to open up an issue she had never before broached in writing: a woman's secret desires.

A question about the untested possibilities of woman's nature again slides out from under the cover of a man's story in 'Mr Gilfil's Love Story'. Readers in her part of Warwickshire at once recognised the Revd Bernard Gilpin Ebdell, also of Chilvers Coton. His middle name is an obvious source for 'Gilfil'. Ebdell had married a collier's daughter, Sarah Shilton, who had been educated by Lady Newdigate and trained as a singer. Instead of the collier's daughter, the story invents an Italian wife, Caterina Sarti, and her story – encased in her husband's love story – comes out thirty years after her early death. We encounter first an aged clergyman, living like a bachelor but with a shut chamber upstairs, a woman's room with leavings from the past century – a cherry bow and faded black lace. The old man sipping his gin and water and scattering the ash from his pipe, and the relics upstairs, tell us too little. The comedy of parish folk surrounds him, the gossip and fragmented memories of a foreigner with large black eyes that had a blank look of someone who's not present in the life she's leading.

Gilfil has closed off his past. It's left to the narrator to take us back into the full-on heat of a girl's unrequited longing for another man. The tale could appear a warning against the consuming effect of desire, but George Eliot, like Claire Clairmont, expects readers to enter into what the social code repressed.

Her control of empathy – channelling a woman's silenced drama through the old man's silenced memory of his own tenacious love – makes this tale a masterpiece of unfolding intimacy. She stakes out the ground for the interior drama of Henry James – the tension of what does not come out.

Caterina has been taken on as a child by landed English gentry, Sir Christopher and Lady Cheverel (based on Sir Roger and Lady Newdigate, whose nephew and heir had appointed George Eliot's father as his agent). Cheverel Manor is an exact picture of the grand Arbury Hall, which of course George Eliot knew from her youth. A fictional nephew and heir, the studiedly elegant and effete Captain Wybrow, makes up to Caterina (Tina, as she's called) and awakens an attachment. When he's expected to marry a high-born and moneyed lady, he wants Tina to forget the tenderness between them. But her attachment holds. What makes this all the harder is that she has to keep it under wraps. Wybrow's fiancée, the dominating Miss Assher, and her small-minded mother have come to stay, and for Tina to witness every gesture of betrayal is a torture she must contrive not to show. Alone in her room she tears a handkerchief to pieces and sets her teeth against a windowpane.

George Eliot reveals how destructive it can be when a creature is forced to be unnatural. The pressure of Tina's silenced feeling is as convincing as Charlotte Brontë's for Monsieur Heger, re-created in her fictions (most painfully in *Shirley*, when well-conducted Caroline Helstone feels as though she's closing her fist on a scorpion). George Eliot's exposure of Tina's moment-by-moment agony reveals what no Victorian lady could utter aloud.

Tina's gift as a singer is a glorious mode of expression but it lasts only so long as the aria, and it counts for nothing beside her rival's class and wealth. To her patrons, Tina's voice qualifies as drawing-room entertainment – no more. Affectionately, Sir Christopher calls her 'little monkey'; in effect she's a performing monkey. She's no freer than a pet – a possession. Her owner, Sir Christopher, is entitled to hand her over to Mr Gilfil. She knows how good Gilfil is, but her attachment to Wybrow is permanent. In this set-up, there's no inkling a girl might have leanings of her own. If she did, it must be female caprice. Reflection about what is due to her benefactor will surely restore her to obedience.

This code has shaped Tina's tame, grateful manners. Since she has internalised the code, it devastates her to find herself unable to contain her rage with Wybrow. He fences his fragile self with a commonplace: females are light creatures who can shift from man to man according to where their bread is buttered.

When Tina can't play out this convenient narrative, Wybrow forces it on her in prompting Sir Christopher to marry Tina to Gilfil. Forced marriage is the final betrayal of her feelings. It's in fact the prospective bridegroom, Gilfil, who tries to protect her.

Gilfil's empathy is the cue for the reader to enter into the effect of force on a girl disempowered to the point of madness and murderous fury. John Blackwood missed this cue when he suggested that Gilfil's devotion was too 'abject' for 'a man of character'. George Eliot refused to alter this. She explained to Blackwood the psychological inevitability of each character's moves in this tragedy where Gilfil's devotion has no reward, and tension between Tina and Wybrow rises to a level fatal to both.

It adds to the tension that Wybrow is no villain. He's too languid for sexual exertion. Tina continues to be drawn to him because of his vein of tenderness; she'd like to call it back because it's still there, though not strong enough to stand up to the social expectations that pressure him as much as her. He's genuinely fond of Tina, but too self-protective to love fully.

As Wybrow's affronts to Tina build up, rage takes her to the point of breakdown. She fears that she can hardly contain the politely grateful façade her dependent position requires. It makes me think of the rage of the adopted orphan Tattycoram in *Little Dorrit* (serialised 1855–7). Dickens made it clear that rage is not an acceptable emotion. He can see that Tattycoram has feelings beyond her control, but he invites us to shake our heads. He doesn't look into these feelings in the way George Eliot sees into Tina's soul.

After Wybrow dies of heart failure, Tina goes through the motions of moving on. She marries good Mr Gilfil – he's offering her a life – but it's a false narrative. Bruised, without the will to live, she dies in childbirth, and we are brought to understand the inevitability of this end.

The temperate John Blackwood baulked at Tina's murderous fury. In particular he objected to the scene where Tina seizes a 'dadger' [dagger] from Cheverel Manor's collection of old weaponry. Blackwood wanted Tina to dream this instead and so retain some shred of 'dignity'.

George Eliot couldn't resist mocking the 'dadger' in her reply. 'It would be the death of my story to substitute a dream for a real scene', she wrote. She wished to grant the inconsistencies in real people[*] and refused to alter Tina's frame of mind. 'So many of us have reason to know that criminal impulses may be felt by a nature which is nevertheless guarded by its entire constitution from the commission of crime, that I can't help hoping my Caterina will not forfeit the sympathy of all my readers.'

My Caterina: 'my' says something about her closeness to this character. Later, she would say that she had done things in *Scenes of Clerical Life* that she would never attempt again. If she was opening up a woman's desire, and if we wonder why she never does this again in so maddened a way, the answer must lie in what she'd surrendered between 1852 and 1854: her thwarted desire for Spencer. In 'Gilfil' George Eliot both revived this pain and distanced it from her own history by making Caterina un-English, at least by birth. All the same, Tina's emotional heat is fuelled by an Englishwoman's rising temperature during the heatwave of July 1852, when Spencer met her with 'lumps of ice'.

Both Spencer and Wybrow are preoccupied with their health: Wybrow has a weak heart and Spencer a nervous complaint. And their temperature is similar: tepid to cold. Marian Evans had marked Spencer's 'tremendous glacier'. The fact that he remained single bears out her sense of a chill that had more to do with him than with her supposed lack of attraction. Of course, it would have had entirely to do with him if he was too wrapped up in fear of ill-health to find sexual energy.

The word 'die' exploding out of her rational plea to Spencer is telling. Her experience of a to-die-for attachment took her into Tina's fatal love. But then, unlike Tina, she'd saved herself, first through work and then by

---

[*] George Eliot would have concurred with Emerson's idea that 'a foolish consistency is the hobgoblin of the little minds'. This would also apply to her idea of 'half-tints', above.

slowly feeling her way into a tie with another man who did not initially attract or impress her. It was no light flit; it was no less than an emotional feat.

She was able to lend her sense to the goodness and loyalty in Lewes. A less mature and rational woman could have been undone, as Tina is. What she eventually found in Lewes, a well-connected mentor, was extraordinarily fortunate – it was the ground from which her flight into fiction could take off – but it was not the wild ardour she had to leave behind.

In the wake of Tina, George Eliot owned her affinity for wildness – that character so unlike the wise woman she became. At this point she was overcome by the portrait of Emily Brontë in the newly published *Life of Charlotte Brontë*. 'Emily has a singular fascination for me,' she confided to Mrs Gaskell, 'probably because I have a passion for lions and savage animals, and she was une bête fauve in power, splendour and wildness.' I see it as the last, backward look of a transformed creature to what she had been.

The price of transformation was family. Isaac Evans has always had bad press for cutting his sister out of his life. It appeared to be an act of self-righteous conformity once he ascertained through his lawyer that she was not legally married, and was sealed by the pathos of Maggie Tulliver's longing for her philistine brother in *The Mill on the Floss*. Yet the real-life tension between brother and sister had been building up well before Isaac cast her off.

The first sign of this, we recall, happened when Marian Evans returned from Geneva in 1850 and did not feel right in her brother's home. There followed a series of family crises on which she closed the door. The first was when Chrissey's husband died, and Marian infuriated Isaac by scooting back to London. Then, when Chrissey's second son drowned in 1854, Marian was in Weimar, giving her all – including earnings – to Lewes, yet with a guilt over divided loyalties that made her more troubled over her sister's distress than by the scandal building up in London. While Marian was reaching the crisis of Tina's passion, a different but equally pressing family crisis tugged at her in March–April 1857.

She heard from Isaac of typhus ravaging Chrissey's household. Pretty, fair-haired Frances (Fanny), aged eight, died on 26 March. A younger child, Kate, Chrissey herself and their servant were all dangerously ill. At this time, Marian was writing the finale to 'Gilfil', which was due to be delivered to her publisher. This professional commitment seemed to her 'more important', yet even after she finished 'Gilfil' on 8 April, it did not occur to her to leave off helping Lewes with marine research at St Mary's, the largest of the Scilly Isles – too far away, she thought, to go to her sister. All the while the sun literally shone on Marian, Chrissey's crisis was, she said, a 'shadow to me'.

On 16 April, on hearing from Isaac that Chrissey and Kate were better but not out of danger, she asked Isaac to advance fifteen pounds of her next half-year's income to Chrissey so that she could take herself and Kate away 'from that hotbed of fever'. She enclosed a note for Chrissey, signing herself 'Marian Evans'.

The name matters. Nearly three years after she began to live with Lewes, she still wished to keep it from her family. But secrecy about her situation exposed her once again to the expectation that a maiden aunt would take on the duty of nursing the sick. This time Marian had no reply from her brother.

So their estrangement was already in place when she finally wrote on 26 May 1857, from Gorey in Jersey (yet another seaside locale for Lewes), to explain her changed situation to Isaac: 'You will be surprised, I dare say, but I hope not sorry to learn that I have changed my name, and have someone to take care of me in the world.' One reason she gives for not coming to Chrissey is her own 'very frail' health, which benefits from sea air. And she now claims to have been 'in ignorance of [Chrissey's] extreme illness'.

These excuses sound oddly lame. For a compassionate woman, her withdrawal from her brother and sister appears out of character. One possible clue is her need for what she mildly calls 'approbation', though she means something much stronger: a family's heartfelt approval. Could it be that with kin she lost the effective self who had defied her family image as 'a failure of Nature'? If so, she had to keep away. Fear, perhaps, was part of it: an outlaw's fear of being drawn back into the net of kinship.

Even with her one-time rescuers, the Brays, the distance yawned in 1857 when Cara wondered how her friend's face had changed in the course of their separation over the last three years.

'Doubtless it is older and uglier', Marian replied, 'but it ought not to have a bad expression, for I never have anything to call out my ill-humour or discontent – which you know were always ready enough to come on slight call – I have everything to call out love and gratitude.'

At length, Cara did invite her to visit Ivy Cottage, the home of Mrs Hennell and Sara, where the Brays had moved in hard times. Again, Marian made an excuse. Instead she sent a photograph (taken on 26 February 1858) inscribed 'To my sisters Cara and Sara'. And so she let go her ties with the Midlands, to be visited only in memory.

Victorian men had no inhibitions about tears. Lewes cried over Milly Barton, and George Eliot let this be known. Proud of his emotion, she took it as her breakthrough: a sign confirming her power to move her reader. A London lecturer called Alfred Smith told Blackwood that he'd 'blubbed' over 'Amos Barton'. At forty, he too was proud of having that many tears to shed. George Eliot herself liked to cry. She had cried with Lewes over the deathbed of Mrs Barton. She cried again, 'hot tears', as the inspired words of a woman preacher, Dinah Morris, came surging up in *Adam Bede*.

She thought of this as 'My Aunt's Story'. At seventeen she had been 'deeply affected' when Elizabeth Evans told her story of a condemned girl who had murdered her baby and refused to confess. Her aunt had stayed with the girl, praying through the night before her execution, until the 'poor creature' burst into tears and confessed her crime.

Her niece never spoke of this murder in 1802 till December 1856, when she relayed the story to Lewes and he suggested a novel building up to the pre-execution scene in the prison. Where her aunt had spoken of a coarse, ignorant girl, George Eliot recasts her as Hetty Sorrel, niece of a farmer, vain in her prettiness and happily placed in the dairy of a respected family, until she succumbs to the idle love-making of Squire Donnithorne. Pregnant, she runs off with nowhere to go, and when she gives birth, her outcast situation is too much to bear. A tempting solution is to be rid of the baby. She doesn't want to kill the child; she simply lays down a bundle in the woods and shuts off to its cry.

By way of contrast, Hester Prynne in *The Scarlet Letter* (1851) holds on to her baby even as she's shunned by her Puritan community. Hetty's name is too close to Hester's to be an accident (as her lover Arthur Donnithorne's name is close to that of Hester's lover, Arthur Dimmesdale, who too stands at the apex of local society as its minister), and George Eliot did hugely admire Hawthorne's novel. For Hester, in America, there's the frontier, close to seventeenth-century Boston, offering a chance of escape from her outcast plight. For Hetty, in England, there's no escape from society; all roads lead back to Hayslope and enduring shame.

In October 1857, twenty years after Mary Ann encountered Elizabeth Evans, she began *Adam Bede* with a scene inspired by her aunt: a young woman preaching outdoors to country folk. When she read the scene aloud to Lewes he was so moved that he urged her to make Dinah central to the story. In the end, when Hetty is in prison, Dinah will help her to find her soul before she dies.

This book's extraordinary effect on readers was not unlike the touch of soul on soul, as Dinah, in her plain black dress and net Quaker cap, mounts a cart to preach. 'There was no keenness in the eyes; they seemed rather to be shedding love than making observations; they had the liquid look which tells that the mind is full of what it has to give out, rather than impressed with external objects ... She was not preaching as she heard others preach, but speaking directly from her own emotions ... '

The 'feminine delicacy' of Dinah's expressiveness blending with fellow feeling for her fallible listeners was as though the living pulse of her aunt's 'spirit of love' had been channelled through the author — as though in Dinah's voice she found her vocation as a writer.

When it came to publication early in 1859, George Eliot discovered how little fame mattered; what mattered was to find readers touched enough to feel transformed. Many felt as 'ardent' as Jane Carlyle did, 'in charity with the whole human race'. The same feeling welled in Dickens, who let George Eliot know that *Adam Bede* had marked 'an epoch' in his life. And then, unexpectedly, Herbert Spencer, whom the author had teased long ago for his 'tremendous glacier', declared himself unusually affected. When, later, he wished to ban novels in the London Library, he exempted George Eliot's – their emotional healing outdid the genre itself.

*Adam Bede* was a best-seller. The name George Eliot came to be known everywhere and yet a mystery remained as to who George Eliot was. She guarded the nom de plume even more firmly than Charlotte Brontë had guarded her identity as Currer Bell. Where certain of Currer Bell's titles point to portraits of women at the centre of her novels – *Jane Eyre*, *Shirley**  – George Eliot extends her male identity to her titles. 'Amos Barton', 'Mr Gilfil', *Adam Bede* and *Daniel Deronda*, are to some extent covers for portraits of women: Milly Barton, Caterina Sarti, Dinah Morris, Hetty Sorrel and Gwendolen Harleth. 'Sister Maggie', the working title of *The Mill on the Floss*, remained the focus of that novel, but disappears from the final title. The strategy gained George Eliot a huge readership. At the start of 1859, *Adam Bede* was widely acclaimed, even by Queen Victoria. The scandal around Miss Evans, had readers known who the author was, might have precluded such acceptance. Then in the course of that year her male image was broken.

Herbert Spencer was the only one to whom George Eliot had confided her identity as the author of *Clerical Life* and *Adam Bede*. But Spencer succumbed to a prod from Chapman – not one to keep a secret. Once George Eliot was known to be a woman there was an attack by William Hepworth Dixon, editor of the *Athenaeum*, declaring *Adam Bede* to be a tale 'such as

---

* *The Professor* (originally 'The Master'), her first novel, is an exception. Claire Harman points out that when Charlotte Brontë grafted onto the opening, scenes from her brother Branwell's story about fraternal enemies ('The Wool is Rising'), she was 'trying to establish a more vigorous, masculine tone' so that the novel would not look like woman's work, and to distract attention from the autobiographical core (p. 200).

a clever woman with ... an unschooled moral nature might have written ... a rather strong-minded lady, blessed with abundance of showy sentiment and a profusion of pious words'. She was merely copying her aunt in Dinah, some said; others, that she was parroting the pithy sayings of the farmer's wife Mrs Poyser. Lewes repeatedly warned Blackwood that George Eliot was so sensitive to slights that they could stop this author from writing.

All the same, 'a vocation to speak to one's fellow-men' was born, never to leave her so long as she lived. Filled with 'deep, silent joy', she sang to herself a quiet *Magnificat*. And for the public, the balm of her moral voice, the emotion it generated, made it unthinkable to regard her as an outcast. It was a book to reclaim her reputation. The large sums that Lewes secured for her, along with the prospect of a larger income from future books, allowed the author and Lewes to move back to London, to a home of their own at Holly Lodge in Wandsworth. This was a time to feel fulfilled and secure, but once more a family trouble raised its head.

Though Chrissey recovered from typhus, she then sank into consumption. Two months before her death in March 1859, Chrissey regretted the silence on her side – a silence dictated by Isaac. A loving apology from her dying sister 'ploughed up' Marian's heart. Even so, she did not visit Chrissey, though the train from London to Coventry took only two and a half hours. Her excuse this time was wifely duty. She and Lewes could not find a servant who would relieve them of household cares. Mr Lewes, she claimed, was 'stoutly' resisting the prospect of her leaving him for two days with their present servant.

'It is a terrible sacrifice to leave home at all', she told Bray, and she could not entertain an idea of coming to them en route. The need to return after two days, she explains, 'will forbid that pleasant renewal of the past. People who have been inseparable and found all their happiness in each other for five years are in a sort of Siamese-twin condition that other people are not likely to regard with tolerance or even with belief.'

After Chrissey died, her sister paid for her two daughters to go to boarding school in Lichfield. She did not adopt them, and these orphans remained at a distance. To visit them once at school was as much as she could manage. It relieved her to receive 'nice' letters from Emily, the elder daughter, whom George Eliot thought old enough at fourteen to take care of her younger sister Kate. Having been at boarding school throughout her own childhood, it may not have occurred to her what children need.

It's usual to commend her generosity to the three Lewes sons, but she speaks of the youngest, Bertie, as 'stupid' as well as sickly. She does not extend her sympathy to a boy who's not thriving in a broken home and whose mother is rearing a second family. What does not happen could be as telling as what does happen: the stepmother does not intervene with Lewes to offer Bertie a space to gain health in his father's home; he's to go instead to join his older brothers in a Swiss boarding school. George Eliot's growing income as a writer would have helped to pay for that school. But the children were not to return to England for most holidays. They behaved as cheerfully as their father could wish when he visited Switzerland about once a year. If they were homesick, if they were deprived of nurture, we can't know. Manliness (associated with imperialism on the Roman model) forbade complaint.

She was now writing at high tide, and to do this she had to protect her time and privacy. There were many ways that a sense of duty could divert the private purpose of a Victorian woman. When Florence Nightingale returned from the Crimea and meant to set up nursing as a profession, her sickbed protected her from social obligations as effectively as an outlaw position had protected George Eliot.

To achieve what she did, given her headaches and depressions, her emotional energy had to be reserved for her work and for Lewes who was vital to her work, acting as her agent and giving her, as she put it, 'the perfect love and sympathy of a nature that stimulates my own to healthful activity'.

The public's embrace of *Adam Bede* made her glad for her birth. Success gave her courage to explore her own experience as that 'unpromising woman-child' she had appeared to be. She was now confident enough to relive what she'd called the 'terrible pain' of her past through the medium of fiction. *The Mill on the Floss* (1860) is filled with personal memory. It relays the story of a clever girl as misfit, at odds with her small-minded mother, her mother's clannish family and the provincial society of St Ogg's. This is the Midlands as it had been a generation before in the time of George Eliot's Pearson aunt, 'Aunt Glegg' in the novel, who deplores a girl who can't conform. Much like George Eliot herself, Maggie Tulliver is tugged by the backward-yearning of those who move on and, at the same time, 'are tied by the strongest fibres of their hearts' to kin who had presided in childhood and who jar them with every movement.

Maggie's father calls her his 'little wench', the same pet phrase Robert Evans had for Mary Ann. Though proud of Maggie's brains in contrast with those of her 'slowish' brother Tom, Mr Tulliver knows brains will be useless in a grown-up woman. 'It's no mischief much while she's a little un, but an over-'cute woman's no better nor a long-tailed sheep – she'll fetch none the bigger price for that.'

Mrs Tulliver disagrees. 'Yes it is a mischief while she's a little un, Mr Tulliver, for it all runs to naughtiness ... wanderin' up an down by the water, like a wild thing'.

This wayward girl is told that she looks like a gypsy, and so, lonely for like-minded beings, she runs away to join the gypsies, hoping naively to find an alternative milieu to admire her for what she is. What the gypsies in fact see is Maggie's otherness: a clueless middle-class girl ripe for picking.

Maggie is unkempt. She's often infuriated by the passivity forced on girls who are expected to sit still with their hair in curls. Nagged by her mother's pleas to tidy her wild locks, she cuts them off – a short cut, literally, to having to brush and primp.

When Maggie visits Tom at his expensive tutor's, her quickness can't be denied but the tutor contrives to belittle brainy girls; their quickness is said to be shallow.

George Eliot is defining Maggie's situation nine years before the first Oxbridge college opened its doors to women. What was Maggie to do – a question the author herself had been forced to face. Here is another potential crosser of the female frontier: restless, intermittently defiant and eloquent.

Maggie Tulliver became something of a cult figure for aspiring women with no prospects outside the home in the 1860s. Among them were Emily Dickinson and her sister-in-law, Susan Dickinson, next door. Brainy, curtailed Maggie reads avidly, and Sue's wants were Maggie's wants: books with '*more*' in them. When Sue set up a salon at her home in Amherst, one member refused to read *Adam Bede* on hearing of its author's ungodliness. Defiantly, Sue bought the novel for Emily in 1860, and then both bought copies of *The Mill on the Floss*. Their friend, the newspaperman Sam Bowles (who published a few of Emily's poems in the early 1860s), read aloud a favourite passage: 'The great problem of the shifting relation between passion and duty is clear to no man who is capable of apprehending it.' Emily Dickinson put a picture of George Eliot on the wall of her room (along with Elizabeth Barrett Browning). Privately, she called her father's intrusive sister Elizabeth 'Aunt Glegg' after Maggie's carping aunt.

Another follower of Maggie was Henry James's vibrant cousin Minny Temple. Here was another untamed, honest creature hungry for life, who urged, 'Let us fearlessly trust our whole nature'. I've wondered if Minny was actually imitating Maggie when in 1861, at the age of sixteen, she cut off her hair with 'a vandal hand', as Henry's brother William put it. William James, Mrs James, Alice James and Minny's teachers all disapproved of her singularity, but Henry observed her as 'an experiment of nature'. She was to be the source for James's American girl who 'affronts her destiny'. Following George Eliot, he was drawn to the possibilities of 'a *grande nature*'.

When Henry James was leaving for England in 1869, Minny asked him to kiss George Eliot for her. Confined to bed with consumption, she had picked up *The Mill on the Floss*. It left her with 'an overpowering admiration and affection' for George Eliot. 'I see that she understands the character of a *generous* woman, that is, of a woman who believes in generosity, & who must be that or nothing, & who feels keenly, notwithstanding, how hard it is practically to carry it out.'

As an adult, Maggie is unable to return the love of a disabled man, Philip Wakem, a potential mentor who does see her for the 'large-souled' creature she is. Instead she takes off with Stephen Guest, her cousin's suitor. They haven't gone far when Maggie, conscience-stricken, turns back. This moral act is not appreciated by the people of St Ogg's, who cast her out.

Both Mary Shelley and George Eliot found women more obstinate and barbed than men when they cast out a member of their sex. Where Mary Shelley could speak only in the privacy of her *Journal*, George Eliot released uncontained sarcasm against 'the world's wife' in her newly confident public voice: a chapter entitled 'St Ogg's Passes Judgement'. In contrast to the calm letters Marian Evans had written from her outposts in Dover and Richmond, saying in measured tones that she accepts what's coming to her, George Eliot, speaking from behind the screen of fiction, could lash out at the stupidity of scandal. To the small-minded it's not what Maggie does that counts in the end; it's whether she is married or not. 'Maggie had returned ... without a husband, in that degraded and outcast condition to which error is well known to lead; and the world's wife, with that fine instinct which is given her for the preservation of society, saw at once that Miss Tulliver's conduct had been ... detestable!'

Maggie's most persistent critic is her brother, the companion of her earliest years. Tom tells her she no longer belongs to him. In the end sister and brother are reunited when the river floods and they drown holding to each other: 'In their death they were not divided', it says on their tomb. For some, this finale is too cataclysmic; for others, Maggie had to go down because there was no future for her gifts of mind and character in that place and time. But those who lend themselves to the sister-brother tie will be moved by the counter-story resonating in George Eliot's past — what might have been: the unbroken bond with scenes of childhood and a sister who did not leave her native place.

George Eliot's great power to move readers comes from the emotions of her past: the silenced passion she had known; the spirit of love in her aunt; and the pain of the social outcast.

Her miser character in *Silas Marner* (1861) is another who lives at the margins. This novel is like a biblical parable. Marner hoards his gold, but selfish greed cuts him off from his community. Then a different sort of gold comes to him in the shape of a baby, Eppie, with golden hair. She is left on his doorstep, and his growing love for this child acts like a miracle: it transforms his being. The biblical reading of George Eliot's youth came to infuse her new religion of humanism: 'an ideal of goodness entirely human'.

Humanism was one of the two leading ideas of her time. Shelley had annexed new authority for the poet when he echoed Mary Wollstonecraft's elder daughter, Fanny, who claimed that poets are the unacknowledged legislators of mankind. George Eliot transfers this to the novel: a profound spiritual revival. Imagination – imaginative sympathy – is to replace ill-feeling, scoring, greed, all base forms of aggression.

The other leading idea was evolution. *The Origin of Species* came out in 1859. It's long been known that Darwin did not originate the idea of evolution; it goes beyond his grandfather, Erasmus Darwin, as far back as Aristotle, who defined nature as change as distinct from stasis. Yet a creature that undergoes metamorphosis does retain the givens of its make-up. If we translate this into human terms – call it biography – it makes sense that when Marian Evans entered her outcast chrysalis and Sara Hennell felt she was writing to a stranger, Marian protested that she was what she'd always been.

If we follow the nature of the 'insurgent' she had appeared to be as a young woman in Chapman's house and, consistent with that, the rebel against society who had cast her lot with a married man, then why does she change her name to 'Mrs Lewes' and then 'George Eliot'? Simply, I think, her need for acceptance. In her journal and letters she repeatedly owns to that longing for 'approbation', a longing understandable in an outsider – though she blames herself for 'egotism'. Her novels send out a message of selflessness, a counter to egotism, most profoundly in *Middlemarch*.

George Eliot draws us into the silent struggles of a disappointed wife, Dorothea Casaubon, as she strives against fits of repulsion for her husband. And as she does so, she hones and perfects the fellow feeling of a potential St Theresa born in the wrong time and place. As an intellectually eager young woman locked in a static provincial life, Dorothea finds it in her to pity her stultified husband. He is dimly aware of his wife's evolving mind and character, and stretches out his 'dead hand' to block her even from beyond the grave.

Virginia Woolf said, famously, that *Middlemarch* is a novel for grown-up people: the power games of mediocrities – the blinkered scholar Casaubon; the wastrel son Fred Vincy; his sister Rosamond, the spoilt wife; the landowner Mr Brooke, who does nothing for his tenants but has a notion to go into politics; and the rich, manipulative elder Mr Featherstone – all show up against the calibre of the elder's carer, able Mary Garth, and the ardently willing Dorothea, who are moral beings on the margins. Without a vote, and with education reserved for well-born men, they have no access to power – self-perpetuating public power. As outsiders they present an alternative power that does not care to show its face; they persuade us that this could be, that in fact it already exists. When George Eliot tells us of Dorothea's unmarked acts of goodness, the lost voice of Elizabeth Evans continues to reach an all-time audience. The outsider ethos led George Eliot to resist 'the man of maxims'. To live by doctrine, to lace oneself up in ready-made formulae, she said, is 'to repress the inspirations that spring from growing insight'.

Through the insight of Dinah and Dorothea, the author herself came to be regarded as a counselling angel, but naturally her own effort to measure up was imperfect, as in her relations with Isaac, Chrissey and the bereft children who looked to her and to whom she was dutiful only up to a point.

Given the support of Lewes and her own wealth – the publisher George Smith paid her no less than seven thousand pounds for her least readable novel, *Romola* – she went on helping her three stepsons from a convenient distance. They were informed of her tie to their father in 1859, five years after Weimar, and there was a cordial exchange of letters. Poor Bertie struggled to express himself and his spelling is haphazard; he understood how inadequate his offering would appear. George Eliot was gratified that the boys were prepared to call her 'Mutter', along with 'Mama', their mother. She met them for the first time in Bern in 1860, when she and Lewes were en route to Italy. It was decided that the eldest, Charlie, who affirmed Mutter with ready affection, was to live at home, while the second son Thornie, also due to leave school, was to stay there for the summer. Sadly, Thornie, the most ambitious and playful of the three, thought he and his brothers might accompany their father and Mutter to Italy, but that was not to be. He had only three days in London in September before Lewes took him to live with a substitute family in Edinburgh, where he was to prepare for the Indian Civil Service examinations. He passed two and failed the third.

Charlie meanwhile was placed in the Post Office, while Bertie remained at Hofwyl school for three more years. When he came home finally in May 1863, Marian remarked, 'we are up to our ears in Boydom'. In October, Thornie was shipped off to Natal with a view to farming (the Leweses decided that it must be easier to farm in the colonies) and later Bertie went out to join his brother. The farming failed and the money their parents had given them drained away.

It must be said that the continued remoteness of the two younger sons fitted ideas of manhood at the height of the Empire. But the fact remains that both of them died young. Thornie came home to die over the course of six months in 1869. It was the only period when he lived in this home. And George Eliot found it difficult. She was put out when Thornie came downstairs, though she did assist the hired nurse and was with Thornie when he died.

Bertie struggled on in Natal, married a young woman against her father's will, and fell into a decline similar to Thornie's. A report that he looked like a ghost of himself did reach London, but there was no idea of his coming home. In 1875 he sought medical care in Durban where he died alone while his wife gave birth to a second child. George Eliot said (and no doubt believed) that there was no ground for self-reproach since she and Lewes had thought a colony with a fine climate offered Bertie 'the only fair prospect within his reach'.

Her attachment to Lewes meant that she was all but broken when he developed bowel cancer in October–November 1878. Just then, Henry James called to leave a copy of his new novel *The Europeans*, and Lewes tossed it back, saying 'away, away' – he was driven to protect George Eliot from the need to respond to a book whilst they endured the pain together.

When Lewes died two weeks later, she howled for days on end and shut herself away; it was a trial to see people. These included 'the Africans', Bertie's young widow and children (named Marian and George), who arrived uninvited in London. It was painful to tell them that they could not (as they hoped) live with her. Lewes had sent them two hundred pounds a year and they needed continued support. The one visitor she welcomed was her long-trusted friend and financial adviser John Walter Cross, whom she'd called playfully 'nephew'. The proposal from a good-looking supporter came to her as comfort.

So long as she'd lived with Lewes, her brother did not communicate with her. For Isaac, his sister's fame did not blot out her transgression. He maintained silence from 1857 until 1880 – twenty-three years – when, at the age of sixty, she married the devoted John Cross, a bachelor in his forties. His closest tie had been to his mother, who had died nine days after Lewes.

Grief then was part of it: two bereaved people finding a measure of relief in each other. Yet, inevitably, she struggled with doubt. On 17 December 1879 she copied Emily Brontë's poem 'Remembrance' into her *Journal*. An Only Love is 'cold in the earth', but then when loss proves 'powerless to destroy', the speaker learns 'how existence could be cherished, / Strengthened and fed'. But significantly the new-found love is 'without the aid of joy'.

All this is understandable, and yet there's something odd, unreal in George Eliot's marriage. Not in the wish to revive, nor in the age gap, nor even in an impulse to rewrite the story of her life, as she'd done before in three outlaw acts: when she had refused to go to church; when she had left the Midlands to seek her fortune in London, and buried in that act, distanced herself from the claims of her family; and when she had defied law and convention in taking off with Lewes. There is secrecy in the run-up to these acts; and whatever she said afterwards, even in the privacy of her journal, is somewhat veiled. There is oddly little of Cross.

What strikes me as unreal is the conventionality of the marriage, starting with a wedding in the fashionable St George's, Hanover Square. It was like a romance with respectability, after not quite passing as a married woman for a quarter of a century. It mattered hugely to George Eliot to set herself right with her brother, and, given this legal and highly public marriage, Isaac Evans consented to wish her well. George Eliot's voice is very, very careful and Isaac's stiffly formal. It's as though brother and sister sing an aria of reconciliation, trying to bridge their estrangement, yet remain divided. The stiltedness of their exchange cannot measure up to the throbbing finale to the wishful fiction of *The Mill on the Floss*.

There followed George Eliot's honeymoon in Venice and the inexplicable incident on 16 June 1880 when Mr Cross jumped or fell from a window and had to be fished from the Grand Canal. He was said to be ill. 'Delirium', Mrs Cross said. A 'nightmare', said Mr Cross. Those who saw them in Venice preserved a respectful silence.

George Eliot continued to refer to Cross as 'my dear husband' but it's my impression – in the absence of facts it can be no more – that she was shaken by this union, as he was. Her voice as counselling angel invited idolising attachments – Cross was not alone – but in the intimacy of a shared room he would have found more to his new wife, more than the benevolence and the vulnerability that had called out his protectiveness. We've marked her ardent nature, and her confidence to Barbara Leigh Smith back in 1856 had made it clear that Lewes as a lover had proved confident enough to be 'considerate'. It's worth decoding the decorous language of the 1850s. My guess would be that Lewes, for all his extrovert exuberance, was sensitive when it came to sex, ready to encourage a woman to express a desire not necessarily the same as his own and to pace himself with her. 'Unsensual' conjoined with 'considerate' did not imply sexless; on the contrary. Sexual confidence seems to me to generate her image of a pale stag in the tapestry of the room assigned to the ardently willing Dorothea in Casaubon's home where she is to find herself his less than satisfied wife.

From the time of George Eliot's return from the near-disaster in Venice, she was never quite well again. The couple moved into a large, beautiful house at 4 Cheyne Walk, overlooking the Thames. And then, soon after, the marriage was cut short when George Eliot caught a chill and died in December 1880.

———

We know what awaits Promethean provincial girls. Craving knowledge or art or a chance to voice their desires, they run into obstruction. George Eliot mined this plot — it might have been her own — in Caterina Sarti, with her soaring songs and suppressed utterance; in the reader Maggie Tulliver, bound to her philistine brother; in Dorothea Casaubon, that St Theresa of the Midland Flats, who comes to be 'a foundress of nothing'; and finally in the proud-spirited Gwendolen Harleth, who is turned into a victim of marriage by the sadistic Grandcourt. For the Victorians marital rape was not deemed to exist but it's implied in the domestic humiliation of Gwendolen and that of Isabella by Heathcliff in *Wuthering Heights*.

George Eliot was writing from the perspective of her rare liberation. Maggie was the provincial self she'd left behind, a young woman with eyes 'full of unsatisfied intelligence and unsatisfied, beseeching affection', who longed 'for something that would give her soul a sense of a home'. There is a private counterpoint, as with the unseen endurance of Claire Clairmont's life running parallel to Mary Shelley's public achievements. George Eliot's thwarted women are versions of what might have been had she not turned into 'George Eliot', the counselling angel. It's tempting to tell a fairy tale: humble girl wins fame and fortune. Bray liked to play this up, calling her an untaught farmer's daughter, an image she rejected for her father's sake. It's truer to ask: what story did she tell herself? The test, as she saw it, was whether her nature could unfold from within.

Unlike the Brontë children, it took her a long time to venture into fiction. Unlike Mary Shelley, she did not grow up in a home filled with books, nor, in her youth, did she have always before her eyes a high-flying model, the portrait of Mary Wollstonecraft in Godwin's study (and now in the National Portrait Gallery). George Eliot picked up the *Vindication of the Rights of Woman* in her mid-thirties. It was then that she seized on Wollstonecraft's challenge: women had to stretch themselves to deserve rights. No one understood better just how far she had to stretch. She was not born a genius; she became one.

# 4

# ORATOR

## Olive Schreiner

In a bare room, a woman prods memory with her pen. The shutters are closed against the sun and by night against the voices of the guards under her window. It was 'so dark that even the physical act of writing was difficult'. Future readers will know how she has to 'crush down indignation' if she is to write.

Constrained under martial law, she means to remake a book that took many years and now has been burnt by troops looting her home in Johannesburg. Report has reached her that the manuscript cannot be salvaged: the first half burnt away; the rest charred — the pages crumbled when touched. For nine months she has put it from her mind, but isolated as she is now in March 1901, regrets for her lost work stir. What memory can retrieve for a short book — she will call it *Woman and Labour* — can occupy this time of confinement and darkness by night when the law forbids a candle and even to strike a match. A resolve firms to rescue her challenge to authority from the ashes.

Twenty years ago she'd sat alone in another room with miles of veld stretching to the horizon. There too, filled with purpose, her pen had travelled over the page as she finished her novel *The Story of an African Farm*. She'd carried it to London and, pressing her manuscript under her waterproof, trod from one London publisher to another. Chapman & Hall, who had turned down another of her novels, accepted the *African Farm* on the advice of their reader, the novelist George Meredith. The publisher of Dickens, Thackeray and Anthony Trollope, they paid this unknown colonial only eighteen pounds, in contrast with the hundreds of pounds that George Henry Lewes had secured for each of the *Scenes* by the unknown George Eliot.

Chapman & Hall's sole editorial suggestion was that the heroine marry her seducer, otherwise 'Smith's, the railway booksellers, would not put it on their stalls'.

The author refused. And she was right, for political and literary figures like Gladstone, Wilde and Shaw had only praise for the *African Farm*. Workers liked its care for obscure lives, and women its outrage over subjection. Its moral vision had the appeal of scripture. The uneducated shepherd boy Waldo and the orphan girl Lyndall, whose souls are awake, continue to suffer: Waldo in silence; Lyndall compelled to raise a voice not heard before. This is no counselling angel. She becomes a fearless speaker, defying authority and refusing to marry an unworthy man even though he has fathered her child.

For all its courage, the novel came out under a man's name, Ralph Iron. As with Ellis, Currer and Acton Bell, and of course George Eliot, a woman publishing in 1883 still had to conceal her gender if she was to secure unbiased reading of her work. The *African Farm* sold ninety-seven thousand copies, followed by the feminist *Dreams* (1890), which sold almost as many[*] and was widely translated. The pseudonym did not hold for long, however, and the author's female identity became, if anything, an asset with the rise of the New Woman in the 1890s.

The woman writing in the dark years later, back home in a British-held *dorp* or hamlet in the northern reaches of the Cape Colony, is a world-wide celebrity. When imperial troops come upon her in this remote place, they telegraph their Commander, Lord Kitchener, 'Have got Olive Schreiner here.'

Whatever happened to her was bound to be reported in the British press. He telegraphs back, 'Leave the woman alone.'

---

[*] Ninety thousand copies.

———

Native ground was, at first, a mission station, Wittebergen, on the border of Basutoland. Like Emily Brontë, Olive Schreiner was a creature of her terrain and also the daughter of an evangelical preacher who was a stranger in a strange land.

A German, his name Gottlob – lover of God – marked him out for a different course from his shoemaking origins. He trained as a missionary, first in Basel, then with the Church Missionary Society in London.[*] There was obstinacy, arguments, fallings out, and at the age of twenty-two Gottlob Schreiner joined the London Missionary Society.

Two further moves secured his future: he was naturalised as a British citizen, and in 1837 married an accomplished London girl from the Lyndall family of doctors and clerics. Rebekah Blom Lyndall[†] was too young, at eighteen, to know what she was taking on in marrying this penniless foreigner with grey-blue eyes, broad shoulders and curls clustering on his forehead, whose angelic singing voice may have suggested more than he could be. A shared religious language elided whatever was lost in translation.

Rebekah's late father had been the charismatic Revd Samuel Lyndall, a Non-Conformist with Calvinist leanings, who had led a chapel in Old Jewry in the City of London. He was said to be eccentric, with an eye full of fire and given to 'strong truths, strongly spoken'. This was a different sort of Dissenter from George Eliot's preacher aunt who spread a spirit of love. The Calvinism left its mark: a fixation on sin, guilt, denial of pleasure and a belief that depravity had to be beaten out of children. Olive Schreiner's writings speak of this or that 'little' child who is subjected to

[*] This Society has a place in the family history of Virginia Woolf. Her great-grandfather, John Venn, was one of the founders, and his son, Henry Venn, was honorary secretary of the Church Missionary Society at the time that Gottlob Schreiner joined it.
[†] The name Blom, or Blum, is common in northern Europe and also amongst Jews. It's often said that Olive Schreiner had a Jewish look, and the same goes for her mother, especially a photo in old age, but so far there is no evidence to back this.

righteous sadism. The father of Samuel Lyndall had flogged him for riding a donkey on a Sunday. This image of her great-grandfather, 'cane in hand', was all Olive knew of him. As a child throbbing with rage, she made up stories about 'Poor Uncle James', her grandfather's eldest brother, flogged at school and flogged when he came home, so that he ran away to sea, never to be heard of again.

But Samuel Lyndall grew up to be as stern as his father. A child would be marched to the top of the gloomy house in Hoxton to pass the day on bread and water for as little as laughing on Sunday. Yet Samuel softened to his daughter Rebekah, a child of his old age. Seated behind him on the pulpit as he preached, she dared to tickle his long silk stockings. She tucked her uneaten crusts under his plate. He warmed to this child who had his face, with large, dark eyes.

Before he landed in England, Gottlob had seen in a dream the face of a beautiful woman with large, dark eyes. The widow of Samuel Lyndall sometimes invited foreign students to dine, Gottlob amongst them, and there on the wall was a portrait of Samuel. Gottlob was stunned to see the very face in his dream. Rebekah happened to be away that night, and on her return Gottlob was ready to marry her. She was short, with those dark eyes, and dark hair scooped to one side of a cocked head and looped in modish ringlets. She loved reading, music and flower-painting.

For her wedding she wore dove-grey satin and pinned a bride's customary flowers under her bonnet. When they were signing their names in the vestry of Moorfields Tabernacle, the minister saw fit to tear the wreath out. Flowers were 'frivolities', not for a missionary's wife.

Rebekah left England with an album full of farewells, and no notion of what awaited her on an African frontier. There, at the age of twenty, among bush-covered mountains along the Kat River, she gave birth to her first child. They were far from a doctor. Her ignorant husband, assisting at the birth, sent for an untrained tribal midwife. The experience taught Rebekah never to repeat this situation.

Before Olive was born, the family trundled northward in an ox-wagon, which came to a stop on a treeless plain between stony hills. Why were they stopping?, Rebekah asked. The answer was that her husband had taken it into his head to start a mission in the wilderness.

Rebekah wept when she saw this spot, which Gottlob blithely named Basel in memory of his joy in Swiss walks and flowers. The reality of a dry, sandy plain might do for a hermit, but Gottlob had a wife and children. He built them a house of sticks tied together at the top, Olive heard from her older brothers and sisters. The cover was so low it looked like a roof standing on the ground. Naked men danced near by. A lion chose this spot to doze with his head on his paws.

The Schreiners moved on; three children died: Albert soon after birth, Oliver at five, Emile aged two — the last two within six months of each other in 1854. Emile's death happened while Rebekah was pregnant with her ninth child. She walked up and down, up and down, and when the baby was born on 24 March 1855 she named the new child after her lost ones: Olive Emilie Albertina Schreiner. Her three-fold name was freighted with the Schreiners' grief, and they seem to have distanced her, as though she could not replace her brothers. As she grew older she found it in her to pity her parents.

Her father, to her, was a holy innocent whose 'child's heart' unfitted him for adult existence. He moved from one position to another, switched from employment under the London Missionary Society to the Wesleyan Missionary Society, and traded when the rules of his post forbade it, and then when he lost that post he failed in business. While his wife regretted the absence of learning in his sermons, Olive saw him as an unworldly dreamer (fictionalised as Otto in the *African Farm*). When it came to converts Gottlob did stress attendance and ritual: baptism, confirmation and Christian marriage. He ticked off these outward markers of faith — the numbers game a missionary had to play.

Apart from his child's heart, what mattered most to his daughter was Gottlob's moral courage. When a runaway slave, bleeding and mutilated, turned up, he refused to return her to her master, who came to claim his property, pointed his rifle at Gottlob's chest and threatened to shoot. Gottlob at length paid for Sarah, the sum eked out with sheep, and she remained with the family.

Discipline lay with Rebekah.

Swinging on the door one fine day, Olive said, '*Ag*, it's so nice outside.'

The local '*Ag*', open-mouthed with the 'g' sounded as a fricative far back in the throat, was a forbidden way to say 'oh'. Rebekah thought it proper to speak with lips almost closed. (At exactly this time, Dickens has Little Dorrit, in training to be a lady, taught to repeat words that will bring her lips into a rosebud: papa, prunes, prism, potatoes.) For uttering an unmannerly sound — a sign of the girl's adaptation to a colonial norm — her mother beat Olive with her switch of twigs tied together. This beating the child never forgot. It filled her with hate, extended to God. Ever after, she made up scenes where a child's innocence meets with thrashing. Abusers in her fictions take out their inadequacy or degradation on their dependants: children, wives and dark-skinned workers.

Olive did not dwell on her mother's harshness. Instead she thought of her as a 'genius' thwarted by marriage. Rebekah might have been an advocate, cleric or doctor, her daughter thought. She observed how keenly her mother read medical books. Olive likened her to a grand piano locked before it's ever played and used instead as a dining table. Throughout its existence it has a sense of another use it might have had. Emily Dickinson distils such a fate in a single line: 'Born — Bridalled — Shrouded — in a Day'. It's a narrative Olive meant to resist.

As a child, Olive asked a Basuto woman if she believed in God.

She'd heard of the white men's God, the woman replied, but she did not believe in him.

'Why?'

'Because they say he is good, and if he were good, would he have made woman?'

She then poured out her bitterness at her subjection. Olive watched another tribal woman be beaten by her husband — her legitimate owner, who had bought her with cattle — then silently pick up her baby and, tying it to her bleeding back, return to work. Such women were fatalistic – this was the way the world was.

The immediate catalyst for her early loss of faith was the death of her baby sister Ellie (Helen) in 1864.

Olive and baby Ellie had a special bond, common in big families where a mother's attention is stretched thin. Olive would look back on this child as proof that perfection did exist. She slept with the body before Ellie was buried. She dedicated her unfinished novel *From Man to Man* to 'MY SISTER LITTLE ELLIE WHO DIED, AGED EIGHTEEN MONTHS, WHEN I WAS NINE YEARS OLD 'Nor knowest thou what argument / Thy life to thy neighbour's creed hath lent'. In 'The Child's Day', a 'prelude' to this novel,* a Karoo child of five called Rebekah – an 'incarnation' of Olive herself – comes upon the body of a new-born sister (one of twins) in a back room, and finds the baby's hand cold. Little Rebekah is treated with impatience by a servant who can't take in the child's feeling, similar to that of the philosophic child Waldo in *The Story of an African Farm*, when he awakens to mortality.

Where George Eliot, in her outcast years, had developed a rational kind of sympathy (requiring, she tells us, a hard-won justness towards people like Maggie Tulliver's repressive aunts or Dorothea Casaubon's unresponsive husband), Olive Schreiner came to sympathy as a child; she felt spontaneous compassion for victims. In this, she herself bears out the belief, put to the test in *Frankenstein* and *Wuthering Heights*, that human nature is wholesome until it is corrupted.

As a child, sympathy came to her as a renegade emotion that could not accommodate a God who determines the undeserved death of innocents. She also deplored Christianity's lack of concern for animals as sentient creatures. When Olive was losing her faith at the precocious age of ten, she could still take comfort in the non-violent message of the Sermon on the Mount. But her mother was not pleased.

---

* Olive Schreiner circulated 'The Child's Day' to many, including her mother and brother Will, as well as friends. She thought it the best thing she wrote. It came to her in a single burst.

At twelve, when her parents could not afford to keep her, she was sent to live in Kruis [Cross] Street, Cradock (a Karoo town in the dry interior of the eastern Cape) with her older brother Theo. The house had a dung floor and a yellow-wood ceiling, and the kitchen, according to rural custom, was painted turquoise to repel flies. An older sister, Ettie (Henrietta), kept house. Physically, Ettie and Olive manifest the difference of their parents: Ettie fair, broad-faced, rather Wagnerian; Olive, five years younger, small and glowingly dark like their mother.

Theo (Theophilus Lyndall Schreiner) was in the mould of the stern Lyndalls, with a face as hard as the stones where he was born – so Olive thought. He saw no obstacle in the path of duty. Olive refused to go to church, to the fury of her uncomprehending brother and sister. Olive stood her ground, as Mary Ann Evans had done in Coventry, and then Olive too relented for the sake of family peace. To pass the time in church, she would look at her hand in the way a child might look at a leaf as something new and strange. She called this 'looking at things really', as a child might, without the interference of 'a few preconceived ideas hang[ing] like a veil between the child and the outer world'. Her reading of Shelley would later confirm this for her: 'that men of genius are always childlike', and that *'Genius does not invent, it perceives!'*

Theo was principal of the government-aided school in Cradock, while Ettie started a school for girls. So Olive may have had some schooling between the ages of twelve and fifteen. It's conceivable because it would have cost her parents nothing. She said later that not sixpence was spent on her education – not as a girl, she meant, in contrast to the education of her brothers. Her eldest brother, Fred, was sent to boarding school in England. Her youngest brother, Will, was with her in Cradock but then was sent away to school and eventually to Cambridge University.[*]

Over the next few years Olive was dispatched from one to another of her older siblings. She hardly lived with her parents again. Her earliest surviving letters are to her eldest, married sister, Catherine Findlay,

---

[*] William Philip Schreiner would eventually succeed Cecil Rhodes as Prime Minister of the Cape Colony in 1898.

in Fraserburg, a country town towards the western Cape. For the most part, these are carefully untroubled letters, offering affection and asking nothing. A second elder sister, Alice, also in Fraserburg and married to wealthy Mr Hemming, did have Olive to stay from time to time, but never for long. These two sisters were always pregnant and a frightful number of their children died. Alice gave birth to sixteen, and only four survived childhood. Not surprisingly, Alice was dead by her forties, and Catherine ended her life in an asylum, maddened by grief. These eldest sisters did not offer Olive a home.

In Fraserburg, this girl with black hair down her back was seen pacing up and down the Hemmings' long *stoep*. She always looked for a 'walking up and down place', whether as a child of three, pacing the coconut matting of the mission-house passage while she made up stories, or as a young woman of eighteen, her hands clenched behind her back, treading out silent ambitions in that small-town setting. The movement between two points, not restless but measured, forms the intellectual pattern of her life.

The mental isolation of a thinking girl was as extreme in the sleepy provinces of a colony, as it had been for Mary Ann Evans in the English Midlands a generation before. Olive recognised herself in George Eliot's autobiographical novel: 'I love *The Mill on the Floss*', she said. During the years when she was moved around and deprived of formal education, she was reading Darwin (*The Descent of Man*), Mill (*Principles of Political Economy*) and the life of Jesus (translated from the German by the unnamed Mary Ann Evans), which drew her to Jesus as a 'loving human soul' who was 'so tender to others'.

In June 1871, when she was staying with an aunt in Basutoland, fifty miles from anywhere, a stranger knocked at the door one rainy winter night and had to be given shelter. It was Willie Bertram, whose father had preceded Gottlob Schreiner at the Wittebergen mission. Bertram lent her Herbert Spencer's *First Principles* and Olive lay all night in front of the fire, reading avidly about the idea of evolution.

'I always think that when Christianity burst on the dark Roman world it was what that book was to me', she said later when she identified this as the book a stranger gives the young boy Waldo in the *African Farm*. Such encounters are indeed like the biblical meetings of strangers in the wilderness. Her mother had taught her to read, but she craved knowledge.

At sixteen Olive joined Theo and Ettie at the diamond fields of New Rush (later Kimberley). This rough spot was her base for the next two years: a mining camp with jostling 'digs' and 'claims', racist clashes, drink and disease. One New Year's Day, with the harsh sun trained on the trampled ground, Olive boasts to be one of a minority *not* sick in bed. Dysentery raged,* but these unsanitary conditions did not deter her. For New Rush was where she began to write. Prostitutes and violence: with such material to hand, she was taking in raw life where, strange though it may seem, it was not threatening for her and her sister Ettie to lose their way at night in the sprawl of dusty tents. Their ladylike appearance and manner sufficed for protection, in the same way that Mary Kingsley's corsetry and full-skirted Victorian dress kept her safe throughout her travels in West Africa.

Theo meant to find a great big diamond that would change the family fortunes. If it came his way, he told Olive kindly, he would send her to America, to study at a women's college. Olive decided that she wished to study medicine, a fulfilment of her mother's unused bent. 'It is the great wish of my life,' Olive confided to her eldest sister, 'and I hope that it is destined to be realized one of these days, and not like so many of our hopes to come to nothing.' While Cecil John Rhodes, there at the same time, laid hands on enough diamonds to take over the De Beers mining company and kick-start the fortune that would make him one of the richest men in the world, for Olive's family the dig did come to nothing.

Needing to earn her keep, Olive began to work as a governess. She was still only sixteen when she negotiated a salary from the Robinson family in Dordrecht. 'They wished me to live with them just as one of the family

---

* My great-great-grandfather died of dysentery in the similar conditions of Johannesburg in the 1880s.

but I preferred coming to some definite arrangement', she said. 'I think it is always best.' She insisted on thirty pounds a year, a meagre sum in 1871. A century earlier Mary Wollstonecraft had earned forty pounds a year as a governess in County Cork.

Though the Robinsons were kind enough, she felt useless and longed to leave, 'but where to go to I don't see just at present', she burst out to her sister Catherine. 'I feel so anxious, miserable and distracted just now . . . I am thoroughly sick of this life always having to move on and never know-ing where to move on to.' She could not turn to her indigent parents, and neither of her eldest sisters responded to this cry.

It's not surprising that when a stranger came along and opened his arms she fell into them. At the Robinsons' she met a German immigrant, Julius Gau. After a brief acquaintance in the winter of 1872, they set off together in early August with a view to announcing their engagement to Olive's parents who were now living in Herzog, a hundred miles east-wards. An unchaperoned journey with a man, especially overnight, was not what well-conducted girls did. George Eliot had treated a similar situation in *The Mill on the Floss*, where Maggie goes off with Stephen Guest and comes back unmarried – which is to say ruined. Gau, ten years older, would have known as much. Olive, only seventeen and desperate for a life, was naïve enough to trust him, even though his prospect of marriage was vague: it might be in January, he told her, or it might be postponed for a year or more. His enticing plan was to carry her off to England, but he neglected to say what he'd do there.

Soon after reaching the Schreiners, Gau departed. Olive reports a head-ache when she informs her eldest sister, rather flatly, of the engagement. Rebekah must have warned her daughter to keep quiet, for Olive mentions the danger of small-town gossip. Then silence falls. Plainly a cover-up, apart from one fact: the engagement was off. Was Gau, who became man-ager of an insurance company, put off when he saw the Schreiners' poverty? Or did Gau get all he wanted on the strength of his promise? The heroine of the *African Farm* has this to say about sexual betrayal: 'A man's love is a fire of olive-wood. It leaps higher every moment; it roars, it blazes, it shoots out red flames; it threatens to wrap you round and devour you . . . You are self-reproached for your own chilliness and want of reciprocity. The next day when you go to warm your hands a little, you find a few ashes!'

For the next few months Olive lay low with her parents, until Theo invited her back to New Rush at the end of 1872. From this time and for years to come, Olive was averse to marriage, and she would dramatise her aversion in the *African Farm* where Lyndall rebuffs an offer of marriage from the Stranger who seduced her.

At eighteen, she fell into conversation with a tribal woman, who confirmed her view:

> She was a woman whom I cannot think of otherwise than as a woman of genius. In language more eloquent and intense than I have ever heard from the lips of any other woman, she painted the condition of the women of her race; the labour of women, the anguish of woman as she grew older, and the limitations of her life closed in about her, her sufferings under the condition of polygamy and subjection; all this she painted with a passion and intensity I have not known equalled; and yet . . . there was a stern and almost majestic attitude of acceptance of the inevitable; life and the conditions of her race being what they were.

For the next two years she shifted between New Rush and her wealthy sister Alice in Fraserburg. Then, minus a plan, Olive had again to fall back on her parents – knowing that they were too poor to keep her. At nineteen she felt suicidal as she set out on the sea route via Cape Town. One day while she was there she read Emerson's exhilarating essay 'Self-Reliance', which restored her. Like Mary Shelley in her outcast situation, she found sustenance in books.

Her boat landed at Algoa Bay [Port Elizabeth] and from there it took a further four days of overland travel to reach her parents. During this journey she had water but no money to buy food. And when she finally reached them, her parents gave her a cold reception. Trying to swallow was difficult, and suddenly she found it hard to breathe. It was probably then that she had her first asthma attack.

Gottlob and Rebekah themselves had not enough to eat, and lived entirely on hand-outs from their older children. Her father wore a son's cast-offs. Olive, shamed to burden them, had to take the first post she could find; at nineteen she went to work for Mr Weakley, a shopkeeper, auctioneer and local newspaper editor in Colesberg, a country town to the north.

Writing to her mother, Olive reports on her spacious room in a fine house with two servants. She does not complain, but her record of her working day reveals what the Weakleys exacted from dawn till late at night. There were household tasks to be completed before breakfast; then teaching the children till one, before a quick change into outdoor clothes to accompany Mr Weakley to his shop where she worked till sunset – this was the hardest part of the day – then a quick supper, the children to be put to bed and, to complete her working day, household sewing with Mrs Weakley until 10.30 at night. Not a moment, then, to read or write. Mrs Weakley worked in the shop in the mornings, and Olive was expected to oversee the servants (and their care of the baby) and get through more sewing while she taught. The baby and older children caught measles, so Olive added nursing to her duties.

Afterwards she recalled Colesberg as the vilest place on earth. This unusual loathing, I suspect, was not the exacting hours; about those she wrote with composure. Something else forced her to leave suddenly.

We must remember how beautiful she was, with her alight black eyes, silken black tresses and olive sheen. A Weakley family photograph shows a rather washed-out Mrs Weakley with thin, crimped ringlets. Olive's unplanned departure, so determined that she had to forgo her salary, suggests that Mr Weakley made a pass at this ardent girl living in his home. The law, the police and social opinion tend to blame the victim, and Olive was already guarding her reputation after the Gau episode. She had to beg her sister Catherine for the coach fare. Without that, she told Catherine, she didn't know what would become of her.

Olive was rescued by a recommendation to a Dutch family living in wild terrain about forty miles south of Cradock: Mr Christiaan Christoffel

Fouché, who farmed at Klein* Ganna Hoek, was in need of a governess for his daughters.

Here, Olive came to know a way of life she could draw on for the *African Farm*. It was self-sufficient, wild, remote from civilisation; the bumpy gravel road was (and still is) rough, almost forbidding, and there were few visitors. Nor were visits made — only when a baby was born did the Fouchés trek to Cradock for the baptism. During 1875 Olive went on writing her first novel, *Undine* (unpublished during her lifetime), in a lean-to room with its own outside door. The roof leaked so badly that she sometimes wrote under an umbrella and she was grateful for an old waterproof Catherine had passed on to her. The farmhouse was perched high on the side of a mountain and facing other bush-covered mountains, then and now with no habitation as far as the eye can see.[†] If, like Olive, you were bent on washing, it had to be outdoors in a mountain stream. She liked to sunbathe naked on a rock; 'there is nothing so restful as a rock', she declared. No one could see her, only the enfolding mountains and low bush stretching for miles under a bared, all-seeing sun. Like Emily Brontë, this woman is formed by a timeless landscape.

It was one of the happiest times of her life. The family was hospitable and respectful; their girls affectionate and the eldest a serious learner; their progress with English was rapid. After the Weakleys, the workload was light, only five to six hours a day, and then she was free to 'study'.

The Fouchés wanted her to stay but paid too little: only thirty pounds a year. She thought ruefully that she would have to save until she was eighty to have the means to go to America. So when her promised year came to an end, she found a better-paid post as governess to the daughters of a Dutch Reformed minister turned farmer — but just for a year, as the Fouchés lured her back with an offer of fifty-five pounds' annual salary when they moved to a farm, Leliekloof, on a mountain, the Winterberg,

---

* 'Klein' literally means 'small', but in this context it is the adjoining farm to the large Ganna Hoek, owned by Olive Schreiner's friend Mrs Elrida Cawood.
† The Klein Ganna Hoek farmhouse has now been demolished, but Ganna Hoek is still there. It can't be seen from the site of Klein Ganna Hoek, as there is mountainous terrain between the two. Ganna Hoek, to this day in the hands of the Cawoods, is now a hunting lodge.

to the north-east of Cradock. These farms are even more remote. The tracks are still almost impossibly rough with baked, prickly miles of bush stretching to the horizon.

Solitude suited Olive Schreiner. Her early twenties were her most fertile years for writing fiction. One of the attractions of her novels is a directness that seems to come from a soul waking in the veld. Speaking from so remote a place, she felt free to express what she urgently wanted to say about cruelty and injustice. In giving voice to the voiceless, a child or a woman, there's a release of pent-up power in her resonant words.

She knew or learnt some Dutch words and expressions, which enter her writing. She remained always something of an orphan and homeless wanderer, making an imaginative home in the landscape. Some employers feared Olive's free-thinking might endanger her charges. The Fouchés, in contrast, could be at once devout and tolerant.

She grew fonder of the children, and their parents invited her to stand as godmother to their new baby. This in itself tells us about her status in this family, rare for a Victorian governess — we recall how Charlotte Brontë, as a governess, was placed on the servants' floor. At Leliekloof this governess could live in books; and as the pages of her novels piled up, she had no wish to change places with anyone in the world.

One day she came upon a coloured* prostitute in labour, lying behind a hedge, with a child of two watching. Olive assisted at the birth. This episode may have been a source for *From Man to Man*,† a novel she began in 1876. It tells of two sisters: the one, Bertie, seduced and abandoned to prostitution; the other, Rebekah, prostituted in a marriage to a philandering man who impregnates their servant. Rebekah brings up his dark daughter without his knowing who the child is, and the story builds towards a

---

* Mixed race, as distinct from the Bantu-speaking peoples further east and to the north.
† An early title was 'Saints and Sinners'. Published posthumously in 1926.

confrontation when he reproaches his wife for introducing a bastard child of colour into his respectable home.

She wrote as well *The Story of an African Farm* while she was a governess. Lyndall of the novel, as a child, lives with a Dutch woman and with her cousin Em, but as a thinking creature she's alone. When Tant' Sannie, the girls' mindless guardian, holds Em's head against her knee and strikes the child on one cheek, then on the other, Lyndall promises herself that when she is grown and strong 'I will hate everything that has power, and help everything that is weak'. Those about her see her strength without comprehension. She is like Jane Eyre as a child: both are in a weak position as girl orphans dependent on unloving guardians.

Once the Lyndall of the novel is an adult, she tells men that an authentic woman is not what they assume. 'Men are like the earth and we are like the moon; we turn always one side to them, and they think there is no other, because they don't see it — but there is.' Most females have been warped by an upbringing that trains them to '*Seem*'. Finishing schools finish girls off so that what they 'are not to use' becomes 'atrophied'. (John Stuart Mill, one of Schreiner's heroes, said the same: unwanted qualities, presumably intellect and agency, are cast out into the cold until they freeze.) Lyndall shows up a colonial Englishman, Gregory Rose: posturing, self-deluded and weak, propped by stale phrases of love and supremacy. And then there's the Stranger. She would rather die than put herself in the power of such a man, even though he attracts her physically.

'If you do love me,' he asked her, 'why is it that you will not marry me?'

'Because, if I had been married to you for a year, I should have come to my senses. . . . You call into activity one part of my nature; there is a higher part that you know nothing of, that you never touch. If I married you, afterwards it would arise and assert itself, and I should hate you always, as I do now sometimes.'

When she writes this, the young Olive is aware of the sexual drive and the risk it poses. Through the humiliating Gau episode alone she would have discovered that – in this time and place – if a woman gratifies desire, or even appears to do so, she is trapped and unable to move forward as a free-thinker. She plays this out in the *African Farm*.

The novel is more concerned with the shaping of character than with plot. Though we move from childhood to adulthood, this is not the usual sort of *Bildungsroman* because the public world doesn't matter. The closest model is the Bible, where character feeds into moral debate and parable, and where stories turn into revelation and exhortation delivered by a prophetic voice. The *African Farm* exposes grotesque, almost comic evil in a confidence trickster, Bonaparte Blenkins, with his gleeful cruelty; and another form of evil – seductive, insidious, educated – in the Stranger, Lyndall's seducer. The novel is allegorical, the veld a setting for figures of endurance and degradation.

Schreiner explores the forced degradation of black functionaries about the farm; the complementary degradation of their employer, the Dutch *vrou*, no more than a small-brained animal, wadded in flesh; and the casual degradation of the black wife because her husband has bought her with heads of cattle (*lobola*), and what's more, she is not the less bound to him when he kicks her, nor does he walk with less quiet dignity across the veld.

And yet, in the midst of this there exists extraordinary goodness. There is Lyndall who bears an illegitimate child and there's her soul's brother, the unworldly Waldo, another thinker, who spends his life in menial occupations, unnoticed, mocked, once hideously thrashed by Blenkins, once sodden with drink. These two, Lyndall and Waldo, are shaped more by the veld than by humans, and so are rather remote to us. They do declare their thoughts, but don't draw us into intimacy. Nelly Dean's confiding voice in *Wuthering Heights* makes a friend of the reader; Lyndall speaks more deliberately to the future.

She speaks in particular about the fate of woman: to Waldo, as revelation; to Gregory Rose, as a voice soaring above his reach; to her seducer, with resolute contempt. A voice like this, rising in the midst of an imitative colony, cannot expect to be heard by those around her. This frees her to talk past them, most impressively when she imagines an ideal relation that might exist between the sexes, based on the 'interknit love song' of a species of bird, the *kokkeviet*, which Schreiner listened to in the veld.

In 1880, at Leliekloof, she was revising the *African Farm* each morning before dawn, wretchedly unsure of it. She had to control an impulse to throw it into the farm dam. Then, at the age of twenty-six, she made a dramatic decision: to leave the Colony and go to Britain. As she put it to her family (who contributed to the cost of travel), her aim was not primarily publication. There was the long-held wish to be a doctor. Since she could not afford the fees for medical training, she had resolved to become a nurse and had found a place to train at the Edinburgh Royal Infirmary.

But it was not to be. After only four or five days in Edinburgh she had an asthma attack and her eldest brother, Fred, by now a schoolmaster in Eastbourne, took her away. She came to rely on him as 'Dadda'.

Instead she went to lectures at the London School of Medicine for Women, established in 1874 by the pioneering women doctors Sophia Jex-Blake, Elizabeth Garrett Anderson and Elizabeth Blackwell, together with Thomas Huxley. Two years later the British Parliament had passed an act to licence qualified graduates irrespective of gender.

Eighty years earlier, in 1796, Jane Austen, aged twenty-one, had to be joking when she threatened to turn doctor if she were to find herself alone in London. Now professional futures were opening up through the efforts of advancing women: the Quaker feminist and abolitionist Lucretia Mott; Margaret Fuller, the intellectual journalist who was a model for George Eliot; and those who broke through the resistant doors of the medical establishment, starting with Florence Nightingale's reforms of army negligence in the sick-wards of the Crimea.

Sadly, asthma attacked Olive again, and Fred advised her to stick to writing (propped by a generous offer to support her with fifty pounds a year). Her novel of an outsider, determined to find and live by what she is, was published in 1883 by a not very hopeful Chapman & Hall. The 'kind reception at the hands of the critics here surprised me much', she said in an elated reply to an engaging letter from a young man called Havelock Ellis, forwarded by her publisher. 'My dear Sir,' she wrote, 'There is too much moralising in the story', but she wanted him to know 'the pleasure your expression of sympathy' had given her. In no time the author from the back of beyond was swept up in London's free-thinking, socialist and utopian circles.

———

Henry Havelock Ellis, the future psychologist of sex, first saw Olive sitting 'with hands spread on thighs, and above, the beautiful head with large dark eyes, at once so expressive and observant'. She was small – just five foot – with a quick, mobile mouth, an eager expression and animated eyes, pointed at the corners. Her dark, curly hair was cut in a high fringe across a low forehead, with the rest drawn back behind the ears. Her figure appeared soft and round; not encased in the proper, hard-edged corset, its bones forcing breasts upward and squeezing the waist to emphasise the hips. She was the kind to support dress reform, but it's more likely that she wore loose clothing, smocks, pinafores, wrap-arounds, to ease breathing.

Ellis was at this time a medical student in London, where Olive lodged for the most part during the 1880s. He was a member of a reforming group called the Fellowship of the New Life and became an early member of the Fabian Society when it was founded in 1884, along with Beatrice Potter (later Beatrice Webb), George Bernard Shaw and the poet Edward Carpenter. Their progressive socialism was an alternative to Marxist revolution, and later would turn into the Labour Party.

When Ellis arrived at her door on 19 May 1884 to escort her to a meeting of the Progressive Association (a small group of ethical free-thinkers), she had to conceal her disappointment that he looked 'sad in body' but nonetheless an intimate friendship developed: Ellis delighting in the strength he saw in her; she delighting in his discernment. She called him 'my other-self'. He wanted, he told her, 'an *immense realisation* of you'.

As soon as his exams were done in the summer of 1885, he joined her on holiday at Bole Hill above Wirksworth in the Peak District. She was aware of George Eliot's girlhood visit to Wirksworth, the encounter with her aunt, the original of the preacher in *Adam Bede*, and it intrigued her to hear that Elizabeth Evans 'lies buried here'.

What spoilt the holiday was the arrival of Edward Aveling along with Eleanor Marx, the youngest daughter of Karl Marx. They were on honeymoon without being married. Tussy (as Eleanor was called) and Olive Schreiner had made friends quickly in 1882, before the *African Farm* was published, but Aveling was a swindler, scrounger and ladies' man who drew Tussy into a long-term liaison that eventually ended in her suicide. (Aveling had a wife from whom he was separated, and when she died he married again under a pseudonym without telling Tussy.)

Olive had intimations of '*horror*' in Aveling's company. 'Every time I see him this shrinking grows stronger', she confided to Ellis, and she had to see Aveling every day. 'I love her, but *he* makes me so unhappy', she went on. 'He is so selfish, but that doesn't account for my feeling of dread.'

There was gossip about Olive and Ellis but their tie eludes a label. She didn't want to kiss him and she told him so, yet they were physically close in a way that was easy and comforting. When she felt alone, an expatriate single woman, she longed for him to be in her bed, and she could tell him this without a sexual risk. She was extraordinarily candid about her sexual nature as Ellis made notes. She confided her terror of sexual involvement: a fear that it demeaned her and that to be aroused made her feel like a prostitute. She spoke of her attraction to employers, their advances and her passionate desires, including her longing for a soulmate.

With Ellis, there was the closeness of a love affair without expressing themselves through sex, or not fully. It's impossible to draw the line between friendship and love-play. Ellis was at once a confidant, a comforter, a medical investigator and a therapist. As an orphan of sorts from the age of twelve, what Olive craved was 'tender' love. Ellis offered a gentle, even maternal kind of love and she offered him something of the same.

She was drawn to Englishmen who wished to overcome gender conventions: as well as Ellis there was Edward Carpenter, who was openly homosexual; and, importantly, the mathematician Karl Pearson, a professor at University College, who sent her a paper he had written on women's nature and prospects. In the mid-1880s they were both members of a club that Pearson and Schreiner wished to name 'the Wollstonecraft' after Mary Wollstonecraft, but others called the Men's and Women's Club. Schreiner's manner was visionary; her gestures emphatic; her dark eyes glowed as she spoke. Mary Wollstonecraft, she said, is 'one of ourselves'. Wollstonecraft 'knew': she'd foreseen a transformation of gender, 'the mighty sexual change that is coming upon us'. The two sexes seemed still a mystery: 'What in the inmost nature they are . . . Future ages will have to solve it.'

Her eloquence broke in on the earnest deliberations of the club. She was curious about the way that Wollstonecraft had managed to retain her independence during her marriage to Godwin.

In May 1886 a publisher approached Olive Schreiner to introduce a new edition of the *Vindication* to mark the centenary of its publication in 1892. She in turn approached Pearson, hoping he might collaborate. 'She is the greatest of English women because she saw a hundred years ago with regard to sex and sex relationships what a few see today, and what the world will see in three hundred years' time.'

That May, during a visit to Bournemouth, she heard that Wollstone-craft and Godwin were buried there, in St Peter's churchyard, together with their daughter. Schreiner, loving Shelley's poems, went to view a memorial to him and Mary Shelley at Christchurch Priory. To her dismay, what she saw was a marble corpse lying in the lap of an idealised Mary. Sir Percy and Lady Shelley had commissioned this beatifying image based on Michelangelo's *Pietà*.

Monument by Henry Weekes, Christchurch Priory (1853–4)

'That ghastly dead thing', Schreiner protested. 'Shelley couldn't die: he never died. "I change but cannot die."' She thought of Shelley's skylark, and the blue sky outside 'spoke much more of him'.

She asked Pearson to lend her the *Vindication* and Godwin's memoir of Mary Wollstonecraft, admitting that 'the great point of interest in her to me is her life'.

What should have been a preface expanded to a running commentary on Godwin's memoir; and then expanded (she confided to Mrs Philpot, a member of the Pearson circle) into 'the substance of all my thoughts on the man and woman question'. The scope of such an undertaking overwhelmed her. Schreiner was too akin to Wollstonecraft for her entire comfort: both had pitied their mothers; both had rejected marriage as disabling to women; both were so outspoken that their writings verge on oratory; both were committed to independence yet at the same time promoted women's traditions of domestic nurture; and both were given to intense and sometimes disabling attachments.

Schreiner believed that an independent woman affronting her destiny could not easily expect to find an appropriate mate. In January 1886 she turned down her doctor, the distinguished physician Horatio Bryan Donkin,* thinking, 'I must be free, you know, I must be *free*.' This rejection of an English gentleman by an expatriate young woman is curiously like Henry James's recent fiction about aspiring Isabel Archer, from Albany in upstate New York, who wants to be free to open up a new path of existence, so refuses kind, nice, but traditional Lord Warburton.

Schreiner's fret over Donkin's love suggests how much there was to recommend him. Not only would she have had medical care at hand but such a marriage would have taken her out of makeshift lodgings. She may have been deterred by her wish for freedom, but I think more likely by an attachment to Pearson, who was not inclined to return the feeling.

---

* Horatio Bryan Donkin (later Sir Horatio) was physician, psychologist and friend to both Karl Marx and Friedrich Engels. He was appointed Medical Commissioner for Prisons, and took great interest in the psychology of criminals.

During this attachment she struggled to maintain the limited, intellectual friendship, which was all he wanted of her — and then stopped wanting even that. Long letters to him repeatedly re-position herself as a writer who relied on their intellectual spark to ignite her work. Schreiner sent Pearson an inspired outline for *From Man to Man*. By linking prostitution with prostitution in marriage she meant to make a difference to women's lot — no less. But it seemed to her that she could not measure up to this without Pearson's support. Unfortunately, she embedded this in an emotional plea that reflects Pearson as an awkwardly cerebral person.

Pearson backed away. Her needing and at the same time needling him over his emotional absence was insufficiently disguised as teasing.

He misunderstood her, she retorted. What she wanted was emphatically not 'sex-love'.

Was she protesting too much? There was, I think, a strong desire involving the body as well as the mind. And then there was the neediness of an orphan pleading for attention.

Olive had met Pearson in June 1885, at just the time her Dadda, Fred, withdrew his affection. A few months earlier it became plain that he did not want to visit. 'If he would come and see me and be a little tender to me then I think I would live and get well again,' she confided to Havelock Ellis. Her brother did continue to support her with an annual sum, but the schoolmaster deplored the *African Farm* with its defiantly unmarried mother. In July 1885 Fred asked his sister not to contact him.

This situation was a painful repeat of Theo's withdrawal when Olive, as a child, had lost her faith. Both brothers, both schoolmasters, reacted against what were really high-minded, though unconventional, moral positions. Olive's situation was like Mary Godwin's rejection by her father and George Eliot's by her father and then by her brother. These are acts of erasure, as though by denying the connection, and thus reminders of these women's very existence, brothers and fathers rub out a perceived stain on the family. They force others in the family to comply: Mary Godwin's sister Fanny and George Eliot's sister Chrissey, both helplessly dependent on their menfolk. The home sisters try and fail to keep the errant sister in sight but the severance cannot be healed. So it is that rising sisters and daughters must seek attachments and mentors outside the family.

Olive hoped for sustained closeness to the intellectually superior Pearson. George Eliot had hoped the same from Herbert Spencer. There was a similar interplay of independence and dependence, evoking different responses in the men they approached: Pearson's withdrawal and, in contrast, Spencer's unbroken friendship, as well as George Eliot's good fortune to find an alternative in Lewes. Olive had no such luck.

She was jealous, almost maddened, when she chanced upon Pearson at the British Museum with another woman, called Mrs Cobb and a member of the Men and Women's Club. Her instinct was not entirely misplaced, for Pearson would eventually marry a relative of Mrs Cobb.

Olive lived alone under a shadow for the next three years, mainly in Alassio on the Italian Riviera. She would have hoped that a warmer climate would ease her breathing, and the regular stipend from Fred would have made this feasible. During these years she was too low to complete her work on Mary Wollstonecraft, nor her intended revision of *From Man to Man*. Back in London, she stood in the rain outside University College, but there was no glimpse of Pearson. Later that year, in October 1889, she sailed for Africa in a state of deadness.

In March 1890 she came to a wide long plain with rocky mountains running down both sides. Matjesfontein, in the Karoo about two hundred miles north of Cape Town, had recently appeared on the map as a dry place to ease impaired lungs. At night myriad stars are visible to the naked eye. No trees, only low bush scattered over the baked, yellow earth and the odd *koppie*. No farms. No homesteads. Nothing but the Main Line of the railway and behind the station, across the short road, a hotel and a row of single-storey cottages. One was to be hers: a gate and short path to a living room with a fireplace, a bedroom and a kitchen-cum-wash-place at the back. All her meals she took a step across the gravel at the station's tearoom — the standard fare: coffee, eggs, bread, sweet-milk cheese with its red rind, perhaps *boerewors* [local sausage], lamb chops, slices of *melktert* [Dutch milk tart] and oranges from the western Cape.

The events of the day were the two trains. Each morning the train, on its way up from Cape Town to the diamond and goldfields of Kimberley and Johannesburg, stopped for half an hour for passengers to stretch their legs and have breakfast. Then in the evening there was the other train on its thousand-mile return journey of two nights and a day. That evening train secured the proximity of her public: a parcel of her writing — one of the African allegories she called 'dreams' — could be in Cape Town next morning. It appealed to her, 'this mixture of civilization and the most wild untamed freedom; the barren mountains and the wild Karroo and the railway train'.

Her poetic sense of solitude quickened her voice. As with George Eliot, forward looking went with backward yearning. Each felt how her deepest fibres held fast to the scene that framed them. A tide of memory sweeps us into George Eliot's Midlands setting: 'I remember', the narrator repeats in the opening of *The Mill on the Floss*, 'I remember the dipping willows'. What she recalled was the very fabric of the old rural England sealed for ever in *Scenes of Clerical Life*, *Adam Bede* and *The Mill on the Floss*. This is how Virginia Woolf would see it, 'the only romance that George Eliot allowed herself — the romance of the past'.

So, too, Schreiner's forward-looking dreams of women's rise are located in the landscape of her past: flat, yellow earth stretching to remote horizons; fierce African heat that throbs slowly against the skin; scorched, prickly bush; dust drying the nostrils. It was to this that she returned, not to the colonial towns or lush valleys of the western Cape.

In the early morning she would write at her window with the sun just rising and the hilltops dull purple. Then she would put on her hat and go out for a walk. 'Such a sense of wild exhilaration and freedom comes to me when I walk over the Karroo', she wrote to Ellis on her first morning in Matjesfontein.

The apparent oddity of where she settled after her London celebrity was not only the need of her asthma but fits a pattern of solitude we see in the lives of certain original women who position themselves at the outposts of existence where the clamour will not reach them: Emily Dickinson saying, 'The Soul selects its own Society / Then shuts the door' or the artist Gwen John alone in Meudon, expressing 'this desire for a more interior life'.

As Emily Brontë had to return to her Yorkshire moor, so Schreiner had to return to the veld. It was more than an escape from the Pearson blight; it was a prerequisite for a return to writing. This drew its strength from the very bareness of the place. She invokes nature alone as validation: the veld is her ground for self-discovery. 'The effect of this scenery', she said, 'is to make one silent and strong and self-contained. And it is all so bare, the rocks and the bushes, each bush standing separate from others, alone, by itself.' From there she put together a collection of *Dreams* (1890).

Her visionary prophecies and biblical cadences shape an alternative scripture for readers who had lost their faith. One of the dreams, 'The Hunter', is a variation on Exodus, where Moses communes with the divine spirit on Mount Sinai while the multitude below worship a golden calf, and then, moving towards a Promised Land, he dies – entry is for others. Schreiner's is an allegory of a hunter who sees, on the surface of a lake, the shadow of a great silver bird flying overhead. This is Truth, a creature no one has seen. Seeking Truth, the Hunter must take his way into endless night and then climb a mountain. With his last strength, he cuts foot-holes into the rock, so that seekers who follow in the future can climb higher. But as he dies, a silver feather from the bird of Truth comes down to him. Herbert Spencer, whose *First Principles* had gripped the young Olive Schreiner, was so taken with 'The Hunter' that eventually he had it read to him on his deathbed.

'Three Dreams in a Desert' would later be read aloud by suffragettes on hunger strike in Holloway prison. Constance Lytton said that there, in the women's prison, it seemed not at all figurative, more 'like an ABC railway guide to our journey'. *Dreams* is the holy text for the young working woman in the 2015 film *Suffragette*, who finds herself drawn to the Cause.

A tale called 'The Buddhist Priest's Wife' (1891–2) is a post-Pearson meditation on sexual difference. An independent single woman cultivates a position on the impossibility of an adequate mate. Silencing her attachment, she takes

herself away from a man's missed opportunity for a marriage of true minds.
The message to her sex is to expect nothing. The stoicism is willed, but if a
woman is to retain her self-respect there is no other way.[*]

It so happened that soon after she crafted this statement of resignation, she went to stay with her old friend Mrs Cawood at Ganna Hoek and
there, in December 1892, she met the Cawoods' neighbour, who managed
a farm, Krantz Plaats, in the same region south of Cradock.

She saw a muscular young man of twenty-nine in riding breeches and
top boots. Samuel ('Cron') Cronwright had an outdoor look of vigour,
lean-hipped, lithe, with a thatch of black hair and a clipped beard. He had
to fire only one bullet, he said, to bring down an antelope. Here appeared
to be her Hunter incarnate, as though her fiction had called him to life.
He was tense, opinionated, but his views on women's rights struck her as
surprisingly advanced. This was an enlightened man and a reader – in
fact, an admirer of the *African Farm*, who had written to her about it. He
had the passion for books of a thinker deprived of higher education – like
Olive herself. And then too he had strong, sunburnt arms (she kept a
photo of him with his sleeves rolled up).

She was not in love, and had to consider whether she could marry this
Mr Cronwright, in somewhat the way that Charlotte Brontë and Marian
Evans took time to consider whether they might take on men who were
not their intellectual equals yet offered consolation for unrequited love.
In 1893 Olive Schreiner went back to England and thought over this move.
She had once confided to Pearson how intensely she wanted to have a
child and now was nearing an age when it might no longer be possible.
Here was a strong suitor exuding youthful virility – he was physically
attractive, and though no Godwin, he was decidedly bookish, a thinker
who respected her. At length she agreed to marry Cron.

The wedding day in February 1894 was a non-event. She wore a grey
dress and the couple went to the registry office in the pleasant country

---

[*] The same position is evident in the single-woman stories of the American writer Constance
Fenimore Woolson in the 1880s and early 1890s, and in the late twentieth century in the lone,
stoic women in the fictions of Anita Brookner.

town of Middelburg, where she was living at the time. Their marriage certificate fudges the age gap: Cron's age is given as thirty-one, though he was thirty; Olive's age is given as thirty-seven, though she was a year older. He is registered as a farmer; her occupation is left blank. Unusually, even now, he took her celebrated name: Cron Cronwright-Schreiner was a man comfortable with her fame.

There was no honeymoon. After the brief ceremony they travelled a number of hours to Krantz Plaats, arriving at about 7.30 by which time, even in summer, it would have been dark. Olive was pleased to find the farmhouse clean and orderly, with a table laid in the hall and a roasted chicken. The long white farmhouse was on an exposed bluff with a sheer drop to the Great Fish River below, with its rocks and reeds. Next morning they climbed down – it looks perilous – and had themselves photo-graphed on a rock in the middle of the river: in one photo Cron, with his hard stare, heavy moustache and shaven chin, stands forward with hands thrust down into his jacket pockets; in another, on a hotter day, he sits next to Olive, who is standing in one of her unstructured pinafores, hand on hip, at ease in her new home as though she had lived here always. For

the sake of the picture she has taken off her shady hat. She liked to swim here, the river quiet in summer — more like big, steady pools than running water. That day, when the February sun would have been fierce, Cron drove her under cover in a two-wheeler around the extensive farm. It included ostriches and, in a far pasture, his cherished angora goats under a mountain called Buffels Kop. One day Cron took off from work in order to climb the Kop with her, a matter of several hours, and at the top they found a far-reaching view of mountaintops. The sight filled Olive with so much joy that she resolved to be buried here.

Their differences, coming at once into play, were challenging, but not divisive. Olive saw Cron as simple, direct, making for the light ahead, in contrast with her own glancing instinct, 'flashing side-lights upon everything'. She jokes how she was born lacking an epidermis. Her sensitivities were jarred by Cron's toughness, yet he could be tender in private. She made a point of 'tender', knowing her friends would be surprised by her marriage to a bossy man — but he had progressive self-improvement in mind. Cron's nephew said that he exercised his mind like a Gustav Zander machine, a Swedish contraption then popular for developing biceps.

Her asthma worsened at Krantz Plaats. Which was a great pity, because their relationship of some equality didn't ever regain its equilibrium after that. Within months, Cron gave up the farm and they moved to Kimberley, where they bought a pretty house, the Homestead, with three acres. It was hard for Cron to give up his ostriches and angoras, and his surrender of employment put pressure on Olive Schreiner to produce the books he expected in marrying an author. She was always about to complete the 'big' books, *From Man to Man* and a 'sex book' that came out of discussions with Pearson in the 1880s. But Cron did stand by her, she said, in the darkness of their grief at the death of a much-wanted baby with 'such a calm, strong face'. She would never forget her child's serious eyes.

The baby was found dead the morning after her birth, 1 May 1895. Cron carried her, closed-eyed, outside into the sun for photographs: she was well-formed in a long, white robe. Olive's grief was lingeringly sad. A letter from Olive to her sister Ettie a fortnight later hints at neglect as the cause of death. Had her sister been at hand, she believed, her baby would have been saved. But she chose not to dwell on this so as to cherish rather her closeness to the child.

> The Homestead
> May 16 / 95
> My darling old Ettie,
>
> I am sending you three pictures of my little one ... They are only taken by Cron's little hand Kodak, but they are all I have. Ettie, if you had been here when my little baby was born I should have had it with me still ... What I say is for your heart alone. I don't want one moment's suffering to be caused to any human creature by that beautiful, holy little life of mine; it is gone now, but one day I will write to you & tell you everything. It lived 16 hours. . . . I had so much milk for it ... the milk ran through the cloths they put on my breast, & down my sides. I had enough milk for two babies. Do you remember how we used to play at having babies when we were little girls? I lie here & think of you often ... People say 'forget'. They don't know that the one joy is that one can never forget: that as long as I live I shall feel that little dead body lying in my breast comforting me.

She told a friend, 'Neither Cron nor I dare ever say to each other what is in our hearts. There are some thoughts we shall carry with us to our dying day.'

There could be another cause for the child's death: the new-born was abnormally large, nine pounds and nine and a half ounces — almost double an acceptable weight. Given that size (usually associated with maternal diabetes) and with a home delivery, the birth was difficult; Olive was unconscious under chloroform for two and a quarter hours, so could not push, and the forceps used tore her so badly that a month later she still could not sit. If so much force had to be used, the child could have suffered a birth trauma.

She resolved that 'Baby' would one day be buried with her on Buffels Kop, and in the meantime could not bring herself to bury her in any final way. Some ten years later, when she and Cron were living temporarily in different places, she wrote to him that if she died he would find the baby in a box at the foot of her bed. She mentions this without explaining if it's a real body in the box, and how it came there. Her most cherished work, *From Man to Man*, is eventually dedicated to two babies: her sister Ellie and 'my only daughter'.

At first, when Olive Schreiner had returned to South Africa, she'd been attracted by the energetic power of Rhodes, but she was outraged when, as Prime Minister of the Cape Colony, he had backed the 1891 'Strop' or Flogging Bill, which proposed to allow white employers to lash blacks for minor offences like disobedience or not turning up for work or riding a master's horse.* Though the bill failed to get a majority, Rhodes's legislative victories, one of which was to disenfranchise Cape Africans, are precursors to apartheid. A famous cartoon of 'The Rhodes Colossus' in 1892 pictured this racist tycoon astride Africa, from Cape to Cairo. From then on, Schreiner would not speak to Rhodes. He admired the *African Farm* as 'a work of profound genius', and would have liked to speak to her. She'd refused an invitation and had shut her door to him when he came to Matjesfontein in the early 1890s.

In 1895 Schreiner was shocked by Rhodes's collusion in the Jameson Raid, an attempt to grab the gold-rich Boer republic of the Transvaal. The raid proved a fiasco. Rhodes dodged censure in the enquiries that followed because his co-conspirator Joseph Chamberlain, the Secretary of State for the Colonies, intervened. Telegrams implicating Rhodes, Chamberlain, members of the British Cabinet and the aristocracy conveniently disappeared. Schreiner continued to detect the worms of

---

* At this date Rhodes was playing to the Boers because he had designs on what they had.

corruption, encouraged by Rhodes's sycophants who, she said, 'sucked dust from his feet'.

Her unpopular parable of 1897, *Trooper Peter Halket of Mashonaland*, indicted the men of Rhodes's British South Africa Company for the violence with which they suppressed rebellion in a new colony to be named Rhodesia. The land's inhabitants, the Ndebele and Shona peoples, had stood in the way of Rhodes's dream of cutting an imperial swathe across the entire continent. Schreiner signals her documentary intention with a frontispiece to the first edition: a photograph of three almost naked black men strung up on 'the hanging tree' outside Bulawayo. The neck of one is hideously dislocated, while Rhodes's men stand by with hats at jaunty angles, idling, at ease with their handiwork. It's a horrendous image, unprecedented for a woman to put in a book, exposing the sort of atrocity kept from protected white ladies. This was the violent reality of colonisation. Meanwhile, back in England, Rhodes was lauded for empire-building and invited to receive an honorary degree from Oxford University.

Instead of posting the Halket manuscript, Olive and Cron carried it to London. Rhodes happened to be a passenger on the same ship, and his manservant searched their cabin. After the novel came out, Rhodes put it about that Schreiner had written in the pay of the Transvaal Republic.

'Of all the lies Rhodes & his followers have spread about me', she told her friend Jan Smuts, the Attorney-General for the Transvaal, 'none has cut me so deeply as the lie circulated in England that I had received £4,000 from the Transvaal Government for writing Peter Halket. It cut straight at the use & value of what I have written & what I may yet write.'

Rhodes still wanted the Transvaal, and he played up the grievances of the English and other foreigners who were living there. Schreiner watched 'engorged capitalists' led by Rhodes foment war. She called them 'the wild dogs of gold'. In a letter to an American newspaper, she denounced a policy that 'would murder a nation to fill a few pockets'.

Sir Alfred Milner, the Governor of the Cape, stood by Rhodes. Olive

Schreiner confronted the absurdity of Milner's dispatches to London, alleging a plan in Africa to overthrow England and suggesting that the Boer Republics (almost encircled by British lands) threatened the peace of the world. First, she drafted a sixteen-page protest to Milner, then discarded it for a more politic approach. Instead, she offered Milner a book, a biography of an earlier Governor, Sir George Grey, inviting him to look at a predecessor who did not lose the trust of the Colony. She was inviting Milner to be greater than he was. No luck.

Olive writes fondly of Cron so long as they lived in Kimberley, but where she was busy with an international career, what was he to do with himself? Though her writing brought in some money, it was not remotely enough for him to fulfil his wider responsibilities. His need to care for his wife's health vied with his commitment to supporting his widowed mother and unmarried sister, and providing for them should he die. He resolved to become an attorney in Johannesburg. Olive did not want to go there but she must have seen Cron's need for some future of his own.

She loathed Johannesburg, 'this great fiendish hell of a city sprung up on our sweet pure rare African velt. A city which for glitter and gold, and wickedness – carriages, and palaces and brothels, and gambling halls, beats creation.' It proved hard for Cron to find a firm to see him through his articles, and when one did, he earned only fifteen pounds a month until he should qualify. For the time being he was still dependent on his wife, and annoyed that she didn't publish the 'big books' which she was always about to complete – books so ambitious to change the world that she kept revising them.

Her brother Fred had stopped his annual support once she married, and though the *African Farm* brought in royalties, they were not a lot – Schreiner said that if she'd been treated fairly by Chapman & Hall she should have been rich. Then came an unexpected claim for forty-seven pounds from Little, Brown in Boston, following its merger with her American publisher, Roberts Brothers. Unless she paid this sum, Little, Brown threatened to publish her *Stray Thoughts on South Africa* in an unrevised state. She had her brother-in-law look into this but they got nowhere.[*]

Once she and Cron settled in Johannesburg, another and more difficult claim confronted her. Johannesburg turned out to be a beacon to her mother-in-law. Cron's mother planned to come and live with them at 2 Primrose Terrace, Berea Estate, and to bring her daughter too, at least for the summer. Mrs Cronwright further suggested that Cron's two brothers might board there. To take in Cron's whole family would have wrecked Olive's life as a writer. Unlike Lewes, who'd protected George Eliot's writing life from his sons' domestic needs, Cron wished to provide a home for his family. So it was that the onus fell on Olive to say no.

She did have to say no, she told Betty Molteno, the principal of a girls' school in Port Elizabeth. This was by way of explaining why Olive could not invite Betty and her partner Miss Greene to stay with her – it would further offend 'the old lady' if she invited friends as house guests. Olive saw her mother-in-law as a woman minus 'an aptitude for seeing that other people also have their lives to live'. She could not help knowing that 'all the family are feeling pained with me'.

At this awkward time, she fell pregnant. The way she pictures her marriage in a letter to Havelock Ellis does not sound companionable. When Cron returned to their lodgings after his long day at the office, he would read after dinner, and so 'It's a curious solitary life I live here, seldom speaking to or seeing a human being . . . I have never led such a solitary life, because when I was a girl I had Nature and in Europe I had friends.'

Cron's professional venture ended in the run-up to war. His law office was closing. Depleted of funds, they left Johannesburg to stay with Cron's relation Edward Wright on Kareekloof, a farm in the Karoo. This was one

---

[*] Robert Hemming was by then living in Johannesburg. He may have been a lawyer for a while, then became Librarian for the Johannesburg Public Library. Emily Dickinson was another casualty of this merger: her work, published by Roberts Bros, went out of print because her poetic *Letters* had not been profitable.

reason to leave the city, and another was that Olive needed to recuperate following a miscarriage compounded by heart and breathing troubles. The farm was remote, ten hours westwards by cart from the nearest station, Kraankuil, north of De Aar on the Main Line.

Back in the dry Karoo, she found herself 'in heaven', on top of her powers and seething with purpose. Heaven was to breathe easily, to gallop across the veld at sunset, to see the sharp outlines of the *koppies* against the darkening sky, to lift her head to the brilliant starlight and to make herself at home in their host's study. With rising alacrity she sat down to a two-part essay on the Woman Question for a New York monthly called *The Cosmopolitan*, who published it in November and December 1899. She received a hundred pounds, vital to her and Cron's support.

It's likely that the essay arose from her 'sex book', the bound manuscript which she had left at Primrose Terrace, expecting to return. But British soldiers stopped them en route on 13 October 1899. War had broken out two days before. The way back to Johannesburg was barred, and from then on her life took another direction.

It was during the weeks at Kareekloof that her friendship with Jan Smuts turned into a political tie. When Cron and Olive had moved to Johannesburg, Smuts had asked what he could do for them. Olive had replied smartly with a counter-offer: 'how glad I should be to assist the Transvaal Government in the fight'. A sparky after-thought is to lay out a price of sorts: the one thing Smuts might, in fact, do for her is to grant the vote to the burghers' wives and daughters as the 'back-bone' of the Republic.

She had paid a visit to Smuts in Pretoria, and had taken to his wife, Isie, who combined, she saw, the strength of the old Boer woman with the culture and refinement of a New Woman. The Smutses invited the Cronwright-Schreiners to stay with them during the coming war, but Olive had found Pretoria bad for her asthma. ' . . . Thank you for your loving wish to have me,' she wrote to Isie Smuts, 'I should only be a trouble to everyone if I could come.'

On 24 September 1899, seventeen days before the outbreak of war, Olive Schreiner, still at Kareekloof, makes an intriguing approach to Smuts. She tells him that the *New York Post* has cabled an offer of £110 a month to be a front-line war correspondent. She wants to present 'our side', and asks Smuts two questions: first, 'whether the Transvaal authorities will give me facilities for gaining information, and for going with the Burghers to the front'; and, secondly, underlined, 'where . . . you think I had better go at first?' She intimates that, health permitting, she is prepared to go anywhere, and repeats this question: 'it would greatly add to my usefulness if I could receive advice as to where I could be most useful.'

Smuts is to telegraph her in a prearranged code with just two words: 'Yes' (the answer she expects to her first question) and the name of the place where she is to go. She commits herself to secrecy. 'Any information you may give me will be kept strictly private of course.'

Further, she takes the precaution of asking for a letter with a legible signature either from himself or from the ex-president of the Orange Free State, Francis Reitz, now State Secretary of the Transvaal Republic.* This letter must verify who she is in case some unknowing Boer mistakes her and Cron for 'rooineks' [red necks] – a derogatory word for the English.

Her only fear is for Cron. Her knowledge of him warns her to act alone. He's too aggressive, too outspoken to be a safe partner in whatever she will undertake. If Cron is with her, he will get shot, she thinks. And she's explicit about Cron's lesser commitment. 'It would not matter at all if I died in a cause which I have so much at heart, I shall never die in a better. But I can't feel it right that he should die in a cause which though he is sympathetic is not one of life and death to him in the same sense as to me'.

Smuts wired his agreement. She was to join the Boers at the front. But when she saw a doctor, he confirmed the heart issues prior to her miscarriage: the left side had now dilated more than before. So, instead of roving

---

* Reitz was a family connection, the father of her affectionate sister-in-law, Frances (Fan), married to Will Schreiner.

as a war reporter, she found two alternative forms of action: platform protest and a lone placing near the northern border of the Colony, in advance of what was to be an unpleasant surprise for the imperial army: the guerrilla phase of the war during which Smuts led one of the most elusive commandos.

Schreiner first discovered her speaking voice when a crowd called her out at a *Volkskongres* in Graaff-Reinet, a country town in the eastern part of the Cape Colony. It was 31 May 1900, the day when British troops invaded the two independent republics of the Boers, to the north of the Colony. Her asthma and the effort of breathing had raised her shoulders, but this in no way impeded her words. Her fists beat out her rhythm against the rail in front of her. Pro-war newspapers reported this gesture as unwomanly. Ladies kept gloved hands close or folded. A lady did not raise her voice so as to be noticed. If she did, she was said to 'shriek', however low her tone. Though she addressed the crowd as 'a writer and not a speaker', what she said was to the point. 'We feel that our friends in South Africa need our help and we must give it.' That word 'help' is careful to keep clear of treason. She was not inciting violence, yet a restrained violence in her manner fired the crowd.

She spoke in English, declaring her stand against her own sort. The largely Dutch-speaking crowd cheered.

Early in June, after seizing Johannesburg, the British then marched on Pretoria. 'We are marching to Pretoria – Pretoria – Pretoria', was the popular song of the day.* The fence-sitting government of Olive's brother Will Schreiner, Prime Minister of the Cape, had to resign in the face of war-fever. His sister decided it was time to stop troubling herself about 'quaking' politicians. 'The women must act,' she said. 'If we stupid women had been running the country for the last nine months we couldn't have made a greater mess of things than the men have done.'

---

* As a child in 1940s Cape Town I would hear my Auntie Isobel tinkling the tune at the piano and singing in a nostalgic manner. Her husband, my great-uncle, had left the Transvaal as a very small child on the outbreak of the war.

Her career as an orator had taken off when she was alone for six months while Cron, after losing his work, undertook (in place of his wife) an anti-war mission in England. It was particularly sporting of him, since he didn't have Olive's death-defying commitment and his pro-British family was not behind him. A prolonged lecture tour brought him low; jeering, heckling jingoes (war-enthusiasts) cut down his confidence. He was visibly aged when he came back in July 1900, and for some months lived with his mother in the Cape Town suburb of Mowbray. Olive meanwhile went her own way.

A war correspondent for London's *Daily Chronicle* reported on her speech of 9 July 1900 to fifteen hundred at a peace protest in the Metropolitan Hall in Burg Street, Cape Town. He saw a short, brown-eyed woman rise to speak amid a silence of expectation. Though she stood still, he said, her words were like a 'molten torrent of white hot rage' as she singled out 'the men who, to satisfy personal greed and ambition, had produced the war'. Speculators like Rhodes were England's real foes, debasing what was decent in the English character: 'every farmhouse which the British soldiers are burning down today is a torch lighting the British Empire ... to its doom'. She's referring to the new tactic of Lord Kitchener to burn the farms of Boer families who resisted imperial rule. Eventually as many as thirty thousand houses were destroyed. Women and children, moved to 'concentration camps', were dying of malnutrition and disease. Kitchener adopted a winning tactic in the American Civil War: Sherman's decision to destroy the supplies of the enemy. Kitchener sent out troops not only to burn down homesteads but also to destroy produce and kill livestock. Mutilated animals were left to die in the veld.

News of farm-burnings reached England. Emily Hobhouse, who had organised a big women's protest against the war at the Queen's Hall in London, felt called upon to help destitute Boer women and children. In September 1900 she began to collect a distress fund.

It was at this critical time, on 16 September – sixteen days after Britain annexed the Transvaal, the second of the Boer republics – that Schreiner made her way to Hanover. It was about two hours by train to the east of the main British force encamped at the railway junction of De Aar. The Boer War was in some ways a railway war with blockhouses along the lines vital to communications and supplies across vast stretches of unpopulated Karoo. Hanover, founded in 1854 (with a nod of colonial deference to the Hanoverian succession), consisted of some fifty-six basic single-storey houses, with blacks and coloureds as always set apart. Schreiner had never been here before and knew no one. Why she chose to live in this spot, bared to the harshest sun, is not entirely obvious.

A plausible reason she gave was asthma: on arrival she claimed to be better for the dry air, five thousand feet above sea level. She was pleased with the climate in springtime, not as yet too hot, with trees in blossom along the few gravel streets. But there are numerous other places at that altitude with the same dry air.

Could there be another motive for her move to this particular *dorp* only two miles from a railway link to the British encampment at De Aar on the Main Line running north? This strategic east–west line for transport of soldiers, arms and equipment was a sitting target within striking distance of the border with the officially conquered Free State. Sleepy as Hanover appeared in September 1900, it would be a military hotspot three months later. I think of Schreiner's offer to Smuts to be sent wherever he directed, and her pride in another Boer leader, Wynand Malan, whose commandos would sweep into the area around Hanover.

If Olive Schreiner thought to help the Boers, who at this stage were still on the other side of the Cape border, she would have kept this to herself, with nothing on paper. To act as a 'rebel' against imperial rule was to risk the death penalty. This was no idle threat. The British executed some forty-five so-called 'Cape rebels', preceded by public sentencing in market squares, a warning to citizens who were compelled to attend. Many, like Olive, had links with the Boers.

Meanwhile, on 12 October she pushed the right to freedom of speech to an inflammatory point. From Hanover she sent a 'letter' to be read aloud at a widely reported women's protest in Somerset East, in the eastern Cape, on the anniversary of the war's start. Her words are designed to resound far beyond a country town: the world must hear. This 'letter' transforms a genre open to women into political oratory, traditionally the preserve of men.

Recalling the eight years she had lived in England and 'the many men and women bound to me by ties of affection and sympathy', she confronts her one-time belief, shared with others in the Colony, that the just element in the British would control 'the baser and more servile'. Her point is that the bulk of the British people have allowed the baser to take control, and she names Rhodes in the first place, also Joseph Chamberlain and Alfred Milner. How, she asks, can it be that the majority of just Englishmen were sitting still 'while private houses were burnt down and women and young children turned homeless into the wilds, in order that through wounding the affections and sympathies of the [Boer] men[,] their arms might be paralysed for further warfare'?

Boer women tried to evade the British after their farms were burnt. They lived rough, hiding in the veld, before these 'undesirables' were rounded up and placed behind Kitchener's barbed wire. Men in the camps who'd laid down their guns were rewarded with better food than was allowed for the undernourished children and wives of men still in the field. The lives of children have not much concerned men with military objectives. It did not occur to Kitchener that the babies of depleted mothers would need milk. A French cartoon of the day shows a mother with shrivelled breasts hanging in despair over dying and dead children. Epidemics of dysentery and typhoid were rife. Twenty-two thousand of those who died in these camps were under the age of sixteen; a comparable number of black children died in their separate and even worse concentration camps.

When protests came from people of conscience in England, Kitchener's answer was that 'civilised nations' do have to do such things in time of war. It was this pretension to virtue, Schreiner said, that destroyed her attachment to a motherland that she, like many English-speakers, had called 'home'.

'Now England is dead to me', she declared to the women gathered at Somerset East. The personal charge of this refrain carries her oratory. 'But for me the England of my love is dead.'

It was one thing for Boers to resist England; quite another for a woman whose English mother sported a framed photo of Rhodes beside her chair. Olive's older siblings Theophilus and Ettie were also staunchly on the side of the Empire. So, in siding against England, Olive Schreiner set her sights apart from these members of her family. Rhodes had been gleeful to receive a wire in his support from Olive's eighty-year-old mother. He'd read this out in one of his war-provoking speeches from his base in Cape Town.

Olive Schreiner's speech recalls 'the blunder of George III and his servile Ministers when they sought to crush by force the instinct for independence and self-government in the men and women of the American Colonies'. And she wonders how England could again allow herself to 'fall into the hands of unscrupulous men, and under their guidance attempt to set her knee on the necks of two small, brave peoples, striving to force life from them, while with eager hands she grasped their gold and lands'.

This long, resounding speech against the motherland goes far beyond Schreiner's first platform appearance with its call for 'help' for the victims of British conquest, and develops further her molten words in Cape Town. This is an accomplished literary writer reviving a lost art with an audience of women: the art of oratory, as practised by the ancients and through the Middle Ages when rhetoric as a subject continued part of higher education. She revived this care for the spoken word and is one of the great letter-writers in our language, with the distinction of turning the private genre of the letter into a public instrument, a form of politics – much as the Romans did and Zola in his 1898 letter, *J'Accuse*, exposing high-level corruption and anti-Semitism in the Dreyfus Affair.

When Schreiner, like Zola, writes a public letter, it's a letter to the world, and reported as such. That element of oratory is present also in her novels and allegories. She is an imaginative writer with a liberating political vision, as Shelley was.\* The vision and the writing are inseparable.

---

\* In April 1886 Olive Schreiner gave a copy of Shelley's *Letters* to her mother. It was edited by Edward Garnett (1882) with a frontispiece from a watercolour (*c.* 1840) by Dina Williams, the artist daughter of Edward Williams who was drowned with Shelley.

Schreiner and Rhodes were the only two public figures to command attention outside southern Africa. And where Rhodes, misty-eyed about Anglo-Saxon superiority, had a fortune to back his imperialism, Schreiner, with no money, had the greater power of words in the form of speeches and 'letters'.

She penned another of her oratorical letters for a women's peace congress in Paarl on 10 November, and she attended a mixed protest in Worcester, a country town near Cape Town, on a rainy 6 December. Spells of fainting, caused by her heart condition, prevented her taking the floor and Cron, once more by her side, spoke in her stead. A caricature in a pro-war paper shows her shaking an umbrella. Cron's relations blamed her for the disabling result of his pro-Boer stance, and he did not return with her to Hanover. She left uncertain if their separation was to be temporary or permanent.

On 14 December she arrived in Hanover, acutely conscious that she was now on her own. The following night – a Sunday – the first two Boer commandos from the Free State crossed the Orange River, the border of the Cape. One of the commandos swept into the region between Hanover and the more substantial Middelburg. Planning for these raids had been secret and they had the advantage of surprise: the vital railway bridge south of the vast British encampment at De Aar was destroyed and the telegraph wires to the north were cut.

The timing of Olive Schreiner's return to Hanover raises a question as to whether she was party to enemy plans to enter the Colony. There's a steely confidence in the way she said 'the war is not over'.

A thousand British soldiers took over Hanover, and their commander, Colonel de Lisle, arrived at Olive Schreiner's door where she was staying in the *dorp*'s hotel. The interrogation lasted two hours. She was aware that jingoes had been urging the British to take action against her and, she puts it plainly, 'arrest me for high treason'.

De Lisle opened with an allegation. Was she calling on the Republican burghers to invade the Cape?

Schreiner's answer was carefully judged. She did not deny siding with the Boer Republics. On the contrary, she told de Lisle that if she could secure the Republics' independence by going into the market square to be shot by his soldiers, she'd do it. Candour, she knew, is best with a sensible Englishman. Afterwards, de Lisle remarked to the mayor, who was present, that he liked people to speak out.

All the same, Schreiner did protect herself by saying that she was against a 'war' in the Colony because – she put it emphatically – '*the bloodshed would be too terrific*'.

This was not a ploy of the moment; she was indeed appalled by war. But what she didn't say – and this we can't know – was how far she supported what is not 'war' as armies understand the word: not full-front invasion, certainly not occupation nor harm to civilians, but an aim to keep the British busy. This mighty army in high-curved helmets and polished boots, with its train of beautifully groomed horses needing daily fodder, would not want to be kept here, indefinitely on the alert, in what looks like an interminable nowhere.

'It's the spirit of the women that will win back the independence of the Transvaal and Free State', Schreiner took this opportunity to enlighten de Lisle. When women have such spirit they are not open to conquest.

'Oh, yes!' he ruminated, turning it around. 'The women are something awful; they are not afraid of anything.'

After her interrogation, Schreiner's position in Hanover changed. Jingoes in her hotel glared. When she wished them good morning, they cut her. She received threatening letters and insulting cards. From now on she was shunned, and not only by the jingoes but also by the Dutch-speaking community. A British soldier told a Dutch child that Olive Schreiner was leading on the Boers, and public notices to this effect went up. Her exclusion made her want to cry when she passed along the street and saw people sitting at their doors together.

Solitude had once been a boon as a young governess on remote farms. In Hanover, it was different: here she was isolated against her will. Everywhere else, especially in England, she had dear friends. She had a gift for friendship, an abundance of love. She was also used to adulation, though she never sought it. As a celebrity, she had been welcomed at first by the Dutch-speaking inhabitants. But once British troops arrived, the fact that she'd lived in England made her suspect. Gossip had it that Schreiner's English background won her special privileges.

On 18 January 1901 Olive left the hotel for a room on the north-east edge of the *dorp*. But why leave a hotel, with meals and water laid on, for a bare room where she had to fend for herself? An obvious answer is that the hotel forced her to leave; she said later that she'd have preferred a boarding house to a room, that is if any boarding house would have taken her. She had no wish to scrub her floor and fetch water. This kind of work was invariably done by servants, and it's curious that 'natives', she says, 'boycotted' her, a woman unusually sympathetic to their exploitation. It's likely that they were intimidated by her taboo status, and in any case there was alternative employment to be had with the British army, and in particular as part of the armed night guard.

Since letters were censored, facts are sparse. The crucial fact in Hanover was the massed pith helmets on its doorstep: at first a thousand, and then a vast increase as the Imperial Light Horse, twenty thousand strong, rose over the horizon and rode into the vicinity. And the other fact: the death penalty for 'rebels'. Locals of all persuasions could not be seen to associate with a woman thought to be in the pay of the enemy. As an outcast, Olive came to depend on the affection of her dog, Neta, who was 'almost human'.

Forced to camp in her room, she bought a blanket, a paraffin lamp for cooking, two plates and a washing bowl. There was a stretcher and two packing cases for furniture. She had no permit to leave Hanover. She was denied newspapers — shut off from information — and could leave her room only once a day to fetch water. News of her plight did reach London, and sympathisers, including Herbert Spencer, contributed to a fund for her, amounting to about £150.

Schreiner's room is still at the edge of the *dorp*, unmarked, looking out on the veld. It was a corner room in a house built by thin, gentle Miss

Aletta Viljoen, who also suffered from asthma. Her brother farmed nearby and an eight-year-old nephew, Dirk, stayed with her for company. The room itself was small and comfortless, and the window let in little light, but it faced towards a stretch of terrain to the north – in the direction of the Free State. This stretch of veld was not as deserted as it looked. British cannon could be heard from behind the *koppies* in the distance.

Barbed wire surrounded Hanover, and walks were barred. But Schreiner would already have scouted the terrain – whether purposefully or not, we don't know – in the course of her daily walks during the three preceding months from mid-September to early December 1900. She hints as much in January 1901, in a request to Lord Kitchener to meet her for half an hour. The smallest wild duck, she said, knows its own tarn better than the biggest swan from elsewhere. The bait is that she could tell Kitchener a thing or two, but her purpose was always to speak for the women and children he'd made his prisoners of war.

Late that same month, Emily Hobhouse began her journey to the 'concentration camps' with a train truck of bedding, clothing and food. In May 1901 she returned to England to lay before the government and the public her report on the lethal conditions.

The military retaliated by deporting her under martial law when she came out to South Africa again in October 1901. Hobhouse proceeded to write *The Brunt of War and where it fell*. The military, incensed by adverse opinion at home, executed a non-combatant lawyer, the one-time Prosecutor for the Transvaal Republic, for reporting on the scale of deaths in the camps.

So it happened that freedom of speech was turned into treason. Schreiner observed how easy it was for rulers at a distance of six thousand miles to do wrongs in England's name that would not be condoned at home. Given the modelling of the British Empire on the Roman Empire, it's apt that Schreiner re-read Gibbon's *Decline and Fall of the Roman Empire* at this time.

The guerrilla war intensified from January 1901 with the commando of Wynand Malan 'running rings around Hanover', as she put it. She liked his restraint of strong passion and had been close enough to mark his drooping left eye. Such was his daring, he would pick up scouts, give them coffee and return them unharmed to Hanover. He remained in the area for a year and a half, till he was captured (fortunately for him, only a few days before the end of the war).

After one raid, citizens of Philipstown (north of Hanover) heard the Boers singing psalms in the *koppies*, their voices coming through mist and rain. 'They are a strange people these,' Schreiner comments, 'how little the world understands them.'

When Smuts's commando was ranging north-east of Cradock, one of his men pointed out the lonely farm, Leliekloof, where Schreiner had completed *The Story of an African Farm*. Smuts thought how she loved that 'fierce, forbidding' landscape 'that gave birth to her intense soul'. This was the moment when he felt closest to her, conscious that – unlike himself – she was alone, 'perhaps in internment'. When he remembered this scene in later years he likened Olive Schreiner to Emily Brontë. Both were clergy daughters, both loners, both interfused with their terrain; during her years in England, Schreiner had an impulse to go and lie face down on the Yorkshire moor because she thought it would be like the veld. Her early life reminded Smuts of his favourite book, *Wuthering Heights*.

Military fury grew as raids into the Colony spread in all directions. The British had won the war, according to their lights: war as a trained phalanx marching to Pretoria, marching to the Free State, and taking them for the Crown. But now, guerrilla commandos were ambushing troops and trains, then galloping away into the veld with its high-piled outcrops of rocks. Gun-holes were constructed in the yard behind Schreiner's room, and to the west of it was a stock-house. There are still gun-holes in that blank wall, pointing towards a gravel road leading from the edge of the veld, where Schreiner lodged, towards the centre of the *dorp*. Its inhabitants listened to the pom-poms from the armoured trains and to the voices of the guards, a hundred in all, as they called out 'who goes there?'

One night Schreiner heard as many as six guards talking under her window. To them she would have appeared an unruly woman trespassing on matters of war, but they were not necessarily targeting her; the whole place was on edge, expecting some kind of attack.

It came on the night of 25–26 February. A train was derailed and plundered about twenty kilometres from Hanover, at Taaibosch. The military chose to punish Hanover men who were sleeping in the outhouse of a farm, even though the army itself had sent them there to collect fodder. Schreiner knew they were innocent and was desperate to intervene. Her attempt to reach the high command failed, and access to public opinion, an unfailing resource in the past, was blocked. To her dismay, three of the men were executed by a firing squad on 19 March. This fatal miscarriage of justice weighed on her in a way she could not quite explain except to say that the horror, for her, was worse than that of the concentration camps. My guess is that there was some sense of guilt. It was Wynand Malan's commando who had carried out the sabotage.

Her plight under martial law was, it seems, not widely known locally. In Cape Town a group of women, who hoped to form an international women's peace union, came together at Marie Koopmans-de Wet's, an elegant, early eighteenth-century house (now a national monument) in Strand Street. They elected Olive Schreiner in absentia to the committee. The pro-war press wondered at this absence. Why had Schreiner disappeared from the political scene? One newspaper had the answer: she was 'tied up' like a rebellious hen 'bent on scratching up her master's garden'.

Cut off from her many friends amongst pacifists, feminists and intellectuals, she was cut off too by the military censor in a way that brought a stop to her public voice so long as the war went on. Silenced for the present, Schreiner turned to address the future. She had long wished to explore what her sex might contribute to society.

The prime aim of *Woman and Labour* is not so much about claiming '*all labour for our province*', any more than the *Vindication of the Rights of Woman* is primarily about rights. Both books dream of a future women must strive to bring into being: not only equal pay for equal work and status for domestic

care like mothering, but above all the task, far off in the future, to put an
end to war, careless as it is of mothers' labour in making the bodies war
expends. Schreiner calls on her sex to act on its 'life-dispensing power'. To
what extent might woman's instinct and practice as mother and nurturer
be tapped for the public good?

Schreiner is not advocating imitations of men – the easier course.
She is not concerned with queens and other exceptions. Her unfinished
introduction to a centenary edition of the *Vindication* seeped into *Woman and
Labour*. Both she and Mary Wollstonecraft want to elicit what is distinctive in woman's experience with a view to constructing a different world.
Their thinking is visionary in its boldness, looking beyond more immediate aims. Schreiner had long believed that 'the question of women's
having the vote, and independence and education, is only part of the
question, there lies something deeper'.

She claims that a woman can't be known by appearance, and to illus-
trate this she invents an allegory. Once upon a time people find a bird's
egg, and when it hatches, they tie its leg so that it can't disappear. They
proceed to argue as to what kind of bird it is: can it be a waterfowl whose
nature is to swim? Or a barn-fowl whose nature it is to scratch around?
Or are its wings for flight? The bird, preening its wings, looks up into the
sky in which it had never been, 'for the bird – the *bird*, knew what it would
do – because it was an eaglet!'

John Stuart Mill had broached the same question about innate endow-
ment. A man, he concedes, can't know a woman's nature unless he talks
to a woman worth knowing and nothing in him makes her afraid to
reveal what she is. 'Hardly anything', he adds, 'can be more rare than this
conjunction.'

Such a conjunction had happened when Mary Wollstonecraft
knocked on Godwin's door for advice. As a one-time minister, he was
a keen counsellor, and she one of many to respect his wisdom. Then,
as we've seen, there was Shelley's conjunction with Mary Godwin,
who could show what she was to no one else; and there was Charlotte
Brontë's experience with her teacher M. Heger in Brussels, which lent
its actuality to Mr Rochester's invitation to Jane Eyre to be 'as natural

with me as I find it impossible to be conventional with you'. We've seen too the 'Siamese twin' of George Henry Lewes and the journalist who emerged from this union as George Eliot. Each of these men, different though they were, had the confidence to encourage a woman to be what she felt herself to be.

Schreiner waves off the kind of brute strength that was useful to primitive societies, together with the share speculator whom she defines as a man of a certain kind of 'low intelligence' who despoils a society. Instead, she calls for the man who is 'furthest removed from the dominant male type of the past'. His qualities will be welcome to the discerning: mental activity, reflective keenness, self-control and other non-'pugilistic' traits found also in developed women.

Her suffragette friend Lady Constance Lytton, who combined strength of will with tenderness, embodied Schreiner's ideal. This friend would later endure force-feeding in prison, after she disguised herself as a working-class woman so as not to be exempted from jail because her father had been an earl and Viceroy of India.

Schreiner's voice is a link in the chain coming down to us from Mary Wollstonecraft, whose watchword was 'tenderness', and George Eliot, whose watchword was 'sympathy'. From 1894 it was recognised that a breed of 'New Woman' had emerged and was continuing to evolve, and Schreiner had led the way with such a woman in the *African Farm* ten years earlier. Yet, like Wollstonecraft and George Eliot, she was not soft on women's failings: assumed silliness, a weakness for strutting brutes and their simplistic ideologies, and 'parasitism' as an occupation. Schreiner sees through idle wives cultivating helplessness so as to appeal to male protection. As we know, she aligns the prostitute with the wife who must exchange her body for hand-outs.

Schreiner foresees that her thoughts will seem obvious to the future. She doesn't ask to be singled out for special attention, only that we feel her solicitude that we should 'go on'; and the touching way she finds 'comfort' in the future: 'All I aspire to be, and was not, comforts me.' Her voice deliberately cuts through time to reach us in the present:

I should like to say to the men and women of the generations, which
will come after us – '. . . You will wonder at passionate struggles that
accomplished so little . . . but what you will never know is how it was
thinking of you and for you, that we struggled as we did and accomplished the little which we have done; that it was in the thought of
your larger realisation and fuller life that we found consolation for
the futilities of our own.'

These words beat her message through the closed shutters and out
into the night, where the moon pours its light onto the wide, lonely plain.
Nowhere is the pulse stronger than in her call for women to resist and in
some far-off future to ban 'the bestiality and insanity' of war.

It can't be a coincidence that she began the book 'with war all about' in
March 1901, the very month when military superiors at a distance ordered
the execution of the three Hanover men, who died declaring their innocence. The failure of her attempt to intervene confounded her. She was
silenced in a way she'd never been before, and I think the power of the
military to shut off her voice led to her determination to co-opt the rest of
her sex. *Woman and Labour* was her way of reaching out through the barbed
wire with a political 'letter' to the future, fuelled by her will to empower
a counter-force to war: the whole community of women 'who have in all
ages produced, at an enormous cost, the primal munition of war' – men's
bodies.

She witnessed the wounded and dying bodies of British soldiers
brought into Hanover. 'So many mothers' sons! So many young bodies
brought into the world to lie there! . . . So many baby mouths drawing life
at women's breasts . . . that men might lie with glazed eyeballs, and swol-
len faces, and fixed, blue unclosed mouths,' so that Karoo bushes might
spring up greener where they have lain, or that the sand might have the
glint of white bones. 'Without an inexorable cause, this must not be!'

She had no illusions about the base reason for almost all wars: people
must die so that a few money-men might increase their gains. She understands that women are not morally superior to men; even though they
know the cost of human flesh, they can be 'seduced' into support for

war. The patriotic aspect of war is a blind – she'd been in Cape Town
when Lord Roberts (Kitchener's predecessor as Commander-in-Chief)
had paraded like a victor in Adderley Street on 8 December 1900, before
embarking for England. She means to strip the image of vainglorious
manliness, the drilled, orderly lines, to expose the chaos soldiers unleash.

'No tinsel of trumpets and flags' should 'seduce women into the insanity of recklessly destroying life, or gild the wilful taking of life with any
other name but that of murder.'

Her oratory – for this reads like oratory – is pointed by parables, as
befits a missionary's daughter. Say, she argues, a town is invaded by an
enemy and its citizens throw anything onto the barricades to block the
advance. They would think nothing of throwing statues onto the pile, but
to the sculptor the statue he's made would not be nothing. Every mother
is such a maker, she asserts. 'Men's bodies are our women's works of art.'

It's a wake-up call. Were they valid, the figures of women looming
ahead, she wondered, or 'is it all a dream?' She suffered as an outcast no
less than Mary Shelley and George Eliot did. She tells herself it's worth it
for the sake of future generations.

How much of *Woman and Labour* was done in Hanover is not known. It
was not published for another ten years. The obverse of her courage was
uncertainty – she would revise her most cherished work endlessly. Her
hesitations were compounded by illness.

Early in May 1901 she collapsed with asthma on hearing that her
English brother Fred had died. It was sudden, on 7 May. The telegram
reached her in Hanover two days later. Alone, a pariah far from her family,
she wanted to howl aloud, 'as if I could go wildly calling for him', and
found herself struggling for breath.

The local commander, Colonel Gedye, hearing she was stricken,
turned out to be civil and considerate. He offered a permit for Cron to
make a visit, and gave Olive permission for a candle and for exercise in
the market square. That winter she had a permit to visit her aged English
mother. The squeezed inhabitants of Hanover murmured louder against
her: she used her Englishness, they said, to extract these favours. In the
no man's land of her room, some British officers from the railway station

at Hanover Road visited her towards the end of the war, and their 'refinement' came as balm for her loneliness.

Was Olive Schreiner changing sides? Was she contradictory? I see her
as strongly consistent in her compassion for victims (as the Boers were at
this time), and her distinction between imperialist greed and the deep ties
of the past that bound her to the mother country. Before the war some
of the dearest humans she had met were English, she had told Havelock
Ellis. 'And this is not taking into view the great army of the dead, from
Shakespeare and Milton to Shelley, Darwin, George Eliot and Browning.'
She thought the worst type of English man or woman a 'canting hypo-
crite', yet in the best English natures saw 'a curious power of obliterating
selfish interests, that is rare, rare indeed.'

A year after she came to Hanover Cron joined her once more, in
September 1901. Her determined, wartime stance and his futile acts of
loyalty to her in the face of family opposition had led to a hardening in
each that separated them even as they shared her small room.

She said in May 1902, 'As all hope in one's personal life dies out one
clings more & more to nature. It seems all in all to one as it was when one
was a little child.'

Even when the war ended that same month, on 31 May 1902, she
remained an outsider. No one in Hanover spoke to her in the street. The
'natives' continued to boycott her. I suppose that Olive was aware how
much Cron had sacrificed in being married to a radical. The plan now
was for Cron to regain standing and confidence by deploying his legal
and administrative skills in a place where the defeated were helpless, as
were the 'natives' who had sided with Britain in the vain hope of a less
racist regime than the Bantu, Khoi and San peoples had suffered under
the Dutch. Cron set up as a land and paralegal agent in a tiny office in
Loop Street in the middle of Hanover, across the way from the Market
Square.

There was plenty of reparation work, though few could afford to pay. In 1903 Cron was elected to the Cape Parliament. The Cronwright-Schreiners bought a house on Hanover's Grace Street, in the same block as Olive's room, but looking in the other direction, away from the veld, and then built on a *stoep* where she liked to cool off, walking up and down, after her day's writing. Though the *stoep* faced towards the *dorp*, no one looked her way. Never had she felt so alone, surrounded by small-minded people who talked to one another about clothes and servants. The defeated, switching-off memory, crawled under a blanket of trivia.

From 1907 Cron set up as an agent in De Aar when this defunct military base — still strewn with relics of the war — declared itself a town. It had never been more than a railway junction, a place of dust, flies and extreme heat in summer, with temperatures of 110° in the shade. At the end of 1907 Olive joined Cron there, first in a room on the edge of what she called the 'camp', and later in a house with a pillared *stoep* at 9 Grundlingh Street. The same solitary pattern prevailed, with both absorbed in their work. Cron took up golf.

She continued to defend outsiders: the victims of anti-Semitism (in 'A Letter on the Jew' in 1905), and the disenfranchised black majority in the Union of South Africa, newly constituted in 1910. Women's separate mission informs *Woman and Labour*. This book came out eventually in 1911. The date of publication is telling, for she was checking proofs at the end of 1910, after an historic event in women's history: 'Black Friday', 18 November 1910, when a WSPU* delegation to the House of Commons, calling itself a 'Women's Parliament', met with violence by the police and male bystanders, who twisted and pinched women's breasts, lifted their skirts, groped them and knocked them to the ground. *Woman and Labour* follows *Dreams* as the holy text for the suffragettes. Vera Brittain said that it became the bible of the women's movement.

But Schreiner resigned from the Women's Enfranchisement League in 1912. She had long opposed its platform on equality with men which in effect excluded women of colour. From this time it was downhill for

---

* Women's Social and Political Union, the militant wing of the suffragettes, founded in 1903.

her. Cron was increasingly disaffected by her failure to complete the 'big' books, which should have compensated financially for his sacrifice. Their estrangement came to a flashpoint over his relationship with Mrs Philpot, whom Olive had known in London as part of the Pearson circle. From 1913, when Olive settled again in England, she and Cron lived apart.

The Great War came as a climax to a series of political events that blighted her hopes of humanity: the pogroms in Russia; the racist constitution of the Union of South Africa, which she foresaw as a disaster like a cart rolling backwards down a hill; the covert racism in the suffrage movement and its short-sighted imitation of men. She deplored the 'theatrical' Mrs Pankhurst who sanctioned the war, Olive thought, to stay in the limelight, though she remained close to her pacifist daughter Sylvia. She spoke up for conscientious objectors, and reproached Gandhi and the ANC for sending troops. When Smuts arrived in 1917, she accompanied him on war business to France and afterwards he recalled how they argued, how she pleaded with him to stop the slaughter. 'I opposed this war', she said in 1918, 'because of the evil I foresaw it would produce for generations to come.'

Her German surname made her unwelcome in London boarding houses – a repeat of her outsider situation in Hanover. The poor food, fuel shortages and the difficulty of breathing in the Underground further undermined her health, so that the war years aged her before her time.

In 1920, when she was sixty-five, Cron arrived in London. They had not seen each other for seven years and Cron could hardly recognise the wife he had known. Although it pained Olive that he should visit Mrs Philpot, he insisted there was no reason to distrust him. They did not live together and Cron did not change his retirement plan for a world tour.

In August 1920 she sailed back to Cape Town, wanting to end her life among her own people. She found a small room in a guesthouse in a leafy southern suburb, but it didn't feel like Africa, and she longed to be back on the veld. On 11 December she died in the night with a book in her hand. She was buried with her baby daughter and dog Neta on Buffels Kop.

---

If Olive Schreiner is remembered mainly for her feminism, hers was independent of a party line. Her central strain is prophetic. Everyone who met her was rapt by her utterance. The British Labour leader Keir Hardie (whose party was the first to support votes for women and possibly the only party ever led by a pacifist), travelled hundreds of miles to Hanover to hear her opinions, as did Fred and Emmeline Pethick-Lawrence, editors of the WSPU journal, who visited her in De Aar. Emily Hobhouse too travelled to De Aar to spend four days in this dusty spot with a fellow protester during the Boer War. Olive seemed 'wrapped in silence', and then would vent speech more eloquent than Hobhouse heard from any other woman.

She belonged to a generation of women who found a public voice. Hers had the resonance of a known writer speaking from an unmasked soul to the souls of readers. It came to them like a voice from the outermost wilderness – unpeopled stretches of veld, a landscape almost unbroken by human habitation. Her dreams of women to be are like dispatches from an unmapped land, a country everyone knew existed, but still unseen.

# 5

# EXPLORER

## Virginia Woolf

Virginia Woolf's fame took off thirty years after her death. In the seventies, with the rise of the Women's Liberation movement, a new generation of readers quickened to her public voice in *A Room of One's Own*, her talks to women at Cambridge in 1928, where she lays out the history of women's subjection. Ten years later, taking a more trenchant tone in *Three Guineas*, she speaks as though she were a leader of the Opposition in Parliament, making the case for closing the pay gap and the right to professional equality. At the same time her attraction to women and her celebration of sex-change in the novel *Orlando* spoke to a burgeoning acceptance of what in her time was considered deviant. Undoubtedly, her daring did its bit to change the face of our world, and the passage of time has brought her closer. We look into the mirror of her writings and find what we are now. All know this Virginia Woolf who was ahead of her time. But co-existing with this image is a writer who understood what she owed to women who lived before the vote. What did she detect in looking back to certain undefined potentialities?

She was ever on the track of gaps and obscurities in past lives. Born on 24 January 1882, a year after George Eliot died, and living into the first half of the twentieth century, she is positioned between nineteenth-century womanhood on the one hand and, on the other, younger women with better access to higher education. Given that position, I want to hear her voice as it picks up the metamorphosed women who preceded her and asks, what is the true nature of woman? I want to read *Three Guineas* as a book that co-opts Emily Brontë's uncowed spirit for its venture to change the world in a revolutionary way. And I want to understand her own sense of her eccentricities and madness, for critics can no longer push her aside as the precious, invalid lady out of touch with the real world.

In the year of her government's Equal Franchise Act of 1928, granting the vote to all citizens over the age of twenty-one, she spoke to newly or soon-to-be enfranchised students at the two women's colleges, Girton and Newnham. They struck her as a sturdy species, making do in a serviceable dining hall, downing their prunes and custard, minus the flow of vintage wines and gamey sauces in centuries-old men's colleges in Cambridge.

She was familiar with Cambridge; all the males in her family were educated there, and her cousin, Katharine Stephen, had been Principal of Newnham from 1911 until 1920, just eight years before. She was the daughter of Sir James Fitzjames Stephen, a hanging judge. Virginia pictures this cousin, a generation older, as hard to know and 'strangely unaccented', with a hat pulled down over her eyes. Her shoes looked as though they were sculptured; a sealed carapace made bare feet unimaginable.

As an unmarried daughter, Katharine Stephen would have been expected to make herself useful at home, but had persuaded her father, who did not favour women's rights, to permit her to work. In the mid-1880s, when she was thirty, she had taken a post as secretary to the Vice-Principal of Newnham, Athena Clough, a classicist who was niece to Anne Jemima Clough, the first Principal. In 1888, when the college built a library, Katharine Stephen became Librarian.

In 1923, the year before her cousin died, Virginia had visited her in South Kensington. Miss Stephen, sitting as though she were 'all of a piece, unjointed', told Virginia that on her deathbed she would order her char to burn the neat row of her diaries started when she was twenty-one. She conveyed this with a sort of 'mute sagacity'.

A diarist herself, Virginia Woolf was struck by this planned act of self-obliteration. But, looking back, she remembered an external invisibility forced upon her cousin when she'd stepped outside her community of women in college. Her father's brother, Leslie Stephen, who had been a Cambridge don, had snubbed this Newnham niece when she came for lunch in London. It was not lost on his daughter Virginia at that family table in Kensington. The Stephen brothers were senior members of Cambridge University, which in those days and for decades to come – beyond Virginia's lifetime – did not grant women degrees, even if the university did tolerate their higher education in separate colleges.

At the time of the snub, Leslie Stephen was educating Virginia at home. It was hugely to her advantage to have this accomplished reader, writer and editor discuss books as they walked each morning around the Round Pond in Kensington Gardens. But only his sons were sent to school and Cambridge. Virginia had to mop up Greek as best she could at home. At the age of twenty, determined (like Mary Godwin and Mary Ann Evans before her) to master words reserved for men, she engaged a private tutor, Janet Case, who had been amongst the first generation of Girton students. Reading Euripides in Greek, Virginia was gripped by the heroic independence of Electra, 'harsh & splendid'. Emily Brontë seemed to her the English counterpart.

Leslie Stephen was a contradictory character, much like Virginia Woolf's portrait of him as Mr Ramsay in *To the Lighthouse*. He had a fearless intellectual honesty. At the same time, he didn't take to opinionated women, and for that reason in her teens she never showed him what she wrote. When he said that Ginia was to be a writer, he adds, 'That is a thing for ladies'. He simply had no idea what she harboured as a writer.

He had scaled the Alps – Thomas Hardy had likened his lean, craggy build to an Alpine peak in his poem 'The Schrekhorn'. In Clarens in 1887 Leslie Stephen had met Olive Schreiner and was charmed by her black eyes, but her critical talk 'riled' him. No, despite popular regard for *The Story of an African Farm*, Miss Schreiner, he remarked to his wife, 'is not my kind of young woman'.

He reserved his most withering put-downs for his sister, Caroline Emelia Stephen. She was a Quaker convert and theologian. In the Society of Friends, a woman had equal right to express her convictions, and

Caroline Stephen had published three books. The best known, *Quaker Strongholds* (1890, reprinted three times), was a summation of the Quaker ethos, including pacifism, a cause her niece Virginia would later take up. Yet though Miss Stephen had the verbal readiness of her eminent brothers (both of whom were knighted), to Leslie she was merely 'Silly Milly', who occupied herself by writing 'little' books.

But it was 'Silly Milly' who, at the age of seventy, took in Virginia, aged twenty-two, after a breakdown following her father's death in 1904. And, then, when Miss Stephen herself died five years later, she left a will that singled out two unmarried nieces, Virginia and Katharine, to receive each £2500. Not a lot, just five hundred pounds more than George Eliot had from her father, which had allowed her to set up as a writer in London. Miss Stephen left a token one hundred pounds to Virginia's sister Vanessa Bell, who was married, and the same to their brother Adrian. It was this legacy from an aunt that had made Virginia Woolf's life as a writer possible, she told her student audience in 1928.* It had meant more to her than the vote, she added, and was the basis for her famous claim that a woman will need five hundred pounds a year and privacy — a room of one's own — if she is to write.

This was only a partial answer to a question she struggled to pose, while entertaining the students with men's nonsensical definitions of women, and freely owning her anger. But when she came to revise the lectures for publication she admitted that she could not solve 'the great problem of the true nature of woman'. There could be no answer for another hundred years, she said, not until women had been tested in politics and the professions. A hundred years brings us to the question now.

George Eliot had concluded that, so long as women's potentialities could not be determined with any accuracy, in view of their thwarted

---

* In *A Room of One's Own* (1929), the book that emerged from the Cambridge talks, Virginia Woolf fictionalises her aunt as 'Mary Beton', who lived in Bombay. In addition to the money from her aunt, Virginia Woolf also had money from her father's estate, so that the bequests together amounted to nine thousand pounds, giving her an income of four hundred pounds a year. By contrast, before George Eliot began to write fiction she had two hundred pounds a year.

lives, they must remain in question. 'Meanwhile', she said, 'the indefinite-ness remains.'

A generation later, Virginia Woolf picks up this matter of indefinite-ness, which she believed takes us beyond the simple politics of rights. In George Eliot's heroines, Virginia Woolf sees 'the ancient consciousness of woman . . . for so many ages dumb' brim with a 'demand for something – they scarcely know what – for something that is perhaps incompatible with the facts of human existence'.

No one knew George Eliot better than she did, she told herself as she read the Cross biography in preparation for the centenary of Eliot's birth in 1919. No one was more awake to the Maggie Tulliver plight of the generation before her own. She had an eye to women who could not express themselves. It's what she herself might have experienced. When she fictionalised her Victorian family in *To the Lighthouse* (1927), she notes in her *Diary* that had her father lived longer, as he might have done, there would have been no books. It comes as a bolt: no books. The writer we know as 'Virginia Woolf' would not have been. Just so Shakespeare's hypothetical sister in the sixteenth century, whom she calls up for the benefit of the Cambridge students: a woman so pulled apart by a gift to write, at variance with womanly obligations, 'that she would certainly have gone crazed' or lived on the margin, demonised and mocked.

In 1927, the year before she talked to the students, she spoke of Jane Carlyle with 'brilliant gifts – which had borne so little visible result'. She quotes Mrs Carlyle's friend, the mid-nineteenth-century novelist Geraldine Jewsbury, assuring Jane that they were *not* failures: 'We are indi-cations of a development of womanhood which as yet is not recognised. It has, so far, no ready-made channels to run in . . . There are women to come after us, who will approach nearer to the fullness of the measure of the stature of women's nature.'

Virginia Woolf's approach to the world and to her writing was both bold and, to her contemporaries, strange. One night, crossing Russell Square, she saw 'the infinite oddity of the human position', and sensed, she said, 'my own strangeness, walking on the earth'.

Her strangeness can come over as eccentricity, so endearing to the English sense of humour, so validating as to authentic character. I think Virginia Woolf's strangeness is stranger, and has to do with the evolutionary frontier.

'Approaching fullness' professionally as a leader of innovative fiction, Virginia Woolf told the students how she'd walk about, alert to unspoken lives, 'the pressure of dumbness'. As she passed, onlookers would stare, giggle and nudge one another. It was not only that her dress was not bright and sleek in the style of the twenties – she might perhaps be wearing a wrinkled pale grey like 'a young elephant' – there was something strange and disquieting in her opened, owlish eyes and in the trance-like way she moved with a slightly shuffling tread. To walk each afternoon through the streets of London was to sharpen her sense of the past and also to open her mind to what she would write next morning.

The city beckoned like an unexplored land. A 'restless searcher', she liked to imagine a voyage of discovery or the fin of a submerged form lurking in the waves. 'Why is there not a discovery in life?' she wrote in her diary. 'Something one can lay hands on & say "This is it"? . . . I have a great & astonishing sense of something there . . . '

To the students at Newnham and Girton in October 1928 she declared that the challenge for them would be language. The words future generations will need are 'hardly syllabled yet'. New words will have 'to wing their way into being'. But when words are wanting, silence must sound. It must not be lost in the tea-table talk she and her sister had been trained to deploy to keep conversation flowing for the benefit of elderly Victorian gentlemen seated in their drawing room at Hyde Park Gate.

In her first novel, *The Voyage Out*, she has a male character predict that it will take six generations for women to surface. On board a ship to South America, an unformed young woman, Rachel Vinrace, imagines a deep-sea creature, 'a monster of the lower waters', who'd explode if brought to the surface. This creature can exist only out of sight and hearing: a highly endangered species, yet for all the danger there's exhilaration in sensing that other existence. To look into those lower waters for unknown modes of being was the imaginative edge that Virginia Woolf walked all her life. This was to tread the edge of insanity.

When does the strangeness become mental instability?

Once, as a child, she couldn't step across a puddle for thinking, 'how strange – what am I?' From childhood she felt life is 'the oddest affair'. The oddity she perceived reflected oddity back on her; the more oddity, the farther out she was in mental solitude. The risk threatened to destroy the gain: the bouts of what she and her family called 'madness'. What she dreaded most, filling her with anticipatory horror, was to be put away in a 'home'. At such times she was even more apart than other risk-takers: Mary Godwin, cast out by her father, or 'Mrs Lewes' shunned in the late 1850s, or Olive Schreiner confined under martial law. Like these risk-takers she found the fruit of her soul in writing. 'I generally get a spurt on after one of these collapses,' she said. 'That[']s what pulls me through – And psychologically they have their advantages – one visits such remote strange places, lying in bed.'

Virginia was fifteen when she suffered her first breakdown. It followed a terrible blow: the death of her half-sister Stella, at the age of twenty-eight. Stella and her two brothers, George and Gerald Duckworth, were the offspring of their mother's first marriage. After the early death of their mother Julia in 1895, Stella took her place for the four children of her mother's second marriage to man of letters Leslie Stephen. She scrubbed the two youngest, Virginia and Adrian, visited her stepfather's child, Laura Stephen, in an asylum, and soothed his widowed grief – taking it on herself behind closed doors to spare the younger children.

So long as their mother had lived, Stella had resisted marriage. She was intensely close to her mother, and then, after Julia Stephen's death, she lost interest in living. So it seemed to an alert Virginia, who thought Stella beautiful, with horns of fair hair like the pale cow-parsley that grows by the road in spring. She had no colour in her skin, and as time went on grew paler in her black dress. Virginia went with Stella when she consulted Elizabeth Garrett Anderson, the first woman doctor in Britain, and Stella told her anxious sister that it was merely 'fidgets' (the family's term for nerviness).

Stella then resigned herself to what her mother had urged: to accept her foremost suitor, Jack Hills. He had the credentials of Eton and Balliol College, Oxford, and his parents lived in a castle in the north. This was a good, though dogged man, inviting respect, not ardour – rather like George Eliot's Mr Gilfil. Virginia Woolf uses the passive form years later when she touched on Stella's fate in *To the Lighthouse*: Prue Ramsay is 'given' in marriage.

Virginia broke her umbrella 'in half' when Stella left on honeymoon, and went to bed 'very furious and tantrumical', she says in her first, 1897 diary. When Stella returned, Virginia herself got the 'fidgets' and Stella kept Virginia with her. Stella, soon pregnant, had a companion; Virginia had the balm of maternal care. When Stella felt better, the sisters took drives around the Serpentine in Hyde Park, but more often Stella lay on the sofa and Virginia sat by her. She stayed overnight in July, sleeping in Jack's dressing room, with Stella stroking her until she slept. Next morning before breakfast Stella, looking quite well, came in her dressing gown to check on her sister. She came for only a moment, Virginia records in her diary, 'and I never saw her again'.

Three days later two new doctors decided to operate for peritonitis, and their patient died. That is all that's known. No one could bear to talk. Virginia's diary is painful to read: how Jack took her and her elder sister Vanessa to Highgate cemetery to see Stella's grave (next to her mother) covered with wilted flowers.

The fact of death came as a betrayal of the hold on life that Stella had given her. 'The blow, the second blow of death struck on me, creased, sitting with my wings still stuck together, on the broken chrysalis.'

Six months later, just before she turned sixteen, her diary observes that she needed a rhino's skin to go on living, 'and that I have not got'.

An added ordeal for the two remaining sisters was that, without Mrs Stephen and Stella, the men in the household began to prey on them. Leslie Stephen subjected Vanessa to outbursts of rage over housekeeping accounts as she stood by mute. But much worse was the sisters' exposure to fondling by their half-brother George Duckworth. Virginia described a scene in a Memoir Club paper: he would tiptoe into her bedroom and when she started up in alarm, he would fling himself on her, crying 'Beloved'. It was made out to be over-mastering brotherly love. This is a sinister kind of predator, who appears, even to himself, as a benevolent protector: now and then the sisters gave him the trust he invited. It was a sequel to Virginia's abuse as a child small enough to be lifted onto a table by her other grown-up half-brother, Gerald. The sisters, who said nothing, formed 'a very close conspiracy': in a glassed room at the back of their home at 22 Hyde Park Gate, Vanessa would paint while Virginia read aloud from Thackeray and George Eliot.

The years from 1897 to 1904, their last at Hyde Park Gate, were unhappy – 'the Greek slave years', Virginia was to call them. The Stephen sisters, who just wanted to paint and write, did not go willingly to society balls with George Duckworth. Before they stepped into the carriage he would scrutinise their appearance for infringements of the social code; he was a stickler for correct dress, and wore a 'slip' under his waistcoat to provide a spotless white edging. No one asked Virginia to dance, and at one ball she crept behind a curtain to read Tennyson. As an onlooker, she wondered at the artifice of society girls, designed for the marriage market. The dinner bell striking eight seemed to call them into existence.

After her father's death in 1904 things got much worse. She heard voices: King Edward VII defiling the language and birds singing in Greek. On 10 May she threw herself out of a window.

When Virginia calls her condition 'madness', we can't recover the exact tone, but we can pick up a jocular nuance to this bluntness, deprecating those who might fall back on crude diagnosis. There is no word for madness that is not pejorative, but undoubtedly Dryden's famous line, 'Great wits are sure to madness near allied' applies, as does Charles Lamb's distinction between the flights of great and small wits.* There was a genetic

---

* 'On the Sanity of True Genius' (1826). His sister, Mary Lamb, co-author of their *Tales from Shakespeare* (published by William Godwin, as part of his Juvenile Library) was subject to bouts of madness. The brother sorrowfully leading his sister to an asylum was a familiar sight in London.

predisposition from her grandfather, Sir James Stephen, who apologised to his wife for being 'moonstruck'. As Colonial Under-Secretary, his anxiety over the colonies was so overwrought as to be 'a test of insanity'.

A nervous temperament was thought to unfit people, females especially, for public office. But John Stuart Mill rebuts this truism: he believed it was this very quality that made for 'great orators, great preachers, impressive diffusers of moral influences'. From boyhood James Stephen felt the rhythms of language and carried 'a great stock of words' in his head. 'I can arrange them without any trouble, when my occasions require it', he remarked to his wife. After he drew up the Parliamentary bill against slavery, working under enormous pressure, he had what his daughter calls 'a severe nervous illness'.

Virginia ascribed 'black melancholy' to the Stephens' Scotch origins — the Scotch, she believed, have melancholy 'in their bones', which was 'turned to madness in some of us'. The predisposition was there in what Sir James's son Leslie Stephen called his own 'Berserker fits'. Virginia was closer to her father than his other children were, and she could not adopt the stony resistance of her sister. He had formed her tastes and she spoke often of his lovability while he was dying. 'It was the most exquisite feeling to be with him, even to touch his hand', she said after he was gone. 'He was so quick, and that one finds in no one else.'

The late-Victorian medical establishment in matters of mental health was led by Dr Maudsley and Dr Savage. The latter was the author of the standard textbook on the subject, and as the Stephen family doctor, one of the practitioners to treat Virginia. These doctors warned against higher education of the weaker sex, including self-education — what Virginia Stephen was doing when she learnt Greek in her bedroom. For, these doctors decreed, if a girl is allowed to educate herself at home, conceit and the want of social friction would unfit her for her function as a woman and could lead to insanity.

The doctors of her youth were sniffing out that room of her own where she learnt and worked, as though privacy itself were an act of deviance.

Only later did she find the courage to say publicly that to diverge from the image of female inferiority in the arts was a form of mental 'torture' that a man cannot imagine. Though 'madness' can't be explained, the word 'torture' does suggest how pressure against deviance can bring on collapse.

This explains the depth of her submergence so as to hold to what she was. Even decades later, when she became a leading novelist, she notes in her diary, 'I must be private, secret, as anonymous and submerged as possible in order to write.' Her essay *On Being Ill* claims illness as an 'act' of separation from the compliant herd, 'outlaws that we are'.

The illness of 1904, severe though it was, did not last all that long. She was not put away in a 'home'; instead she was sent for nearly three months to Welwyn in Hertfordshire to stay with Stella's Quaker friend Violet Dickinson — 'my Violet', Virginia always called her. She was seventeen years older than Virginia, a single woman in her late thirties, who had served briefly as mayor of Bath and had a particular concern for mentally ill women with a criminal record. It amused Virginia to observe the way this friend would screw her face into comical grimaces. Violet was the 'harum-scarum' granddaughter of Lord Auckland, tall (six foot two), sympathetic and indispensable to her many friends.

By the time she nursed Virginia in 1904 a 'romantic friendship' had been in play for the six years since Stella had died. The word 'tender' resonates in Virginia's letters, touched up with erotic teasing. She had 'tender memories of a long embrace, in a bedroom' and ended one letter saying 'I will lick you tenderly', but her infantine need was uppermost. Its insistence makes it difficult to label this as a sexual relationship. With Violet she played the 'wallaby', a kind of snuffling baby whose soft nose wrinkled: 'would you like to feel the Wallaby snout on your bosom?' she asked. Would Violet be a mother kangaroo with an enfolding pouch? Now and later she was inclined to fall in love with an older woman who offered her petting and cherishing.

In October 1904, she went to stay with another Quaker, her aunt Caroline Emelia Stephen, in Cambridge.* Though she missed her sister

---

* At Cambridge Caroline's father, Sir James Stephen, had held an honorary appointment as Professor of History. He should not be confused with his son, the judge James Fitzjames Stephen, who was Caroline's brother.

Vanessa and her brothers, Thoby and Adrian, who were making a new home in Bloomsbury, she came to find The Perch 'an ideal retreat for me'.

Her aunt believed that to 'retire from the surface to the depths of life is sure to bring help and strengthening'. To retire was to be the precaution Virginia adopted for the rest of her life whenever premonitions of break-down – headaches, agitation, sleeplessness – took her over. In her aunt's book, to retire, in a spiritual sense, was not to give up; on the contrary, to switch off the clamour of public voices was to retrieve integrity and, with that, peace of mind.

Miss Stephen would calm strain with a humorous phrase her high-flying circle used to one another: 'Now, dear, do not be sublime.'

Her niece went with her to Meeting, and thought of writing it up. One day she and her aunt talked, Virginia reports, 'for some nine hours; and [she] poured forth all her spiritual experiences. All her life she has been listening to inner voices'.

Her aunt's trust in 'the witness within' was a sound alternative to mad voices that appeared to bear out doctors' warnings. Later, Virginia would confide to another novelist, Gerald Brenan, that there was something to be gained from her 'insanities', which had 'done instead of religion'. And later still, as she pitted art against death in the bravura finale to her masterpiece *The Waves*, her pen seemed to stumble after voices flying ahead 'as when I was mad'. In this instance, the fusion of madness and art certainly has to do with an inner voice carried through to public utterance. This work co-opts the art of poetic soliloquy for the novel; it sheds the outer life of action to hear six voices, three men and three women, who, collectively, take us through the lifespan of one generation.

Caroline Stephen had herself experienced a collapse in 1875, after performing what society expected of her, which is to say what she expected of herself as an unmarried daughter at home: to nurse her dying mother and, that same year, to care for her brother Leslie and his child after the death of his first wife. She understood the danger of what she termed morbid introspectiveness leading to a painful 'baptism'. There were truths, she found, too deep for definition, to be discovered only through death. Caroline Stephen was prepared to say that she did actually wish for death. This frame of mind fits Virginia Woolf's predisposition to suicide. To make one's way through death to join with the dead is hinted in fragments she crossed out from her treatment of her suicidal character, Septimus Warren Smith, in *Mrs Dalloway*.

To suggest that Caroline Stephen prompted these positions would not be entirely true, since they were already part of her niece, but for a space there was comfort, and it's conceivable that the model of her writer-aunt heartened her as she started to write for publication.

It was while she lived with her aunt that she picked up her pen to write professionally for the first time in November 1904. Violet had introduced her to the editor of a women's supplement to a church newspaper called *The Guardian*, who commissioned a piece. The topic Virginia chose is a pilgrimage to the Brontë Parsonage in Haworth. Will her 'friend' Charlotte Brontë be the same, she wonders a little uneasily as she comes upon what looks like a too-ordinary Yorkshire village. At the Parsonage, she peers into the oblong recess beside the staircase where Emily drove and pinned Keeper, her fierce dog, and pummelled him for sleeping on her bed. In the museum above a bank on the steep street, she's 'thrilled' to see the little oak stool 'which Emily carried with her on her solitary moorland tramps, and on which she sat, if not to write, as they say, to think'.

During that time of retreat, Virginia also did a portrait of her father for publication, at the request of his biographer, F. W. Maitland (a Cambridge don who had been one of Leslie Stephen's band of hikers or 'Sunday tramps'). It was part of her recovery to distil what she most wished to retain of her father as a voice reciting poems to his children: 'as he lay back in his chair and spoke the beautiful words with closed eyes, we felt that he was speaking not merely the words of Tennyson or Wordsworth but what he himself felt or knew. Thus many of the great English poems now seem to me inseparable from my father; I hear in them not only his voice, but in some sort his teaching and belief.' These two sentences welling up to bear witness, the feeling they communicate, together with her rhythmic grace, are equal to the greatness to come. We don't need to be told that she was perfectly sane when she wrote that.

She says little of her aunt, and often it's tinged with irony. Leslie Stephen had licensed his children to talk down his sister. Caroline Stephen would not defer to authority – nor to the priesthood. Her 'admission' to 'the ministry of women' – that was how she spoke – freed her words to flow 'naturally' from 'the disuse' of appointed power.

That politely toned-down phrase, 'disuse of power', links her with two political movements. Though the Quaker faith aligns her with Dissenters, the challenge to power aligns her with Stephen kin in the Clapham Sect, evangelicals in the early years of the century who were bent on reforming the established church from within. Caroline Stephen's grandfather, the first James Stephen, was a Scotch lawyer who had visited the West Indies to inspect the conditions of the slaves. On his return, he had joined opponents of slavery, including their leader, William Wilberforce, who settled in the vicinity of the Rector of Clapham, John Venn, south of London. John Venn was Caroline Stephen's other grandfather, and great-grandfather to Virginia. Both of these men, together with the Smith forebear of George Eliot's intimate Barbara Leigh Smith and her cousin Florence Nightingale (as granddaughters of William Smith, MP), were central to the abolitionists, who proved effective in manning pulpits and delivering speeches in Parliament. They succeeded in abolishing the slave trade in 1807. In the following generation, James's son Sir James (Caroline Emelia's father and Virginia's grandfather) drew up the bill to abolish slavery throughout the Empire in 1833, facing down resistant slave-owners. This voice of protest found its way into the female line. Virginia was proud to say that by nature 'both Vanessa and I were explorers, reformers, revolutionists'.

When it came to the Woman Question, their aunt's 'disuse' of power found a political home in Mrs Humphrey Ward's alternative to women who narrowed in on the vote. Miss Stephen was a signatory to a different plan in an 'Appeal Against Female Suffrage' (1889). Though for some this expressed a conservative backlash, for others there was the high aim of women's 'public usefulness'. Caroline Stephen, who had established a women's refuge, aligned herself with her sister-in-law Julia Stephen (Virginia's mother was a volunteer nurse who wrote a book on the management of sickrooms), Octavia Hill (co-founder of the National Trust), Beatrice Potter (later Webb, the pioneering socialist) and Elizabeth Wordsworth (the founding Principal of Lady Margaret Hall, the first women's college in Oxford).

This put Virginia Stephen's kin amongst a hundred and four upper-middle-class Englishwomen (linked to the political class, the civil service, dons and teachers), who initiated what became a growing movement (forty-two thousand by 1914) against the fifty thousand suffragists who, they foretold – accurately, as it turned out, once women gained the vote – would dissipate the woman's voice in the established political parties. They looked on Parliament as an alien debating club concerned with the army and navy, mines and railways. Reforming or 'forward' members of the movement abjured the copycat aims of the militants, which would tug women towards personal struggle and rivalry. The antis saw women's potential contribution (alongside that of civilised men) as being to develop altruism and morality to counter balance public power resting on force.

At the core of this debate was the question of woman's nature: the antis favoured 'true' as distinct from 'new' womanhood. This was in the air when Virginia Stephen came of age. In an article on 'Women and Politics' in 1907 and again in the *Anti-Suffrage Review* in 1909, Caroline Stephen proposed a 'third House' of Parliament. She conceived it as a separate con-sultative chamber of wise, experienced women, elected by women only. For the first time, Miss Stephen said, 'we should hear a really feminine voice in national affairs – a voice . . . that the Suffrage could never give.'

Virginia Woolf made much of her aunt's legacy – perhaps too much – when she declared to Cambridge students that it had 'unveiled the sky to me'. But her aunt provided more than money to fund her future. Though Caroline Stephen's movement lost out to party politics, Virginia Woolf's writings would reinvigorate that alternative idea of women's mission. In her obituary of her aunt, she praised 'a life which had about it the har-mony of a large design'.

———

The Stephen sisters had their own large design when they set to work at 46 Gordon Square in Bloomsbury. Writing and painting were to come first: no more balls; no white gloves; no more dressing for dinner. Instead, 'shabby, crony talk' over cocoa, talk till all hours with their brother Thoby's Cambridge friends. Gurth, their sheepdog, was sole chaperone. Photographs of their mother, a whole row of them, by another aunt, the pioneering photographer Julia Margaret Cameron, looked down from the walls of the hall, opposite her famous photos of Tennyson (an image known as 'The Dirty Monk'), Darwin, Hershel, Lowell, Meredith and Browning (wrapped in a dark blanket setting off his shapely beard).

The bonds with Thoby's friends tightened with yet another family tragedy: in 1906 large, confident Thoby died of typhoid caught on a journey to Constantinople. The following year Vanessa married his friend Clive Bell. Virginia believed herself in love with another friend, the future biographer Lytton Strachey. He proposed to her in February 1909, but even as he spoke she sensed homosexual unease, and next day released him.

Strachey suggested to Leonard Woolf that he take his place.

'You must marry Virginia', his letter said. She was the only woman with sufficient brains. 'It's a miracle that she should exist.'

Lytton described Virginia for Leonard's benefit in August 1909: she was 'young, wild, inquisitive, discontented, and longing to be in love'.

Leonard responded with alacrity. 'Do you think Virginia would have me?', he wrote. 'Wire to me if she accepts. I'll take the next boat home.'

Virginia was somewhat intrigued by reports of Leonard Woolf, who had been in her brother's Cambridge circle, but was now far off in Ceylon. Thoby had pictured him as a misanthrope who shook his fist at the world and vanished into the jungle, never to return. But, meanwhile, she had other admirers, including her sister's husband Clive Bell. At Bloomsbury parties she entertained friends with dashing flights of fancy. Lytton, for instance, should be a Venetian prince in blue tights lying on his back and balancing an exquisite leg in the air. Her playfulness gained her a reputation for unreliability when it came to facts. But away from parties she was serious, going back to her enthusiasm at seventeen for a book her father had brought her from the London Library. It was *The Principal Navigations, Voyages, Traffiques and Discoveries of the English Nation* (1589) by Richard Hakluyt. (The title of her first novel, *The Voyage Out*, is no coincidence.)

Her own wish to explore is not primarily a fact-collecting impulse; it's a search for meaning by a witness who abstains from ready-made definitions. Virginia Stephen was twenty-four when she produced a few pages on 'The Mysterious Case of Miss V.' (1906). The narrator is a detective or spy of sorts, who cannot catch elusive Miss V. Her life flits by, unknown. The detective poses a posthumous question: is it possible 'to track down the shadow'?

It's a crucial question about a woman's unseen life, analogous to that endangered monster of the lower waters. The first act of detection is to mark that this form of life does in fact exist.

Miss V. appears a nonentity, the obscurest of the obscure, a vanishing shadow – the word 'shadow' recurs like an insistent rat-tat on a drum: a shadow of an unmarked life. Miss V.'s conversational fillers about the weather provide no clue to who she is. Her reported death seems to close off a blank, yet that blank reverberates as a challenge 'to see . . . if she lived, and talk to her'. It's tantamount to addressing a ghost. The author calls it 'a mysterious case', using Sherlock Holmes terms. Virginia Stephen does begin to detect Miss V., if only by circling her absence (as, in her post-war novel *Jacob's Room*, she will go on to circle the absence of Jacob Flanders, representing the lost generation of the Great War, who is killed on Flanders fields before he comes into his own).

Once, when the novelist asks herself what exactly she is writing, her hesitant answer is 'elegy'. Her recurring drama is indeed loss and striving to know, and yet the effort to track the footprints of the dead becomes itself the story. These are not great men, not candidates for the *Dictionary of National Biography* founded by her father. A counter-story waits in the wings, the untried potentialities of lives 'in the shade'. The phrase calls up the candlelit confidences of two sisters called Phyllis and Rosamond, whom Virginia imagines in a story of 1906, and in that same year, a fifteenth-century mother and daughter holed up against soldiers on the rampage during the Wars of the Roses. Then, in 1909, she imagines a woman writer of an earlier generation whose works won't survive. She submitted the last, 'Memoirs of a Novelist', to the *Cornhill*, the literary journal her father used to edit. The story was turned down.

In 1910, during a threatened bout of madness, she had been put away in a private nursing home at Twickenham. How she hated it: the ugliness of the walls in mottled green and red; the director, Miss Jean Thomas, 'always culminating in silent prayer'; the staff as small-witted as the patients, gushing over the royal family. A person who Vanessa thought might be a homicidal maniac turned out to be a nurse.

'To be 29 and unmarried – to be a failure – childless – insane too, no writer,' Virginia groaned to her sister in June 1911.

At this low point, enter Leonard Woolf.

That very month, June 1911, he returned on leave from his Colonial Service post, where he had been for seven years. By then he had attained the position of Assistant Commissioner in Hambantota District in southern Ceylon, and was acting as magistrate in courtroom hearings. He was the son of a Jewish barrister, Sidney Woolf, a moral being whose watchwords came from the prophet Micah: to deal justly and love mercy and walk humbly with your Lord. Sidney Woolf had died in his prime, leaving his wife, the Dutch-born Marie de Jongh, with nine children and little money. The brainy, responsible Leonard had won classical scholarships to St Paul's School and then to Trinity College, Cambridge. There, in Thoby Stephen's rooms, he had met the remote and beautiful Stephen sisters dressed in white, carrying parasols, when they visited their brother.

Now, on Leonard's return from the East, he found them part of an artistic group bent on breaking Victorian taboos, airing the words 'semen' and what they gravely termed 'copulation' in mixed company where women were equals – it was hardly possible to treat them otherwise in the presence of the Stephen sisters. When Leonard dined with the Bells at 46 Gordon Square in July 1911, Virginia came in afterwards. She saw a man who had been friends with Thoby; as such she felt him to be like her brother, though physically he was very different: dark, thin, with intent blue eyes and a hawk-like profile. When he laughed it seemed as though the hawk rose in the air.

He felt at once at home in the Bloomsbury set, and began to see a lot of Virginia, who had moved with her brother Adrian to Fitzroy Square. As a friend, she invited him for a weekend at a place she rented at Firle in Sussex.

Later in 1911 Leonard took the top floor in a communal house that Virginia set up at 38 Brunswick Square (yet another of Bloomsbury's squares). Meals on trays for the various inmates (all members of the set, including the economist John Maynard Keynes) were provided by Sophie, who had been the Stephens' cook at Hyde Park Gate. This experiment in communal living was considered shocking: an unchaperoned young woman living with men friends.

This was when Leonard Woolf decided to pursue Virginia, even if it meant staying on beyond his leave. It would put an end to his post in Ceylon and, with no income of his own, he took a huge risk. For though Virginia lent an ear to his offer of marriage, she remained unconvinced and could be, at times, aloof and distant. Given her history with her half-brothers, she had reason to be wary of male sexuality and had rejected a number of suitors – all Cambridge men from backgrounds like her own.

During this time of coming to know Leonard in a day-to-day way, there were two points of accord to be tested: themselves and their novels. Virginia Woolf's greatest short story, 'Lappin and Lapinova', looks back to this uncertain time in so far as it's about the fate of an orphan bride who takes on the character of a woodland creature with big staring eyes, at once playful and elusive. Flitting by night through the thickets, she reveals herself as 'Lapinova' – hare-like with her dangling paws, as Odette in *Swan Lake* is swanlike with arms behind her like wings.

In 1911 Diaghilev brought the Russian Ballet to London, and the repertoire included the woodland Act II of *Swan Lake*.* Vaslav Nijinsky was Siegfried, who comes upon this mysterious creature in the wild – forced to appear a swan by day, she is freed only by night to be the woman she is, utterly

---

* The Lev Ivanov-Petipa choreography was revised by Michel Fokine, and Mathilde Kschessinska was the Swan Queen.

unlike the indistinguishable ladies at court – and he falls in love with her.

It was during this first London season that the Russian Ballet 'became a centre for both fashionable and intellectual London', Leonard Woolf recalls in his autobiography. 'Night after night we flocked to Covent Garden, entranced by a new art', and the people he liked best in the world were all there, as moved as he was. 'I have never seen anything more perfect, nor more exciting, on any stage than Scheherezade, Carnival, Lac des Cygnes, and the other famous classics.' According to his diary, he saw *Swan Lake* on 7 December and again, together with Virginia, saw 'Russian dancers' on 24 June 1912.

Lapinova's locus comes from those acts of discovery and transformation in the night woods. There a woman reveals her true being, and there a male of character, King Lappin, will find her. Away from the world, on honeymoon, Lapinova shows who she is to her bridegroom: here is 'the real Rosalind', a name that calls up an outcast young woman in the Forest of Arden, an orphan, who makes shift to survive.

The success or failure of marriage will depend on a bridegroom's willingness not only to recognise his bride's 'real' self when they are alone, but to carry that knowing back into the day-to-day life that follows the honeymoon. It's a crucial test of love, but since the outcome can't be foretold, the bride takes a risk: will she survive in the husband's world outside her natural habitat? This was Virginia's question.

They were both mature enough to know that they could not know themselves in the situations marriage would present. A surer test of accord must be what they made of each other's novels. In March 1912 Virginia Stephen read aloud extracts from her still unpublished *Voyage Out*. Leonard thought it extraordinarily good.

A young woman, Rachel Vinrace, is surfacing in the course of her 'voyage out', and then dies before her shape is clear. Leonard Woolf was then writing his first, Ceylon novel, *The Village in the Jungle*. The integrity of a Sinhalese peasant called Babun is unreachable by a colonial court. The accused, in turn, cannot comprehend British justice, which ends his life. The jungle dominates the book, both in its power to obliterate the clearings and as a metaphor for the obfuscation of justice. The tale shows how impossible it was for British rule, however well intentioned, to penetrate the jungle of the ruled, how superficial that rule was and, in a way, absurd. (*The Village in the Jungle* also proved that the Colonial Service had lost one of its most thoughtful magistrates.)

So it was that the two writers found their territories touched, as do those of Lappin and Lapinova, despite the fact that they 'were the opposite of each other'. Lapinova's habitat was 'a desolate, mysterious place' where she ranges 'mostly by moonlight', while King Lappin 'ruled over the busy world of rabbits'.

When Virginia continued to hesitate in late April 1912, Leonard owned to 'many beastly qualities', especially lust. He repeated, 'I have faults vices beastlinesses but even with them I do believe you ought to marry me and be in love –'.

From this there arose a beast language that made them intimates in a world of their own making and convinced Virginia to marry. She was sometimes a variegated Bird given to courtship display but mainly she was a Mandrill (a large West African baboon), known also as 'the great Brute', and Leonard was mainly a Mongoose (called affectionately 'my rapid, bold Mong' whom the Mandrill takes into service). Their love letters speak through their animal characters before and after their marriage, which took

place not long after, on 10 August 1912. The Mandrill makes free to boast
of the fine condition of her flanks and rump, and invites the Mongoose
to an exhibition. The grovelling Mongoose takes courage to lay before the
Mandrill a legal contract whereby the Mandrill has to obey certain rules
while he is away. These are Leonard Woolf's precautions against mental
illness: not to excite herself unduly, to drink a *whole* glass of milk every
morning, to rest on the sofa if she has a period, to 'be wise', to 'be happy'.

Here is a relationship in which character drums up enduring interest.
They were far less free than others in their set. They were miserable apart.
Their letters express flatness and longing: 'It's so frightfully tame without
you', Virginia complains. Leonard's Trinity College roommate, Saxon
Sydney-Turner, was keeping her company in their rented country house,
Asheham, in Sussex, but he seemed like a tame pussycat 'after my own
passionate & ferocious & entirely adorable M'.

The marriage was crucial to Virginia not so much for the practical reason
of Leonard's protection, but because marriage itself presented a complementary challenge to becoming an artist: to be creative in private life.
Here is a mate not as mentor, like Shelley was for Mary, but as Lewes was
for George Eliot – an equal. She presents the case of a writer who believes
that creativity must not be reserved for work. Her letters to her husband
show how much verbal skill went into daily conduct. Obviously, the marriage was infused with Virginia's flair for characterisation. What is less
obvious is Leonard's contribution to the artist, especially her treatments
of just action.

In her novels, just feeling is the basis for just action, and the more just
the feeling, the more humane the action. To her, action was a practical act of loving kindness, like Mrs Ramsay knitting a brown stocking
for the lighthouse keeper's boy who has a tuberculous hip. What the
world calls action – legal, imperial, belligerent or economic action – is
disregarded as worthless and worse, so much strutting and mouthing.

Leonard Woolf's first novel sets out this premise, which his wife took up.

Though Virginia and Leonard Woolf agree on the futility of that kind of public action, and share too an acute awareness of the unknown, their works treat love somewhat differently. Where Leonard fixes on the physical act, Virginia dwells on a subtle rapport.

In an early, unsigned review of the Carlyles' love letters, Virginia perceived that 'the more we see the less we can label' and again, 'the further we read the less we trust to definitions'. To see the Woolves' (in their humorous way, they used the plural 'Woolves', not 'Woolfs') marriage on its own terms, it is essential to take in the rapport that was called into being through words and to isolate, as subsidiary, a terrible period of trial from 1912 to 1915, what Virginia later called the 'prelude' to the marriage proper.

They managed to keep the game going in the run-up to a breakdown in the summer of 1913. When Virginia forced herself to stay in the nursing home at Twickenham, the Mongoose asks Mandrill to be 'a brave beast lying quietly in its straw', while he sings her a Mongoose song which begins

> *I do adore . . .*
> *I do adore . . .*

But lovers' language, bonding though it was, could not enter into a divisive issue. The love-play of two beasts, which liberated that erotic invitation on Virginia's part, came into conflict with the sleeping beauty myth: the regard for a hero who makes his way through a thicket to the sleeping princess, whom he must wake with one kiss. In this fairy tale there's an obligation for a man to wake a woman on the instant. The first time Leonard Woolf kissed Virginia, when she agreed to marry, she told him that she felt 'no more than a rock'. This is too common to be ominous. In fact, when Virginia's father had approached her mother, Julia had confessed to deadness – after losing her first husband, she lacked 'proper passion'. Leslie Stephen responded sensibly: he reassured Julia that nothing must be forced. William Godwin did the same when Mary Wollstonecraft was, at first, put off. He spoke calmly, affirming their union.

Leonard Woolf was in many ways like these men, but not completely. He tended to be impatient and gloomy and cared a lot – perhaps too much – about a woman's desire. Virginia did find the transports of sex exaggerated and owned to being unchanged by the loss of chastity: 'I might still be Miss S'. Yet her letters from Somerset, Spain and Italy confirm her confidence in their union. They had become permanently 'monogamic'.

Her voice is contented, quite at ease, untroubled by mosquitoes which 'interrupted the proper business of bed', until a month after their marriage, while they were still in Spain, she woke to the fact that she disappointed Leonard and, what's more, he was preparing to announce this in print. On 4 September, he was writing the first chapter of a new novel that was to explore the issue of unresponsiveness in an artistic woman, Camilla, whom the Jewish hero, Harry, longs for and adores in vain. It is widely acknowledged that what emerged as *The Wise Virgins* is a *roman-à-clef*, and that Camilla is a portrait of the author's wife. How much she knew or guessed of this work in progress is impossible to say, but Leonard's disappointment was plain. On their return to London, they went together to Vanessa for advice on orgasm.

Vanessa declared her sister to be incurably frigid. This decided judgement went into Leonard Woolf's novel, a chapter called 'Katharine's Opinion of her Sister'. Katharine warns Harry that even to attempt to arouse Camilla would be fraught with danger to them both. Katharine thinks no man should marry her sister, and that the only solution to her untenable existence is to die young.

Leonard Woolf did not consider or possibly did not know the extent to which Vanessa's opinion, though born of concern, could have been retaliation for Virginia's flirtation with Vanessa's husband during the first years of the Bells' marriage – a marriage that didn't last. It's conceivable that an unattached Virginia, intent on her own needs and nursing jealous ardour for her sister, as well as competing for Clive Bell's attention, did jar Vanessa.

Bell teased his sister-in-law about her 'emerald sleeping passions'; their habit was to 'bill and coo'. When she became engaged to Leonard, Bell said he would always cherish a thought that he loved her more than her husband did. She didn't take this amiss. Bell's infidelities would not have made for the tie Virginia could count on with Leonard.

Heartening though the flirtation had been for the sister who often claimed inferiority, what mattered as much or more was the encouragement Bell gave to early drafts of her novel. 'You were the first person who ever thought I'd write well', she reminded him ten years later. He acted as a mentor for a time, questioning her predilection for 'shadow', and if we recall the mentoring of Shelley and Lewes, we can't overrate the advantage of such a connection to a rising writer. With Mary Godwin and Virginia Stephen, we see how single-minded this course could be, necessitating a degree of selfishness if they are to succeed in the face of all that's stacked against women with as yet untested aspirations: Mary Godwin's disregard of the children of Shelley's first marriage, George Eliot's maintaining Lewes's sons at arms' length, and, more painfully blatant, Schreiner's refusal to house her husband's mother and Virginia Stephen's heedlessness of Vanessa Bell's dependence on the father of her sons.

Virginia envied her sister's motherhood, and when she was engaged to Leonard she hoped to have a child the following year. She was delighted when her friend Violet Dickinson gave her a cradle. Her childlessness was a one-sided decision taken on Leonard's initiative, in consultation with doctors.

Marriage to so enlightened and committed a man as Leonard Woolf was a triumph for Virginia – a rather unexpected triumph, it might be thought, given her 'madness', George Duckworth's fondling and her romancing women like 'my Violet'. These are all indeterminate elements in a young woman who, in her own treatments of characters, questioned labels. When Vanessa Bell painted her faceless portraits of Virginia Stephen in 1911–12, just before her marriage, she shows the woman who remained unknown. And Leonard Woolf too pursues that elusiveness in his portrait of Virginia as Camilla. She was like Hakluyt's rovers – he's that explicit about the likeness to Virginia. 'Her life was an adventure, the joy of moving among experiences that were ever new under the shifting and changing of chance.'

Camilla is an art student who is said to be more suited to writing, and like Virginia, she comes from the confident upper middle class, a cut above the suburban background of moody Harry Davis. His pursuit of the elusive Camilla awakens Harry to a kind of love he's never known. How should he reconcile this romantic love with a man's sexual nature? He sees Camilla in the way that Leonard Woolf saw Virginia, 'like a hill covered with virgin snow'.

The branding of Virginia as frigid persisted through the last century, reinforced by her admissions that she was a sexual failure. When she declared this to Vita Sackville-West, or to Gerald Brenan in Spain, she may have hoped for contradiction. Since 'frigid' was a criticism of women who did not respond to a masculine need, it has to be questioned. We live now in an era where it's accepted that there are many ways to make love, and some elude simplistic labels.

In *The Wise Virgins* Harry wants 'what the male wants, a certain fierceness of love ... a flame that shall join and weld together'. He thinks of a primitive female who would come to a male's cave to possess and be possessed, and bear his children. Romance and sex are, for him, in separate categories. Camilla, adept at romance, only 'knew vaguely, felt vaguely what he meant. But it was not in her, a woman and unmarried to know the want.'

'Perhaps you were never made to be able to say "I love you",' Harry writes in a letter to Camilla.

She assents in her reply. 'I can't give myself. Passion leaves me cold.'

How is a man to read a virgin's hesitations over marriage? Would sexual union and other demands of marriage damage the possibilities of a gifted woman's singleness and freedom?

'There's so much in marriage from which I recoil', Camilla tells Harry. 'It seems to shut women up and out. I won't be tied by the pettinesses and the conventionalities of life. There must be some way out. One must live one's own life'.

*The Wise Virgins* was written at the height of the women's suffrage campaign. Harry declares himself 'pro-suffrage', and Leonard Woolf called feminism 'the belief or policy of all sensible men'. As Harry muses over the phenomenon of a venturesome, not vacant virgin, he imagines her 'voyage out'. The most appealing element in Leonard Woolf's novel – whatever it says about Virginia Woolf's sexuality – is this alertness to what was far-out and alone in authentic womanhood.

Most women at some time or other would hear a man ask what women want. It was an awkward question, often rhetorical, in a tone that implied, do women know what they want? I have yet to hear a woman say that she wants what many men think she wants: size, muscle, power, self-importance. Those may be acceptable as signs that massage her public image, but can't, in the absence of character, satisfy her. No, when women talk in private, they agree that what they want is to be known for what they sense themselves to be (and this may be what men want too). In *Wuthering Heights*, Catherine Earnshaw has an affinity for Heathcliff because he knows and shares her far-out nature as no conventional gentleman can. Harry has something of Heathcliff's alien quality, his outsider's awareness, together with his surly energy. In Harry this is a Jewish kind of energy, a need to *know* – the poetic word for sexual union in the Hebrew Bible. Like Heathcliff too, Harry loses his soul when he shuts his eyes in order to marry a conventional girl. This is where Leonard diverged from Harry: he had the courage to take on the far-out Virginia and see her through. Deliberate though he was in this intention, he did not, could not, foresee differences he could not at once solve. The novel came out of his stubborn side, a quality that, as staying power, is a virtue.

Virginia's mental health deteriorated from the time that Leonard completed a draft of his novel in the spring of 1913. Shut away that summer in hateful Twickenham, she offered Leonard a separation.

'Dearest One,' he replied on 3 August 1913, 'if I <u>have</u> done anything wrong to you, & which has displeased you, you would tell me, wouldn't you?'

There is no evidence of what followed, except a typically brief entry in Leonard Woolf's diary for 30 September 1913 that Virginia 'confessed' to him. What she confessed he does not say, but it may not have been much because it brought no relief. She was, he noted, 'v. violent in night'.

All this time, they were in some way speaking to each other through *The Wise Virgins* and *The Voyage Out*, with both books held back from the finality of publication. It's as though Leonard's Camilla speaks to Virginia's Rachel, saying that after all she cannot marry. The crux is Camilla's confession to Harry that she cannot give herself. If so, the problem lies not with Harry but with this particular kind of woman. Virginia's letters to Leonard likewise insist on her 'fault' – she takes the onus for her breakdown on herself (as she must, given her history). Yet a breakdown can be in itself an act of communication, as is the speaking silence around that word 'fault'. It was impossible for her to resist the publication of *The Wise Virgins* because the book was consistent with Bloomsbury's code of candour.

Leonard's eldest sister, Bella Woolf, did feel free to resist the book. She took a dim view of Harry when she read a draft in August 1913, and told Leonard she thought he had his 'worst characteristics multiplied to the nth degree': an 'ill-mannered cub'. There is an accurate self-portrait in Harry's 'look of discontent, discomfort, almost of suffering in his face, as he sat with crossed legs staring at the carpet'.

Virginia was in a bad way when she emerged from Twickenham. Leonard took her back to the Plough Inn in Somerset where they began their honeymoon, and where she had been happy. It was a disaster. On the return journey to London he feared that she would throw herself from the train.

In September 1913 there was a consultation with Sir Henry Head, a mind doctor who had recently sent Henry James 'down into hell'. Virginia Woolf went home and swallowed an overdose of veronal. Her stomach was pumped in time, and for a year she appeared to recover. Then, in October 1914, the publisher Edwin Arnold went ahead and brought out *The Wise Virgins*.

When Virginia was allowed to read it in mid-January 1915, three months after publication, she had to face, there in print for all to read, a contradiction of Leonard's love letters and the love-games of Mandrill and Mongoose. Her restrained comment in her diary is that the book is very good in some ways and very bad in others. Two weeks later, she broke down. It was the worst of the four or five episodes in her life, and the only one when she rejected Leonard.

It is tempting to make a connection between the book and break-down, but it's inadequate for two reasons. For one thing, the biographical situation was more complex. Her adoring letters to her husband and her two fictional portraits based on him (the unconventional lawyer, Ralph Denham, in *Night and Day* and the alien, Louis, in *The Waves*) vindicate a man who responds to a woman's 'night' — what is dark, invisible, but coming into focus in her nature. Such a man is 'indispensable', not so much because he takes care of a woman but because he sees her. There were imaginative as well as harsh aspects to the real Leonard. He was abrasive — alarming — with employees. He had a critical kind of stubborn-ness, and his wife coped through jokes that weren't only jokes, as when she named his room 'Hedgehog Hall'. Leonard Woolf's bristles and gloom went into Harry Davis; not his expressive ardour. All the same, the ardour was there in the Woolves' marriage, as well as a remarkable susceptibility to a woman's imagination.

Then, too, in Leonard's novel 'cold' is but one of several versions of the single woman unattached to a man — what the book terms a 'virgin'. The title itself posits a 'wise' virgin. This is a more promising character than the 'wise virgins' of the New Testament, where duty not virginity is in question. 'Wise virgins' fill their lamps with oil; 'foolish virgins' neglect to do so. This trivialising model of womanhood as a functional but vacant shell fades before the phenomenon of Camilla. She combats Harry's crass idea of a 'spinster' as a dried-up freak with hairs sprouting from her chin. Camilla demonstrates how free a single woman can be — unlike mar-ried 'cows'. Harry carries with him the sensitiveness of her forehead and mouth, the sensuousness of her lips, the light and sadness and aloofness of the eyes. The whole novel builds on the ambiguities of what appears more a state of being than a female membrane.

Though Harry ruins his life by impregnating a foolish virgin, he car-ries with him the memory of the wise one and her voyage-out question of woman's unknown potential. Leonard Woolf conceived a flawed and lost hero who can convince us that one man *did* want to know.

Another cause of Virginia's breakdown had nothing to do with *The Wise Virgins*. It was the forthcoming appearance of *The Voyage Out* in March

1915. Now and later the exposure of publication under the author's real name (a new practice for women writers in her generation) brought on illness. When Virginia Woolf came to speak to students at Cambridge in 1928, she tried to convey to the next generation the stress women of past had experienced: 'Currer Bell, George Eliot, George Sand, all victims of inner strife as their writings prove, sought ineffectively to veil themselves by using the name of a man. Thus they did homage to the convention, which if not implanted by the other sex was liberally encouraged by them (the chief glory of a woman is not to be talked of, said Pericles, himself a much-talked-of man), that publicity in women is detestable'.

This aversion to naming in the public arena goes in fact further back, to Jane Austen, who published anonymously. Despite her need for the income writing brought, Mary Shelley, we recall, was familiar with 'the desire to wrap night and the obscurity of insignificance around me', rather than to be in print and 'the subject of *men's* observations'.

In the course of 1915 Virginia needed two nurses to look after her. Report has it that she was violent. I find it hard to believe, unless she fought off coercion. It was a mistake to place her, a one-time victim of George Duckworth, in his home. His offer to have her at Dalingridge Place would have appeared benevolent and an expense-free solution that would save her from a return to Twickenham. But while she was there, she refused to eat, and it's suggested that she was force-fed. The argument is that a three-stone increase in her weight could not have been gained by patient spoonful.

In late May 1915 Virginia turned, Leonard said, 'very violently against me' and for a month, beginning on 20 June, refused to see him. By August she was well enough to go out in a bath chair, and Leonard was allowed to wheel her through Kew Gardens. He continued to do his best by his own lights, which was to defer to medical advice that, from a later perspective, was ignorant and which Virginia rightly distrusted.

How, after this, did she come to accept Leonard again?

———

To observers, she simply recovered against all expectation. And yet recovery must have turned on hope of healing unspoken but extreme differences. Madness there was, and some including Leonard label it manic depression, but diagnosis has to be inadequate if it fails to see her exceptional resilience ('I have a power of recovery — which I have tested,' she affirmed); and diagnosis is inadequate too if it fails to see, beneath the loss of control, common gender differences, especially to do with women's submerged desires — a question Virginia Woolf would open up later in a 1931 speech to another all-women audience, the National Union for Women's Service.* She pictures a fisherwoman casting her line. The fish of desire slips away through the silver stream. Reason hauls the line back, and she comes to the surface 'panting with rage and disappointment'. Men, she claims, were not yet ready to hear what women could tell them.

For his part, Leonard saved their union by his response to the beast game and by affirming a passion that lay deeper than their differences. 'Beloved,' he wrote, 'I adore every feather on your magnificent form.' These beast letters and, on one occasion, her diary suggest that there were times when marriage gave her some sort of physical pleasure. On 10 November 1917, after a dispirited day together, they recovered their 'illusions' in the evening, before the fire, and were 'going merrily till bedtime when some antics ended the day'. Quite soon after Virginia recovered they began to be 'divinely happy'.

For her part, Virginia saved their union by yielding control over her health — a very difficult move, given her distrust, even loathing, of doctors. Her conciliatory gesture is evident in a reassuring letter to Leonard posted six months after she began to recover. She writes from Richmond, at the periphery of London, where long before George Eliot had found refuge as an 'outlaw' and where Leonard had now settled himself and Virginia, to keep her from the buzz of Bloomsbury.

---

* The successor to the WSPU, after women gained the vote.

Hogarth [House, Richmond]

Monday April 17th [1916]

Precious Mongoose,

This is just to tell you what a wonderfully good beast I am. I've done everything in order, not forgetting medicine twice. [Dr] Fergusson came this morning . . . He had been seeing [Dr] Craig, who had sent a message to tell me to stay in bed every morning, and always have a sleeping draught at hand, to take at the least wakefulness – and altogether to be very careful for a fortnight. Fergy said my pulse was quite different from last summer – not only much steadier, but much stronger. I am to go on spraying my throat . . .

That's all my news, but I lie and think of my precious beast, who does make me more happy every day and instant of my life than I thought it possible to be. There is no doubt that I'm terribly in love with you. I keep thinking what you're doing, and have to stop – it makes me want to kiss you so . . .

It will be joyful to see your dear funny face tomorrow.

The Marmots kiss you.

Yr MANDRILL

Then, in the summer of 1916, she made an even greater gesture when she planned a novel that talks back to *The Wise Virgins*. Although the issues between this couple are familiar, it's their handling of the issues that's admirable, not only because they succeed, but because, as authors, they can say the unsayable through books talking to books. This is not ordinary talk; not psychological discourse; nor marriage counselling; it's using fiction to explore or create a fuller truth. If *The Wise Virgins* spoke to *The Voyage Out*, saying that marriage was untenable with a cold virgin, Virginia found herself equal to an answer. From 1916, the year following the threat of permanent madness, she began to explore a positive answer in a new novel, *Night and Day*.

It starts with the meeting of a man and woman from different social backgrounds: Katharine Hilbery lives in Cheyne Walk, Chelsea (where George Eliot had lived at the end of her life, and later, Henry James – both were friends of Leslie Stephen). Katharine belongs to the intellectual aristocracy, ultra-respectable, polished in its rituals and civilities. Invited there for tea, enter Ralph Denham, an edgy lawyer from a noisy, frayed home in Highgate. He is very like Harry with his outsider abrasiveness. The novelist explores their differences so as to bring out Katharine's covert apartness, her strangeness and affinity for a moody man – as though Catherine Earnshaw and Heathcliff can come together after all.

The surface or 'day' scenes have a rational social realism in the documentary manner of George Eliot; the 'night' is more suggestively poetic, more Emily Brontë.

Virginia Woolf's diary and essays give us entrée to that shadow-life, as she put it in 1917 while reviewing the posthumous volume of Henry James's autobiography: 'the shadow in which the detail of so many things can be discerned which the glare of day flattens out'. 'Night' comes first in the title of the book she was writing, for it's at night that Katharine does mathematics upstairs, in secret, away from her tea-table role as daughter of the house. Mathematics is the sign for the alternative existence Vanessa and Virginia had devised during their Kensington girlhood, when they rebelled against the lady-hood for which they'd been destined. Katharine's upstairs activity, her invisible 'night', is counter to her visible downstairs life by 'day'.

For much of the novel Katharine remains a divided being. In her downstairs aspect she becomes engaged to William Rodney from the same cultivated milieu. He's limp, rather like Lytton Strachey, and pleasantly familiar, a well-mannered gentleman. Such a marriage would set in motion a life definitely marked out in advance – the traditional course of wives who lose themselves.

Katharine muses over women who 'pretend' their way through married life as a way of satisfying husbands. A wife's stock of commonplaces is laid on to fill silences; they had 'little to do with her private thoughts'. Was being engaged to marry someone with whom you are not in love an 'inevitable step in a world where the existence of passion is only a traveller's story brought from the heart of deep forests'? Or was marriage 'an archway through which she must pass to have her desire'? I take 'desire' to mean a wish to fulfil her bent, in the way that George Eliot's Dorothea, at eighteen, marries the deadly Casaubon, imagining him an archway into the realm of knowledge. Katharine has that longing. 'At such times the current of her nature ran in its deep narrow channel with great force'.

Completed in 1918, *Night and Day* coincides with the vote for women over thirty, and there is a parallel drama of a suffragist, Mary Datchet. Mary, who supports herself as a single woman, is respected by intelligent men like Ralph Denham and William Rodney. She wants what men want; she's the political activist who will open the way for the equal-rights feminism of our time. But what do we make of the more indeterminate Katharine?

Ralph asks himself this question as they walk together in London by night. 'What woman did he see? And where was she walking, and who was her companion?'

Her answers to Ralph's questions are enigmatic:

*Ralph*:      Has Mary made a convert of you?
*Katharine*:  Oh no. That is, I'm a convert already.
*Ralph*:      But she hasn't persuaded you to work for them [the suffragettes]?
*Katharine*:  Oh dear no – that wouldn't do at all.

Answers lurk in Katharine's unspoken trains of thought. Her night-time mathematics are symbols, literally and figuratively, of an unknown quantity. Katharine belongs with 'indefinite' women who do not imitate men. Her cousin, the pointedly named Cassandra, sees her as 'a being who walks just beyond our sphere'.

Through Katharine, Virginia Woolf looks back to unfledged Virginia Stephen, hovering between an unknowable Miss V., or a socially acceptable marriage within her family's professional milieu, or a surprising marriage to 'a penniless Jew'. The last was Virginia Stephen's joke to single friends Violet Dickinson and Janet Case, when she'd announced her engagement to Leonard Woolf.

Her fictionalised Katharine tempts readers to write her off as a nebulous daughter at home, but there is something distinctive – imaginative – in the way she holds off from Mary Datchet's replay of power politics.

Virginia Woolf's position was similarly detached when she remarks on her 'natural disposition to think Parliament ridiculous'. It's a comment in the privacy of her diary in 1918, when Leonard Woolf was invited to stand for the Labour Party. She goes on: 'If one didn't think that politics are an elaborate game got up to keep a pack of men trained for that sport in condition, one might be dismal; one sometimes is dismal.' Her dismissal of power games is as much to the point today as it was to a victorious warrior-nation towards the end of the Great War. She brushed off the vote, granted at that stage, as a non-event in view of four years of slaughter perpetrated by politicians. It's as if Virginia Woolf is saying the fighter for the vote may be less advanced than her speculative character.

At the close of the novel, Katharine and Denham come together by night as a bus carries the pair about London. 'They shared the same sense of the impending future ... infinitely stored with undeveloped shapes which each would unwrap for the other.' As such, they are 'exploring indefinitely' in the oncoming shadows.

The scene reminds me of the play of Lappin and Lapinova by night in the woods. That tale was drafted at about the time *Night and Day* went to press. I like to think this took place when the Ballets Russes returned to London for the 1918–19 season. Both Leonard and Virginia record in their diaries seeing 'Russian Dancers' at the Coliseum on Thursday 28 November 1918. The prima ballerina was Lydia Lopokova, whose name may lie behind 'Lapinova'. In *Swan Lake*, the shadowed woods and the brilliantly lit court prove irreconcilable, and so too the wild hare in Lapinova cannot enter into the mundane daytime routines of the partner she had known in the woods as King Lappin. Back in his busy daytime world, Lapinova does not exist for him in her imaginative being, and he turns from sporting with her in the dark to hunting her.[*] 'Dead' he confirms, and sets her up as a trophy: a stuffed hare with staring eyes.

Virginia could have ended thus a mad hare in the summer of 1915,

---

[*] A hunting scene had lodged in Virginia Woolf's memory since August 1908: it's in a letter from Vanessa who, accompanying her husband and his family on a shooting party in Scotland, had watched him shoot three rabbits: 'Poor little furry beasts. It surpasses my imagination entirely, this wish to kill – does it yours?'

when she and Leonard were estranged. Had she not recovered, she could have been shut in an asylum for the rest of her life like her older half-sister, Laura Stephen.* Where *Night and Day* celebrates a fortunate outcome in Katharine's union with a man who can 'see' her, 'Lappin and Lapinova' is a dark and horribly plausible fable of marital disaster. I think Virginia Woolf could devise this with the clarity of one saved from impending madness.

When Katharine and Ralph come together, what do they say to each other? There's an exchange by night that brings us close, I think, to the long-term tie the author devised with Leonard Woolf. Katharine's reserve had 'left a whole continent of her soul in darkness', so intimacy was a kind of exposure. 'Was he not looking at something she had never shown to anybody? Was it not something so profound that the notion of his seeing it almost shocked her?'

In *Night and Day*, Katharine looks at Ralph in silence, 'with a look that seemed to ask what she could not put into words'. This asks more than love. It's more a 'compact'. The relationship looks forward to the conspiratorial tie of the awkward Rhoda and the Australian man of business, Louis, outsiders who will come together as improbable lovers in *The Waves*.

These fictions are fascinating re-creations of what Virginia and Leonard Woolf negotiated in the face of difference and the kind of ordeal that could end a marriage. He could be harsh — she considered Jewish gloom in a class of its own — and yet he saw and sanctioned her voyage-out character. He really did want her to write to the farthest reach. And she in turn saw that he loved justice and was humane as well as interesting. 'I like coming back to Richmond after Gordon Sq[ua]re', she confides to her diary. 'I like continuing our private life, unseen by anyone.'

The conclusion to *Night and Day* is Virginia Woolf's vindication of her

---

* No one really knows what ailed Laura, only reports of her father's impatience with her slowness to learn after her mother's sudden death, then reports of rage and misbehaviour after her father's remarriage (when she was side-lined by the cutting cleverness of her father's new family and also perhaps by her stepmother's occupation as a nurse), followed by the distorting effects of incarceration.

marriage to a 'penniless Jew'. It's an optimistic riposte to Leonard's casting of 'Camilla' as too uncontrollable, too classy, too non-Jewish. Her novel conceives a marriage of true minds. It's a hard-won answer to the harshness of Leonard's pessimism, and to write it was an act of recovery.

But to return to sanity was to wake up to the senselessness of a world at war. Lord Kitchener, whose concentration camps had destroyed thousands of women and children during the Boer War, was now, as Secretary of State for War, throwing his men's lives away. It was his uniformed image that was used to recruit doomed soldiers in the finger-pointing poster, 'Your country needs you'.

Under conditions of trench warfare, the English and the Germans were slaughtering a whole generation of young men over minuscule gains of a few feet of ground. At the time Virginia recovered, the disastrous battle of the Somme had yet to come, conscription was in the offing, and tribunals for conscientious objectors, amongst them members of the Bloomsbury Group, were taking place. Leonard Woolf was not a pacifist, but he was released from military service because of a tremor of his hands and also because, given his wife's mental health, it was thought that her life would be at risk if he went away.

Soon after the last nurse left in November 1915, Virginia wrote on 23 January 1916 to Margaret Llewelyn Davies, who ran the Women's Co-operative Movement, 'I become steadily more feminist, owing to the Times, which I read at breakfast and wonder how this preposterous masculine fiction keeps going a day longer – without some vigorous woman pulling us together and marching through it – Do you see any sense in it? I feel as if I were reading about some curious tribe in Central Africa – And now they'll give us votes'. The last refers to Mrs Pankhurst's calculation that if the suffragettes supported the war – that is, if these women consented to millions of deaths – rulers would relent on the matter of women's suffrage.

German prisoners of war were visible when Virginia walked with her brother Adrian in Sussex. Adrian spoke to 'a lean and hopeless one', while she smiled at him and he smiled in return since the sentry was not there. He seemed to like talking. War propaganda demonised Germans as 'Huns'; that is, barbarians. 'By rights,' she comments in her diary, 'he and Adrian should be killing each other.' Reading, she mused, is the reverse of military training which makes an 'enemy' unimaginable as a human being. 'The existence of life in another human being is as difficult to realise as a play of Shakespeare when the book is shut. The reason why it is easy to kill another person must be that one's imagination is too sluggish to conceive what his life means to him − the infinite possibilities of a succession of days which are furled in him, & have already been spent.'

Already in 1906 her pacifism had shaped a story, 'The Journal of Mistress Joan Martyn', about a female historian who is looking for records of women's domestic existence during the Wars of the Roses. Her pacifism intensified in three post-war novels. *Jacob's Room* (1922) keeps its focus on the pre-war life of a boy who, the novel constantly reminds us, must die on Flanders fields. The novel is an elegy for doomed youth. In *Mrs Dalloway* (1925), the focus is on the maddening after-effect of the Front (what used to be called shell-shock and now is called post-traumatic stress). And then in *To the Lighthouse* (1927) Andrew Ramsay, one of the Victorian children, is killed, shockingly in brackets, during the blind course of the Great War. Unlike *War and Peace* and other books and films that take up war as part of life, Virginia Woolf denies war the validity of a subject because she believed that to view or read about killing invites a vicarious participation that habituates the mind to bloodshed. It pretends to excite indignation but that's a shallow cover for the insidious blunting of sensibility.

To refuse to treat war is to take a political stand: to resist the patriotic 'fictions' of the dominant group. In an innovative central section of *To the Lighthouse*, like a blank corridor between the Victorian and Modern periods, individual faces, including Andrew's, are swallowed up by a passage of time, when civilisation, epitomised by the Ramsay home, decays. Andrew's obliteration is forecast by the absurd heroism his father had upheld as a public memory of the Crimean War, celebrated by the poet laureate. 'Boldly we rode and well', Mr Ramsay had liked to recite, thrilling to Tennyson's idealisation of military disaster as he blunders into an artist's easel and almost knocks it down.

The Charge of the Light Brigade is the kind of action history will not overlook. But what is history, Virginia Woolf will ask the students at Newnham and Girton. Opening Trevelyan's history of England, she observes that it is about the Hundred Years War, religious strife, the Armada and the House of Commons. History selects for violent change, not a mother preserving an island of domestic order. In 'The Journal of Mistress Joan Martyn', Virginia Woolf invents a document that historians thought worthless because it looks away from the Wars of the Roses to fix attention on domestic life. This journal reveals that it's not thugs on the rampage but a woman like Joan's mother who secures her country:

> And she went on to expound to me what she calls her theory of ownership [Joan records]; how in these times one is as the Ruler of a small island set in the midst of turbulent waters; how one must plant it & cultivate it . . . and fence it securely from the tides; and one day perhaps the waters will abate & this plot of ground will be ready to make part of a new world. Such is her dream of what the future may bring to England . . .

Virginia Woolf's friend Maynard Keynes returned disillusioned from the so-called Peace Conference at Versailles in 1919 after the end of the First World War. Virginia heard him speak of 'the dismal & degrading spectacle . . . where men played shamelessly, not for Europe, or even England, but for their own return to Parliament at the next election'. They were not wholly vicious, Keynes said, they had 'spasms of well meaning', but no one had the strength to resist the punitive terms forced on the Germans – rolling out the ground for another world war.

The Woolves had long wished to take up printing. In 1917 they bought a hand-press and took it home to Hogarth House in Richmond. And so the Hogarth Press was born. Their first choices were books that will last for ever. Publication number one was their own *Two Stories*: 'A Mark on the Wall' by Virginia Woolf and 'Three Jews' by Leonard Woolf. Publication number two was *Prelude*, a frieze of scenes from a New Zealand childhood by Katherine Mansfield, and number three was T. S. Eliot's *Poems* (1919). Originality was to have precedence over sales, so they were taken by surprise to be deluged with orders for Virginia Woolf's *Kew Gardens* (1919).

The Hogarth Press made it feasible to open out her expressive gifts in a more experimental form. Up until then, Gerald Duckworth had published her work; now, she told herself, instead of worrying about writing for sixteen hundred readers, she could write just for six if she wanted. She doesn't specify who the six are, but they'd be the like-minded of her circle (Leonard; Vanessa; her one-time mentor Clive Bell; Lytton Strachey, who had made a splash with four candid portraits of *Eminent Victorians*; Katherine Mansfield; and the novelist E. M. Forster). Forster's critique of *Night and Day* struck home. The character of Katharine Hilbery could not hold a reader, he said, because she was not lovable. Virginia, he told her, must now create a lovable character. She did so in *Mrs Dalloway*, the book that established her as a leading novelist.

It's usual for critics to see a switch in Virginia Woolf's oeuvre as she became overtly experimental. But the unseen kernel of lives in the shade was there from the start, and the same subject drove the post-war books and the experimental form best adapted to her investigation: a fragmented narrative registering gaps and tantalising half-glimpses. This form itself implies a question: what will be revealed when the narratives imposed on a life are peeled back? When Mrs Dalloway walks through London by day, she feels perpetually 'out, out, far out to sea and alone' — in the recesses of her mind she is not entirely the supportive Westminster hostess she appears. The mould taken by the wife of an MP, Mrs Richard Dalloway, is haunted by the vivid girl she once had been.

Virginia Woolf takes us through a day and night in the middle age of Mrs Dalloway. In a sense this is a mellower version of Lapinova taken over by a husband who rules in 'the busy world of rabbits'. It's pointedly at night and alone, away from the guests at her party, when Clarissa Dalloway can lend her imagination to the suicide of a man driven mad by war.

She divines the menace of Dr Bradshaw, the Harley Street mind-doctor, who drives Septimus to escape incarceration in the doctor's 'home' by throwing himself from a window. Mrs Dalloway can see that this doctor, a social climber and one of her guests, is 'obscurely evil'. As the clock strikes midnight, a sort of Cinderella switch happens: Mrs Dalloway is divested of her trappings as her husband's hostess-wife. As such she can commune with an ex-soldier who could not move on from the Great War. Septimus Warren Smith has been living with the dead, while public figures contrive to forget. It was his distinction not to be complicit with the heroics of virtuous aggression; refusing the humbug of decoration for his wartime service, he was compelled to confess his insensibility after four years of killing. A sense of wrong bound him in particular to his dead commanding officer, Evans, coming towards him through the barbed wire.

There is a curious sentence that Virginia Woolf eventually eliminated from the manuscript: 'A naked soul looking at emptiness has its independence,' Septimus thinks, and he 'has the desire to test it further', if necessary by death. She discerns that he sees himself as an explorer in the interface of life and death, passing through 'a green mist' to discover that 'the dead were alive'. Others will follow: '& now, through evolution, a few of the living have access to this world'.*

Septimus had posed the word 'war' in an interrogative way that Dr Bradshaw would not permit. This ex-soldier is questioning the political order that makes war, an order held in place by the artifice of clock time. Big Ben strikes the hours, which fall like leaden rings, holding citizens in place. The novel contrasts expanded time, stretching out the past in the present of Septimus and Mrs Dalloway, who never meet but have in common their sense of time's losses.

In the day and night of this scenario, Mrs Dalloway makes her climactic appearance at the darkest hour of the night. Darkness blots out her public face as she joins with a man who held out against humbug. This

---

* Cancelled line.

is 'Clarissa', continuous with the girl she had been, not the Westminster wife. Here is an emotionally animate being, a counterpart to Septimus, whose finer perceptions are untapped and denied in public life.

Unlike Septimus, Mrs Ramsay, the Victorian mother in *To the Lighthouse*, accepts what society requires her to be. This makes her all too visible, too identifiable as the domestic angel for a true portrait. So the artist Lily Briscoe surprises the angel with a visit at night. This was Virginia Woolf's attempt to feel a way towards her mother, Julia Stephen – in accord with her advice to the students to 'think back through our mothers'. (Strikingly, *Vogue* magazine photographed her in her mother's Victorian dress. The image is suggestive: can a Modern woman, who plainly doesn't belong in that puffy-sleeved, rustling taffeta dress, enter into her Victorian mother's frame of mind? Perhaps in the same way that Lily has to find the kernel of Mrs Ramsay if she is to shape her on canvas?)

Alone with Mrs Ramsay in the dark bedroom, Lily 'imagined how in the chambers of the mind and heart of the woman ... were ... tablets bearing sacred inscriptions, which if one could spell them out, would teach one everything, but they would never be made public'.

Inscribed in this woman is a hidden nature, a kind of DNA, tantalising to an artist or writer. Long before, Mary Shelley's secret self had seemed to her 'a sealed treasure' and Charlotte Brontë too had detected a nature concealed in secret script, in almost the same terms.* Her feminist character Shirley, based as we know on Emily, both reveals and conceals her innate freedom as a curiously 'graven' stone 'whose mystic glitter I rarely permit even myself a glimpse'. Even the unconventional Shirley can barely discern closely guarded elements in herself.

Mrs Ramsay, likewise, barely discerns an undisclosed element in herself – the one the artist senses. When her day and doings are done, she sits alone, under the beam of the lighthouse, whose third stroke falls on the unread script. Lily will register it on canvas as 'a wedge-shaped core of darkness'. This abstract Modernist shape reveals what is 'almost unclassified'.

Virginia Woolf set out to generate a new model of womanhood. The position is similar to that of the Irish orator in *Ulysses*, refusing to serve the dominant civilisation. His model is Moses coming down from Sinai with a new code 'graven in the language of the outlaw'.

Through Lily's encounter with Mrs Ramsay in the speaking silence of the night, I think Virginia Woolf co-opts her mother from the compliant narrative her mother had followed and she infuses into this scene of artist and subject what was as yet unuttered: the outlaw language of intelligent madness. Here is her mother released not only from the conventions of Victorian womanhood, but also from the artifice of language itself.

This author is not the first to frame this challenge to language. It's brilliantly anticipated by Emily Dickinson's use of dashes, pushing received words literally apart to let in the silence of the unsayable.

The use of silence goes back to *The Voyage Out*, where Terence Hewitt

---

* See Chapter 2, above.

wants to write about 'Silence, the things people don't say'. But, he adds, 'the difficulty is immense'. In 1930, in an introduction to the writings of working-class members of the Co-operative Women's Guild, Virginia Woolf said, 'These voices are beginning only now to emerge from silence into half-articulate speech. These lives are still hidden in profound obscurity.'

She told the Cambridge students to watch women when they were alone, 'unlit by the capricious and coloured lights of the other sex'. Whatever our field, whether it be fiction or biography or history or art, we might catch 'those unrecorded gestures, those unsaid or half-said words' which form like the shadows of moths on the ceiling. We might go with our feelers waving, on the lookout for 'this organism that has been under the rock these million years': a variety of elusive Miss V. or Katharine Hilbery doing mathematics by night, or Lapinova's love-play in the moon-lit woods, or the 'core of darkness' in Mrs Ramsay picked up by the third stroke of the lighthouse.

Virginia Woolf's early focus on shadow prepares the way for her attentiveness to voices speaking in private under cover of night. Darkness invites the emergence of imaginative traits not on show in daylight. By day, wives like Mrs Ramsay and Mrs Dalloway are disempowered, yes, but to see them by night does bring out kinds of creativity that are not recognised or named. For Virginia Woolf believes that 'the power to change and the power to grow, can only be preserved by obscurity; and ... if we wish to help the human mind to create and to prevent it from scoring the same rut repeatedly, we must do what we can to shroud it in darkness'.

In the same year, 1929, that Virginia Woolf reworked her Cambridge talks as *A Room of One's Own*, she wrote a biographical essay on Mary Wollstonecraft. It's designed to do justice to Wollstonecraft's spirit of renewal instead of the brand of unruly womanhood stamped on her at the close of the eighteenth century, an image perpetuated in biographies demeaning this pioneer of women's rights as depressive and wanton. It took Virginia Woolf only three pages to show how Wollstonecraft 'cut her way to the quick of life', and that what matters is not melancholy, which is common, but experiment, which is rare, 'above all that most fruitful experiment, her relation with Godwin'. These are strengths Virginia Woolf shared. Rising again and again from the trough of illness, she did not allow herself to be a silent 'case'.

In her second feminist treatise, *Three Guineas*, published in 1938, the year before the outbreak of the Second World War, she positions herself as a triumphant 'Outsider' and member of the Outsiders' Society. This is a secret and anonymous organisation of women, potentially a political party. Members work for the same aims as their brothers: 'liberty, equality and peace'. But they do this separately, 'by their own methods', following that band of outstanding women who resisted militancy and imitation of men. At one point Virginia Woolf thought of putting out an illustrated sheet called *The Outsider*.

In *Three Guineas*, as spokeswoman for the Society, she confronts 'Sir', representing the dominant party. 'Sir' is a lawyer who requires facts and logic.* She's at her most oratorical as she poses scriptural authority, the words of Jesus Christ declaring men and women to be no different in the spirit, versus the assumed authority of the Church, specifically a recent decision by the Anglican clergy to exclude women above the lowly rank of deaconess. Emily Brontë's spiritual gift could have no professional place in such a hierarchy. To question this absurdity, Virginia Woolf has only to mark the reach of that sublime voice:

---

* The painstaking logic of her evidence-based argument is so insistent that it's as though she has to rebut male prejudice – summed up most famously by Sir Almroth Wright, a medical tyrant, in 1913, who alleged that women arrive at conclusions on incomplete evidence, and who deplored their 'intellectual immoralities and limitations' as the secondary sexual characters of women. He excluded female medical students from his lectures. It must be said that he was not an isolated old fogey. The young T. S. Eliot, arriving in Oxford in 1914, wrote home to Boston to say that he was shocked to see female students coming to lectures in male colleges.

*No coward soul is mine,*
*No trembler in the world's storm-troubled sphere;*
*I see Heaven's glories shine,*
*And faith shines equal, arming me from fear.*

*O God within my breast,*
*Almighty, ever-present Deity!*
*Life — that in me has rest,*
*As I — undying Life — have power in Thee!*

In her duet with this voice, Virginia Woolf comes into her own as the leading Outsider she felt herself to be, heir to Stephen forebears. To fuel the oratory of *Three Guineas*, she paid a visit to Stoke Newington to see her great-grandfather's grave: a table-tomb with his name James Stephen (1758–1832) carved 'large & plain, as I suspect he was large & plain'. There was a long inscription about his tie with William Wilberforce. 'I was much refreshed by all this,' she notes in her diary.

Mounting her platform, she recasts the role of Outsider as a position of strength and defiance. Even illness can be deployed to advantage. When the lights of health go down, she said, we leave those ruts of normality; it's an opportunity to plot a solitary course of action. 'Ancient and obdurate oaks are uprooted in us by the act of sickness.'

These are the aims of the Outsider Society:

Not to make war, nor make munitions, nor back those who bear
    arms with moral or political support.
To wither fighters with indifference.
To work to support oneself, abjuring greed and exploitation.
    (One model is Barbara Leigh Smith, who used the three
    hundred pounds a year from her father to found an 'out-
    sider' school for children of both sexes, and for Catholics,
    Jews and whomever their faith might exclude from main-
    stream education.)
To resist dominance at home and abroad i.e., end imperialism.

To campaign for equal pay and remuneration for unpaid jobs like
mothering.

These are political voices unconcerned with personal power. Virginia
Woolf cuts free from patriotism since in the past her fatherland had
denied half its citizens education, property, income and a place in history.

Publication in June 1938 roused a 'racket': angry letters, telephone
calls, rage from reviewers like 'butting buffaloes'. G. M. Young, author
of *Victorian England*, bellowed in the *Sunday Times*, 'I wish Mrs Woolf would
resign herself to the necessity of being an Insider and not an Outsider:
and let that spark fly freely among the moth-eaten feathers and tarnished
*passementerie* of Edwardian feminism.'

Controversy raged. The *TLS* called her the most brilliant pamphleteer
in England. Quakers and governesses cheered her with letters of thanks, as
did Lady Rhondda (founder of *Time and Tide*), who signed herself her 'grateful Outsider', and Philippa Strachey (who back in 1907 had organised the
first women's suffrage procession in London). Meanwhile Queenie Leavis
was vituperating in the Cambridge journal *Scrutiny*. Mrs Woolf had let
down her sex; she was 'dangerous' and putting out 'preposterous claims'.

Bookshops, at first, would not carry *Three Guineas*. Readers, they said,
would not buy something so controversial about women.*

'I think the sales have struck a rock of rage, and won't go further',
Virginia remarked to Ethel Smyth, who had composed a marching song
for the suffragettes and conducted it with a toothbrush from a window in
Holloway Prison.

All the while, she sat 'calm as a toad in an oak at the centre of the
storm'. She had her Hogarth Press; this was what it was for: to free her
voice irrespective of received opinion. 'I am an incorrigible outsider', she
insisted, though she did feel the hostility and did privately call Young a
'mincing old pedant . . . lapped in book dust humbug' (echoing her father's
groans over contributions from 'Dryasdust' for the *DNB*).

During the Battle of Britain, as German bombers flew nightly over the

---

* In fact, eight thousand copies were sold.

Woolves' country home in the Sussex village of Rodmell, she sustained the stand of *Three Guineas* with one of her most original essays. 'Thoughts on Peace during an Air Raid' (August 1940) shifts the focus from the enemy to the instinct of aggression in the English as well as Germans. In the *Times*, she read Lady Astor (the first woman to enter Parliament) saying, 'Women of ability are held down because of a subconscious Hitlerism in the hearts of men'.

Seizing that phrase, she deplores propagandist rhetoric that locates an insane love of power in one man. No, she thought, this is a universal problem throughout human history. How to compensate men for the loss of their guns is the question she poses to posterity. An answer, she ventures, might be to give gun-toters a creative task.

A new wave of feminism in protest against the rise of domestic violence revives Virginia Woolf's resistance to the 'Hitlerism in the hearts of men'. Might women, more than half the human race, come together to criminalise arms as well as those monsters of greed who make and sell them, rating human life as expendable for the sake of profit? Three hundred million pounds is the profit Virginia Woolf cites in the late thirties.

Reframing her forebears' campaign against slavery, she suggests that we are all enslaved, irrespective of nationality, by a wish to dominate. The word 'slavery' reverberates through 'Thoughts on Peace in an Air Raid', and of course that blight goes on in the work-slaves of the present.

In 1940, when German invasion seemed imminent, Leonard proposed suicide to a somewhat reluctant Virginia. Leonard's apprehension was justified: as a Jew, he and his wife were already on Himmler's list for immediate arrest.

'There would be no point in waiting', Leonard told Virginia. His first idea was that they asphyxiate themselves, and he laid by a supply of petrol for that purpose. 'We would shut the garage door and commit suicide.' As an alternative in June 1940, he obtained a vial of 'protective poison' – a lethal dose of morphine – from Virginia's brother Adrian.

'No,' Virginia said to the first suicide pact, 'I don't want the garage to see the end of me. I've a wish for ten years more, and to write my book which as usual darts into my brain.' *Between the Acts* was written during the Battle of Britain, and there were war-planes advancing shark-like overhead, for Rodmell was in the path of German bombers making for London. Their Bloomsbury home in Mecklenburgh Square had been hit and they were living permanently at Monk's House. One day she went up to London and took the Tube to Temple, then wandered around the bombsites. 'All that completeness ravished', she wrote in her *Diary*.

*Between the Acts* enacts a pageant of English history in the grounds of a country house, Poinz Hall, before a village audience. The dramatist, Miss La Trobe, lives in the village but as an outsider — jeered by the locals for being lesbian. She passionately wants to convey to her audience that England's past, the ages of Queen Elizabeth and Queen Victoria in particular, and its literature constitute England's real treasure. Chaucer's pilgrims weave behind each successive scene, suggesting the continuity of English characters: Mrs Manresa putting on lipstick in the audience is a present-day version of Chaucer's man-hunting Wife of Bath. The question resonating through the scenes is whether England's treasure will survive.

There are moments when Miss La Trobe can't convey this and, wretched with failure, she gashes her nails along a tree trunk. Virginia Woolf too felt a conviction of failure as she came to the end of her own attempt to reach out to a grassroots audience. No reassurance from Leonard could lift a depression that settled on her in the early months of 1941.

She was not mad when she ended her life at the age of fifty-nine. She feared madness. The letter she left for Leonard expresses a considerate wish to spare him. She assures him of her gratitude for all he did. On Friday 28 March 1941, she weighted her pockets with stones and waded into the fast-running River Ouse near Rodmell. Her body was recovered three weeks later, but in the interim none of her family, neither Leonard Woolf nor Vanessa Bell, could doubt that she had drowned herself.

The Hogarth Press published *Between the Acts* posthumously in July 1941. For the next three decades Virginia Woolf's reputation dropped. She was disparaged as a nervy invalid, a snobbish aesthete withdrawn from real life. Her close friends Forster and Eliot, with their enormous prestige, did not exactly stand up for her greatness, while Leonard Woolf's claims for her in his preface to *A Writer's Diary* – published twelve years after her death – are constrained by her dented image. Fifty years later, a movie called *The Hours* (2002) starts its Virginia Woolf episode with slamming re-takes of a scene no one saw: the writer wading deeper into the river. Look at it! Look at it! the scene insists, as though this manner of death were the prime fact of this life.

Virginia Woolf argues back in her essay on 'The Art of Biography' (1938): a biographer, she says, 'can give us much more than another fact to add to our collection'. A biographer can give us rather 'the creative fact; the fertile fact; the fact that suggests and engenders'.

An example leaps from her diary: 'The spirit of delight' visited her when she woke early on 4 September 1927. It's the solitary, creative spirit Shelley had embraced and lamented when it left: 'Rarely, rarely comest thou, spirit of delight'.* She recalls singing that line ('and sang so poignantly that I have never forgotten it') a year before, on 30 September 1926, when that same spirit had visited her and she'd first had her 'vision of a fin rising on a wide blank sea'. This was her inspiration for *The Waves* (1931).† No biographer', she adds, 'could possibly guess this important fact about my life in the late summer of 1926: yet biographers pretend they know people.'

The popular fixation on insanity and suicide muffled the reasoning voice that Virginia Woolf developed in the 1930s, extending the feminism of the 1920s to a confrontation of power itself. Not only did she speak out against vainglorious rhetoric, militarism, medals and the strutting aspect of honour, she also despised honorary degrees (on offer in 1933 and 1939) as 'mere baubles distributed by the pimps of the brain-selling trade'. In the same way she refused public honours coming her way – the Clark lectures at Cambridge for 1933 and a Companion of Honour in 1935 – because 'it is

---

* From Shelley's 'Song: Rarely, rarely, comest thou'.
† In Shelley's 'Song', the following lines may bear on *The Waves*: 'I love waves, and winds, and storms, / Everything almost / Which is Nature's, and may be / Untainted by man's misery.'

an utterly corrupt society'. Her rejection of public life is as sure and fearless as Emily Brontë's.

In the context of the post-Crash 1930s, she aligned herself with the disempowered, while she tried out a voice designed to address a national audience. The idea was to be no less than arbiter of the national conscience and preserver of what she judged the national treasure — its civilisation, chiefly its books. In 'The Leaning Tower' (a talk for the Workers' Educational Association in Brighton in May 1940) she exhorted workers and women, 'the commoners' and 'the outsiders', to join forces: 'we are not going to leave writing to be done for us by a small class of well-to-do young men who have only a pinch, a thimbleful of experience to give us'.

She asked her WEA audience why it is that a family like the Shelleys or the Brontës suddenly bursts into flame. What conditions bring about that explosion? There is no way, she admits, that we can explain 'the germ of genius', but she does make a claim for the kind of alternative education she herself had, a kind open to workers as well: reading, listening and discussion.

The most fertile of the facts remains that frame of mind she shared with her Quaker aunt: the priority she granted the inner light and, too, the courage with which she upheld pacifism. In the run-up to the Second World War, this position was unwelcome to Maynard Keynes, to Vanessa's son Quentin Bell and other members of her milieu. She quarreled with her one-time adorer and Hogarth author Vita Sackville-West, who accused her of 'misleading' readers. Virginia took this to heart as an accusation of dishonesty. Some friends stopped speaking, her sister was ambiguous and Leonard lukewarm. *Three Guineas* was not on a par with the novels, he told her. But she shrugged off opposition: 'I do my best work & feel most braced with my back to the wall. It's an odd feeling though, writing against the current: difficult entirely to disregard the current. Yet of course I shall.'

As it turned out, her pacifism would survive the current of the time, and speak to civilised Americans of the late 1960s, who opposed the Vietnam War. The great wave of her posthumous fame would rise there and then.

———

To me, the point of her life lies not only in the great novels, essays, diary and letters, but also in an oratorical voice yet to be heard by both sexes. Honing her political position, Virginia Woolf moved from addressing women on their own to a conversation with men, whom she calls 'our brothers'.

This has been a story of a speaker who emerged from shadow and silence. For a woman of her generation, born to go on without a vote, denied formal education and brought up to be a quietly spoken lady with a tea-table manner, it took tremendous resolve to raise a public voice.

In 1937–8, as she called up her Outsiders' Society in her writing room at the bottom of her garden, the ground would crack and this tremendous voice would erupt ('epoch-making', the *TLS* said, if read seriously). And each afternoon, when she took her walk from two to four, a new sense of freedom would whirl her 'like a top[,] miles upon miles over the downs'. Never had she spurted words under the lash of such compulsion, she said, not caring if this toppled her from her literary pedestal. Completing the final proofs of *Three Guineas* on Thursday 28 April 1938, she conceived a right to vote not for one party or another, but against the whole edifice of power. Ahead of her sex, ahead of generations to come, she felt herself 'enfranchised till death, & quit of all humbug'.

# THE OUTSIDERS SOCIETY

The Outsiders Society claims half the human race. Virginia Woolf's insistence on a 'society' implies ties; she reversed the romantic or pained idea of an isolated outsider and proposed instead a common cause.

I warm to that idea. We have long known the greatness of these five as individual writers, but here we have looked at them collectively. A recurring issue has linked them. These outsiders do not make terms with our violent world; they do not advance themselves by imitation of the empowered. Instead they speak out against the humbug of authority and its 'baubles' – the decorations and honours – disguising the mess rulers have made. These voices say no to arms and patriotism. "'For,' the outsider will say, "in fact, as a woman, I have no country. As a woman I want no country. As a woman my country is the whole world.'"

'Outsider', 'outlaw', 'outcast': as writers, the five front-runners made these their own, taking advantage of their separation from the dominant political and social order throughout the world and through the ages. To see thus widely went beyond politics; it meant an empathic mind, and it took moral courage for silenced women to carry this into public utterance.

I admire these writers for not shaking their heads over the human species, even though they face the recurrent strain of violence: economic aggression, domestic violence and war. It's there in Frankenstein's monster, who can strike the terrified at any time, and in the vindictive hatred at Wuthering Heights. These books reveal how violence spills from narrowed mind-sets: self-pity or blame or the will to power.

My outsiders are the reverse of narrow. If they were isolated from people, they were not from books. I think of Mary Wollstonecraft's insistence on the development of character through reading as vital to women's rights, and the benefit of enlightened fathers who encouraged their daughters to be readers. The lives of these five exceptional daughters have shown how books and intelligent conversation more than made up for what they lacked by way of formal education.

Certainly, to be an outsider had its negative aspect. Leonard Woolf noticed how people nudged and chortled as his wife drifted along the street thinking out her next day's writing. Emily Brontë and Olive Schreiner also appeared odd, dressed in derisory ways. Neither seems to have worn the corsets obligatory for respectable nineteenth-century ladies, locking bodies in upright postures and restricting movement. We know that schoolgirls in Brussels thought Emily pitifully unfashionable, and some men jeered as Olive Schreiner passed. As a girl, Emily Brontë declined at school where she could not adapt, and Olive Schreiner shed tears when shunned in Hanover. All had to bear the jeers of those who looked askance at people unlike themselves. The small-minded held up diminishing mirrors, so that George Eliot as a girl felt herself 'a failure of Nature'. And yet these five writers summoned the will to explore oddity in ways that speak to us about our unseen selves.

How selfish should a woman be? How far should she reserve her time and privacy — what Virginia Woolf called, famously, a room of one's own? George Eliot admitted to herself some mismatch between the model of sympathy and the demands of art. She did not take in bereft children in the family, as a non-writing aunt and stepmother might have done. Olive Schreiner was in a more divisive situation because her husband pressed her to fulfil duties which she could not, as a writer, undertake.

Of course they had flaws, often behaving badly towards their own, more passive sisters: Mary Godwin's put-downs of her loving sister, Fanny; George Eliot's neglect of her ill sister, Chrissey; Virginia Woolf's flirtation with her sister's husband; Olive Schreiner's refusal to house her sister-and mother-in-law. Then there was Emily Brontë's rudeness to people in

Brussels as well as religious intolerance. But all did have the courage to find original voices.

What do they tell us?

The alternative these women embody and offer to readers is the quality of their feeling: to enter into the lives of others with 'tenderness' (Mary Wollstonecraft's watchword) and 'sympathy' (George Eliot's). Some feel this spontaneously, but for most of us it comes through the fellow feeling of stories. Next to parental love, as we know, small human creatures sop up stories. What makes Frankenstein's monster most human is his initial taste for stories, the empathy that rises in him through reading. What turns him into a monster is when self-pity takes hold, and empathy switches off.

We love their books, which draw us close to women who are both believable and more evolved. Olive Schreiner used the words of Tennyson in dedicating *Woman and Labour* to the friend she revered most, the suffragette Constance Lytton: 'Give her the glory of going on and still to be.' Serious voices cut a channel through time to where we are now. I feel their presence, not as phantoms of the past but a beat on the pulse. In literature, where 'every fibre of nature' is involved, George Eliot said, a woman has something specific to contribute. 'It is an immense mistake to maintain that there is no sex in literature,' she insists. 'A certain amount of psychological difference between man and woman necessarily arises out of the difference of sex.'

One after the other, their books talk up domestic affection, listening, empathy and forms of desire consistent with lasting friendship — all qualities that the civilised of both sexes already share.

And they understood female sexuality. The desire and sexual bravery in their own lives gave them the raw material for their novels. I admire the play of character in their treatments of passion, both in the to-die-for ardour that George Eliot put into Tina Sarti and in Mary Shelley's reflections on her tie with Shelley — her erotic use of 'unveil' to suggest her freedom with him to be what she felt herself to be. She, George Eliot and Virginia Woolf show us how it feels to be seen in no ordinary way; they choose men who have the will and power to satisfy women in that way.

In 1929 Virginia Woolf thought it impossible to state 'the true nature of woman'. The answer, she said, must wait until women had been tested in politics and the professions. Yet even now, in the next century, an answer is still uncertain, and the reason, I think, is this: women are still finding a concerted voice of our own. In the meantime, we can look to the determined apartness of five writers who mined women's separate sphere, and listen to those who were alert to the unspoken, 'the roar from the other side of silence'.

# SOURCES

ABBREVIATIONS

CB          Charlotte Brontë
CBL         *The Letters of Charlotte Brontë*, vols i–iii, ed. Margaret Smith (Oxford: Clarendon Press, 1995–2004)
CC          Claire Clairmont
CCJ         *The Journals of Claire Clairmont*, ed. Marion Kingston Stocking (Cambridge, MA: Harvard University Press, 1968)
ClCor       *The Clairmont Correspondence*, vols i–ii, ed. Marion Kingston Stocking (Baltimore: Johns Hopkins University Press, 1995)
EB          Emily Brontë
EBP(H)      Emily Brontë, *The Complete Poems*, ed. C. W. Hatfield (New York: Columbia University Press, 1941)
EBP(G)      Emily Brontë, *The Complete Poems*, ed. Janet Gezari (Harmondsworth: Penguin Classics, 1992)
EBP(R)      *The Poems of Emily Brontë*, ed. Dennis Roper with Edward Chitham (Oxford: Clarendon Press, 1995)
EB/WH       Emily Brontë, *Wuthering Heights*
GE          George Eliot
GEJ         *The Journals of George Eliot*, ed. Margaret Harris and Judith Johnston (Cambridge: CUP, 1998)
GEL         *The George Eliot Letters*, ed. Gordon S. Haight (New Haven: Yale University Press; Oxford: OUP, 1954)
GESE        George Eliot, *Selected Essays, Poems and Other Writings*, ed. with introduction by A. S. Byatt (London: Penguin Classics, 1990)
GESL        *Selections from George Eliot's Letters*, ed. Gordon S. Haight (New Haven: Yale University Press, 1985)
GHL         George Henry Lewes
LW          Leonard Woolf
MW          Mary Wollstonecraft

| | |
|---|---|
| MWS | Mary Wollstonecraft Shelley |
| MWS/F | Mary Wollstonecraft Shelley, *Frankenstein or The Modern Prometheus: The 1818 Text*, ed. Marilyn Butler (London: Pickering, 1993; repr. for the World's Classics, OUP, 1994). Also published as the first volume of the eight-volume *The Novels and Selected Works of Mary Shelley*, ed. Nora Crook with Pamela Clemit, with introduction by Betty T. Bennett (London: Pickering, 1996) |
| *MWSJ* | *The Journals of Mary Shelley*, ed. Paula R. Feldman and Diana Scott-Kilvert, 2 vols (repr. pb: Baltimore: Johns Hopkins University Press, 1980–8) |
| *MWSL* | *The Letters of Mary Wollstonecraft Shelley*, i–iii, ed. Betty T. Bennett (Baltimore: Johns Hopkins University Press, 1995) |
| OS | Olive Schreiner |
| OS/AF | Olive Schreiner, *The Story of an African Farm* |
| *OSL*, i | Olive Schreiner, *Letters 1871–1899*, ed. Richard Rive (Oxford: OUP, 1988) |
| *OSL*, ii | Olive Schreiner, *The World's Great Question: Olive Schreiner's South African Letters 1889–1920*, ed. Liz Stanley and Andrea Salter (Cape Town: Van Riebeeck Society, 2014) |
| OS/OLP | Olive Schreiner, Online Letters Project, ed. Liz Stanley and Andrea Salter |
| OS/*W&L* | Olive Schreiner, *Woman and Labour* (Mineola: Dover Publications, 1998), a republication of the work originally published by Frederick A. Stokes Company, New York, in 1911. |
| PBS | Percy Bysshe Shelley |
| *PBSL* | *The Letters of Percy Bysshe Shelley*, 2 vols, ed. Frederick L. Jones (Oxford: Clarendon Press, 1964) |
| PBS/*SPP* | Percy Bysshe Shelley, *Selected Poetry and Prose*, ed. Donald H. Reiman and Neil Fraistat (New York: Norton Critical Edition, 2002, 2nd edition) |
| Seymour | Miranda Seymour, *Mary Shelley* (London: John Murray, 2000) |
| VW | Virginia Woolf |
| VW/*AROO* | Virginia Woolf, *A Room of One's Own* |
| VW/*CSF* | Virginia Woolf, *The Complete Shorter Fiction*, ed. Susan Dick (New York: Harvest/Harcourt, 1989, 2nd edition) |
| *VWD* | *The Diary of Virginia Woolf*, 5 vols, ed. Anne Olivier Bell (London: Hogarth Press, 1977–84) |
| *VWE* | *The Essays of Virginia Woolf*, ed. Andrew McNeillie (vols i–iv) and Stuart N. Clarke (vols v–vi) (London: Hogarth Press, 1986–2011) |
| *VWL* | *The Letters of Virginia Woolf*, 6 vols, ed. Nigel Nicolson and Joanne Trautmann (London: Hogarth Press, 1975–80) |
| VW/*ND* | Virginia Woolf, *Night and Day* |
| VW/*TG* | Virginia Woolf, *Three Guineas* |
| WG | William Godwin |

## FOREWORD

1 *'the world without' and 'the world within'*: 'To Imagination' (3 Sept 1844). Published in *Poems* (1846). *EBP*(R), 25.

2 *'No coward soul is mine'*: *EBP*(H), 243.

3 *staying at home*: Emily Dickinson was fortunate in a father who excused her from household duties, freeing her to write in the morning. That liberty was unknown to other homes, apart from that of the poet Elizabeth Barrett, in Wimpole Street, London, where she was treated as an invalid. At the age of twenty, Emily Dickinson had consulted the pre-eminent Boston doctor and there is circumstantial evidence to suggest that she too had a physical condition, one reason for keeping to her room and which allowed her special consideration.

3 *motherless*: Mary Godwin's mother died when she was ten days old. Mrs Brontë died when Emily was three. Mary Ann Evans's mother died when she was seventeen; she had been away at boarding school throughout her childhood and never mentions her mother. Virginia Woolf's mother died when she was thirteen. Schreiner's mother lived into her eighties but was not present for Olive after the age of twelve, when the child was sent away.

4 *'the madness of art'*: 'The Middle Years' (1893).

5 *'Speak I must'*: *Jane Eyre* (1847), ch. 4.

## 1. PRODIGY

7 *'All being decided . . . '*: *MWSJ*, 6. In the hand of PBS. At first Mary and Shelley wrote a joint journal. The entries for 28 July until 13 Sept 1814 were revised and, together perhaps with extracts from correspondence, published in Dec 1817 as a *History of a Six Weeks' Tour through a part of France, Switzerland, Germany and Holland*. Afterwards the *Journals* were written by Mary alone.

7 *'somewhat imperious'*: WG to a stranger, E. Fordham, who had asked him about his daughters, 13 Nov 1811. Bodleian Library, Abinger Papers: Dep.b.214/3.

7 *'the productions of her mind'*: (30 July 1814), *MWSJ*, 8. In the hand of PBS, reporting on what MWS promised him.

8 *'I who love him . . . '*: (24 Jan 1815), *MWSL*, i, 9.

8 *'soft as a woman . . . '*: (26 Apr 1823), *MWSJ*, 463. Her best images come after his death. Living with his memory, she distils her idea of him.

8 *'interpenetrated'*: (10 Nov 1822), *MWSJ*, i, 443.

8 *'my divine Shelley'*: *MWSL*, i, 253–4.

9 *'. . . what art thou?'; 'I know . . . '*: 'To Mary –', PBS/*SPP*, 104. Dedication to *The Revolt of Islam*, first published under this title in Jan 1818, addressing MWS.

Shelley's refusal to be too articulate recurs in other poets: Emily Brontë, Emily Dickinson, Hardy and T. S. Eliot (in 'Prufrock', when he says 'It is impossible to say just what I mean').

9 *'unveil'; 'sealed treasure'*: (2 Oct 1822), *MWSJ*, 429–30.

9 *voice applauds her*: (7 Oct 1822), *MWSJ*, 436.

9 *'exquisite pain'; strange thoughts*: (8 Feb 1822), *MWSJ*, 396.

9 *'natural modulation'*: (7 Oct 1822), *MWSJ*, 436.

9 *'communicate with unlimited freedom'*: (2 Oct 1822), *MWSJ*, 429.

9–10   *'peculiarities', 'unfold in secret', 'like one in a distant and savage land', 'inmost soul', 'one delightful voice':* Essay 'On Love', PBS/*SPP*, 503–4.

10   *'Mary, look':* M WSJ, 7.

10   *'insensible to all future evil':* (7 August 1814), *M WSJ*, 11. In the hand of PBS.

11   *fifteen years later:* MWS's 1831 preface to MWS/F, republished in the Colburn and Bentley Standard Novels series. Seymour, 408, rightly questioned the story in MWS's preface: 'even today, Mary's description of the birth of *Frankenstein* is quoted without scepticism. And yet . . . she was, when she chose, a singularly convincing liar.'

12   *'a woman I shudder to think of ':* (27 Oct 1814), *M WSJ*, 40.

12   Clermont: By Regina Maria Roche.

15   *Shelley was heartened:* William St Clair has a fine chapter on Shelley's arrival on the scene. Miranda Seymour's biography, *Mary Shelley*, is alert to the nuances of a complex drama, where the full truth cannot be known. She includes the fact that we can't know what was in Shelley's mind in the early months of 1814, and suggests plausibly that his confusion might have verged on insanity.

16   *'thrilling' voices:* Hogg reported this scene and the one at MW's tomb, *Shelley*, ii, 538.

16   *'sublime':* PBS to Thomas Jefferson Hogg (4 Oct 1814), *PBSL*, i, 401–3.

16   *hints of marital unhappiness:* According to CC in a late-in-life conversation with the Shelley devotee Captain Edward Silsbee. Silsbee Papers, Peabody Museum, Salem, Massachusetts.

16   *Any hesitation:* PBS to Thomas Jefferson Hogg (4 Oct 1814), *PBSL*, i, 401–3. 'I was vacillating & infirm of purpose: I shuddered to transgress a real duty', and Mary, he reports, dispelled this.

17   *M WS's hair: CCJ*, 431. Often said to be auburn, but the lock in the Pforzheimer Library has no red in it. I thought it looked nut brown, but CC's description of its varied colours is lovely. Smallpox, as Seymour recounts, took the life and body out of her hair.

17   *'name', 'aspiring Child':* 'Dedication to Mary' in 'Laon and Cythna', written at the end of the summer of 1817, revised as *The Revolt of Islam*, published Jan 1818 (the same month as MWS/F). PBS/*SPP*, 104.

18   *'He had the madness':* Godwin to John Taylor (27 Aug 1814), *PBSL*, i, 391 note 258.

18   *wicked:* Reported to MWS by Charles Clairmont that WG had said Shelley was so beautiful it was a pity he was wicked. (23 March 1815), *M WSJ*, 72.

18   *'it is no reproach to me . . . ':* To Harriet Shelley (14 July 1814), *PBSL*, i, 390.

19   *Godwin's letter of 25 July to PBS:* This exists only as an extract in a sale catalogue. St Clair, 550, notes that the whereabouts of this letter, as that of an earlier letter to PBS on 10 July, sold in the same lot, are unknown. Cited also by Seymour, 581.

21   *erase her:* Isobel Dixon provided this phrase.

21   *'We returned . . . '; 'She rested on my bosom':* (2 Aug 1814), *M WSJ*, 9.

22   *'the first of a new genus':* To sister Everina Wollstonecraft (7 Nov [1787]). *The Collected Letters of Mary Wollstonecraft*, ed. Janet Todd (London: Allen Lane, 2003), 139–40.

22   *aim in Mary:* MW's prologue.

22   *'dart into futurity':* Mary (1788), ch. 4.

22   *'still does my panting soul . . . ':* Ibid., ch. 20

22   *'Those who are bold enough . . . censure':* Thought to be letter to Mary Hays, *c*. April 1797, *Collected Letters*, 410.

22–3   *M WS on the distress in the wake of war: M WSJ*, 12. See also the war-ruined towns in MWS's novel *The Fortunes of Perkin Warbeck* (1830).

23   *'Brutal force . . . ':* A Vindication of the Rights of Woman, ch. 2.

23  *'Nothing could be more entire . . . '*: MWS and PBS, *History of a Six Weeks Tour* (1817), 19.

23  *MWS refusal of leaves to dry herself*: *Shelley and his Circle*, iii, 350. CC recalled this later. Not in the version of the journal published in *CCJ*.

24  *'I was thinking of my father'*: Ibid., 348. Not in *CCJ*.

24  *'vulgar abuse'*: (21 Oct 1838), *MWSJ*, 554.

24  *'spirit of the elements' and her own apartness*: (17 Nov 1822), *MWSJ*, 445.

25  *'uncleansable animals', 'loathsome creepers'; 'Twere easier . . . '*: (28 Aug 1814), *MWSJ*, 20–1.

26  *Rousseau's coquette*: (9 Sept 1814), *CCJ*, 40. While in Holland and writing her story, CC was reading *Emile*.

26  *CC's 'Ideot'*: *CCJ*, 40. More on her story in letter to Byron (Mar or Apr 1816), *ClCor*, 33.

27  *seated at her mother's tomb*: On 22 Oct 1814.

27  *professed friendship*: (15 Apr 1815), *MWSJ*, 75.

27  Journal *as record of reading*: With very occasional entries by PBS. Jane Austen, as it happens at this very time, 1814, takes the same position that properly directed reading – on the part of her exemplary Fanny Price – 'must be an education in itself' (*Mansfield Park*, vol. i, ch. 2).

28  *'subterraneous community of women'*: Shelley's entry in *MWSJ*, 32. Anticipates by more than a century Virginia Woolf's proposal (in *TG*) of an 'Outsider Society' of those who cultivate the buried links between women in their authentic character. See ch. 5, below.

28–9  *record of 'the horrors' on 7 Oct.*: Shelley's record. *MWSJ*, 33.

29  *liberating 'two heiresses'*: (30 Sept 1814), *MWSJ*, 30.

30  *'hopping about town'*: *MWSJ*, 45.

30  *'eternity'*: *PBSL*, i, 416.

31  *'fright the steeds . . . '*: Shelley blends lines from two scenes in *Romeo and Juliet*: III.ii.1 and II.ii.31. *PBSL*, 413.

31  *'Mary's many embraces . . . '*: PBS (29 Jan 1815), *MWSJ*, 61.

31  *genius 'transcending mine'*: (2 Oct 1822), *MWSJ*, 429.

31  *surpassed him in originality*: To Thomas Jefferson Hogg (4 Oct 1814), *PBSL*, i, 265.

31  *Garnerin lecture*: *MWSJ*, 56.

33  *PBS's fear of pursuit*: A Godwinian drama in *Caleb Williams*.

33  *Dr Clarke*: His brother was also in practice.

33  *'many things'*: (13 Mar 1815), *MWSJ*, 69. 'Things' is consistent with the tight-lipped records of the early *Journal*, as when Mary held up the chaise on 28 July 1814, to do 'something'.

34  *CC in Lynmouth*: Seymour, 131–3, 136–7. The lack of verifiable facts makes it just as plausible to see Claire as innocent at this stage. All we can know is that CC's departure was under discussion from March 1815, with MWS finding her presence unbearable, and that her refusal to return to Skinner Street made MWS wretched. While CC was away, Shelley had a protracted stay in London and Mary, at a distance, feared CC had joined him. Sunstein thinks she feared correctly. From Oct 1815 CC travelled with her brother to Dublin.

William St Clair gives another reason for the exile to Lynmouth: a visit to Godwin by MW's sister Mrs Bishop, saying that Fanny, her niece, was tainted by the scandal of CC, and that Fanny's future as a teacher at her school would not be possible so long as CC remained in the Shelley ménage. St Clair sees the stay in Lynmouth as a kind of social quarantine.

34–5  *'Will you judge candidly . . . '*: CC to Byron (Mar–Apr 1816), *ClCor*, 33. The half-written novel had been set down at intervals and in scraps.

35 *influence of Gibbon on CC's novel*: CC was citing a controversial chapter (16) in the first of the six volumes.

36 *ten minutes happy passion*: CC in Moscow to Jane Williams in London (Dec 1826), *ClCor*, i, 241.

36 *'I shall ever remember . . . '*: (16? Apr 1816), *ClCor*, i, 36.

37 *Shelley voice as rain*: (Recalled 19 Oct 1822), *MWSJ*, 439. Otherwise described (above) as high and cracked. At that time, after Shelley's death, MWS was living near Byron in the Albaro suburb of Genoa, and hearing Byron's distinctive voice.

38 *CC present on 16 June*: The cover-up ensured that her presence would go unmentioned.

38 *'When I placed my head on my pillow . . . '*: Preface to 1831 edn of MWS/F.

39 *'the deep consciousness . . . '*: MWS/F, ch.1.

39 *'feelings of affection . . . '*: Ibid., ch.3.

39 *encounter at Chamonix*: Ibid., ch.8.

39 *'hate' at Chamonix*: Ibid. The monster says later, 'All men hate the wretched . . . '

40 *'miserably alone'*: Ibid.

40 *Jemima as 'outcast' from society*: The Wrongs of Woman, chs 1 and 5.

40 *the Creature hides in the hovel*: MWS/F, ch. 14.

40 *'because I found the world deserted you . . . '*: (20 May 1816), *ClCor*, i, 49.

43 *'that hateful novel thing'*: To Byron (19 November 1816), *ClCor*, i, 92.

43 *'my unhappy life'*: (29 July–1 Aug 1816), *ClCor*, i, 58.

43 *'My heart is warm . . . '*: To MWS (3 Oct 1816), *ClCor*, i, 82.

44 *'I have long determined . . . '*: *ClCor*, i, 86.

44 *'the three girls were all equally in love'*: Godwin told Mrs Gisborne, an intimate friend of MWS in Italy, who had looked after Fanny and Mary after their mother died: (9 July 1820), Gisborne, *Journals and Letters*, 39. CC offered the same explanation in an interview when she was old. Silsbee Papers, box 7, folder 2. Cited in *ClCor*, i, 88–9.

44 *Harriet thought PBS a 'monster'*: Recalled by CC. Silsbee Papers, box 8, folder 4.

45 *PBS's excess*: Charles Clairmont to CC (17 Sept 1815), *ClCor*, 14–15. Passage noted by Charles E. Robinson, Introduction to *The Frankenstein Notebooks*, lxvi.

46 *'mine own heart's home'; 'prophecy'; 'thou and I'*: dedicatory stanzas 'To Mary –', written at the end of the summer of 1817, to 'Laon and Cythna', revised as *The Revolt of Islam* and published at the same time as MWS/F, Jan 1818. PBS/SPP, 101.

46 *PBS's felicitous touches to the ms of* Frankenstein: In 1996 Charles E. Robinson brought out a facsimile edition of Mary Shelley's manuscript novel, 1816–17 (with alterations in the hand of Percy Bysshe Shelley) as it survives in draft and fair copy in the Bodleian Library, Oxford (Dep.c.477/1 and Dep.c.534/1-2). At the time PBS was composing what came to be called *The Revolt of Islam* with its sympathetic feminist leader, erotic freedom and a revolution that is determinedly pacifist.

47 *PBS never exercised his legal right to see his children*: St Clair, 420.

48 *doppelgänger*: Anne K. Mellor (54–5) links MWS with the time-scheme of *Frankenstein*, as does Charles E. Robinson, ed. of *The Frankenstein Notebooks*, Introduction, vii. The introduction offers an ingenious idea that the dates of the story bear on MWS's own life (p. lxv). The novel starts with Walton's letter dated 11 Jan 1796, which would be the date of MWS's conception, and the novel ends with Walton's last letter of 12 Sept 1797; that is, thirteen days after MWS's birth and two days after her mother died. Might this make the author (privately) a doppelgänger herself?

48 *Frankenstein's abortion*: MWS/F, ch. 14. Law professor Carol Sanger sifts issues of gender

and the law in *About Abortion: Terminating Pregnancy in Twenty-First-Century America* (Cambridge, MA: Belknap Press of Harvard University, 2017).

48 *'The remains of the half-finished creature . . .'*: MWS/F, ch. 16. Frankenstein views this in the light of the day following the abortion perpetrated in the murk of night.

49 *PBS editing the final lines of* Frankenstein: *The Frankenstein Notebooks*, ii, 817.

49 *PBS offered CC's novel to publishers*: PBS to MWS (6 Oct 1817), *PBSL*, i, 561. Charles E. Robinson notes the possibility that this 'novel' might be CC's response to the horror-story challenge of 16 June 1816. (Her probable presence at the Diodati that night is not mentioned by the participants, as the cover-up would have required.)

52 *publication date of* Frankenstein: 1 January is the official date. In fact, the book was issued late in 1817.

53 *Shelley party at Bagni di Lucca*: At this time, Shelley wrote a narrative poem, *Rosalind and Helen*, about the loneliness of two women whose beliefs and behaviour have made them outcasts. MWS made a fair copy.

53 *letter to Mrs Hoppner*: From Pisa (10 Aug 1821), *MWSL*, i, 205–8. This letter, due to be forwarded by Byron, remained amongst his papers.

53 *'a most tremendous fuss'*: (28 Feb 1819), *MWSJ*, 249. Would there have been such a fuss if the situation had been as Sunstein, 163, suggests: that Shelley undertook secret charge of an illegitimate baby, not his own, hoping possibly that Mary would agree to adopt Elena after she got over baby Clara's death.

54 *PBS 'this bark of refuge'*: (7 Oct 1922), *MWSJ*, 438.

54 *'Misery: A Fragment'*: Otherwise known as 'Invocation to Misery' (c. June 1819), *The Poems of Shelley*, ii, ed. Kelvin Everest and Geoffrey Matthews (Harlow: Longman, 2000), 703–5.

54 *'Love, from its awful throne . . .'*: Finale to *Prometheus Unbound*, Act IV. Shelley's title undoes that of Aeschylus in his play *Prometheus Bound*.

55 *'To forgive wrongs . . .'*: PBS/*SPP*, 285–6.

56 Matilda: The narrator's preoccupation with her death may go back to Richardson's *Clarissa*, which MWS read between June and August 1819, immediately after her son died.

56 *'Oh, my beloved father . . .'*: *Matilda* in *Mary Maria Matilda*, ed. Janet Todd (London: Penguin Classics, 1992), 149–210.

57 *'often did quiescence . . .'*: MWS, 'Life of William Godwin', 97. A collection of preliminary fragments (1836–40) amongst the Abinger Papers, Bodleian Library. In Pamela Clemit et al, *Lives of the Great Romantics*, iii, i: *Godwin*, 95–115.

57 *'alone!'*: (2 Oct 1822), *MWSJ*, 429. MWS's first entry in a new volume of her *Journal* after PBS's death in July.

57 *'the chain of existence'*: MWS/F, ch. 14.

57 *'hate more & more'*: To Jane Williams (19–20 Feb 1823), *MWSL*, i, 311.

58 *'disdained' as 'a woman . . .'*: (2 Dec 1824), *MWSJ*, 487.

58 *Why is the companion . . .'*: (Sept 1824), *MWSJ*, 484–5.

59 *'nihil timens . . .'*: Quoted (3 Dec 1824), *MWSJ*, 486. From *De Finibus Bonarum et Malorum*.

59 *'the subject of* men's *observations'*: To Trelawny (Apr 1829), who wished to write a biography of Shelley, which would bring MWS into notice. *MWSL*, ii, 72.

60 *'yields'*: CC in Marlow to Byron (12 Jan 1818, a few days after the publication of *Frankenstein*), *ClCor*, i 111.

60 *'what my tongue . . .'*: 'Miscellanea: Second Leaflet', *CCJ*, 437. Missing pages were destroyed by Dowden, Shelley's first official biographer.

60–1 *'blood and life'; 'Thy voice . . . '; 'Upon the verge . . . ':* 'To Constantia, Singing', PBS/*SPP*, 107–9. Written at Marlow, latter half of 1817–Jan 1818. The 'breath of summer's night' is similar to Byron's words about a voice like 'the swell of summer's ocean' when the breast of the deep 'is gently heaving', in his 'Stanzas for Music'.

61 *Claire claimed . . .*: Silsbee Papers, box 8, folder 4.

62 *CC's pleas to Byron about Allegra*: Silsbee Papers, box 8, folder 4. Shelley did pay one visit and did not perceive anything to alarm him. But it would have been impossible to gauge the feelings of so young a child in the presence of her keepers. I think of Charlotte Brontë's later anger at a ladylike friend of her father, who visited the starved, mistreated, sickening Brontë girls at Cowan Bridge and noticed nothing to disturb her.

62 *Allegra's death*: Said to be either from typhus or 'after a convulsive catarrhal attack'.

62 *'The party of free women'*: (16 Sept 1834), *ClCor*, i, 314–15.

63 *'I beleive [sic] . . . '*: (21 Oct 1838), *MWSJ*, 554.

63 *'Composing . . . '*: (17 Nov [1822?]). Bodleian Library, Abinger Papers: Dep.c.517.

64 *MWS conceived of a women's history*: Proposed (8 Sept 1830) for Murray's *Family Library*: 'the Lives of Celebrated women – or a history of Woman – her position in society and her influence upon it'. Murray archive.

65 *'the most contemptible of lives'*: (25 Feb 1822), *MWSJ*, 399–400.

65 *'a kind of tenderness'*: (8 Feb 1822), *MWSJ*, 396.

## 2. VISIONARY

67 *fancies*: fully and wittily chronicled in *The Brontë Myth* by Lucasta Miller (London: Cape, 2001).

68 *'most lovable women . . . '*: '*Jane Eyre* and *Wuthering Heights*' (1925), *VWE*, iv, 170.

68 *'strangers'*: Letter to the Revd John Buckworth (17 Nov 1821), *The Letters of the Reverend Patrick Brontë*, ed. Dudley Green (Stroud: Nonsuch Publishing, 2005), 43.

68 *'not a single educated family'*: CB to her editor, William Smith Williams (3 July 1849). *CBL*, ii, 227. She was writing after the deaths of her brother and two sisters, so that at this time she would have felt particularly alone.

70 *'my poor children'*: Elizabeth Gaskell heard this from the nurse. To Catherine Winkworth (25 Aug 1850). J. A. V. Chapple, assisted by John Geoffrey Sharps, *Elizabeth Gaskell: A Portrait in Letters* (Manchester University Press, 2012), 138.

70 *'prattle'*: To the Revd John Buckworth, *The Letters of Patrick Brontë*, 44.

73 *'She exhibited . . . '*: Note by Dudley Green, *The Letters of Patrick Brontë*, 55.

73 *'the heart is dead since infancy'*: 'Castle Wood' (2 Feb 1844), *EBP*(H), 194. This is a Gondal poem, and one of the many lines that resonate with private import below the surface of Gondal drama.

73 *'a sound . . . '*: 'Written on Returning to the P[alace] of I[nstruction] on the 10th of January 1827', i.e., she sets back the date to a year and a half after Maria and Elizabeth died. *EBP*(H), 110–12; *EBP*(R), 83–4.

74 *'So hopeless is the world without . . . '*: 'To Imagination' (3 Sept 1844), published *Poems* (1846). EBP(R), 25.

75 *No evidence for contact with Ponden House*: Ellen Nussey's diary records some 'fun' there in 1844 but it's too glancing a comment for any conclusion.

75–6 *Benjamin Wiggins and sisters*: 'My Angria and the Angrians', dated 1834.

76 *Their walk was free and rapid*: Ellen Nussey, holograph ms relating to the Brontës. Berg Collection, New York Public Library.

77 *'humor'*: EB's and AB's manuscript diary paper (26 June 1837). Brontë Parsonage Museum.

77 *'this delusive . . . world' and 'this land of probation'*: The Revd Patrick Brontë to Mrs Franks, about daughters going away to school (6 July 1835). *The Letters of Patrick Brontë*, 100.

78 *EB's decline at school*: CB, 'Prefatory Note to "Selections from Poems by Ellis Bell"' (1850). Appendix to *CBL*, ii, 753.

78 *'those first feelings . . . '*: 'Often Rebuked, yet always back returning', *EBP*(G), 198 (in section of Poems of Doubtful Authorship) and 220 (in section of poems edited by CB in 1850, entitled 'Stanzas'). CB is known to have substantially revised most of the poems she printed in 1850, and since no manuscript of this poem survives, its authorship has been dispute. But it does seem to me to have the vigour of EB rather than the droopy pathos of many of CB's poems.

79 *'Riches I hold . . . '*: Dated 1 Mar 1841. Published *Poems* (1846). *EBP*(H), 163; *EBP*(R), 120–1.

79 *The breath of liberty*: 'Liberty was the breath of Emily's nostrils', CB explained in her Preface of 1850. Appendix to *CBL*, ii, 753.

80 *Tempest roaring, 'voice divine'*: 'Aye, there it is . . . ' (dated 6 July 1841), *EBP*(H), 165.

80 *guest list for Robert Heaton's funeral, 1846*: Heaton Papers, Bradford City Archives: HEA/B/13.

81 *'slave' and 'comrade'*: 'Plead for Me' (14 Oct 1844), published *Poems* (1846). *EBP*(H), 208–9; *EBP*(R), 155–6.

82 *Jacob in the Bible*: Genesis: xxxiii, 24–32.

82 *'worsted God'*: 'A little East of Jordan' (*c.* early 1860). *Complete Poems*, ed. Thomas H. Johnson, no. 59; *Poems: Variorum Edition*, ed. F. H. Franklin (Cambridge, MA: Belknap Press of Harvard University, 1998), no. 145.

82 *'never twice alike . . . more divine'*: Dickinson confided this in a letter (30 Apr 1882) to her suitor, Judge Lord. Letter 750 in *The Letters of Emily Dickinson*, ed. Thomas H. Johnson (Cambridge, MA: Belknap Press of Harvard University, 1958, 1986).

84 *'upright, heretic and English spirit'*: CB, 'Prefatory note to "Selections from Poems by Ellis Bell"' (1850). Appendix to *The Letters of Charlotte Brontë*, ii, 753. Stevie Davies rightly entitles one of her profound and intellectually searching books on EB *Emily Brontë: Heretic*.

84 *Louise de Bassompierre on EB*: Letter to W. T. Field, *Brontë Society Transactions*, v, 23, 26. Cited by Rebecca Fraser, *Charlotte Brontë* (London: Methuen, 1988), 171.

84 *'unconscious tyranny'*: Mrs Gaskell, after interviewing M. Heger, *Life*, ch. 11. A fellow pupil, Laetitia Wheelwright, confirmed this according to Fraser, 171.

86–7 *essays in Brussels*: The *Belgian Essays*, ed. and transl. Sue Lonoff (New Haven: Yale University Press, 1996).

87 *'divinest anguish' and 'indulge . . . '*: 'R. Alcona to J. Brenzaida' (3 March 1845), *EBP*(H), 223.

87 *'Dear childhood's Innocence . . . '*: 'H.A. and A.S.', *EBP*(H), 175.

87 *EB felt obliged to teach music*: Plausible suggestion by Sue Lonoff, *Belgian Essays*.

88 *'singularities'*: To Ellen Nussey (July? 1842), *CBL*, i, 289. Cited by Mrs Gaskell, *Life*, ch. 11.

88 *M. Heger to Patrick Brontë*: (5 Nov 1842), *CBL*, i, 298–302.

88 *EB and Beethoven*: Stevie Davies is superb on the German influences, especially music: *Emily Brontë: Heretic*, 52. She played, as well, piano transcriptions of the fourth and sixth symphonies; also Mozart and Haydn.

88 *Anne's 'world within':* *Agnes Grey*, ch. 22.

88 *'passages in the life of an Individual':* Anne Brontë's diary paper for July 1845 indicates that she was starting what she calls the third volume. Not known exactly when she began this novel at Thorp Green.

89 *Robert Heaton's marriage:* The Heaton family papers, first seen in Keighley in 1993, have since been moved to the Bradford City Archives. The couple were married at Cross Roads in the parish of Bingley, where they continued to live. Mr Brontë baptised all three of their daughters. (These daughters were born at intervals of several years, suggesting an inactive couple trying in vain for a son.)

89 *no record of the precise date:* In *Charlotte Bronte: A Passionate Life* I noted that the record was in the family Bible. Heaton Papers: HEA/B/166. Checking again in 2016, I see that there are indeed records there but only of earlier generations, with one slip with later data laid in. I wonder whether another laid-in slip has somehow vanished. I saw this when the material was in the Keighley archive in 1993.

89 *Earnshaw:* EB, it seems, used a local surname for the central family in her novel. Mary Earnshaw's name appears on the guest list for Robert Heaton's funeral in April 1846, the year EB completed *Wuthering Heights*. Heaton Papers: HEA/B/13.

89 *'thy love I will not, will not share!':* from 'How clear she shines!' (13 Apr 1843), published *Poems* (1846). *EBP*(H), 184–5.

89 *'resentful mood', 'demon's moan':* 'My Comforter' (10 Feb 1844), published *Poems* (1846). *EBP*(H), 195–7. At this time, Feb 1844, EB began to copy her poems (without their prose contexts) into two notebooks. In 1844 she was writing about the parting of loved ones, either by death or by finding themselves on opposite sides in war. (Barker, *The Brontës*, 512.)

90 *aunt's bequest:* See Samantha Ellis, *Take Courage*, ch. 2, for a fresh view of Elizabeth Branwell. She notes that their aunt's bequest paid for the publication of *Poems*, *Wuthering Heights* and *Agnes Grey*.

90 *Dodgson's copy of* Poems: Claire Harman, *Charlotte Brontë* (London: Viking, 2015), 234n.

90 *Nightingale transcribing EB:* Early 1860s. Mark Bostridge, *Florence Nightingale: The Woman and Her Legend* (London: Viking, 2008), 106, 415–16.

92 *sister figure:* Lucasta Miller notes this is somewhat in the manner of idealised brother-sister pairings in Shelley, Byron, De Quincey and Wordsworth. *The Brontë Myth*, 242.

92 *'If all else perished . . . ':* EB/*WH*, i, 9. Link with 'No coward soul' quoted by Lucasta Miller and others.

93 *'Though Earth and moon were gone':* Sixth stanza of 'No coward soul'. *EBP*(G), 182; *EBP*(H), 243; *EBP*(R), 183–4.

94 *'Books, coarse even for men':* 28 Dec 1850. *The Brontës: The Critical Heritage*, ed. Miriam Allott (Abingdon: Routledge, 1995), 292. Extraordinary difference between GHL's virulence towards the Brontës and his generosity to GE. There may be two possible reasons: one is CB's refusal to accept his anti-Romantic mentoring; the other, the anti-Romantic temper itself. He was in accord with GE's scientific temper, her rationality and realism.

94 *EB writing to Lewes:* Mrs Gaskell to George Smith, while writing her *Life* in 1856. 'I *know*', she said, that EB corresponded with Lewes.

95 *'I feel an assurance . . . ':* EB/*WH*, ii, ch. 11.

96 *order from Whitehall:* letter from H. Waddington, as directed by the Secretary of State, to Messrs Heaton of Cross Road, near Haworth (the address of Robert Heaton). Heaton Papers: HEA/A/548.

99   *'poisoning doctor'*: CB to Ellen Nussey (10 Dec 1848), *CBL*, ii, 152.

99   ' . . . *relentless conflict* . . . ': CB to William Smith Williams (25 Dec 1848), *CBL*, ii, 159.

99   *'he says I drive him to it* . . . ': *The Tenant of Wildfell Hall*, ch. 35.

100  *'My greatest source of uneasiness* . . . ': Ibid., ch. 39.

101  *'Because Ellis's poems are short* . . . ': To William Smith Williams (16 Nov 1848), *CBL*, ii, 140.
     CB writes after reading an adverse review in the *Spectator* of Smith, Elder's recent
     reprint of the Bells' *Poems*.

101  *'Stronger* . . . ': Currer Bell's 'Biographical Notice of Ellis and Acton Bell'. Appendix
     to *CBL*, ii, 746. Smith, Elder published a one-volume edition of *WH*, *Agnes Grey* and a
     selection of their poems in Dec 1850.

102  *'In showing my treasure* . . . ': *Shirley*, ch. 26.

102  *'undying life'*: From 'No coward soul', op. cit.

103  *Emily Dickinson on 'Gigantic EB'*: Letter 742 to Mrs Holland, *The Letters of Emily Dickinson*. In
     *c.* 1884 she spoke again of 'marvellous' Emily Brontë to Smith College teacher Maria
     Whitney (letter 948).

103  *VW on EB as 'gigantic'; 'She looked out* . . . ': *'Jane Eyre* and *Wuthering Heights'* (1925), *VWE*, iv,
     169.

103  *'Why ask to know what date* . . . ': *EBP*(H), 252–3. This poem reworks a long, unfinished
     poem, dated 14 September 1846, which is a dramatic monologue by a soldier admit-
     ting how he 'grew hard' and 'learnt to wear/ An iron front to terror's prayer'.

104  *poetry of situation*: 'Phases of Fiction' (1929), *VWE*, v, 78–9. Intended as a critical book on
     the craft of fiction for a Hogarth series but came out in *The Bookman* (NY).

## 3. 'OUTLAW'

107  *'one marvel'; 'counselling angel'*: To father, Henry James Sr (10 May 1869), *The Complete
     Letters of Henry James*, i (1855–72), ed. Pierre A. Walker and Greg W. Zacharias (Lincoln:
     University of Nebraska Press, 2006– ), 311.

107  *'like a species* . . . ': To mother, Mary James (13 Oct 1869), *The Complete Letters of Henry James*,
     ii (1855–72), 145.

107  *The Priory*: 21 North Bank, where GE and GHL lived from 1863 to 1878. Here she wrote
     *Middlemarch* and *Daniel Deronda*.

108  *'who has been* . . . ': 'George Eliot' (1919), written for *TLS*, celebrating the centenary of
     GE's birth; published in *The Common Reader* (1925); repr. *VWE*, iv, 170–80.

108  *protest from William Hale White*: A. S. Byatt, Introduction, *GESE*, ix.

108  *'outsiders' school'*: VW/*TG*, ch. 3.

110  *'an unpromising woman-child'*: To Sara Hennell (3? Oct 1859), *GESL*, 226.

110  *'failure of Nature'*: To Sara Hennell (3 June 1854), *GESL*, 134.

110  *'the nature of women* . . . ': John Stuart Mill, *The Subjection of Women* (1869), ch. 1.

111  *'the daughters of educated men'*: VW/*TG*. See ch. 5, below.

112–13 *report of Elizabeth Evans*: To Sara Hennell (7 Oct 1859), *GESL*, 226–8.

113  *'spirit of love'* and *'a truly religious soul'*: Ibid.

113  *'I make the most humiliating* . . . ': (5 Mar 1839), *GESL*, 18–19.

113  *'insatiable desire'* and quote: Genesis 49:4. (6 Feb 1839), *GESL*, 14.

117  *'crude state of free thinking'*: To Sara Hennell (7 Oct 1859), with recollections of her aunt,
     *GESL*, 228.

118  *'Dr Brabant being its archangel'*: To Cara Bray (20 Nov [1843]), *GEL*, i, 165.

119   *'I am sure . . . twinges of alarm'*: (18 June 1844), *GESL*, 30.

120   *'soul-stupefying'*: To Sara ([6 Apr 1845]), *GEL*, i, 185.

121   *'I am determined to sell . . .'*: (1 Apr 1850), *GESL*, 71.

121   *'I thought . . . horrible stories . . .'*: To Cara Bray (12 Jan 1852), *GEL*, ii, 3.

123   *'to pay our respects to the Cow'*: To Sara Hennell (27 May 1845), *GESL*, 33.

123   *'All sacrifice is good . . .'*: To Charles Bray (11 June 1848), *GESL*, 51.

123   *strong, sharp, adamant*: Words of Isobel Dixon.

123   *instructed Chapman to tell his wife . . .*: (4 Apr [1851]), *GEL*, i, 348.

124   *'Pray be candid'*: (9 May [1851]), *GESL*, 79.

126   *response to 1848 revolts; 'slow crawlers'*: To John Sibtree Jr (8 Mar 1848), *GESL*, 46–8.

126   *'I am training myself . . .'*: (3 Oct 1851), *GESL*, 83.

126   *'groaning with books'*: (2 Nov 1851), *GESL*, 86.

128   laideur divinée: When she met Liszt in Weimar, 1854.

128   *'proof-hunting'*: To Sara Hennell (29 June 1852), *GESL*, 99.

129   *'life-preservers'*: To Mrs Peter Taylor (27 Mar 1852), *GEL*, ii, 15.

130   *Margaret Fuller's journal touched her*: Ibid. The review of the *Memoirs of Margaret Fuller* in the *Westminster Review* (Apr 1852) seems to be by GE. Gordon Haight, editor of the *Letters*, notes that she's quoting somewhat inaccurately.

130   *'a good, delightful creature'*: To the Brays (27 Apr 1852), *GESL*, 95.

131   *'haggard'*: (5 and 27 May 1852), *GESL*, 96, 97.

131   *if Spencer married she would again be frozen out*: Thanks to Isobel Dixon.

131   *'lumps of ice'*: To Herbert Spencer (8 July 1852), *GESL*, 100.

132   *'I know this letter will make you very angry'*: (14? July 1852), *GESL*, 102.

133   *Spencer confided*: To E. L. Youmans, *GESL*, 101–2.

133   *'Dear Mr Spencer . . .'*: (29? July [1852]), *GESL*, 105.

135   *'I live in a world . . .'*: (22 Aug 1852), *GEL*, ii, 52.

135   *tableaux devised by GHL*: To Herbert Spencer (8 July 1852), *GESL*, 100–1.

135   *'defective'*: To John Chapman (24–25 July 1852), *GESL*, 105.

137   *GHL's unsigned review of* Villette: *Leader* (12 Feb 1853). *The Brontës: The Critical Heritage*, ed. Miriam Allott, 181–3.

137   *GHL 'wonderfully' like Emily Brontë*: CB to Ellen Nussey (12 June 1850), *CBL*, ii, 414, and quoted in Mrs Gaskell, *Life*, ch. 20.

137   *GHL on Charlotte Brontë as old maid*: To the Brays (5 Mar 1853), *GESL*, 118.

137   *GE's response to* Villette: To Cara Bray (15 Feb 1853), *GESL*, 116. *GEL*, ii, 87. *'Villette – Villette – '* she exclaimed to the Brays (c. 12 Mar 1853), *GESL*, 119.

138   *'unsatisfactory'*: To Charles Bray (18 Mar 1853), *GESL*, 120.

138   *'half tints'*: To Mrs Peter Taylor (1 Feb 1853), *GESL*, 115.

138   *quarrel with Isaac Evans*: To the Brays (31 Jan 1853), *GESL*, 113.

140   *GHL 'genial and amusing'*: To Sara Hennell (28 Mar 1853), *GESL*, 120.

141   *behind the scenes in his personal life*: With thanks to Isobel Dixon.

141   *GE sees Rachel act*: To Cara Bray and Sara Hennell (17 June 1853), *GESL*, 122.

142   *'a heathen and an outlaw'*: (29 June 1853), *GEL*, ii, 107.

144   *'home'; 'evening red . . .'*: (20 July 1854), *GEJ*, 15.

144   *'lying melting . . .'*: (25 and 26 July 1854), *GEJ*, 16.

145   *'Strauss looks so strange'*: (16 Aug 1854), *GEL*, ii, 171.

145   *'blackguard Lewes . . .'*: (4 Oct 1854), *GEL*, ii, 175–6. Woolner would later call many times at the Priory.

147–8   *GE on Liszt*: (10 Sept 1854), *GEL*, ii, 173. She also heard Clara Schumann play in Weimar.

149   *'Woman in France: Mme de Sablé'*: *GESE*, 8–37.

149   *'sympathy'*: *GESE*, 8–9.

149–50   *translation of Spinoza's Ethics*: The commission was for Bohn's Library. In the end the publisher seems to have defaulted on the deal. The translation was not published, and remained in a Yale archive until it was published in 1981, a century after GE's death.

152   *'someone in a book'*: (15 Nov 1854), *GEL*, ii, 186.

153   *'It is one round of a long ladder . . .'*: (28 Jan 1856), *GEL*, ii, 227.

153   *GE on Margaret Fuller*: 'Margaret Fuller and Mary Wollstonecraft' appeared in the *Leader* (13 Oct 1855). *GESE*, 332–8.

153–4   *'"Enfranchisement of Women" only makes creeping progress'*: To Mrs Peter Taylor (1 February 1853), *GESL*, 116.

155   *'we seem to have gained . . . new ideas'*: To Charles Bray from Ilfracombe (6 June 1856), *GEL*, ii, 252.

155   *caterpillar*: 'Recollections of Ilfracombe' (8 May–26 June 1856), *GEJ*, 269.

155   *zoology interrupted her work*: (13 June 1856), *GESL*, 157.

156   *'the roar from the other side of silence'*: *Middlemarch*, ch. 20.

157   *'unusually sensitive'*: GHL to John Blackwood (22 Nov 1856), *GEL*, ii, 276.

162   *GE on wildness*: To Mrs Gaskell (15 Apr 1857), *GEL*, ii, 315.

163   *'shadow to me'*: To Cara Bray (5 Apr 1857), *GEL*, ii, 314.

163   *'approbation'*: To Sara Hennell (5 June 1857), *GESL*, 172.

164   *'older and uglier'*: To Cara Bray (5 June 1857), *GESL*, 171.

164   *'blubbed'*: John Blackwood to GE (10 Feb 1857), *GEL*, ii, 293n.

164   *'hot tears'*: To Sara Hennell (7 Oct 1859), *GESL*, 228.

164   *'My Aunt's Story'*: *GEJ* (30 Nov 1858). *GEL*, ii, 502. *GESL*, 197–9.

165   *Dinah preaching*: *Adam Bede*, Book I, ch. 2.

166   *'ardent'; 'in charity . . .'*: To John Blackwood (24 Feb 1859), *GESL*, 204.

166–7   *Dixon's attack*: Quoted in *GESL*, 217.

167   *'vocation'*: To John Blackwood (24 Feb 1859), *GESL*, 204.

167   Magnificat: To John Blackwood (10 Apr 1859), *GESL*, 209.

167   *'ploughed up'*: To Cara Bray (24 Feb 1859), *GESL*, 203.

167   *'terrible sacrifice'*: To Charles Bray (28 Feb 1859), *GESL*, 206.

168   *GE and her stepsons*: Rosemarie Bodenheimer's chapter, based on the papers in the Beinecke Library, Yale, provides absorbing detail of this sad tale of the two younger sons.

168   *'the perfect love'*: To Mrs John Cash (6 June 1857), *GESL*, 173.

169   *'terrible pain'*: To Mrs John Cash (6 June 1857), *GESL*, 173.

169   *'are tied . . .'*: *The Mill on the Floss*, Book IV, ch. 1.

169   *'Yes it is a mischief . . .'*: Ibid., Book I, ch. 1.

170   *'Let us fearlessly trust our whole nature'*: To John Chipman Grey. From transcript of twenty-three letters (1869–70), mss destroyed by Henry James, in Houghton Library, Harvard: bMS Am 1092.12. Extensively quoted in my biography, *Henry James: His Women and His Art*, revised edn (London: Virago, 2012), ch. 5: 'Minny's Dream'.

170   *'experiment of nature'*: Henry James to William James (29 Mar 1870), *Correspondence of William James*, i, ed. Ignas K. Skrupskelis and Elizabeth M. Berkeley (Charlottesville: University of Virginia Press, 1993–4), 153.

170  '*affronts*': Henry James, Preface to *The Portrait of a Lady* (1881).

170  '*a grande nature*': Henry James to William Dean Howells (2 Feb 1877), *The Complete Letters of Henry James*, ii (1876–8), 50.

170  '*an overpowering admiration*' . . . *for George Eliot*: Minny Temple to John Chipman Grey (4 Mar 1869), mss in Houghton Library, Harvard: bMS Am 1092.12. Misquoted by Henry James, *Autobiography*, ii, ed. F. W. Dupee (1956; repr. Princeton University Press pb, 1983), 513.

170  '*a generous woman*': Minny Temple to John Chipman Grey (2 Apr 1869), mss in Houghton Library, Harvard: bMS Am 1092.12.

171  *casting out a woman*: The most brilliant scene is in Edith Wharton's *The Age of Innocence* (1920), when Old New York casts out Ellen Olenska.

171  '*St Ogg's Passes Judgement*': *The Mill on the Floss*, Book VII, ch. 2.

171  '*In their death they were not divided*': Ibid., Book VII, 'Conclusion'.

173  *opposition to* '*the man of maxims*': *The Mill on the Floss*, Book VII, ch. 2.

174  '*the only fair prospect*': *GEL*, vi, 165.

175  *marriage to Cross*: Kathryn Hughes sifts the complex motives for marriage on both sides, rightly deploring the misogynist caricature of a sexually avid older woman chasing a younger man. Haight held to the valid view that GE was not fitted to stand alone, and Bodenheimer reinforced GE's dependence with her stress on this marriage as a practical step, which was certainly one of GE's motives. Phyllis Rose stressed the physical and emotional appeal. Ruby Redinger suggested that GE was afraid of losing her power to love. GE did think of herself as nearly dead, with her coffin, as it were, waiting in the next room, when there came what appeared to her a miraculous, almost fairy-tale offer of revival.

175  '*Remembrance*': *EBP*(H), 222–3, first published in *Poems* (1846). *GEJ*, 188–9.

177  '*full of unsatisfied . . . affection*': *The Mill on the Floss*, Book II, ch. 5.

177  '*a sense of a home*': Ibid, Book III, ch. 5.


## 4. ORATOR

179  '*crush* . . . ': OS/*W&L*, Introduction, xv.

179  *burnt by troops*: Preamble to OS/*W&L*, which gives the history of the ms.

179  *rescue* . . . *ashes*: With thanks to Isobel Dixon for this phrase and for re-shaping this chapter, as did Lennie Goodings.

180  Dreams: This book was to be the holy text for the heroine of the film *Suffragette* (2015), who finds there what women are to be.

180  *New Woman*: The phrase was coined in 1894 by novelists Ouida and Sarah Grande.

181  *Rebekah*: OS's spelling of her mother's name in 'Early Remembrances', written in London 1883–4, *Words in Season*, 1.

181–2  *Rebekah and Gottlob*: OS, 'Early Remembrances', *Words in Season*, 1–11.

182  *missionary's wife*: The couple had been recruited by Dr Philip of the London Missionary Society, and one of his converts, the son of a Basuto chief, brought to London, was a witness at the Schreiners' wedding. The couple's first posting was to be at a place called Philipolis on the edge of Basutoland. It was in the path of resentful Boers trekking away from the British colony at the Cape, which enforced emancipation of slaves as laid down by the British Parliamentary Act of 1833 (see Virginia Woolf's grandfather who drew up the bill: ch. 5, below). Dr Philip, keenly in accord, wished

the colonised peoples and ex-slaves to be educated according to the Christian idea of civilisation. The trekkers saw Dr Philip as an opponent, and he was still vilified in apartheid-era textbooks for South African schools.

184 *'Born . . . '*: From 'Title divine — is mine' (c. 1861), *Complete Poems*: no. 1072, ed. Thomas H. Johnson (London: Faber, 1976; repr. 2003); *Poems: Variorum Edition*: no. 194, ed. F. H. Franklin (Cambridge, MA: Belknap Press of Harvard University, 1998).

184 *Basuto woman and God*: OS's Introduction to *A Vindication of the Rights of Woman*, in *Words in Season*, 27.

185 *'incarnation'*: To Betty Molteno and Alice Greene (31 Jan 1901), writing from Hanover. University of Cape Town: Manuscripts and Archives: OS BC16/Box 2/Fold 4/1901/5. OS/OLP transcription.

186 *house in Cradock*: 9 Cross Street is now a museum, the Schreiner House, and linked with the National English Literary Museum in Grahamstown.

186 *'Genius does not invent . . . '*: She is recalling Shelley's letter to Leigh Hunt (27 Sept 1819), where he quotes a comment by a friend of Coleridge: 'Mind cannot create, it can only perceive.' OS repeats the phrase 'Mind cannot create' to Havelock Ellis (18 July 1884), *OSL*, i, 47. OS sent a copy of Shelley's letters to her mother: now in the Schreiner House, Cradock.

187 *'I love* The Mill on the Floss*'*: To J. X. Merriman, looking back on her reading (29 June 1896), *OSL*, i, 284.

187 *'loving human soul'*: To Havelock Ellis (8 Apr 1884), *OSL*, i, 37.

187 *'I always think . . . '*: To Havelock Ellis (28 Mar 1884), *OSL*, i, 36.

188 *Mary Kingsley: Travels in West Africa* (1897; London: Virago, 1982).

188 *to America, to study*: To Catherine Findlay (30 Apr 1873), *OSL*, i, 10.

188–9 *'They wished . . . '*: To Catherine Findlay (12 Oct 1871), *OSL*, i, 4.

189 *MW's £40*: Admittedly MW worked for landed aristocrats. It's worth noting, though, that forty years earlier, Charlotte Brontë was paid a miserable sixteen pounds a year to work as a governess in 1841. As a man, her brother, working as an assistant railway clerk, was paid seventy-five, more than four times as much.

189–90 *'A man's love . . . '*: OS/*AF*, Part 2, ch. 4.

190 *'She was a woman . . . '*: OS/*W&L*, Introduction, x.

190 *OS on 'Self-Reliance'*: Havelock Ellis's Notes he took from OS, 1884–5, *OSL*, i, 40n. See also letter to Ellis (28 Aug 1884), *OSL*, i, 50.

192 *'There is nothing so restful . . . '*: To Betty Molteno (1 Nov 1898), *OSL*, i, 338.

194 *'I will hate . . . power'*: OS/*AF*, Part 1, ch. 8.

194 *'Men are like the earth . . . '*: Ibid., Part 2, ch. 4.

194 *finishing schools*: Ibid.

194 *Mill: The Subjection of Women* (1869), ch. 1.

194 *'If you do love me . . . '*: OS/*AF*, Part 2, ch. 9.

195 *'interknit love song'*: OS repeated this memory in *Woman and Labour* and in *From Man to Man*.

196 *'kind reception'; 'moralising'; 'sympathy'*: To Havelock Ellis (25 Feb 1884), *OSL*, i, 35.

197 *disappointed with Ellis's appearance*: *OSL*, i, 41n.

197 *'other-self'*: To Havelock Ellis (15 Nov and 1 Dec 1884), *OSL*, i, 52, 55.

197 *'an immense realisation of you'*: First and Scott, *Olive Schreiner: A Biography*, 133.

198 *'horror' of Dr Aveling*: To Havelock Ellis (2 Aug 1884), *OSL*, i, 49.

198 *tie of OS and Ellis*: She likened their friendship to her favourite Montaigne essay, *On Friendship*.

198　*OS's sexual nature*: Havelock Ellis, 'Notes on Olive Schreiner' (1885). Correspondence between OS and Ellis with related material, Humanities Research Center, The University of Texas at Austin.

200　*'that ghastly dead thing', etc; 'spoke much more of him'*: To Karl Pearson (23 May 1886), about the sculpture (1853–4) by Henry Weekes, admired by critics of the day. *OSL*, i, 74.

200　*'"I change but [I] cannot die"'*: 'The Cloud', PBS/*SPP*, 301–4.

200　*'the great point of interest . . . '*: To Karl Pearson (26 Oct 1886), *OSL*, i, 111.

200　*'the substance'*: To Mrs J. H. Philpot (18 Feb 1888), *OSL*, i, 136.

200　*Donkin; 'I must be free'*: To Havelock Ellis, *OSL*, i, 72n.

200　*Isabel Archer and Warburton*: *The Portrait of a Lady* (1881), ch. 12.

201　*'If he would come . . . '*: To Havelock Ellis (1 Dec 1884), *OSL*, i, 55.

201　*brothers' erasure of sisters*: Comment by Isobel Dixon.

203　*letter to Ellis from Matjesfontein*: (25 Mar 1890), *OSL*, i, 167.

204　*'The Soul selects . . . '*: (c.1862), *Poems*, op. cit.: Johnson 303; Franklin 409.

204　*'this desire for a more interior life'*: Gwen John to Ursula Tyrwhitt (4 Sept 1912?). Cited by Cecily Langdale and David Fraser Jenkins, *Gwen John: An Interior Life* (Oxford: Phaidon, 1985), 12.

204　*'the effect of this scenery . . . '*: To Havelock Ellis (5 Apr 1890), *OSL*, i, 168.

204　*'The Buddhist Priest's Wife'*: OS cherished this as an important work, though it was not published during her lifetime. It is collected in *A Woman's Rose*.

207　*'flashing side-lights'*: To Edward Carpenter (8 Oct 1894), *OSL*, ii, 51.

207　*Cron's nephew's opinion*: G. M. C. Cronwright, a biographical essay.

208　*letter to Ettie*: (16 May 1895), *OSL*, i, 252.

209　*coffin of 'Baby'*: Baby had originally been buried in Kimberley close to the house, but was disinterred when OS moved. Letter to Cron in De Aar (July 1907), advising him of her belongings should she 'not come back'. It sounds odd that she had to tell Cron this, as though he was not aware of the child's presence. OS/OLP.

210　*'of all the lies . . . '*: (24 Jan 1899), *OSL*, ii, 114.

210　*'engorged capitalists'*: To Jan Smuts (23 Jan 1899), *OSL*, ii, 115.

210　*'the wild dogs of gold'*: To Will Schreiner (26 July 1899), *OSL*, ii, 127.

211　*OS letter to Milner*: (10 July 1899), *OSL*, ii, 127.

211　*'great, fiendish hell . . . '*: To Edward Carpenter (13 Nov 1898), *OSL*, i, 340.

212　*threat from American publisher*: To sister-in-law Fan Schreiner (16 May 1902), *OSL*, ii, 156. She felt bullied as a woman.

212　*'an aptitude . . . ' and 'all the family'*: (7 June 1899), *OSL*, i, 359.

212　*'It's a curious solitary life'*: (25 July 1899), *OSL*, i, 370. She does not mention her pregnancy in this letter, but had done so on 19 June to Betty Molteno, predicting the birth in January or February 1900.

213　*'how glad I should be . . . '*: (23 Jan 1899), *OSL*, i, 344–5. She was already writing pro-Boer articles like 'The Boer' and 'The Wanderings of the Boer' for the *Fortnightly Review*; 'The Boer Woman and the Modern Woman's Question' for the New York *Cosmopolitan*; and a recent one on the Boer's domestic life.

213　*OS on Isie Smuts*: To W.P. Schreiner (17 May 1899), *OSL*, i, 351.

213–4　*OS to Isie Smuts*: (22 Aug 1899), *OSL*, i, 375.

214　*OS's questions to Smuts*: (24 Sept 1899), *OSL*, i, 380–1.

214　*'It would not matter . . . '*: To W.P. Schreiner (24 Sept 1899), *OSL*, i, 381.

214　*Smuts wired OS*: To W. P. Schreiner (12 Oct 1899), *OSL*, i, 386.

215  'a writer and not a speaker': Words in Season, 112–13.

215  'women must act': To Mary Sauer (15–30 June 1900), OSL, ii, 144.

216  war correspondent: Henry W. Nevinson.

216  speech in Burg Street: Words in Season, 118–21.

217–18  letter-speech in Somerset East: Ibid, 123–32.

218  Joseph Chamberlain: In the coalition government with Lord Salisbury as Prime Minister. Chamberlain was a leading activist in the so-called Khaki Election of 1900.

218  'Now England is dead to me': 'Letter' to the peace meeting at Somerset East. Words in Season. Elsewhere she contradicts this dramatic statement, saying how incomparable was the English character at its finest.

219  Rhodes reading out wire from Rebekah Schreiner: To Will Schreiner (26 July 1899), OSL, ii, 128.

219  rhetoric: a cornerstone of the Trivium in medieval universities, together with logic and grammar.

219  'J'Accuse': By Émile Zola, published on front page of L'Aurore in January 1898. This public letter accused the French military, together with the justice system and Catholic Church, of corruption and anti-Semitism by falsely concocting a case to condemn Dreyfus, who was sent to Devil's Island. The French mob was so worked up that the bravely outspoken Zola had to take refuge in England. OS signed a petition to release Zola's English translator when he was imprisoned.

220  Cron's relations angry with OS: To Frances Schreiner (14 Dec 1900) from Hanover. OS/OLP.

220  first two Boer commandos: Led by Herzog and Kritzinger.

220  'the war is not over': To Edward Carpenter (2 Nov 1900), OSL, ii, 147.

220  'high treason': Ibid.

220–1  de Lisle's interrogation: To Cron (Dec 1900–Jan 1901), cited in Karel Schoeman, Only an Anguish to Live Here: Olive Schreiner and the Anglo-Boer War 1899–1902 (Cape Town: Human & Rousseau, 1992), 139. Not in OSL, nor in OS/OLP.

221  notices against OS posted up: To Cron (Dec 1900–Jan 1901), cited in Schoeman, Anguish, 146. Not in OSL, nor in OS/OLP.

221  exclusion made her want to cry: To Alice Greene (29 Jan 1901). University of Cape Town: Manuscripts and Archives: OS BC16/Box 2/Fold 4/1901/6.

223  OS's request to Kitchener: (9 Jan 1901), OSL, ii, 149. There is no evidence that Kitchener replied.

223  'running rings around Hanover': To Betty Molteno (27 July 1902), OSL, ii, 167. The British forces did finally capture him, wounded, but only days before the end of the war in May 1902. His recollections are included in H. J. C. Pieterse, Oorlogsavonture van Genl. Wynand Malan (Cape Town: Nationale Pers, 1941).

224  Wynand Malan and the scouts: To Betty Molteno (27 July 1902), OSL, ii, 167. OS speaks of 'our' scouts. Since no one could leave Hanover without military permission, these are likely to have been British scouts or volunteers from Hanover whom the British trusted, perhaps members of the town guard. It would then appear a bold act of one-upmanship for a commando leader to treat scouts to unexpected hospitality and consideration – a sort of insouciance.

224  'They are a strange people': To Betty Molteno (Jan 1901), OSL, ii, 148–9.

224  Smuts and OS: Smuts's Introduction to Vera Buchanan-Gould, Not Without Honour: The Life and Writings of Olive Schreiner (London/Cape Town: Hutchinson, 1948).

225  'scratching up her master's yard': Cited by Schoeman, Anguish, 162.

226  'life-dispensing power': OS/W&L, Introduction, xvi.

226  *'The question . . . ':* To Havelock Ellis (2 May 1884), *OSL,* i, 40.

226  *parable of the unidentified bird:* OS/*W&L,* ch. 6, 89.

226  *Mill on the rarity of a 'conjunction':* The Subjection of Women, ch. 1.

227  *'parasitism':* OS/*W&L,* ch. 2, 21.

228  *'All I aspire to be . . . ':* OS/*W&L,* Introduction, xvii.

228  *'I should like to say . . . ':* Ibid.

228  *'bestiality . . . of war':* 'Woman and War', OS/*W&L,* ch. 4, 68.

228  *'with war all about':* To English friend Alf Mattison, *OSL,* ii, 150–1.

229  *'tinsel':* 'Woman and War', OS/*W&L,* ch. 4, 65.

229  *'Men's bodies . . . ':* 'Woman and War', Ibid., 67.

229  *'is it all a dream?':* Ibid., ch. 6, 117.

230  *'refinement':* cited in *Anguish,* 148–9. Not in *OSL,* nor amongst the wartime letters in OS/OLP.

230  *OS on her feelings about the English:* (30 Sept 1899), *OSL,* i, 384.

230  *'As all hope . . . ':* To Betty Molteno (5 May 1902), cited by eds of *OSL,* ii, as instance of her increasing use of the impersonal 'one' as cover for the personal, p. 132.

231  *'A Letter on the Jew':* published in the *Cape Times* (2 July 1906), 8. Repr. *Words in Season,* 144–53.

231  *disenfranchised black majority:* OS's brothers supported black rights. Will Schreiner was returned to Parliament in 1908. Took deputation to London in 1909, including men who were to found the ANC in 1912: Alfred Mangena, Thomas Makipela, Walter Rubusana. Theo too was a supporter of black rights, and in the first Union House of Assembly in 1910 he represented Tembuland, a largely black constituency.

231  *Vera Brittain on OS/W&L:* Testament of Youth (London: Gollancz, 1933, repr. Virago), 28. 'To . . . *Woman and Labour* – that "Bible of the Woman's Movement" which sounded to the world in 1911 as insistent and inspiring as a trumpet-call summoning the faithful to a triumphant crusade – was due my final acceptance of feminism.' See also Mark Bostridge, *Vera Brittain,* 55–6: 'Olive Schreiner replaced George Eliot as Vera's literary mentor and idol; and *African Farm* [when Roland Leighton gave it to her, saying she was like Lyndall] took the place of *Woman and Labour* as Vera's personal "Bible".'

231  *resignation from the Women's Enfranchisement League:* The values of OS are actually close to the more far-sighted feminism of founding members of the Women's Anti-Suffrage Movement. See Christopher Beauman, 'Women Against the Vote', a masterly piece in the *Persephone Quarterly* (winter 2016). This is beautifully written with a novel grasp of this complex movement. See below, ch. 5, for Virginia Woolf's connections.

232  *spoke up for conscientious objectors:* 'On Conscientious Objectors, 1916', *Words in Season,* 198–200.

232  *reproached Gandhi:* 'You know I hate war', she said to Gandhi's associate Hermann Kallenbach, declining Gandhi's invitation to a meeting. (2 Oct 1914), *OSL,* ii, 335.

232  *'I opposed this war . . . ':* 'Letter to a Peace Meeting', *Words in Season,* 201–3.

233  *Emily Hobhouse on OS:* Her memoir recalls meeting on the station at Beaufort West in 1903 and at De Aar in 1907.

## 5. EXPLORER

236  *Katharine Stephen's destruction of diaries:* (15 Feb 1923), *VWD,* ii, 234–5.

237  *'harsh & splendid':* (19 Aug 1918), *VWD,* i, 184.

237   *'not my kind of young woman'*: Letter to Julia Stephen, his wife. Berg Collection, New York
      Public Library.

238   *nonsensical definitions of women: Women & Fiction: The Manuscript Versions of* A Room of One's
      Own, ed. S. P. Rosenbaum (Oxford: Blackwell, 1992).

239   *'the indefiniteness'*: Prelude, *Middlemarch.*

239   *'the ancient consciousness of woman'*: 'George Eliot', *VWE*, iv, 178. First published in *TLS* (20
      Nov 1919), then revised for *The Common Reader* (1925).

239   not *failures, etc*: 'Geraldine and Jane', *VWE*, v, 505–19.

239   *'my own strangeness'*: (27 Feb 1926), *VWD*, ii, 62.

240   *'the pressure of dumbness'*: *Women & Fiction*, op. cit., 130.

240   *VW walking in the streets*: LW, *Beginning Again: An Autobiography of the Years 1911 to 1918*
      (London: Hogarth; NY: Harcourt, 1963), Part I, 29.

240   *'restless searcher'*; *'Why is there not a discovery in life?'*: (27 Feb 1926), *VWD*, ii, 62.

240   *'hardly syllabled yet'*: VW/*AROO*, ch. 5.

240   *'monster of the lower waters' who'd explode . . .*: Emily Dickinson says, similarly, 'My Life
      had stood — a Loaded Gun' and she too speaks of a hidden Existence too strangely
      powerful for 'unshaded' eyes. 'To simulate — is stinging work — / To cover what we
      are'. *Collected Poems*, ed. Thomas H. Johnson (London: Faber, 1976; repr. 2003), 754 and
      443; in the Franklin edition from Harvard University Press, 764 and 522 (the latter
      eliminates the penultimate stanza).

241   *as a child, she couldn't step . . .*: (30 Sept 1926), *VWD*, ii, 113.

241   *'I generally get a spurt . . . '*: To Ethel Smyth (4 Sept 1936), *VWL*, vi, 70.

244   *'moonstruck'*; *'test of insanity'*: To Jane Venn Stephen (July 1816), quoted in Caroline Emilia
      Stephen's portrait of her father, *Sir James Stephen*. London Metropolitan Archives.

244   *Mill on nervous sensibility*: *The Subjection of Women* (1869), ch. 3.

244   *'a great stock of words'*: Caroline Emelia Stephen, quoting a letter from her father to his
      wife Jane Venn. *Sir James Stephen*, op. cit.

244   *'black melancholy'*, *'turned to madness'*: To Vanessa Bell (28 June 1938), *VWL*, vi, 248–9.

244   *'the most exquisite feeling . . . '*: Confided to Stella's friend Violet Dickinson, who kept
      a blank recipe book in which she recorded her conversations with Virginia. Berg
      Collection, New York Public Library.

245   *'torture'*: Appendix III: 'The Intellectual Status of Women', *VWD*, ii, 339–42. This is an
      exchange with 'Affable Hawk' (her friend Desmond MacCarthy) in the *New Statesman*,
      which MacCarthy edited. In 1920 he had backed a book *Our Women* by Arnold
      Bennett, which claimed that women's artistic and intellectual inferiority could not
      be explained by disadvantages.

245   *'I must be private . . . '*: (17 Sept 1938), *VWL*, vi, 272.

245   On Being Ill: (Jan 1926, for T. S. Eliot's *New Criterion*. Then published in Nov 1938 by
      the Hogarth Press as a book. It was one of the last to be hand-printed by VW and LW.
      That year the Press installed a new printing machine.) *VWE*, iv, 317–29, and v, 195.

245   *'tender memories . . . '*: (March 1903), *VWL*, i, 71.

245   *'I will lick you . . . '*: (summer 1903), *VWL*, i, 84.

245   *'Wallaby snout'*: (late Sept 1903), *VWL*, i, 96.

246   to *'retire from the surface . . . '*: Caroline Emelia Stephen, *Quaker Strongholds* (1890), ch. 2: 'The
      Inner Light'.

246   *'do not sublime'*: Caroline Emelia Stephen to Albert Dicey (13 Mar 1893). London
      Metropolitan Archives: A/NFC109/26.

246  *'for some nine hours . . . '*: (15 Feb 1919), *VWD*, i, 240.

246  *'insanities'*: To Gerald Brenan in Spain (21 Jan 1922), *VWL*, ii, 499.

246  *'as when I was mad'*: (7 Feb 1931), *VWD*, iv, 10.

246  *'baptism'*: Stephen, *Quaker Strongholds.*

246–7  *Miss Stephen's wish for death*: Ibid.

247  *fragments crossed out*: Ms of *Mrs Dalloway*, British Library.

247  *on visit to the Brontë Parsonage*: 'Haworth, November 1904', published Dec 1904, *VWE*, i, 5–9.

247  *'as he lay back . . . '*: Frederick Maitland, *Life and Letters of Leslie Stephen* (1906), 476.

249  *'explorers, reformers, revolutionists'*: 'A Sketch of the Past', *Moments of Being: Autobiographical Writings* (University of Sussex Press, 1976), 126–7.

248  *Miss Stephen and the Anti-Suffragists*: See Christopher Beauman, 'Women Against the Vote', *Persephone Quarterly* (winter 2016) for a novel grasp of this complex movement. See also above, ch. 4, for a link between the values of OS and the more far-sighted feminism of founding members of the Women's Anti-Suffrage Movement.

249  *Caroline Stephen's political proposals*: *Nineteenth Century and After*, 61 (1907), 230–1, and *Anti-Suffrage Review*, 2 (Jan 1909), 7. Cited by Julia Bush, *Women Against the Vote* (2007), ch. 9, who points out the overlaps between moderate suffragists and 'forward' antis.

249  *elected by women*: Lovenduski, *Feminizing Politics* (2005), 164.

251  *Miss V.*; 'The Journal of Mistress Joan Martyn'; 'Phyllis and Rosamond'; 'Memoirs of a Novelist': VW/ CSF.

251  *addressing a ghost*: Henry James had recognised such a pursuit in his sophisticated ghost tale about a biographer and his subject, 'The Real Right Thing'.

252  *'To be 29 . . . '*: *VWL*, i, 466.

253  *hawk*: Observed by VW's niece, Angelica Bell. *Deceived With Kindness: A Bloomsbury Childhood* (London: Pimlico, 1995).

254  *'became a centre . . . '*: LW, *Beginning Again*, 37, 49.

254  *LW seeing* Swan Lake: Pocket diary (1911), The Keep, Brighton.

255  *'rapid, bold Mong'*: (31 Oct 1917), *VWL*, ii, 193.

256  *fine condition*: To LW from Asheham (Dec 1913), *VWL*, ii, 35.

256  *legal contract*: Monks House Papers, The Keep, Brighton. Described in Quentin Bell's biography of VW, ii, 19. Photo in *Letters of Leonard Woolf*, ed. Frederic Spotts (London: Weidenfeld & Nicolson, 1990).

256  *'so frightfully tame without you'*: To LW (30 Oct 1917), *VWL*, ii, 193.

257  *'a brave beast'*: (27 July 1913), *Letters of Leonard Woolf*, 185.

258  *'bill and coo'*: (15 Feb 1919), *VWD*, i, 240. Draws on a later encounter, a meal at Verray's in Regent Street, because it gives such a vivid sense of her delight in their flirtation.

259  *'You were the first . . . '*: To Clive Bell (24 July 1917), *VWL*, ii, 167.

260  *'the belief . . . '*: LW, *Beginning Again*, Part II, 101.

262  *'down into hell'*: James to Edith Wharton (4 Dec 1912), *Letters*, ed. Leon Edel, iv (Cambridge, MA: Belknap Press of Harvard University, 1974–84), 643.

264  *'Currer Bell . . . publicity in women is detestable'*: VW/*AROO*, ch. 3.

265  *'I have a power of recovery'*: (27 Feb 1926), *VWD*, ii, 62.

265  *fisherwoman*: Speech before the London/National Society for Women's Service (21 Jan 1931), included in *The Pargiters*, ed. Mitchell Leaska (London: Hogarth, 1977), xxxvii.

265  *'every feather'*: (31 Oct 1917), *Letters of LW*, 218.

265  *'illusions'*: (10 Nov 1917), *VWD*, i, 73.

265  *divinely happy*: (16 Jan 1916), *VWL*, ii, 136. She's referring to their time over Christmas 1915 at their country place they rented, Asheham, under the South Downs in Sussex.

266  *'Precious Mongoose'*: *VWL*, ii, 89–90.

267  *marked out in advance*: See Henry James, *The Portrait of a Lady* (1881), ch. 12. The context is a traditional marriage plot.

267  *'pretend'*: VW/*ND*, ch. 17.

268  *'a being who walks . . . '*: Ibid., ch. 33.

269  *'exploring indefinitely'*: Ibid.

270  *'left a whole continent . . . '*: Ibid., ch. 27.

270  *'I like . . . '*: (11 May 1920), *VWD*, ii, 36.

271  *'I become . . . more feminist . . . '*: *VWL*, ii, 76.

272  *'should be killing each other'*: (27 Aug 1918), *VWD*, i, 186.

272  *'The Journal of Mistress Joan Martyn'*: VW/*CSF*, 33–62. Unpublished in her lifetime.

273  *Keynes*: On the Versailles Conference (July 1919), *VWD*, i, 288.

274  *'out, out, far out to sea and alone'*: Mrs Dalloway (1925). VW said that in part Mrs Dalloway was the kind of woman whom she didn't much like. Her diary shows how consciously she deepened this society hostess with something of herself. 'Far out' is patently herself.

277  *'almost unclassified'*: VW/*AROO*, ch. 5.

277  *'graven in the language of the outlaw'*: James Joyce, *Ulysses*, part II, headed 'FROM THE FATHERS'.

278  *'These voices . . . '*: 'Memories [after seventeen years] of a Working Women's Guild', VW's preface to collection of writings by the Women's Co-operative Guild (1930). *VWE*, v, 176–94.

278  *'the power to change . . . '*: VW/*TG*, ch. 3.

279  The Outsider: (7 Feb 1938), *VWD*, v, 128. As she walked on the downs, she considered an illustrated sheet to be called *The Outsider*: a barrel organ tune and rhymed burlesque. It could be a way of popularising and politicising an Outsider party.

280  *'No coward soul . . . '*: This poem is dated 2 Jan 1846. *EBP*(H), 243.

280  *'much refreshed'*: (12 July 1937), *VWD*, v, 102.

280  *'Ancient and obdurate oaks . . . '*: On Being Ill, op. cit.

281  *'racket'*: To Ethel Smyth (11 July 1938), *VWL*, vi, 253.

281  *G. M. Young on* Three Guineas: Note by Nigel Nicolson, *VWL*, vi, 247.

281  *'grateful Outsider'*: (24 May 1938), *VWD*, v, 141.

281  *Queenie Leavis*: To Ethel Smyth (11 Sept 1938), *VWL*, vi, 271 and n.

281  *'I think the sales . . . '*: To Ethel Smyth (15 July 1938), *VWL*, vi, 255.

281  *'calm as a toad'*: (30 May 1938), *VWD*, v, 146.

281  *'incorrigible outsider'*: To John Lehmann (early July 1938), refusing an invitation to write for his journal and saying she wanted to stay with the Hogarth Press. *VWL*, vi, 252.

283  *not mad when she ended her life*: Nigel Nicolson, Introduction, *VWL*, vi, xvii.

283–5  *latter part of section xiii on VW's death and reputation*: This draws on my essay 'Too Much Suicide', *Canvas: The Charleston Magazine* (Feb 2011), on the seventieth anniversary of VW's death. Revised for the British Library https://www. bl.uk/20th-century-literature/articles/too-much-suicide#

284  *movie called* The Hours: Closely based on a novel *The Hours* (1998) by Michael Cunningham.

284   *'can give us much more . . . '*: *VWE*, vi, 187. Published in *Atlantic Monthly* (Apr 1939).

284   *VW on Shelley and 'The spirit of delight'*: *VWD*, iii, 113, 153.

285   *'The Leaning Tower'*: *VWE*, vi, 259–83. A paper read to the WEA, Brighton (27 Apr 1940).

285   *Quentin Bell on* TG: On 22 Oct 1984 (in a letter to me) he expresses his divergence: 'What did my dear aunt want?'

286   *'epoch-making'*: (3 June 1938), *VWD*, vi, 148.

286   *whirl*: (Recalled 12 Mar 1938), *VWD*, vi, 130. See also 'a motor in the head', *VWD*, vi, 111.

286   *'enfranchised'*: (28 Apr 1938), *VWD*, v, 137.

## THE OUTSIDERS SOCIETY

287   *'baubles'*: VW/*TG*, 171.

287   *'"For," the outsider will say, "in fact . . . I have no country"'*: VW/*TG*, ch. 3, 125.

289   *'every fibre of nature'*, etc: 'Woman in France: Madame de Sablé', *GESE*, 8–9.

290   *'the true nature of woman'*: VW/*AROO*, ch. 1.

290   *'the roar from the other side of silence'*: Middlemarch, ch. 20.

# FURTHER READING

## GENERAL

Appignanesi, Lisa, *Mad, Bad and Sad: A History of Women and the Mind Doctors from 1800 to the Present* (London: Virago, 2008)

——, Rachel Holmes and Susie Orbach (eds), *Fifty Shades of Feminism* (London: Virago, 2013)

Beauman, Nicola, *A Very Great Profession: The Woman's Novel 1914–1939* (London: Virago, 1983; revised Persephone Books, 2008)

Dinnage, Rosemary, *Alone! Alone! Lives of Some Outsider Women* (New York: New York Review of Books, 2004)

Gordon, Linda, *Heroes of their Own Lives: The Politics and History of Family Violence: Boston, 1880–1960* (New York: Viking, 1988; London: Virago, 1989)

Mendelson, Edward, *The Things That Matter: What Seven Classic Novels Have to Say About the Stages of Life* (New York: Pantheon, 2006)

Mill, John Stuart, in discussion with Harriet Taylor Mill, *The Subjection of Women* (1869)

Moers, Ellen, *Literary Women* (London: The Women's Press, 1978)

Nightingale, Florence, 'Cassandra' (1859). Appendix to Ray Strachey, below.

Norris, Pamela, *Words of Love: Passionate Women from Heloise to Sylvia Plath* (London: HarperCollins, 2006)

Rose, Jacqueline, *Women in Dark Times* (London: Bloomsbury, 2014)

Showalter, Elaine, *A Literature of Their Own: British Women Novelists from Brontë to Lessing* (Princeton: Princeton University Press, 1977; revised Virago and Princeton University Press, 1997–8)

——, *The Female Malady: Women, Madness, and English Culture, 1830–1980* (London: Virago, 1987)

——, *Inventing Herself: Claiming a Feminist Intellectual Heritage* (London: Picador, 2001)

——, *A Jury of Her Peers: American Women Writers from Anne Bradstreet to Annie Proulx* (London: Virago, 2010)

Smith, Joan, *Misogynies* (London: Faber, 1989)

——, *Moralities: How to End the Abuse of Money and Power in the 21st Century* (London: Penguin, 2002)

——, *The Public Woman* (London: The Westbourne Press, 2013)

——, *Domestic: A Memoir* (unpublished)

Strachey, Ray, *The Cause: A Short History of the Women's Movement in Great Britain* (1926; repr. London: Virago, 1979), with Appendix by Florence Nightingale

Warner, Marina, *Fantastic Metamorphoses, Other Worlds: Ways of Telling the Self* (Oxford: Oxford University Press, 2004)

## MARY SHELLEY

Bennett, Betty T., 'Mary Shelley's letters: the public/private self', in Esther Schor (ed.), *The Cambridge Companion to Mary Shelley* (Cambridge: Cambridge University Press, 2003), 211–25

Byron, George Gordon, Lord, *Letters and Journals*, ed. Leslie A. Marchand, 12 vols (Cambridge: Belknap Press of Harvard University, 1973–83)

Clairmont, Claire, *The Journals of Claire Clairmont*, ed. Marion Kingston Stocking (Cambridge, MA: Harvard University Press, 1968)

——, *The Clairmont Correspondence: Letters of Claire Clairmont, Charles Clairmont, and Fanny Imlay Godwin*, ed. Marion Kingston Stocking, 2 vols (Baltimore: Johns Hopkins University Press, 1995)

Clemit, Pamela, '*Frankenstein, Matilda*, and the legacies of Godwin and Wollstonecraft', in Esther Schor (ed.), *The Cambridge Companion to Mary Shelley* (Cambridge: Cambridge University Press, 2003), 26–44

Dunn, Jane, *Moon in Eclipse: A Life of Mary Shelley* (London: Weidenfeld & Nicolson, 1978)

Gittings, Robert and Jo Manton, *Claire Clairmont and the Shelleys 1798–1879* (Oxford and NY: Oxford University Press, 1992)

Godwin, Fanny Imlay, letters in *The Clairmont Correspondence*, op. cit.

Godwin, William, Diaries. Bodleian Library: Dep.e.196-227

——, *The Letters of William Godwin*, ed. Pamela Clemit, i–ii (Oxford: Oxford University Press, 2011–14)

——, *Political Justice* (1793)

Gordon, Charlotte, *Romantic Outlaws: The Extraordinary Lives of Mary Wollstonecraft & Mary Shelley* (London: Hutchinson, 2015; London: Windmill Books, 2016)

Hardyment, Christina, *Writing the Thames* (Oxford: Bodleian Library, 2016). Includes the Shelleys' Thames journey and time in Marlow.

Hay, Daisy, *Young Romantics: The Shelleys, Byron and Other Tangled Lives* (London: Bloomsbury, 2010)

Hogg, Thomas Jefferson, *The Life of Percy Bysshe Shelley*, 2 vols (London: E. Moxon, 1858)

Holmes, Richard, *Shelley: The Pursuit* (1974; repr. London: Harper Perennial, 2005)

Imlay, Fanny: see above, Fanny Imlay Godwin

Kucich, Greg, 'Biographer', in Esther Schor (ed.), *The Cambridge Companion to Mary Shelley* (Cambridge: Cambridge University Press, 2003), 226–41

Leader, Zachary, 'Parenting *Frankenstein*', chapter 4 of his *Revision and Romantic Authorship* (Oxford: Oxford University Press, 1996)

Mellor, Anne K., *Mary Shelley: Her Life, Her Fiction, Her Monsters* (New York: Routledge, 1988). Appendix on PBS's revisions of *Frankenstein*.

Sanger, Carol, *About Abortion: Terminating Pregnancy in Twenty-First-Century America* (Cambridge, MA: Belknap Press of Harvard University Press, 2017)

St Clair, William, *The Godwins and the Shelleys: The Biography of a Family* (London: Faber, 1989; Baltimore: Johns Hopkins University Press, 1991)

Seymour, Miranda, *Mary Shelley* (London: John Murray, 2000)

Shelley, Mary Wollstonecraft, *The Frankenstein Notebooks*, 2 vols, ed. Charles E. Robinson (New York and London: Garland Publishing, 1996). MS 1816–17, with alterations in the hand of Percy Bysshe Shelley, as it survives in draft and fair copy in the Bodleian Library, Oxford. This consists of Notebook A (77 leaves) of Continental paper with a light blue tint, probably bought in Geneva, used for draft, August–December 1816. Notebook B has thickish British paper, cream coloured, and was used for revision and copying a fair text for publication, December? 1816–April 1817. The editor assumes there was originally an 'ur-text', begun on 17 June 1816, the morning after MWS's waking dream and including the recognition scene, i.e. the substance of the dream. The ur-text has not survived, and as the editor says, may have been minimal.

——, *Frankenstein, or, The Modern Prometheus: The 1818 Text*, ed. Marilyn Butler (Oxford: Oxford University Press, 1994) with Appendix: 'The Third Edition (1831): Substantive Changes'.

——, *Frankenstein, or, The Modern Prometheus*, ed. Charles E. Robinson (Oxford: Bodleian Library, 2008)

——, *Frankenstein*, ed. Nora Crook, vol i of *The Novels and Selected Works of Mary Shelley*. 8 vols, ed. Nora Crook with Pamela Clemit (London: Pickering, 1996). Crook provides also 'Endnotes: Textual Variants', pp. 182–227.

——, *Matilda*. This novella was unpublished until 1959. Collected with *Mary* and *Maria* in *Mary; Maria*, ed. Janet Todd (London: Penguin, 1992)

——and Percy Bysshe Shelley, *A History of a Six Weeks Tour* (London: Ollier, 1817). Copy in the Bodleian Library; available online.

——, *The Journals of Mary Shelley, 1814–1844*, ed. Paula R. Feldman and Diana Scott-Kilvert, i–ii, (Baltimore: Johns Hopkins University Press, 1980–88). Shelley was her co-diarist in the early entries.

——, *The Letters of Mary Wollstonecraft Shelley*, ed. Betty T. Bennett, i–iii (Baltimore: Johns Hopkins University Press, 1995)

——*Notes to the Complete Poetical Works of Percy Bysshe Shelley*, <http://www.gutenberg.org/etext/4695>

——, *The Mary Shelley Reader*, ed. Betty T. Bennett and Charles E. Robinson (New York and Oxford: Oxford University Press, 1990). Includes a selection of tales and reviews.

Shelley, Percy Bysshe, *Shelley's Poetry and Prose: Authoritative Texts, Criticism*, ed. Donald H. Reiman and Neil Fraistat (2nd edition; New York, London: Norton, 2002)

——, *The Letters of Percy Bysshe Shelley*, 2 vols, ed. Frederick L. Jones (Oxford: Clarendon Press, 1964)

*Shelley and His Circle, 1773–1822*, 10 vols, ed. Kenneth Neill Cameron, Donald H. Reiman and Doucet Devin Fischer (Cambridge, MA: Harvard University Press, 1961–2002)

——Review of *Frankenstein*, appendix to *SPP*, 434–6. Published posthumously in 1832. He argues that the novel is founded on 'nature' and praises the narrative momentum like a rock rolled down a mountain.

Schor, Esther (ed.), *The Cambridge Companion to Mary Shelley* (Cambridge: Cambridge University Press, 2003)

Silsbee Family Papers, The Phillips Library at the Peabody Essex Museum, Salem, Massachusetts

Smith, Andrew (ed.), *The Cambridge Companion to* Frankenstein (Cambridge: Cambridge University Press, 2016)

Sunstein, Emily W., *Mary Shelley: Romance and Reality* (Boston: Little, Brown, 1989; repr. Baltimore: Johns Hopkins University Press, 1991)

Tomalin, Claire, *Shelley and his World* (1980; London: Penguin, 2005)

Wollstonecraft, Mary, *Mary; and, The Wrongs of Woman*, ed. Gary Kelly (Oxford: Oxford University Press, 1980)

——, *The Works of Mary Wollstonecraft*, ed. Janet Todd and Marilyn Butler (London: Pickering, 1989). Includes *Thoughts on the Education of Daughters*.

——, *The Collected Letters of Mary Wollstonecraft*, ed. Janet Todd (London: Allen Lane, 2003). Questionable re-ordering of undated letters implies that MW soon fell into bed with Gilbert Imlay. A different order in the edition below allows for her seriousness in this tie, as in all she did.

——, *Collected Letters of Mary Wollstonecraft*, ed. Ralph M. Wardle (Ithaca: Cornell University Press, 1979)

Wroe, Ann, *Being Shelley: The Poet's Search for Himself* (London: Jonathan Cape, 2007)


EMILY BRONTË

Alexander, Christine and Margaret Smith (eds), *The Oxford Companion to the Brontës* (Oxford: Oxford University Press, 2006)

Barker, Juliet R. V. *The Brontës* (1994; revised edn London: Abacus, 2010)

Brontë, Anne, *Poems* (1846)

——, *Agnes Grey* (1847)

——, *The Tenant of Wildfell Hall* (1848)

Brontë, Charlotte, *Poems* (1846)

——, *Jane Eyre* (1847)

——, *Shirley* (1849)

——, *Villette* (1853)

——, *The Letters of Charlotte Brontë*, i–3, ed. Margaret Smith (Oxford: Clarendon Press, 1995–2004)

Brontë, Emily, *The Complete Poems of Emily Jane Brontë from the manuscripts*, ed. C. W. Hatfield (New York: Columbia University Press; London: Oxford University Press, 1941)

———, *The Complete Poems*, ed. Janet Gezari (Harmondsworth: Penguin Classics, 1992)

———, *The Poems of Emily Bronte*, ed. Derek Roper with Edward Chitham (Oxford: Clarendon Press, 1995)

———, *Wuthering Heights* (1847)

———, and Charlotte *Brontë*, *The Belgian Essays*, ed. and translated by Sue Lonoff (New Haven: Yale University Press, 1996)

Brontë, Patrick, *The Letters of the Reverend Patrick Brontë*, ed. Dudley Green (Stroud: Nonsuch Publishing, 2005)

Brontë, Branwell, *The Works of Patrick Branwell Brontë*, i–iii, ed. Victor A. Neufeldt (New York and London: Garland, 1999)

Chitham, Edward, *A Life of Emily Brontë* (1987; revised edn Stroud: Amberley Publishing, 2010)

Davies, Stevie, *Emily Brontë* (London: Harvester Wheatsheaf, 1988)

———, *Emily Brontë: Heretic* (London: The Women's Press, 1994)

———, *Four Dreamers and Emily* (London: The Women's Press, 1996). A novel

———, *Emily Brontë* (Plymouth: Northcote House/ British Council, 1998)

de Bassompierre, Louise (music pupil of EB in Brussels), Letter about EB to W. T. Field, *Brontë Society Transactions*, v (1913), 23, 26.

Ellis, Samantha, *Take Courage: Anne Brontë and the Art of Life* (London: Chatto & Windus, 2017)

Fermi, Sarah, *Emily's Journal* (Cambridge: Pegasus, 2006). Fiction about a forbidden love affair with a working-class boy called Clayton, an imaginary backdrop to *Wuthering Heights*, with her sisters' responses. Underpinned with facts about Haworth families.

Frank, Katherine, *Emily Brontë: A Chainless Soul* (London: Hamish Hamilton, 1990)

Fraser, Rebecca, *Charlotte Brontë* (London: Vintage, 2003)

Gaskell, Elizabeth, *The Life of Charlotte Brontë* (London: Smith, Elder, 1857). Numerous reprints.

———, *Elizabeth Gaskell: A Portrait in Letters*, ed. J. A. V. Chapple and John Geoffrey Sharps (Manchester: Manchester University Press, 2012)

Green, Dudley, *Patrick Brontë: Father of Genius* (Stroud: History Press, 2010)

Heaton Family Papers, Bradford City Archives, West Yorkshire

Heaton history: Mary A Butterfield, *The Heatons of Ponden Hall and the Legendary Link with Thrushcross Grange in Emily Brontë's* Wuthering Heights (Keighley: Roderick and Brenda Taylor, 1976); Edward Chitham, *A Life of Patrick Branwell Brontë* (London: Nelson, 1961), 43; *Brother in Shadow*, research by Mary Butterfield, ed. R. J. Duckett (Bradford Information Service, 1988), 70, 139–45. The last quotes from Mrs Percival Hayman, 'The Heatons and the Brontës', typescript (1982).

MacEwan, Helen, *Down the Belliard Steps: Discovering the Brontës in Brussels* (Hythe: Brussels Brontë Editions, 2012)

———, *The Brontës in Brussels* (London: Peter Owen, 2014)

———, *Winifred Gérin: Biographer of the Brontës* (London: Sussex Academic Press, 2015)

——, 'Through Belgian Eyes: Charlotte Brontë's Troubled Brussels Legacy' (draft, 2017)

Miller, Lucasta, *The Brontë Myth* (London: Jonathan Cape, 2001)

Mullen, Alexandra, 'Charlotte Brontë: Insurrection and Resurrection', *The Hudson Review*, LXIX:3 (autumn 2016), 432–43

Nussey, Ellen, 'Reminiscences of Charlotte Brontë by a "Schoolfellow"', repr. Appendix to *CBL*, i, 589–610. Texts from *Scribner's Monthly* (1871) and from mss in the King's School, Canterbury. It has long been common to denigrate Nussey, who really did know the Brontës and here writes eloquently about them.

Ruijssenaars, Eric, *Charlotte Brontë's Promised Land: The Pensionnat Heger and other Brontë Places in Brussels* (Keighley: Brontë Society, 2000)

Sanger, Charles Percy, *The Structure of Wuthering Heights* (London: Hogarth Press, 1926). Repr. various collections.

Shackleton, William, 'Four Hundred Years of a West Yorkshire Moorland Family' (1921), typescript, Heaton Papers: HEA/B/164-5.

## GEORGE ELIOT

Ashton, Rosemary *G. H. Lewes: An Unconventional Victorian* (1991; Pimlico, 2000)

——, *142 Strand: A Radical Address in Victorian London* (London: Vintage, 2008)

——, *George Eliot: A Life* (1996; London: Faber, 2013)

Bodenheimer, Rosemarie, *The Real Life of Mary Ann Evans: George Eliot, Her Letters and Fiction* (Ithaca: Cornell University Press, 1994)

Byatt, A. S., Introduction to *Selected Essays of George Eliot* (Harmondsworth: Penguin Classics, 1990)

Chapman, John, Diaries in *George Eliot & John Chapman*. See Haight, below.

Cross, John Walter (ed.), *George Eliot's Life as related in her Letters and Journals*, 3 vols (Edinburgh: Blackwood, 1885)

Eliot, George, *Scenes of Clerical Life* (1857)

——, *Adam Bede* (1859)

——, *The Mill on the Floss* (1860)

——, *Silas Marner* (1861)

——, *Middlemarch* (1871–2)

——, *Daniel Deronda* (1876)

——, *The George Eliot Letters 1819–1881*, 9 vols, ed. Gordon S. Haight (New Haven: Yale University Press, 1954ff)

——, *Selections from George Eliot's Letters*, ed. Gordon S. Haight (New Haven: Yale University Press, 1985)

——, *Selected Essays* (Harmondsworth: Penguin, 1990)

——, *The Journals of George Eliot*, ed. Margaret Harris and Judith Johnston (Cambridge: Cambridge University Press, 1998)

Haight, Gordon S., *George Eliot: A Biography* (London: Clarendon Press, 1968)

——(ed.), *A Century of George Eliot Criticism* (Boston: Houghton Mifflin, 1965)

——, George Eliot & John Chapman: with Chapman's Diaries (New Haven: Yale University Press; London: Oxford University Press, 1940)

Hardy, Barbara, *George Eliot: A Critic's Biography* (London: Continuum, 2006)

Henry, Nancy, *George Eliot and the British Empire* (Cambridge: Cambridge University Press, 2006)

——, *The Life of George Eliot: A Critical Biography* (Malden, MA: Wiley-Blackwell, 2015)

Hirsh, Pam, *Barbara Leigh Smith Bodichon, 1827–1891: Feminist, Artist and Rebel* (London: Pimlico, 1999)

Hughes, Kathryn, *George Eliot: The Last Victorian* (London: Fourth Estate, 1998)

James, Henry, *The Complete Letters*, ed. Pierre A. Walker and Greg W. Zacharias (Lincoln, NE: University of Nebraska Press, 2008–)

Lodge, David, Introduction to *Scenes of Clerical Life* (Harmondsworth: Penguin, 1973 ). Best short introduction to GE.

Redinger, Ruby V., *George Eliot: The Emergent Self* (New York: Knopf, 1975)

Rose, Phyllis, *Parallel Lives: Five Victorian Marriages* (New York: Knopf, 1983; London: Vintage, 1984)

Willey, Basil, *Nineteenth Century Studies: Coleridge to Matthew Arnold* (1949; New York: Harper, 1966). Chapter 8, on GE's translations.

## OLIVE SCHREINER

Bostridge, Mark and Paul Berry, *Vera Brittain: A Life* (London: Chatto & Windus, 1995)

Bostridge, Mark and Alan Bishop (eds), *Letters from a Lost Generation: First World War Letters of Vera Brittain and Four Friends* (London: Little, Brown, 1998)

Brittain, Vera, *Testament of Youth*, ed. Mark Bostridge (1933; repr. London: Virago, 2014)

Cronwright-Schreiner, S. C., *The Life of Olive Schreiner* (London: T. Fisher Unwin, 1924)

Driver, Dorothy, 'Reclaiming Olive Schreiner: A Re-reading of *From Man to Man*', *South African Literary History: Totality and/or Fragment*, ed. Edward Reckwitz, Karin Reitner and Lucia Vennarini (Essen: Die Blaue Eule, 1997), 111–120

——, 'Olive Schreiner's *From Man to Man* and "the copy within"', in *Changing the Victorian Subject* (Adelaide: University of Adelaide Press, 2014). Online.

——, Introduction to her edition of *From Man to Man* (Cape Town: University of Cape Town Press, 2016). See Schreiner, below.

First, Ruth and Ann Scott. *Olive Schreiner: A Biography* (London: André Deutsch, 1980; New Brunswick: Rutgers University Press, 1990)

Hobhouse, Emily, *Boer War Letters*, ed. Rykie van Reenen (Cape Town: Human& Rousseau, 1984)

Holmes, Rachel, *Eleanor Marx: A Life* (London: Bloomsbury 2014)

——, *Sylvia Pankhurst* (forthcoming)

Jenkins, Lyndsey, *Lady Constance Lytton: Aristocrat, Suffragette, Martyr* (London: Biteback, 2015)

Kingsley, Mary, *Travels in West Africa* (1897; repr. London: Virago, 1982)

McClintock, Anne, *Imperial Leather: Race, Gender, and Sexuality in the Colonial Contest* (London: Routledge, 2015)

Pieterse, H. J. C., *General Wynand Malan's Boer War Adventures* (1941). In Afrikaans.

Pretorius, Fransjohan, *The Anglo-Boer War, 1899–1902* (Cape Town: Struik, 1998)

Schoeman, Karel, *Olive Schreiner: A Woman in South Africa 1855–1881* (Johannesburg: Jonathan Ball, 1991)

——, *Only an Anguish to Live Here: Olive Schreiner and the Anglo-Boer War, 1899–1902* (Cape Town: Human & Rousseau, 1992)

——(ed.), *Witnesses to War: Personal Documents of the Anglo-Boer War from the Collections of the South African Library* (Cape Town: Human & Rousseau, 1998)

Olive Schreiner Letters Online (OSLO), http://www.oliveschreiner.org. There are about five thousand extant letters, transcribed by Liz Stanley and Anthea Salter for this prize-winning internet site. Sadly, S. C. Cronwright-Schreiner destroyed some of his wife's letters after selecting extracts for his edition of her *Letters* and his self-interested biography. The two print volumes are well-judged selections.

——, *Letters, 1871–99*, ed. Richard Rive with historical research by Russell Martin (Oxford: Oxford University Press, 1988)

——, *The World's Great Question: Olive Schreiner's South African Letters 1889–1920*, ed. and introduced by Liz Stanley and Andrea Salter (Cape Town: Van Riebeeck Society, 2014)

——, forthcoming: complete works from the University of Edinburgh

——, *From Man to Man or Perhaps Only*, with introduction by Paul Foot (London: Virago, 1982)

——, *From Man To Man, or Perhaps Only …*, ed. Dorothy Driver (Cape Town: University of Cape Town Press, 2015; Edinburgh: Edinburgh University Press, 2018). First published posthumously in London by T. Fisher Unwin, 1926, with an introduction by S. C. Cronwright-Schreiner. His report of the intended conclusion to this unfinished novel is not authoritative, as Dorothy Driver's scholarly edition explains.

——, *Dreams*, illustrated, designed by Elbert Hubbard (East Aurora: The Roycroft Shop, 1901)

——, *The Story of an African Farm* (Oxford: Oxford University Press, 2008)

——, *Woman and Labour* (New York: Frederick A. Stokes; London: Constable, 1911; repr. London: Virago, 1978; repr. Mineola: Dover Publications, 1998)

——, *The Woman's Rose: Stories and Allegories*, introduced and ed. Cherry Clayton (Johannesburg: Ad Donker, 1986)

——, *Words in Season*, ed. Stephen Grey (Johannesburg: Penguin, 2005). Includes speeches, political 'letters' and reminiscences.

Smuts, Jan Christiaan, Introduction (linking Schreiner and *Wuthering Heights*) to Vera Buchanan-Gould, *Not Without Honour: The Life and Writings of Olive Schreiner* (London/Cape Town: Hutchinson, 1948)

Stanley, Liz, *Imperialism, Labour and the New Woman: Olive Schreiner's Social Theory* (Durham: Sociologypress, 2002)

——, and Anthea Salter, editors of online OS letters

VIRGINIA WOOLF

Barkaway, Stephen, '"It's the personal touch": The Hogarth Press in Richmond, 1917–1924', *Virginia Woolf Bulletin*, 55 (May 2017)

Beauman, Christopher, 'Women Against the Vote', *The Persephone Biannually*, 18 (autumn/winter 2015–16), 7–8

Beaumont, Matthew, *Nightwalking: A Nocturnal History of London, Chaucer to Dickens* (London: Verso, 2015). Refers to VW's 1930 essay, 'Street Haunting'.

Bell, Quentin, *Virginia Woolf: A Biography*, 2 vols (London: Hogarth, 1972)

Bell, Vanessa, *Selected Letters*, ed. Regina Marler (London: Bloomsbury, 1993)

Black, Naomi, *Virginia Woolf as Feminist* (Ithaca: Cornell University Press, 2004)

Briggs, Julia, *Virginia Woolf: An Inner Life* (London: Allen Lane, 2005)

Bush, Julia, *Women against the Vote: Female Anti-Suffragism in Britain* (Oxford: Oxford University Press, 2007)

Crawford, Elizabeth, *The Women's Suffrage Movement: A Reference Guide, 1866–1928* (London: University College Press, 1999)

Davies, Margaret Llewelyn, *Life As We Have Known It* (1931; London: Virago, 1977)

*The Death of Virginia Woolf*, The History Hour, BBC World Service, 4 April 2016, <www.bbc.co.uk/programmes/p03p31g6>

Dell, Marion, *Virginia Woolf's Influential Forebears: Julia Margaret Cameron, Anny Thackeray Ritchie and Julia Prinsep Stephen* (Basingstoke: Palgrave Macmillan, 2015)

Dunn, Jane, *Virginia Woolf and Vanessa Bell: A Very Close Conspiracy* (1990; repr. London: Virago, 2001)

Gill, Stephen and Solomon Benatar, 'Global Health Governance and Global Power: A Critical Commentary on the Lancet-University of Oslo Commission Report', *International Journal of Health Services*, 46:2 (2016), 346–65. Ethically enlightened proposal of how our world might be changed through good governance, unlike that of self-interested politicians.

Goldsworthy, Vesna, 'The Bloomsbury Narcissus' (on Bloomsbury life writing), in Victoria Rosner (ed.), *The Cambridge Companion to the Bloomsbury Group* (Cambridge: Cambridge University Press, 2014), 183–197

Harris, Alexandra, *Romantic Moderns: English Writers, Artists and the Imagination from Virginia Woolf to John Piper* (London: Thames & Hudson, 2010)

——, *Virginia Woolf* (London: Thames & Hudson, 2011)

Harrison, Brian, *Separate Spheres: The Opposition to Women's Suffrage in Britain* (London: Croom Helm, 1978). Online via Bodleian Library

Holton, Amanda, 'Resistance, Regard and Rewriting: Virginia Woolf and Anne Thackeray Ritchie', *English*, 57:217 (2008), 42–64

Humm, Maggie, *Snapshots of Bloomsbury: The Private Lives of Virginia Woolf and Vanessa Bell* (London: Tate, 2006)

Kennedy, Richard, *A Boy at the Hogarth Press* (London: Heinemann, 1972)

Lee, Hermione, *Virginia Woolf* (London: Chatto & Windus, 1996)

Lewis, Alison M., 'A Quaker Influence on Modern English Literature: Caroline

Stephen and her niece, Virginia Woolf', *Types & Shadows: Journal of the Fellowship of Quakers in the Arts*, 21 (spring 2001)

Lovenduski, Joni, *Feminizing Politics* (Cambridge: Polity Press, 2005)

Mackrell, Judith, *Bloomsbury Ballerina: Lydia Lopokova, Imperial Dancer and Mrs John Maynard Keynes* (London: Weidenfeld & Nicolson, 2008)

Marcus, Laura, *Virginia Woolf* (revised edn; Tavistock: Northcote House in association with the British Council, 2004)

Nicholson, Virginia, *Among the Bohemians: Experiments in Living 1900–1939* (London: Viking, 2002)

Park, Sowon S., 'Suffrage and Virginia Woolf: "The Mass behind the Single Voice"', *Review of English Studies*, 56:223 (February 2005), 119–34

——, work in progress on Memory and the Unconscious

Santel, James, 'Antonio Muñoz Molina: Narrative Across Time', *The Hudson Review* (autumn 2014)

Sellers, Susan (ed.), *The Cambridge Companion to Virginia Woolf* (2nd edn; Cambridge: Cambridge University Press, 2010)

Smith, Harold L., *The British Women's Suffrage Campaign, 1866–1928* (revised 2nd edn; Harlow: Longman, 2010)

Spalding, Frances, *Vanessa Bell* (London: Weidenfeld & Nicolson, 1983)

——, *Virginia Woolf: Art, Life and Vision* (London: National Portrait Gallery, 2014)

——, *Vanessa Bell: Portrait of the Bloomsbury Artist* (London: Tauris Parke, 2016)

Stephen, Caroline Emilia, Papers in the London Metropolitan Archives, City of London

——, *Quaker Strongholds* (3rd edn; London: Edward Hicks, 1891). Accessed online via Bodleian Library.

Woolf, Leonard, *Beginning Again: An Autobiography of the Years 1911 to 1918* (London: Hogarth Press, 1964)

——, *Downhill All the Way: An Autobiography of the Years 1919–1939* (London: Hogarth Press, 1967)

Woolf, Virginia, *The Diary of Virginia Woolf*, i–v, ed. Anne Olivier Bell (London: Hogarth Press; New York: Harcourt, 1977–84)

——, *A Writer's Diary*, ed. Leonard Woolf (London: Hogarth Press, 1953; repr. London: Persephone Books, 2012)

——, *The Letters of Virginia Woolf*, i–vi, ed. Nigel Nicolson and Joanne Trautmann (London: Hogarth Press, 1975–80)

——, *The Essays of Virginia Woolf*, ed. Andrew McNeillie (vols i–iv) and Stuart N. Clarke (vols v–vi) (London: Hogarth Press, 1986–2011)

——, *Women & Fiction: The Manuscript Versions of* A Room of One's Own, ed. S. P. Rosenbaum (Oxford: Blackwell, 1992)

——, *Essays on the Self*, introduced by Joanna Kavenna (Widworthy: Notting Hill Editions, 2016)

——, *Carlyle's House and Other Sketches*, ed. David Bradshaw (London: Hesperus, 2003)

# ACKNOWLEDGEMENTS

It has been a privilege to live with the women in this book who had the courage and foresight to take risks. I must thank first Siamon Gordon for seeing the extent of the darkness that surrounds facts, with a readiness, as an immunologist, to push back that darkness in the limited ways open to each generation. His search for a dispersed organ of protective cells reminds me of Dr Lydgate's idea of an interconnected web in *Middlemarch*, the guiding metaphor for George Eliot's own wide-flung web of investigation into how people with inward drives function in their intimate relations. The possibility of such a web lies behind my experiment in dispersed biography. Siamon has been a constant reader of drafts, and I want to thank also Anna and Olivia Gordon and agent Isobel Dixon as readers who 'see'. My mother's outsider eye prompted the urge to speak.

Nothing would have been possible without Virago's publisher, Lennie Goodings. Her sense of what a book has to be is akin to collaboration, together with a superb copy-editor, Zoe Gullen. The alacrity and promptness of Johns Hopkins University Press has made it a pleasure to work with Catherine Goldstead and her colleagues, and I want to thank too agents Georges, Anne and Valerie Borchardt. More helpful than I can say has been the quick understanding of Paula Deitz, Robin Baird-Smith, Marie Philip, Pamela Norris, Rachel Holmes, Lovell Friedman, Audrey Russell, Fenuala Dowling and Meg van der Merwe. The words of novelist and spirited feminist Sindiwe Magona, wanting to 'change the world', came as a ray of concord as we sat in the sun on her stoep.

A special thanks to friends whose work has mattered: Lucasta Miller for her enlightening and witty history of Brontë myths; Mark Bostridge for his biographies; Miranda Seymour for her portrait of Mary Shelley; Stevie Davies with her affinity for Emily Brontë; Dorothy Driver on Olive Schreiner; and Nicola Beauman for advancing 'domestic feminism'.

I am grateful to the Stellenbosch Institute for Advanced Study, where I drafted the first chapter; to Mel Cawood of Ganna Hoek and her son Josh for leading us across harsh terrain to the site of Klein Ganna Hoek; to Brian Wilmot at the Olive Schreiner House in Cradock; to Wilby Murray for showing the site of the farmhouse at Krantz Plaats; to Renata Meyer and Clive Kirkwood in Jagger Library, University of Cape Town; to Lynne Grant at the National English Literary Museum, Grahamstown; to Fiona Marshall and Sarah Powell at the West Yorkshire Archives in Bradford; and to the archivists at the Berg Collection, New York Public Library; the Brontë Parsonage Museum; the Keep in Brighton; the Houghton Library, Harvard; the manuscript division of the British Library; the London Metropolitan Archives; and the Peabody Museum archives in Salem, Massachusetts. The impact of *Wuthering Heights* goes back to the lessons of Thelma Tyfield at Good Hope Seminary in Cape Town and to conversations with Colin Williamson at Jesus College, Oxford. Over the years, students at Jesus and St Hilda's College enlivened readings of the books in *Outsiders*.

# INDEX